Contents

William Shakespeare

KING JOHN
and
HENRY VIII

Edited by
David Bevington

David Scott Kastan,
James Hammersmith,
and Robert Kean Turner,
Associate Editors

With a Foreword by
Joseph Papp

BANTAM BOOKS
TORONTO / NEW YORK / LONDON / SYDNEY / AUCKLAND

KING JOHN and HENRY VIII

*A Bantam Book / published by arrangement
with Scott, Foresman and Company*

PRINTING HISTORY
*Scott, Foresman edition published / January 1980
Bantam edition, with newly edited text and substantially revised,
edited, and amplified notes, introductions, and other
materials, published / February 1988
Valuable advice on staging matters has been
provided by Richard Hosley.
Collations checked by Eric Rasmussen.
Additional editorial assistance by Claire McEachern.*

Library of Congress Cataloging-in-Publication Data

Shakespeare, William, 1564–1616.
    King John; and, Henry VIII.

    (A Bantam classic)
    "Bantam edition, with newly edited text and
substantially revised, edited, and amplified notes,
introductions, and other materials"—T.p. verso.
    Bibliography: p.
    1. John, King of England, 1167–1216—Drama.
2. Henry VIII, King of England, 1491–1547—Drama.
I. Bevington, David M.   II. Shakespeare, William, 1564–
1616. Henry VIII. 1988.   III. Title.   IV. Title: King
John.   V. Title: Henry VIII.
PR2762.B48   1988   822.3'3   87–19542
                                         CIP

    ISBN 0-553-21286-9 (pbk.)

Published simultaneously in the United States and Canada

PRINTED IN THE UNITED STATES OF AMERICA

O   0 9 8 7 6 5 4 3 2 1

WILLIAM SHAKESPEARE was born in Stratford-upon-Avon in April, 1564, and his birth is traditionally celebrated on April 23. The facts of his life, known from surviving documents, are sparse. He was one of eight children born to John Shakespeare, a merchant of some standing in his community. William probably went to the King's New School in Stratford, but he had no university education. In November 1582, at the age of eighteen, he married Anne Hathaway, eight years his senior, who was pregnant with their first child, Susanna. She was born on May 26, 1583. Twins, a boy, Hamnet (who would die at age eleven), and a girl, Judith, were born in 1585. By 1592 Shakespeare had gone to London, working as an actor and already known as a playwright. A rival dramatist, Robert Greene, referred to him as "an upstart crow, beautified with our feathers." Shakespeare became a principal shareholder and playwright of the successful acting troupe the Lord Chamberlain's men (later, under James I, called the King's men). In 1599 the Lord Chamberlain's men built and occupied the Globe Theatre in Southwark near the Thames River. Here many of Shakespeare's plays were performed by the most famous actors of his time, including Richard Burbage, Will Kempe, and Robert Armin. In addition to his 37 plays, Shakespeare had a hand in others, including *Sir Thomas More* and *The Two Noble Kinsmen*, and he wrote poems, including *Venus and Adonis* and *The Rape of Lucrece*. His 154 sonnets were published, probably without his authorization, in 1609. In 1611 or 1612 he gave up his lodgings in London and devoted more and more of his time to retirement in Stratford, though he continued writing such plays as *The Tempest* and *Henry VIII* until about 1613. He died on April 23, 1616, and was buried in Holy Trinity Church, Stratford. No collected edition of his plays was published during his lifetime, but in 1623 two members of his acting company, John Heminges and Henry Condell, published the great collection now called the First Folio.

Bantam Shakespeare
The Complete Works—29 Volumes
Edited by David Bevington
With forewords by Joseph Papp on the plays

The Poems: Venus and Adonis, The Rape of Lucrece, The
Phoenix and Turtle, A Lover's Complaint,
the Sonnets

Antony and Cleopatra	*The Merchant of Venice*
As You Like It	*A Midsummer Night's Dream*
The Comedy of Errors	*Much Ado about Nothing*
Hamlet	*Othello*
Henry IV, Part One	*Richard II*
Henry IV, Part Two	*Richard III*
Henry V	*Romeo and Juliet*
Julius Caesar	*The Taming of the Shrew*
King Lear	*The Tempest*
Macbeth	*Twelfth Night*

Together in one volume:

Henry VI, Parts One, Two, and Three
King John and Henry VIII
*Measure for Measure, All's Well that Ends Well, and
Troilus and Cressida*
Three Early Comedies: Love's Labor's Lost, The Two
Gentlemen of Verona, The Merry
Wives of Windsor
Three Classical Tragedies: Titus Andronicus, Timon
of Athens, Coriolanus
The Late Romances: Pericles, Cymbeline, The Winter's
Tale, The Tempest

Two collections:

Four Comedies: The Taming of the Shrew, A Midsummer
Night's Dream, The Merchant of Venice,
Twelfth Night
Four Tragedies: Hamlet, Othello, King Lear, Macbeth

Foreword

It's hard to imagine, but Shakespeare wrote all of his plays with a quill pen, a goose feather whose hard end had to be sharpened frequently. How many times did he scrape the dull end to a point with his knife, dip it into the inkwell, and bring up, dripping wet, those wonderful words and ideas that are known all over the world?

In the age of word processors, typewriters, and ballpoint pens, we have almost forgotten the meaning of the word "blot." Yet when I went to school, in the 1930s, my classmates and I knew all too well what an inkblot from the metal-tipped pens we used would do to a nice clean page of a test paper, and we groaned whenever a splotch fell across the sheet. Most of us finished the school day with ink-stained fingers; those who were less careful also went home with ink-stained shirts, which were almost impossible to get clean.

When I think about how long it took me to write the simplest composition with a metal-tipped pen and ink, I can only marvel at how many plays Shakespeare scratched out with his goose-feather quill pen, year after year. Imagine him walking down one of the narrow cobblestoned streets of London, or perhaps drinking a pint of beer in his local alehouse. Suddenly his mind catches fire with an idea, or a sentence, or a previously elusive phrase. He is burning with impatience to write it down—but because he doesn't have a ballpoint pen or even a pencil in his pocket, he has to keep the idea in his head until he can get to his quill and parchment.

He rushes back to his lodgings on Silver Street, ignoring the vendors hawking brooms, the coaches clattering by, the piteous wails of beggars and prisoners. Bounding up the stairs, he snatches his quill and starts to write furiously, not even bothering to light a candle against the dusk. "To be, or not to be," he scrawls, "that is the—." But the quill point has gone dull, the letters have fattened out illegibly, and in the middle of writing one of the most famous passages in the history of dramatic literature, Shakespeare has to stop to sharpen his pen.

Taking a deep breath, he lights a candle now that it's dark, sits down, and begins again. By the time the candle has burned out and the noisy apprentices of his French Huguenot landlord have quieted down, Shakespeare has finished Act 3 of *Hamlet* with scarcely a blot.

Early the next morning, he hurries through the fog of a London summer morning to the rooms of his colleague Richard Burbage, the actor for whom the role of Hamlet is being written. He finds Burbage asleep and snoring loudly, sprawled across his straw mattress. Not only had the actor performed in *Henry V* the previous afternoon, but he had then gone out carousing all night with some friends who had come to the performance.

Shakespeare shakes his friend awake, until, bleary-eyed, Burbage sits up in his bed. "Dammit, Will," he grumbles, "can't you let an honest man sleep?" But the playwright, his eyes shining and the words tumbling out of his mouth, says, "Shut up and listen—tell me what you think of *this*!"

He begins to read to the still half-asleep Burbage, pacing around the room as he speaks. ". . . Whether 'tis nobler in the mind to suffer the slings and arrows of outrageous fortune—"

Burbage interrupts, suddenly wide awake, "That's excellent, very good, 'the slings and arrows of outrageous fortune,' yes, I think it will work quite well. . . ." He takes the parchment from Shakespeare and murmurs the lines to himself, slowly at first but with growing excitement.

The sun is just coming up, and the words of one of Shakespeare's most famous soliloquies are being uttered for the first time by the first actor ever to bring Hamlet to life. It must have been an exhilarating moment.

Shakespeare wrote most of his plays to be performed live by the actor Richard Burbage and the rest of the Lord Chamberlain's men (later the King's men). Today, however, our first encounter with the plays is usually in the form of the printed word. And there is no question that reading Shakespeare for the first time isn't easy. His plays aren't comic books or magazines or the dime-store detective novels I read when I was young. A lot of his sentences are complex. Many of his words are no longer used in our everyday speech. His profound thoughts are often condensed into poetry, which is not as straightforward as prose.

Yet when you hear the words spoken aloud, a lot of the language may strike you as unexpectedly modern. For Shakespeare's plays, like any dramatic work, weren't really meant to be read; they were meant to be spoken, seen, and performed. It's amazing how lines that are so troublesome in print can flow so naturally and easily when spoken.

I think it was precisely this music that first fascinated me. When I was growing up, Shakespeare was a stranger to me. I had no particular interest in him, for I was from a different cultural tradition. It never occurred to me that his plays might be more than just something to "get through" in school, like science or math or the physical education requirement we had to fulfill. My passions then were movies, radio, and vaudeville—certainly not Elizabethan drama.

I was, however, fascinated by words and language. Because I grew up in a home where Yiddish was spoken, and English was only a second language, I was acutely sensitive to the musical sounds of different languages and had an ear for lilt and cadence and rhythm in the spoken word. And so I loved reciting poems and speeches even as a very young child. In first grade I learned lots of short nature verses— "Who has seen the wind?," one of them began. My first foray into drama was playing the role of Scrooge in Charles Dickens's *A Christmas Carol* when I was eight years old. I liked summoning all the scorn and coldness I possessed and putting them into the words, "Bah, humbug!"

From there I moved on to longer and more famous poems and other works by writers of the 1930s. Then, in junior high school, I made my first acquaintance with Shakespeare through his play *Julius Caesar*. Our teacher, Miss McKay, assigned the class a passage to memorize from the opening scene of the play, the one that begins "Wherefore rejoice? What conquest brings he home?" The passage seemed so wonderfully theatrical and alive to me, and the experience of memorizing and reciting it was so much fun, that I went on to memorize another speech from the play on my own.

I chose Mark Antony's address to the crowd in Act 3,

scene 2, which struck me then as incredibly high drama. Even today, when I speak the words, I feel the same thrill I did that first time. There is the strong and athletic Antony descending from the raised pulpit where he has been speaking, right into the midst of a crowded Roman square. Holding the torn and bloody cloak of the murdered Julius Caesar in his hand, he begins to speak to the people of Rome:

> If you have tears, prepare to shed them now.
> You all do know this mantle. I remember
> The first time ever Caesar put it on;
> 'Twas on a summer's evening in his tent,
> That day he overcame the Nervii.
> Look, in this place ran Cassius' dagger through.
> See what a rent the envious Casca made.
> Through this the well-belovèd Brutus stabbed,
> And as he plucked his cursèd steel away,
> Mark how the blood of Caesar followed it,
> As rushing out of doors to be resolved
> If Brutus so unkindly knocked or no;
> For Brutus, as you know, was Caesar's angel.
> Judge, O you gods, how dearly Caesar loved him!
> This was the most unkindest cut of all . . .

I'm not sure now that I even knew Shakespeare had written a lot of other plays, or that he was considered "timeless," "universal," or "classic"—but I knew a good speech when I heard one, and I found the splendid rhythms of Antony's rhetoric as exciting as anything I'd ever come across.

Fifty years later, I still feel that way. Hearing good actors speak Shakespeare gracefully and naturally is a wonderful experience, unlike any other I know. There's a satisfying fullness to the spoken word that the printed page just can't convey. This is why seeing the plays of Shakespeare performed live in a theater is the best way to appreciate them. If you can't do that, listening to sound recordings or watching film versions of the plays is the next best thing.

But if you do start with the printed word, use the play as a script. Be an actor yourself and say the lines out loud. Don't worry too much at first about words you don't immediately understand. Look them up in the footnotes or a dictionary,

but don't spend too much time on this. It is more profitable
(and fun) to get the sense of a passage and sing it out. Speak
naturally, almost as if you were talking to a friend, but be
sure to enunciate the words properly. You'll be surprised at
how much you understand simply by speaking the speech
"trippingly on the tongue," as Hamlet advises the Players.

You might start, as I once did, with a speech from *Julius
Caesar*, in which the tribune (city official) Marullus scolds
the commoners for transferring their loyalties so quickly
from the defeated and murdered general Pompey to the
newly victorious Julius Caesar:

> Wherefore rejoice? What conquest brings he home?
> What tributaries follow him to Rome
> To grace in captive bonds his chariot wheels?
> You blocks, you stones, you worse than senseless
>   things!
> O you hard hearts, you cruel men of Rome,
> Knew you not Pompey? Many a time and oft
> Have you climbed up to walls and battlements,
> To towers and windows, yea, to chimney tops,
> Your infants in your arms, and there have sat
> The livelong day, with patient expectation,
> To see great Pompey pass the streets of Rome.

With the exception of one or two words like "wherefore"
(which means "why," not "where"), "tributaries" (which
means "captives"), and "patient expectation" (which
means patient waiting), the meaning and emotions of this
speech can be easily understood.

From here you can go on to dialogues or other more challenging scenes. Although you may stumble over unaccus-
tomed phrases or unfamiliar words at first, and even fall
flat when you're crossing some particularly rocky passages, pick yourself up and stay with it. Remember that it
takes time to feel at home with anything new. Soon you'll
come to recognize Shakespeare's unique sense of humor
and way of saying things as easily as you recognize a
friend's laughter.

And then it will just be a matter of choosing which one of
Shakespeare's plays you want to tackle next. As a true fan
of his, you'll find that you're constantly learning from his
plays. It's a journey of discovery that you can continue for

the rest of your life. For no matter how many times you read or see a particular play, there will always be something new there that you won't have noticed before.

Why do so many thousands of people get hooked on Shakespeare and develop a habit that lasts a lifetime? What can he really say to us today, in a world filled with inventions and problems he never could have imagined? And how do you get past his special language and difficult sentence structure to understand him?

The best way to answer these questions is to go see a live production. You might not know much about Shakespeare, or much about the theater, but when you watch actors performing one of his plays on the stage, it will soon become clear to you why people get so excited about a playwright who lived hundreds of years ago.

For the story—what's happening in the play—is the most accessible part of Shakespeare. In *A Midsummer Night's Dream*, for example, you can immediately understand the situation: a girl is chasing a guy who's chasing a girl who's chasing another guy. No wonder *A Midsummer Night's Dream* is one of the most popular of Shakespeare's plays: it's about one of the world's most popular pastimes—falling in love.

But the course of true love never did run smooth, as the young suitor Lysander says. Often in Shakespeare's comedies the girl whom the guy loves doesn't love him back, or she loves him but he loves someone else. In *The Two Gentlemen of Verona*, Julia loves Proteus, Proteus loves Sylvia, and Sylvia loves Valentine, who is Proteus's best friend. In the end, of course, true love prevails, but not without lots of complications along the way.

For in all of his plays—comedies, histories, and tragedies—Shakespeare is showing you human nature. His characters act and react in the most extraordinary ways—and sometimes in the most incomprehensible ways. People are always trying to find motivations for what a character does. They ask, "Why does Iago want to destroy Othello?"

The answer, to me, is very simple—because that's the way Iago is. That's just his nature. Shakespeare doesn't explain his characters; he sets them in motion—and away they go. He doesn't worry about whether they're likable or not. He's interested in interesting people, and his most fascinating characters are those who are unpredictable. If you lean back in your chair early on in one of his plays, thinking you've figured out what Iago or Shylock (in *The Merchant of Venice*) is up to, don't be too sure—because that great judge of human nature, Shakespeare, will surprise you every time.

He is just as wily in the way he structures a play. In *Macbeth*, a comic scene is suddenly introduced just after the bloodiest and most treacherous slaughter imaginable, of a guest and king by his host and subject, when in comes a drunk porter who has to go to the bathroom. Shakespeare is tickling your emotions by bringing a stand-up comic on-stage right on the heels of a savage murder.

It has taken me thirty years to understand even some of these things, and so I'm not suggesting that Shakespeare is immediately understandable. I've gotten to know him not through theory but through practice, the practice of the *living* Shakespeare—the playwright of the theater.

Of course the plays are a great achievement of dramatic literature, and they should be studied and analyzed in schools and universities. But you must always remember, when reading all the words *about* the playwright and his plays, that *Shakespeare's* words came first and that in the end there is nothing greater than a single actor on the stage speaking the lines of Shakespeare.

Everything important that I know about Shakespeare comes from the practical business of producing and directing his plays in the theater. The task of classifying, criticizing, and editing Shakespeare's printed works I happily leave to others. For me, his plays really do live on the stage, not on the page. That is what he wrote them for and that is how they are best appreciated.

Although Shakespeare lived and wrote hundreds of years ago, his name rolls off my tongue as if he were my brother. As a producer and director, I feel that there is a professional relationship between us that spans the centuries. As a human being, I feel that Shakespeare has enriched my understanding of life immeasurably. I hope you'll let him do the same for you.

❖

The two scenes in *King John* that I like best concern the planned murder of young Arthur, the claimant to the throne, by Hubert de Burgh. In the first, Act 3, scene 3, King John is trying to *suggest* to Hubert that the boy be murdered, without actually coming out and saying the incriminating words. It's a gorgeous piece of writing; as the King tosses the issue noncommittally up in the air, Hubert takes it and runs with it:

> KING JOHN
>   Good Hubert, Hubert, Hubert, throw thine eye
>   On yon young boy. I'll tell thee what, my friend,
>   He is a very serpent in my way,
>   And wheresoe'er this foot of mine doth tread
>   He lies before me. Dost thou understand me?
>   Thou art his keeper.
> HUBERT   And I'll keep him so
>   That he shall not offend Your Majesty.
> KING JOHN   Death.
> HUBERT
>   My lord?
> KING JOHN   A grave.
> HUBERT   He shall not live.
> KING JOHN   Enough.
>   I could be merry now. Hubert, I love thee.

Throughout the scene, of which this is the latter part, the King is marvelously subtle and suggestive as he carefully communicates his wishes. And Hubert is quick to pick up on the cue, unlike Buckingham in *Richard III*, who pretends not to understand Richard's hints and forces the King to say, "Cousin, thou wast not wont to be so dull / Shall I be plain? I wish the bastards dead."

Another favorite scene is Act 4, scene 1, when Hubert is preparing to carry out the murder, and the boy tries to dissuade him. To me this is the most moving scene of the play. Young Arthur is sensitive, and precocious, and extremely eloquent as he pleads for his life. Indeed, the little fellow is so endearing that Hubert starts to worry that he won't be able to go through with the murder: "If I talk to him, with his innocent prate / He will awake my mercy, which lies dead. / Therefore I will be sudden, and dispatch."

The tension between the murderous plan in Hubert's mind and the innocence of the young boy who asks, "Must you with hot irons burn out both mine eyes?" builds throughout the scene, as Hubert tries to begin the binding and blinding of Arthur while struggling to master the pity welling up in his heart. He's undergoing a wrenching psychological struggle, but finally his better self wins, and, letting go of the irons, he says, "I'll fill these dogged spies with false reports. / And, pretty child, sleep doubtless and secure / That Hubert, for the wealth of all the world, / Will not offend thee." The lines are so moving, especially when read aloud, that I practically get tears in my eyes every time I hear them.

❖

King John was one of Shakespeare's earliest history plays, and *Henry VIII* was one of his last. In the early play, there's a boy, Arthur, pleading for his life; in the late play, there's a woman, Katharine of Aragon, pleading for her honor. Together the plays provide a nice pair of bookends for the histories.

The courtroom scene where Queen Katharine defends herself against Henry VIII's divorce proceedings is a terrific one. The Queen, being sacrificed to Henry's need for a male heir, is dignified and eloquent. To Wolsey, she says, "Sir, / I am about to weep; but thinking that / We are a queen, or long have dreamed so, certain / The daughter of a king, my drops of tears / I'll turn to sparks of fire." And so she does, angrily accusing Wolsey of engineering the divorce. Finally, exasperated and determined, she leaves the scene of the trial, vowing never to return. It's a splendid scene.

Interestingly enough, *Henry VIII* is the only one of Shakespeare's plays I've never produced. If I were superstitious, I would say it's because the Globe Theatre burned down during a performance of *Henry VIII* in 1613. But that's not the reason; it's just that I never felt a sense of urgency about doing it. I think it would be great fun to put on, for it's full of all kinds of spectacular pageantry and ceremony, and would *look* beautiful in the theater. It's something I'd like to do in the future—Globe fires notwithstanding.

JOSEPH PAPP

JOSEPH PAPP GRATEFULLY ACKNOWLEDGES THE HELP OF ELIZABETH KIRKLAND IN PREPARING THIS FOREWORD.

King John and *Henry VIII*

Shakespeare wrote a total of ten English history plays, all but two of which deal with the critical period of unrest and civil war from about 1398 to 1485: *Richard II, Henry IV Parts 1* and *2, Henry V, Henry VI Parts 1–3,* and *Richard III.* The two exceptions, brought together in this volume, are *King John* and *Henry VIII. King John* goes back to the years 1202–1216; *Henry VIII* deals with more recent history, from 1520 to 1534, so timely indeed that a play on the subject could not have been written and performed during the lifetime of Henry VIII's daughter, Queen Elizabeth. These two plays are thus the chronological beginning and end of Shakespeare's exploration of English history as a subject for the stage. *King John* is an early play (c. 1594–1595), written probably before Shakespeare began his second four-play historical series, going from *Richard II* to *Henry V; Henry VIII* is a late play (1613), separated from *Henry V* (the last of Shakespeare's histories on the fifteenth-century civil wars) by fourteen years or so.

Why did Shakespeare depart on these two occasions from his central interest in the great civil wars that had led up to the beginning of the Tudor reign? One tantalizing possibility is that he planned to write more than one play about England's earlier history; there are fleeting references to now-lost plays called *Henry the First, Henry the Second,* and *The History of King Stephen,* all ascribed (though with what accuracy we do not know) to Shakespeare. It is more likely, however, that Shakespeare found a special pertinence in the reigns of John and Henry VIII. Both reigns had a controversial place in the history of the English Reformation that shaped Elizabethan England.

John, though known to us chiefly as the signer of Magna Carta, was to Reformation England a troubling figure whose conflicts with the Catholic Church marked him as either a tyrant and usurper who deserved the trouble he got or a proto-Protestant hero and martyr defying without success the authority of Rome. John's reign was variously interpreted in accordance with the current political and religious persuasions of fifteenth- or sixteenth-century

Catholic or Protestant historians. He was used as an object lesson pointing to either the folly or the necessity of the Reformation, depending on the point of view of the observer. Shakespeare, without choosing sides in this polemical quarrel, dramatized a conflict that was enormously charged and meaningful to his audience.

In this important respect *Henry VIII* resembles *King John*. Like John, Henry defied the Catholic Church and was regarded variously as a monstrous heretic or hero of the Reformation. Henry had, of course, succeeded where his predecessor had failed, but one result of his divorce and break with Rome was that his Protestant children, Edward and Elizabeth, were declared illegitimate in Catholic eyes and unfit to rule. For that reason the issue of dynastic uncertainty, and its threat to England's political stability in the sixteenth century, applies by analogy to *Henry VIII* as it does to *King John*. *Henry VIII* is finally the eventful story of the birth of Elizabeth and the promise of her future glory. Henry VIII's break with Rome over the issue of the marriage, his dependence on Wolsey and his replacing of him, were all instrumental in bringing about the reign of Elizabeth. Again, Shakespeare's approach is not polemical; his portrait of Henry VIII is mixed, ambiguous, even tentative. Shakespeare has once again chosen to dramatize a conflict with application to the political and religious concerns of his spectators. He examines history not as an abstract subject but as one that can give perspective on the political and human drama of his own day.

The Playhouse

This early copy of a drawing by Johannes de Witt of the Swan Theatre in London (c. 1596), made by his friend Arend van Buchell, is the only surviving contemporary sketch of the interior of a public theater in the 1590s.

From other contemporary evidence, including the stage directions and dialogue of Elizabethan plays, we can surmise
that the various public theaters where Shakespeare's plays
were produced (the Theatre, the Curtain, the Globe) resembled the Swan in many important particulars, though there
must have been some variations as well. The public play-
houses were essentially round, or polygonal, and open to
the sky, forming an acting arena approximately 70 feet in
diameter; they did not have a large curtain with which to
open and close a scene, such as we see today in opera and
some traditional theater. A platform measuring approximately 43 feet across and 27 feet deep, referred to in the de
Witt drawing as the *proscaenium*, projected into the yard,
planities sive arena. The roof, *tectum*, above the stage and
supported by two pillars, could contain machinery for ascents and descents, as were required in several of Shakespeare's late plays. Above this roof was a hut, shown in the
drawing with a flag flying atop it and a trumpeter at its
door announcing the performance of a play. The underside
of the stage roof, called the heavens, was usually richly decorated with symbolic figures of the sun, the moon, and the
constellations. The platform stage stood at a height of 5½
feet or so above the yard, providing room under the stage
for underworldly effects. A trapdoor, which is not visible in
this drawing, gave access to the space below.

  The structure at the back of the platform (labeled *mi-
morum aedes*), known as the tiring-house because it was the
actors' attiring (dressing) space, featured at least two
doors, as shown here. Some theaters seem to have also had
a discovery space, or curtained recessed alcove, perhaps between the two doors—in which Falstaff could have hidden
from the sheriff (*1 Henry IV*, 2.4) or Polonius could have
eavesdropped on Hamlet and his mother (*Hamlet*, 3.4). This
discovery space probably gave the actors a means of access
to and from the tiring-house. Curtains may also have been
hung in front of the stage doors on occasion. The de Witt
drawing shows a gallery above the doors that extends
across the back and evidently contains spectators. On occasions when action "above" demanded the use of this space,
as when Juliet appears at her "window" (*Romeo and Juliet*,
2.2 and 3.5), the gallery seems to have been used by the actors, but large scenes there were impractical.

The three-tiered auditorium is perhaps best described by Thomas Platter, a visitor to London in 1599 who saw on that occasion Shakespeare's *Julius Caesar* performed at the Globe:

> The playhouses are so constructed that they play on a raised platform, so that everyone has a good view. There are different galleries and places [*orchestra, sedilia, porticus*], however, where the seating is better and more comfortable and therefore more expensive. For whoever cares to stand below only pays one English penny, but if he wishes to sit, he enters by another door [*ingressus*] and pays another penny, while if he desires to sit in the most comfortable seats, which are cushioned, where he not only sees everything well but can also be seen, then he pays yet another English penny at another door. And during the performance food and drink are carried round the audience, so that for what one cares to pay one may also have refreshment.

Scenery was not used, though the theater building itself was handsome enough to invoke a feeling of order and hierarchy that lent itself to the splendor and pageantry onstage. Portable properties, such as thrones, stools, tables, and beds, could be carried or thrust on as needed. In the scene pictured here by de Witt, a lady on a bench, attended perhaps by her waiting-gentlewoman, receives the address of a male figure. If Shakespeare had written *Twelfth Night* by 1596 for performance at the Swan, we could imagine Malvolio appearing like this as he bows before the Countess Olivia and her gentlewoman, Maria.

KING JOHN

Introduction

King John is usually dated on grounds of style between Shakespeare's two historical tetralogies, perhaps shortly before *Richard II* in 1594 or 1595. In structure and characterization it is also transitional from the episodic first series (*Henry VI* through *Richard III*) to the more tightly organized second series (*Richard II* through *Henry V*). It stands alone among Shakespeare's history plays of the 1590s in choosing the early thirteenth century for its subject rather than the fifteenth. Yet the political problems are familiar.

Foremost is the uncertainty of John's claim to the English throne. He occupies that throne by "strong possession" and also seemingly by the last will and testament of his deceased eldest brother, King Richard I. But could such a will disinherit Arthur, the son of John's older brother Geoffrey? English primogeniture specified that property must descend to the eldest son; after Richard's death without direct heirs, his next brother Geoffrey would inherit, and then Geoffrey's son Arthur. Significantly, even John's mother, Queen Eleanor, who publicly supports John's claim, privately admits that "strong possession" is much more on their side than "right" (1.1.39–40). All parties concede, then, that young Arthur's claim is legally superior.

Yet such a claim raises serious practical questions, because it challenges the status quo. John is de facto king, and Arthur a child. To make the dilemma complete, Arthur has no ambitions to rule and seemingly no talent for leadership. Without the unremitting zeal of his widowed mother, Constance, Arthur would retire into the private world of kindness and love where his virtues shine. Moreover, Constance's uncompromising defense of her son's true claim requires her to seek alliance with the French for an invasion of England. Such an appalling prospect of invasion and civil war inevitably poses the question: Is the replacement of John by Arthur worth the price? Which is better, an ongoing regime flawed by uncertain claim and political compromises, or restitution of the "right" by violent and potentially self-destructive means?

Shakespeare refuses to simplify the issues. John is neither a monstrous tyrant nor a martyred hero, although both
interpretations were available to Shakespeare in sixteenth-
century historical writings. Catholic historians of the late
Middle Ages such as Polydore Vergil had uniformly condemned John, partly at least because of his interference
with the Church. The English Reformation brought about a
conscious rewriting of history, and in John Bale's play of
King Johan (1538, with later revisions) the protagonist is
unassailably virtuous. Centuries ahead of his time, this
King John comprehends the true interests of the state in
fending off the encroachments of the international Church.
He fails only because his people are superstitious and his
aristocrats are the dupes of Catholic meddling. Bale's play
is transparently a warning to Tudor England. This portrait
of John as a martyr continues unabated in John Foxe's *Acts
and Monuments*, and in the chronicles of Richard Grafton
and Raphael Holinshed that were based on Foxe. Most viru-
lent of all is the play called *The Troublesome Reign of King
John* (c. 1587–1591), once thought to be by Shakespeare and
analyzed by one recent editor as a bad quarto of Shakespeare's text, but now almost universally regarded as the
work of some more chauvinistic playwright such as George
Peele. Although generally close to Shakespeare's play in its
narrative of events, it also contains scenes of the most de-
graded anti-Catholic humor, featuring gross abbots who
conceal nuns in their private rooms, and the like. Against
such a corrupt institution, the Bastard's plundering is
wholly justifiable. John and the Bastard would be invincible, were it not for the base Catholic loyalties of the nobility.

Shakespeare consciously declines to endorse either the
Catholic or the Protestant interpretation of King John. (Interestingly, neither side showed any interest in Magna
Carta; not until the seventeenth century was that event interpreted as a famous precedent for constitutional re-
straints imposed on the monarchy.) To be sure, some
anticlericalism still remains in the play. John grandly pro-
claims that "no Italian priest / Shall tithe or toll in our dominions." John is "supreme head" of church and state (the
actual title claimed by Henry VIII), defending his people
against "this meddling priest" with his "juggling witchcraft" (3.1.153–169). Yet Shakespeare's King John is not vin-

dictive against the Church. He seizes some of its wealth not as a reprisal but to support his costly military campaigns; and, when he is poisoned by a monk, neither John nor anyone else assumes that a Catholic conspiracy is responsible —as it is in *Troublesome Reign*. Similarly, the baronial opposition to John is motivated not by secret leanings toward Rome but by understandable revulsion at the apparent murder of Arthur.

Shakespeare's balanced treatment need not merely reflect his own political allegiances, whatever they were. Artistically, *King John* is a study of impasse, of tortured political dilemmas to which there can be no clear answer. How do people behave under such trying circumstances? Shakespeare's play is remarkable for its sensitivity and compassion toward all sides. His most completely sympathetic characters are those innocently caught in the political crossfire, such as Arthur and the Lady Blanche. Among the major contenders for power, all except the ruthless Dauphin Lewis are guided by worthy intentions and yet are forced to make unfortunate and self-contradictory compromises. Constance, for all her virtuous singleness of mind, must seek a French invasion of England. King Philip of France, bound to Constance's cause by all the holy vows of heaven, changes his purpose when England offers a profitable marriage alliance, and then shifts quickly back again when the papacy demands in the name of the Church that Philip punish King John for heresy. Philip's conscience is troubled about both decisions, but what is a king to do when faced with practical choices affecting his people's welfare and his own political safety?

Even Pandulph, the papal legate, can be viewed as a well-intentioned statesman caught in the web of political compromise. Presumably he is sincere in his belief that King John's heresy—in particular, his refusal to accept the Pope's choice, Stephen Langton, as Archbishop of Canterbury—represents a grave threat to Catholic Christendom. Yet Pandulph reveals an unprincipled cunning when he teaches King Philip how to equivocate a sacred vow, or instructs the apt young Lewis in Machiavellian intrigue. As Pandulph explains, the French can exploit King John's capture of Arthur by invading England in Arthur's name, thereby forcing John to murder his nephew in order to ter-

minate the rival claim to the throne. Arthur's death will in
turn drive the English nobility over to the French side. By
this stratagem, the seemingly bad luck of Arthur's capture
can neatly be turned to the advantage of France and the international Church (3.4.126–181). Lewis learns his lesson
only too well. What Pandulph has failed to take into account
is the insincerity of Lewis's alliance with papal power.
When the legate has achieved through the invasion what he
wants—the submission of John—and then tries to call off
Lewis's army, Pandulph discovers too late that the young
Frenchman cares only for war on his own terms. Pandulph's cunning becomes a weapon turned against himself.

John is, like his enemies, a talented man justly punished
by his own perjuries. His failings are serious, but they are
also understandable. Given the fact that he is king, his desire to maintain rule serves both his own interests and
those of political order generally. The deal by which John
bargains away his French territories of Angiers, Touraine,
Maine, Poitiers, and the rest, in order to win peace with
France, is prudent under the circumstances but a blow to
those English dreams of greatness that John professes to
uphold. When France immediately repudiates this treaty,
John merely gets what he deserves for entering such a deal.
His surrender of the crown to the papacy is again the canny
result of yielding to the least dangerous of the alternatives
available but diminishes John's already shaky authority
nonetheless.

Most heinous is John's determination to be rid of Arthur.
He has compelling reasons, to be sure. As Pandulph pre-
dicts, the French invasion of England using Arthur's claim
as its pretext forces John to consider Arthur as an immediate threat to himself. (Queen Elizabeth had long agonized
over a similar problem with her captive, Mary, Queen of
Scots; so long as Mary lived, a Catholic and claimant to the
throne, English Catholics had a perennial rallying
point.) What is a ruling king to do with a rival claimant in
his captivity? As Henry IV also discovers once he has cap-
tured Richard II, the logic demanding death is inexorable.
Yet such a deed is not only murder, but murder of one's
close kinsman and murder of the Lord's anointed in the
eyes of those believing the captive, in this case Arthur, to be
rightful king. Furthermore, it is sure to backfire and punish

the doer by arousing national resentment and rebellion. John quickly regrets Arthur's death, but we suspect that the regret is in part motivated by fear of the consequences. The same unseen power that protects John against his own worst instincts, momentarily saving the boy from Hubert's instruments of torture, also justly prevents John from obtaining any political benefit from this brief reprieve; Hubert is too late, Arthur dies in a fall, the lords are convinced of John's guilt. With fitting irony, John is punished for his crime after he has decided not to do it and after the murder itself has failed to take place.

The word used to sum up the universal political scheming and oath-breaking in this play is "commodity," or self-interest (2.1.574). The word is introduced by the Bastard, the fascinating choric figure of *King John* whose reactions to the events of the play are so important in shaping our own. The Bastard is an outsider from birth and so not beholden to society for its usual tawdry benefits. As the natural son of the great King Richard Coeur de Lion, the Bastard is a kind of folk hero: he is instinctively royal and yet a commoner, a projection of the audience's sentimental fondness for monarchy and at the same time a hero representing all of society. He is a fictional character in a largely historical world. His quarrel with his effete brother Robert over the inheritance of their father's property comically underscores the futility of the dynastic quarrel between King John and Arthur. In both contentions a will left by the deceased confuses the issue of genealogical priority. Thus John, who defends the Bastard's unconventional claim to his inheritance, discovers a natural ally.

The Bastard is strangely drawn to commodity at first. He finds it exhilarating to trust his fortune to war and the King's favor, rather than to the easy comfort of a landed estate. The wars enable him to pursue a quest for self-identity. After learning from his reluctant mother who his real father was, the Bastard must venge himself upon the Duke of Austria, who killed his father. When the Bastard is first confronted with the moral ambiguity of the war, his response is mischievous, almost Vice-like. He makes the cunning suggestion, for example, that France and England join against the city of Angiers until it surrenders, after which they may resume fighting each other. Clearly this

Machiavellian proposal embodies, even satirizes, the spirit of commodity. Yet the Bastard is not motivated by self-interest or a cynical delight in duping men, as is the bastard Edmund in *King Lear*. This Bastard's illegitimacy has no such ominous cosmic import. Instead he is at first the detached witty observer, wryly amused at the seemingly inherent absurdity of politics. Although he does protest also that he will worship commodity for his own gain, we never see him doing so. Despite his philosophic detachment, he remains loyal to England and to John. In fact he is the play's greatest patriot.

The supreme test for the Bastard, as for all well-meaning characters and for the audience as well, is the death of Arthur. The Bastard must experience disaffection and even revulsion if he is to retain our sympathy as choric interpreter. Yet his chief function is to triumph over that revulsion, and in so doing to act as counterpart to the more rash English lords. They have come hastily to the conclusion that John is guilty of Arthur's death. This is of course true in the main, but they do not know all the circumstances, and truth, as always, is more complicated than they suppose. Only the Bastard consistently phrases his condemnation in qualified terms: "It is a damnéd and a bloody work . . . If that it be the work of any hand" (4.3.57–59). Moreover, the lords have concluded that John's guilt justifies their rebellion. Yet they stoop to commodity of the very sort they condemn. They fight for the supposed good of England by allying themselves with Lewis of France. Once again, the ironies of cosmic justice demand that such commodity be repaid by treachery. The lords are luckily saved just in time by Lord Melun's revelation of Lewis's plan, just as John had been saved from his own headstrong folly by the kindness of Hubert. The Bastard's decision to remain loyal to John thus proves not only prudent but virtuous. He has led our sympathies through disaffection to acceptance. Rebellion only worsens matters by playing into the hands of opportunists. Loyalty to John is still, in a sense, a kind of commodity, for it involves compromise and acceptance of politics as morally a world unto itself. Nevertheless, loyalty is a conscientious choice and is rewarded finally by the accession of young Henry III, who at last combines political legitimacy and the will to act.

The ending of *King John* is not without its ironies. England, having suffered through the dynastic uncertainties of a child claimant to the throne (as also in the *Henry VI* plays, *Richard III*, *Richard II*, and Christopher Marlowe's *Edward II*), must now face a new destiny under the young and unproven Henry III. The irony is often underscored, in modern productions at least, by doubling the parts of Arthur and Henry III for the same juvenile actor. Is there sufficient reason to suppose that the problem will not recur? The Bastard's role in seeking affirmation is a crucial one, and yet he does so from his vantage point as the play's most visibly unhistorical personage. As a fictional character, the Bastard is free to invent fictions around him, to instruct King John in the playing of a part that will benefit England, and to fashion a concluding speech in which there can be hope for the future. What sort of consolation does this fiction provide? To dwell on the conflict between history and fiction is not to subvert all hope by labeling fiction as mere fantasy, but it does call attention to the fruitfully ambiguous relation between Shakespeare's stubbornly historical subject matter and his function as creative artist.

King John
in Performance

Like *Henry VIII*, *King John* is seldom seen onstage today but was a great favorite of the nineteenth century. The key to the former popularity of both plays no doubt lies in the manner in which they were staged. Both plays invited opulent and detailed historical sets of the sort nineteenth-century audiences loved, and both provided big emotional speeches that lent themselves to oratorical and even melodramatic delivery. Productions of *Henry VIII* centered on the piteous falls of Buckingham, Queen Katharine, and Wolsey; productions of *King John* focused on John's defiance of the French King at Angiers, Constance's speech about her absent young son Arthur, Arthur's persuading Hubert not to put out his eyes, Arthur's escape attempt and death, John's encounter with the papal legate, and the last moments of the life of King John. As with other historical subjects, that of *King John* also gave actor-managers the opportunity to stage spectacular tableaux, including scenes that do not appear in Shakespeare's script.

The nineteenth century inherited from the eighteenth a play that had been rearranged with a view to unifying its action and sharpening its thrust at the international political intriguing of the Catholic Church. Only occasionally performed after a long hiatus in the late seventeenth and early eighteenth centuries, *King John* enjoyed its first successful reintroduction to the theater in a version by Colley Cibber called *Papal Tyranny in the Reign of King John* (1745). Cibber's adaptation strove for unity by eliminating Shakespeare's first act and by locating its own first two acts at a camp near Angiers. Other cuts and interpolations followed. Cibber's animus against the meddling of the Catholic Church in English politics is evident in his title and in his avowed purpose to "paint the intoxicated tyranny of Rome in its proper colors," with obvious application to current agitation in 1745 over attempts to place the Catholic pretender Charles Edward on the English throne. Adjustment of the text also made possible considerable scenic display, with individual sets for Angiers, the French court, the Castle of Rouen, the Dauphin's camp at St. Edmundsbury, Swinstead Abbey, and so on. Cibber gave particular attention to two splendid processions, one in which Cardinal Pandulph entered in state to receive and then tread on the robe and crown of English royalty before returning them to a submissive John, and another bit of pageantry (not called for in Shakespeare's text) in which a funeral ceremony for Arthur moved toward Swinstead Abbey in a dead march.

Not to be outdone by Cibber, David Garrick brought forth a more avowedly Shakespearean version of the play at the Theatre Royal, Drury Lane, only five days after Cibber's version opened at the Theatre Royal, Covent Garden. Garrick played John; Susannah Cibber, Theophilus Cibber's wife, played Constance; and Charles Macklin acted the part of Pandulph. The playbill claimed, with an obviously scornful glance at Cibber's play at the rival theater, that *King John* was "not acted 50 years," though in fact there had been a revival—indeed, the first certain production of the play—in February of 1737 at Covent Garden, and in March of that year the Haymarket Theatre saw another production of the play claiming to be "as originally written by Shakespeare. Supervised, read over, revised, and unaltered." Garrick's text also was essentially Shakespeare's, though it interpolated two speeches from the anonymous *The Troublesome Reign of King John.*

In 1751 Shakespeare's *King John* replaced Cibber's version at Covent Garden. Susannah Cibber had now joined that company and acted Constance opposite James Quin as the King. When Mrs. Cibber took ill at the end of February, Peg Woffington replaced her in the four remaining performances of the year. In 1754 Garrick again produced the play at Drury Lane, now taking the part of the Bastard and leaving John to Henry Mossop. The production advertised its characters as "new dressed," apparently initiating the move away from contemporary attire and toward period costume that would become a virtual obsession on the nineteenth-century stage.

After Garrick it was John Philip Kemble who brought the greatest distinction to productions of the play. In December of 1783 Kemble and his sister, Sarah Siddons, first performed *King John* at Drury Lane, and he revived the play in five of the next seventeen years. Kemble produced a version in 1800 at Drury Lane that, although not lavish, was carefully attentive to spectacle, and he was much praised for the production's "mimic art" and for its fidelity to Shakespeare's text. At Covent Garden, meanwhile, *King John* was still a victim of adaptation. Richard Valpy, who had revised the play in 1800 for his students at Reading School, introduced his version on the Covent Garden stage in 1803 with the candid avowal that it had been "altered from Shakespeare." The production starred George Frederick Cooke as King John. Working from both Shakespeare's *King John* and Cibber's *Papal Tyranny*, Valpy followed Cibber in cutting away Shakespeare's first act while ameliorating the sharp anti-Catholic tone of Cibber's play. Later that year, Kemble left Drury Lane to become manager of Covent Garden, bringing his Shakespearean version with him and ensuring its place in the Covent Garden repertory until his retirement in 1817.

Building on the emerging traditions of scenic rearrangement and visual splendor, and no longer restricted to the Catholic issue after the subsiding of the Jacobite challenge of 1745, the nineteenth-century theater managers had great success in bringing a spectacular realism to *King John*. Charles Kemble's revival at Covent Garden in 1823 made use of design innovations proposed mainly by the antiquary and theatrical consultant, J. R. Planché. The opening scene showed John in a costume derived from the effigy of the historical King John in Worcester Cathedral, surrounded, as Planché wrote, "by his barons sheathed in mail, with cylindrical helmets and correct armorial shields, and his courtiers in the long tunics and mantles of the thirteenth century." Other sources for the authentic costuming included Queen Eleanor's effigy at the Abbey of Fonteveraud, the effigy of the Earl of Salisbury in Salisbury Cathedral, and medieval illuminated manuscripts. The designers had done careful research; the playbill boasted of their "attention to costume never equalled on the English stage." To audiences accustomed to actors in wigs and long waistcoats, the historical reconstruction was a revelation and the production a great success.

William Charles Macready, who had first acted the play

in 1823, produced in 1842 a spectacle that was perhaps the most financially lavish of his tenure at Drury Lane. His aim was to bring to the stage, as *The Times* of October 25 put it, an "animated picture of those Gothic times" in which the play was set. Costumes were designed with scrupulous attention to historical accuracy, and, with upwards of two hundred supernumeraries moving against the elaborate medieval backgrounds painted by William Telbin, the stage was "thronged with the stalwart forms of the middle ages." Macready played John and Helen Faucit played Constance; Samuel Phelps was, in the estimation of *The Times*, "an admirable Hubert."

Phelps produced his own *King John* in 1844, his first season at the Sadler's Wells Theatre. With Phelps himself in the role of the King, the play was enthusiastically received. The costumes and sets were favorably compared with Macready's, and Phelps's acting was also highly praised; *The Critic* claimed, for example, that "he has more real genius in him than any actor of our time." Phelps's *King John* was revived in six of the eighteen seasons that he was at Sadler's Wells.

Though Macready and Phelps repeatedly demonstrated how actor-managers could succeed with elaborate visual representations of Shakespeare's locales, other actor-managers before them, such as Cibber and Kemble, had shown that the most promising subjects for stage pictures were not always to be found in Shakespeare's text. Charles Kean, undeterred by *King John*'s virtual ignoring of Magna Carta, interpolated a splendid dumb show of its signing in his 1852 production at the Princess's Theatre. Like Kemble and Macready before him, Kean insisted on historical accuracy in matters of scenery, costumes, and accoutrements, even if his fidelity to Shakespeare's text was something less than scrupulous. From seals, tapestries, illustrated manuscripts, effigies on tombs, and medieval ruins, Kean made authentic copies in his stage design of the Norman architecture appropriate to John's reign. The room of state in Act 1 was an exact replica of the hall in Rochester Castle. In fact, every succeeding location was copied from a specific historical ruin of the twelfth and thirteenth centuries. Kean also had success acting the play, appearing as King John for the first time at the Park Theatre in New York in 1846, and making his London debut in his splendid production of 1852.

Herbert Beerbohm Tree, at Her Majesty's Theatre in 1899, retained Kean's tableau of the granting of Magna Carta, along with striking verisimilar effects. Percy Anderson's costumes impressively reproduced twelfth-century dress, armor, and heraldic devices. The sets were equally elaborate. The walls of Angiers in Act 2 were replete with Norman archways, a moat, battlements, crenelled parapet walls, corbels, and, in the distance, the towers of the medieval castle. A contemporary reviewer praised the "fresh and delicate beauty" of the orchard at Swinstead where John dies. The extensive cuts needed to accommodate the massive scenes and interpolated tableaux of this production fitted well into the actor-manager's wishes to concentrate on moments of intense emotion and high seriousness. The play was performed in a three-act version, each act ending with a scene of pathos: the first with Arthur's capture, the second with his death, and the third with the miserable end of King John.

The twentieth century, by contrast, has witnessed a return to something apparently closer to the staging principles of Shakespeare's own theater. Increasingly, directors have opted for what they perceive to be Shakespeare's rather than the set designer's artistry and are no longer willing to rearrange the text to accommodate massive sets like those of Kean or Tree. Frank Benson's company energetically performed the play in a virtually uncut text at Stratford-upon-Avon in 1901 as part of a season that included five other history plays. Although Benson appeared only in the minor role of the second executioner in Act 4, scene 1, he entered to tumultuous applause. Robert Atkins directed the play in 1920 at the Old Vic in a production whose swift pacing and simplified staging revealed Atkins's training with William Poel, the initiator of the movement away from realistic illusion in producing Shakespeare. In 1926 Andrew Leigh opened the season at the Old Vic with a modest production of *King John*, focused on Baliol Holloway's truculent Bastard, that played to capacity houses. Five years later at the Old Vic, Harcourt Williams directed Robert Speaight as John and Ralph Richardson as the Bastard in a successful production that also demonstrated the new simplicity of staging, though it is unclear whether the sparseness was because of Williams's aesthetic belief or because all of England, which had just gone off the gold standard, was in a deep financial crisis.

During World War II, no doubt in part because of its patriotic rhetoric, the play continued to find eager audiences. Ben Iden Payne and Andrew Leigh directed a lively *King John* at Stratford-upon-Avon in 1940 as "a bright medieval pageant," according to *The Times*. In the following year, the Old Vic Company's production at London's New Theatre, directed by Tyrone Guthrie and Lewis Casson and with Sybil Thorndike as Constance, effectively used curtains, banners, and creative lighting effects to suggest the battlefields, pavilions, courts, and castles called for in the play script. Four years later, a twenty-one-year-old Peter Brook directed *King John*, his first Shakespeare play, at the Birmingham Repertory in a production that centered upon Paul Scofield's portrayal of the Bastard as the play world's harshest critic and ablest champion. The production became notorious for Brook's emendation in the Bastard's soliloquy in Act 2, scene 1: "That smooth-faced gentleman, expediency, / Or, as they say, commodity."

After the war, it became possible to play *King John* with a darker sense of its political vision. Michael Benthall's production at Stratford-upon-Avon in 1948 featured Robert Helpmann as a calculating King John, one who was haunted by the production's most striking visual effect: the menacing shadow of a cross that towered over the stage during the entrance of the papal legation. In 1960 at Stratford, Ontario, Douglas Seale emphasized the vicious opportunism of all but Christopher Plummer's Bastard. Joseph Papp's production of the play in 1967 for the New York Shakespeare Festival established provocative tensions between the bright promise of the colorful pageantry and the deep cynicism of most of the action. At Stratford, Ontario, in 1974, Peter Dews directed Edward Atienza as a paranoid John destroyed by the power he proved unfit to wield. That same year, at Stratford-upon-Avon, John Barton further explored the play's dispiriting political vision in a restructured text incorporating lines that he himself wrote, as well as material from John Bale's *King Johan* and from the anonymous *The Troublesome Reign of King John*.

Though recently there have been significant European productions of the play, for example, in Weimar in 1980 at the Deutsches Nationaltheater and in Berlin in 1985 at the Theater im Palast, the 1980s have not offered the English-speaking world many opportunities to see *King John*. In 1982 Randall Duk Kim acted John with an unusual sensitivity to the complex political situation in which he is caught, in a colorful production of the play by the American Players Theatre on the outdoor stage in Spring Green, Wisconsin. When the Jean Cocteau Repertory company performed the play at New York's Bouwerie Lane Theater in 1983, halfway through the performance the dull tunics that served for medieval costume were rolled up, turning into modern battle fatigues. More traditionally, if somewhat ponderously, the BBC television production in 1984 starred Leonard Rossiter as a desperate John and Claire Bloom as a passionate Constance whose deeply felt grief provided some balance to the inhumanity of the surrounding world of courtly sophistication. In 1985 the play was performed at the Oregon Shakespeare Festival in Ashland, where, in the open-air theater, director Pat Patton used richly colored costumes and a simple set to produce an absorbing historical pageant punctuated by the cynicism of John David Castellanos's Bastard.

Although recent productions such as Patton's have repudiated the cumbersome visual elaboration of Kemble, Macready, Kean, and Tree, the impulse toward pageantlike display is actually a valid response to Shakespeare's text. The scene at Angiers in Act 2, so dear to actor-managers of the eighteenth and nineteenth centuries (at times, indeed, the production's crowning scene), calls for impressive visual effects on the unadorned Elizabethan stage for which it was devised. As King Philip of France and King John of England meet before the walls of Angiers, accompanied by numerous followers, an element of symmetrical opposition organizes the exchange of thrust and counterthrust in the parley before the battle. When Hubert and other citizens of Angiers appear *"upon the walls,"* that is, in the gallery above at the rear of the stage, we are shown in spatially symbolic form the dilemma of the town itself, caught between two powerful nations, willing to offer submission to the victor but not knowing who will win.

Throughout the battle of Angiers, the walls and the citizens
upon them remain as vivid reminders of the occasion of the
quarrel between France and England. Personal loyalties are
divided by the conflict as well: the Lady Blanche, John's
niece, is offered to the French Dauphin as his prize if he will
make accommodation, and so she, like the town, must see
her fate determined by the uncertain outcome of battle.

Later (4.3), the gallery above the stage is imaginatively
transformed into castle walls in England, from which
young Arthur, disguised as a shipboy, attempts escape and
leaps to his death—that is, onto the main stage. No scenery
was used in Shakespeare's theater to create the effects of
castle walls, but the theater building itself, with its impressive architecture, its pillars, its colorful decoration, and
above all its vertical differentiation between gallery and
main stage, offered a plausible space in which the actors'
words and gestures could conjure up a stage picture of
political conflict. Rich costuming and a throne of state,
quickly brought onstage when needed, lent to scenes of interview between John and his irate barons or the papal legate an aura of ceremonial magnificence that contrasted
ironically with the realities of John's dubious claim to the
throne, his underhanded way of dealing with the stronger
claim of his nephew, young Arthur, and his craven capitula-
tion to the papacy. The most visually impressive scenes of
his sitting in royal state are fatally marred, as his nobles
point out to him, by the "superfluous" nature of the double
ritual through which his crown, already bestowed on him
by English law and custom, is rendered him again by Cardinal Pandulph (4.2, 5.1). A theatrical language of ceremony is
vital to any production of *King John*, not for the sake of pageantry or for any attempt to recapture the flavor of medieval life, but because of what it implies through contrast
about John's failures.

KING JOHN

[*Dramatis Personae*

KING JOHN
QUEEN ELEANOR, *his mother*
PRINCE HENRY, *his son, afterward King Henry III*
ARTHUR, *Duke of Brittaine (Brittany), King John's nephew*
CONSTANCE, *Arthur's mother, widow of King John's elder brother, Geoffrey*
BLANCHE *of Spain, niece of King John*

LADY FAULCONBRIDGE, *widow of Sir Robert Faulconbridge*
Philip the BASTARD, *afterward knighted as Sir Richard Plantagenet, her illegitimate son by Richard I (Richard Coeur de Lion)*
ROBERT FAULCONBRIDGE, *her legitimate son*
JAMES GURNEY, *her attendant*

EARL OF PEMBROKE
EARL OF ESSEX
EARL OF SALISBURY
LORD BIGOT
HUBERT DE BURGH, *a citizen of Angiers and afterward in the service of King John*
PETER OF POMFRET, *a prophet*
An English HERALD
Two MESSENGERS *to King John*
FIRST EXECUTIONER

KING PHILIP *of France (Philip II)*
LEWIS, *the Dauphin*
DUKE OF AUSTRIA *(Limoges)*
MELUN, *a French lord*
CHATILLON, *ambassador from France to King John*
A French HERALD
A MESSENGER *to the Dauphin*

CARDINAL PANDULPH, *the Pope's legate*

Lords, a Sheriff, Soldiers, Citizens of Angiers, Executioners, and Attendants

SCENE: *Partly in England and partly in France*]

1.1 *Enter King John, Queen Eleanor, Pembroke,
Essex, and Salisbury, with the Chatillon of
France.*

KING JOHN
  Now, say, Chatillon, what would France with us?   1
CHATILLON
  Thus, after greeting, speaks the King of France
  In my behavior to the majesty—   3
  The borrowed majesty—of England here.   4
ELEANOR
  A strange beginning: "borrowed majesty"!
KING JOHN
  Silence, good Mother. Hear the embassy.   6
CHATILLON
  Philip of France, in right and true behalf
  Of thy deceasèd brother Geoffrey's son,
  Arthur Plantagenet, lays most lawful claim
  To this fair island and the territories,
  To Ireland, Poitiers, Anjou, Touraine, Maine,
  Desiring thee to lay aside the sword
  Which sways usurpingly these several titles,   13
  And put the same into young Arthur's hand,
  Thy nephew and right royal sovereign.
KING JOHN
  What follows if we disallow of this?   16
CHATILLON
  The proud control of fierce and bloody war,   17
  To enforce these rights so forcibly withheld.
KING JOHN
  Here have we war for war and blood for blood,
  Controlment for controlment. So answer France.
CHATILLON
  Then take my king's defiance from my mouth,
  The farthest limit of my embassy.

1.1. Location: England. The court of King John.
1 what . . . us what does the King of France want with us   3 In my
behavior in my person and conduct, through me   4 borrowed i.e., not
belonging by true right   6 embassy message   13 sways manages,
directs.   several titles distinct possessions   16 disallow of reject
17 control compulsion

KING JOHN
Bear mine to him, and so depart in peace.
Be thou as lightning in the eyes of France;
For ere thou canst report I will be there,   25
The thunder of my cannon shall be heard.   26
So, hence! Be thou the trumpet of our wrath
And sullen presage of your own decay.—   28
An honorable conduct let him have.   29
Pembroke, look to 't.—Farewell, Chatillon.
                    Exeunt Chatillon and Pembroke.

ELEANOR
What now, my son? Have I not ever said
How that ambitious Constance would not cease   32
Till she had kindled France and all the world
Upon the right and party of her son?   34
This might have been prevented and made whole   35
With very easy arguments of love,   36
Which now the manage of two kingdoms must   37
With fearful bloody issue arbitrate.   38

KING JOHN
Our strong possession and our right for us.

ELEANOR [*Aside to King John*]
Your strong possession much more than your right,
Or else it must go wrong with you and me—
So much my conscience whispers in your ear,
Which none but heaven and you and I shall hear.

        Enter a Sheriff, [*who whispers to Essex*].

ESSEX
My liege, here is the strangest controversy,
Come from the country to be judged by you,
That e'er I heard. Shall I produce the men?

KING JOHN   Let them approach.
            [*The Sheriff goes to summon the men.*]

---

25 report (1) deliver your message (2) sound like thunder   **26 cannon**
(An anachronism, since gunpowder was not employed in Europe until
the fourteenth century.)   **28 sullen presage** dismal portent, omen.
decay ruin   **29 conduct** escort, guard   **32 How that** how   **34 Upon** in
behalf of.   **party** cause   **35 prevented** foreseen.   **made whole** set
right   **36 arguments of love** amicable negotiation   **37 manage** government   **38 issue** consequence

Our abbeys and our priories shall pay
This expeditious charge.

    Enter Robert Faulconbridge and Philip, [his
    bastard brother].

                What men are you?   49
BASTARD
Your faithful subject I, a gentleman,
Born in Northamptonshire, and eldest son,
As I suppose, to Robert Faulconbridge,
A soldier, by the honor-giving hand
Of Coeur de Lion knighted in the field.   54
KING JOHN   What art thou?
ROBERT
The son and heir to that same Faulconbridge.
KING JOHN
Is that the elder, and art thou the heir?
You came not of one mother then, it seems.
BASTARD
Most certain of one mother, mighty King—
That is well known—and, as I think, one father.
But for the certain knowledge of that truth
I put you o'er to heaven and to my mother.   62
Of that I doubt, as all men's children may.
ELEANOR
Out on thee, rude man! Thou dost shame thy mother,
And wound her honor, with this diffidence.   65
BASTARD
I, madam? No, I have no reason for it.
That is my brother's plea and none of mine—
The which if he can prove, 'a pops me out   68
At least from fair five hundred pound a year.
Heaven guard my mother's honor and my land!
KING JOHN
A good blunt fellow.—Why, being younger born,
Doth he lay claim to thine inheritance?

---

49 expeditious charge sudden expense **54 Coeur de Lion** Lion-heart,
i.e., Richard I **62 put you o'er** refer you **65 diffidence** distrust, suspicion **68 'a** he

BASTARD

I know not why, except to get the land.
But once he slandered me with bastardy.   74
But whe'er I be as true begot or no,   75
That still I lay upon my mother's head;   76
But that I am as well begot, my liege—
Fair fall the bones that took the pains for me!—   78
Compare our faces and be judge yourself.
If old Sir Robert did beget us both
And were our father, and this son like him,
O old Sir Robert, Father, on my knee
I give heaven thanks I was not like to thee!

KING JOHN

Why, what a madcap hath heaven lent us here!

ELEANOR

He hath a trick of Coeur de Lion's face;   85
The accent of his tongue affecteth him.   86
Do you not read some tokens of my son
In the large composition of this man?   88

KING JOHN

Mine eye hath well examinèd his parts
And finds them perfect Richard. [*To Robert.*] Sirrah,
  speak.   90
What doth move you to claim your brother's land?

BASTARD

Because he hath a half-face like my father.   92
With half that face would he have all my land—   93
A half-faced groat five hundred pound a year!   94

ROBERT

My gracious liege, when that my father lived,   95
Your brother did employ my father much—   96

---

74 once in short   **75 whe'er** whether   **76 lay . . . head** leave to my
mother to give account   **78 Fair fall** may good fortune befall.   **the
bones** i.e., the man, now dead   **85 trick** characteristic look   **86 affecteth** resembles   **88 large composition** (1) general constitution (2) big
build   **90 Sirrah** (Customary form of address to inferiors.)   **92 half-face**
(1) profile (2) defective, scant face   **93 With half that face** i.e., with only
half his father's thin face (but with plenty of cheek)   **94 half-faced groat**
i.e., coin bearing the sovereign's profile, and perhaps also clipped and
devalued. (The groat, worth four pence, is a figure for Robert's insig-
nificance, in antithesis to his fortune, five hundred pounds a year.)
95 when that when   **96 Your brother** i.e., Richard Coeur de Lion

BASTARD
  Well, sir, by this you cannot get my land.
  Your tale must be how he employed my mother.

ROBERT
  —And once dispatched him in an embassy
  To Germany, there with the Emperor
  To treat of high affairs touching that time.   101
  Th' advantage of his absence took the King
  And in the meantime sojourned at my father's;
  Where how he did prevail I shame to speak,
  But truth is truth. Large lengths of seas and shores
  Between my father and my mother lay,
  As I have heard my father speak himself,
  When this same lusty gentleman was got.   108
  Upon his deathbed he by will bequeathed
  His lands to me, and took it on his death   110
  That this my mother's son was none of his;
  And if he were, he came into the world
  Full fourteen weeks before the course of time.
  Then, good my liege, let me have what is mine,
  My father's land, as was my father's will.

KING JOHN
  Sirrah, your brother is legitimate.
  Your father's wife did after wedlock bear him,
  And if she did play false, the fault was hers—
  Which fault lies on the hazards of all husbands   119
  That marry wives. Tell me, how if my brother,
  Who, as you say, took pains to get this son,
  Had of your father claimed this son for his?
  In sooth, good friend, your father might have kept
  This calf, bred from his cow, from all the world;
  In sooth he might. Then, if he were my brother's,   125
  My brother might not claim him, nor your father,
  Being none of his, refuse him. This concludes: 127
  My mother's son did get your father's heir;
  Your father's heir must have your father's land.

101 To . . . time to discuss matters that were currently of first importance **108 lusty** merry. **got** begotten **110 took . . . death** i.e., swore
solemnly (the most solemn oath being a deathbed oath) **119 lies on the
hazards** is one of the risks **125 if** even if **127 Being . . . his** i.e., even if
the Bastard were not sired by him. **refuse** disclaim. **concludes** settles
the problem

ROBERT

   Shall then my father's will be of no force
   To dispossess that child which is not his?

BASTARD

   Of no more force to dispossess me, sir,
   Than was his will to get me, as I think.

ELEANOR [*To the Bastard*]

   Whether hadst thou rather be: a Faulconbridge   134
   And, like thy brother, to enjoy thy land,
   Or the reputed son of Coeur de Lion,
   Lord of thy presence, and no land besides?   137

BASTARD

   Madam, an if my brother had my shape   138
   And I had his, Sir Robert's his, like him,   139
   And if my legs were two such riding-rods,   140
   My arms such eel skins stuffed, my face so thin
   That in mine ear I durst not stick a rose   142
   Lest men should say "Look, where three-farthings
     goes!"
   And, to his shape, were heir to all this land,   144
   Would I might never stir from off this place,   145
   I would give it every foot to have this face;   146
   I would not be Sir Nob in any case.   147

ELEANOR

   I like thee well. Wilt thou forsake thy fortune,
   Bequeath thy land to him, and follow me?
   I am a soldier and now bound to France.

BASTARD

   Brother, take you my land. I'll take my chance.
   Your face hath got five hundred pound a year,

---

134 Whether which of two choices   **137 Lord of thy presence** i.e., master of your own person   **138 an if** if   **139 I had . . . him** i.e., I had Sir Robert's shape as my brother now has. (*Sir Robert's his* means "Sir Robert's.")   **140 riding-rods** switches (probably with a suggestion of sexual emaciation and insufficiency, as also in *eel skins stuffed,* l. 141, and *Sir Nob in any case,* l. 147)   **142 stick a rose** (The Queen's likeness on the three-farthing coin was distinguished from that on the three-halfpence by a rose behind her head. The Bastard's taunt is based on the thinness of the coin.)   **144 to his shape** in addition to (inheriting) his physical characteristics   **145 Would . . . place** i.e., may I never stir from this spot if I am not speaking the truth   **146 it every foot** every foot of it   **147 Nob** (Diminutive of *Robert;* with a possible play on *head* in a sexual sense and as head of the family.)

Yet sell your face for five pence and 'tis dear.—
Madam, I'll follow you unto the death.

ELEANOR
Nay, I would have you go before me thither.

BASTARD
Our country manners give our betters way.   156

KING JOHN   What is thy name?

BASTARD
Philip, my liege, so is my name begun;
Philip, good old Sir Robert's wife's eldest son.

KING JOHN
From henceforth bear his name whose form thou
   bearest.
Kneel thou down Philip, but rise more great:
          [*The Bastard kneels and is knighted*]
Arise Sir Richard, and Plantagenet. [*The Bastard rises.*]

BASTARD
Brother by th' mother's side, give me your hand.
My father gave me honor; yours gave land.
Now blessèd be the hour, by night or day,   165
When I was got, Sir Robert was away!   166

ELEANOR
The very spirit of Plantagenet!
I am thy grandam, Richard. Call me so.

BASTARD
Madam, by chance but not by truth; what though?   169
Something about, a little from the right,   170
   In at the window, or else o'er the hatch.   171
Who dares not stir by day must walk by night,
   And have is have, however men do catch.   173
Near or far off, well won is still well shot,   174
And I am I, howe'er I was begot.

---

156 give . . . way yield precedence to our superiors. (The Bastard jokes
that he will not upset social precedence to rush before Queen Eleanor
to death.)   **165–166 Now . . . away** i.e., I thank God that, at the blessed
time when I was conceived, whether by night or day, Sir Robert was
absent   **169 not by truth** not honorably, not chastely.   **what though**
what of that   **170 Something about** somewhat roundabout, clandestinely   **171 hatch** lower half door. (*O'er the hatch* means clandestinely,
out of wedlock.)   **173 have is . . . catch** possession is what matters,
however it is achieved   **174 Near . . . shot** i.e., in archery, hitting the
target is what matters, whatever the distance. (With sexual suggestion.)

KING JOHN

    Go, Faulconbridge. Now hast thou thy desire;
    A landless knight makes thee a landed squire.   177
    Come, madam, and come, Richard, we must speed
    For France, for France, for it is more than need.

BASTARD

    Brother, adieu. Good fortune come to thee!
    For thou wast got i' the way of honesty.

                           Exeunt all but Bastard.

    A foot of honor better than I was,   182
    But many a many foot of land the worse!
    Well, now can I make any Joan a lady.   184
    "Good e'en, Sir Richard!"—"God-a-mercy, fellow!"—   185
    And if his name be George, I'll call him Peter,
    For new-made honor doth forget men's names;
    'Tis too respective and too sociable   188
    For your conversion. Now your traveler,   189
    He and his toothpick at my worship's mess,   190
    And when my knightly stomach is sufficed,
    Why then I suck my teeth and catechize   192
    My pickèd man of countries: "My dear sir,"   193
    Thus, leaning on mine elbow, I begin,
    "I shall beseech you"—that is Question now;
    And then comes Answer like an Absey book: 196
    "O sir," says Answer, "at your best command;
    At your employment; at your service, sir."
    "No sir," says Question, "I, sweet sir, at yours";
    And so, ere Answer knows what Question would,   200
    Saving in dialogue of compliment,   201

---

177 A landless knight i.e., the Bastard, who is willing to trade his inheritance for a knighthood   **182 foot** degree   **184 Joan** (Frequently used to designate any girl, usually of the lower class.)   **185 Good e'en** good evening, good afternoon. (The Bastard imagines himself, in his new title, encountering a lower-class person.)   **God-a-mercy** God reward you **188 respective** considerate   **189 conversion** change of status, acquisition of *new-made honor*. (The Bastard wryly jokes that remembering names is too considerate a thing for a newly made knight to bother about.) **190 toothpick** (An affectation associated with foreign travel and the latest courtly fashion.)   **my worship's mess** i.e., my dinner table. (A knight was formally addressed as "your worship.")   **192 suck my teeth** (i.e., in contrast to the use of toothpick by the *traveler*)   **193 pickèd** (1) refined (2) having picked his teeth   **196 Absey** ABC, primer **200 would** intends, asks   **201 Saving . . . compliment** except in polite but inane conversation

And talking of the Alps and Apennines,
The Pyrenean and the river Po,
It draws toward supper in conclusion so.
But this is worshipful society
And fits the mounting spirit like myself,
For he is but a bastard to the time   207
That doth not smack of observation.   208
And so am I—whether I smack or no,   209
And not alone in habit and device,   210
Exterior form, outward accoutrement,
But from the inward motion—to deliver   212
Sweet, sweet, sweet poison for the age's tooth;   213
Which, though I will not practice to deceive,   214
Yet, to avoid deceit, I mean to learn;   215
For it shall strew the footsteps of my rising.   216
But who comes in such haste in riding robes?
What woman-post is this? Hath she no husband   218
That will take pains to blow a horn before her?   219

Enter Lady Faulconbridge and James Gurney.

O me! 'Tis my mother.—How now, good lady?
What brings you here to court so hastily?

LADY FAULCONBRIDGE
Where is that slave, thy brother? Where is he,
That holds in chase mine honor up and down?   223

BASTARD
My brother Robert, old Sir Robert's son?
Colbrand the Giant, that same mighty man?   225
Is it Sir Robert's son that you seek so?

207–208 but a bastard . . . observation i.e., not a true son of the times
unless he observes and practices courtly obsequiousness   **209 And
so . . . no** and so I intend, whether or not I have a true smack of obsequiousness   **210 habit and device** attire and outward appearance (with
a suggestion too of "coat of arms")   **212 from . . . motion** from my own
inclination. (The Bastard is partly attracted to the use of flattery for
self-advancement, even though he also laughs at it.)   **213 Sweet . . .
poison** flattery.   **tooth** i.e., sweet tooth, appetite   **214 practice to deceive** deliberately plan to deceive others   **215 deceit** being deceived
216 it . . . rising i.e., deceitful flattery will inevitably make easy my rise
in importance, just as rushes are strewn on the floors of great men
218 woman-post female messenger   **219 blow a horn** (The ordinary
signal of approach; with a punning reference to the horn of cuck-
oldry.)   **223 holds in chase** pursues   **225 Colbrand the Giant** legendary
Danish giant slain by Guy of Warwick in a popular romance named
after its hero

LADY FAULCONBRIDGE
  Sir Robert's son! Ay, thou unreverent boy,
  Sir Robert's son. Why scorn'st thou at Sir Robert?
  He is Sir Robert's son, and so art thou.

BASTARD
  James Gurney, wilt thou give us leave awhile?   230

GURNEY
  Good leave, good Philip.

BASTARD   Philip? Sparrow! James,   231
  There's toys abroad; anon I'll tell thee more.   232
                                        Exit James.

  Madam, I was not old Sir Robert's son;
  Sir Robert might have eat his part in me   234
  Upon Good Friday and ne'er broke his fast.
  Sir Robert could do well—marry, to confess—   236
  Could he get me! Sir Robert could not do it;   237
  We know his handiwork. Therefore, good Mother,
  To whom am I beholding for these limbs?   239
  Sir Robert never holp to make this leg.   240

LADY FAULCONBRIDGE
  Hast thou conspirèd with thy brother too,
  That for thine own gain shouldst defend mine honor?
  What means this scorn, thou most untoward knave?   243

BASTARD
  Knight, knight, good Mother, Basilisco-like.   244
  What! I am dubbed; I have it on my shoulder.   245
  But, Mother, I am not Sir Robert's son.
  I have disclaimed Sir Robert and my land;
  Legitimation, name, and all is gone.
  Then, good my Mother, let me know my father;
  Some proper man, I hope. Who was it, Mother?   250

230 give us leave leave us alone   **231 Philip? Sparrow** i.e., call me Philip
no more, a name commonly used for sparrows (because of their "Phip"-
like chirp), since I'm now Sir Richard   **232 toys** rumors, follies, interesting events   **234 eat** eaten. (Pronounced "et.")   **236 do** (With sexual
suggestion.)   **marry, to confess** indeed, to speak truly. (*Marry* was
originally an oath "by the Virgin Mary.")   **237 Could he get** if he could
beget   **239 beholding** beholden   **240 holp** helped   **243 untoward** unmannerly   **244 Basilisco-like** (The character Basilisco in the play
Solyman and Perseda, presumably by Thomas Kyd, insists braggartlike
on his knighthood but nevertheless is called "Knave" by his servant.)
245 dubbed made a knight by a touch of the sword on the shoulder
250 proper handsome, fine

LADY FAULCONBRIDGE
　Hast thou denied thyself a Faulconbridge?
BASTARD
　As faithfully as I deny the devil.
LADY FAULCONBRIDGE
　King Richard Coeur de Lion was thy father.
　By long and vehement suit I was seduced
　To make room for him in my husband's bed.
　Heaven lay not my transgression to my charge!
　Thou art the issue of my dear offense,　　　　　　257
　Which was so strongly urged past my defense.
BASTARD
　Now, by this light, were I to get again,　　　　　　259
　Madam, I would not wish a better father.
　Some sins do bear their privilege on earth,　　　　261
　And so doth yours. Your fault was not your folly.
　Needs must you lay your heart at his dispose,　　　263
　Subjected tribute to commanding love,
　Against whose fury and unmatchèd force
　The aweless lion could not wage the fight,　　　　266
　Nor keep his princely heart from Richard's hand.
　He that perforce robs lions of their hearts　　　　268
　May easily win a woman's. Ay, my Mother,
　With all my heart I thank thee for my father!
　Who lives and dares but say thou didst not well
　When I was got, I'll send his soul to hell.
　Come, lady, I will show thee to my kin;
　　And they shall say, when Richard me begot,
　If thou hadst said him nay, it had been sin.
　　Who says it was, he lies; I say 'twas not.　　　*Exeunt.*

❖

257 dear (1) precious, costly (2) loving　**259 get** be conceived
261 do . . . earth i.e., are excusable, venial　**263 dispose** disposal
266 aweless lion (During his imprisonment by the Duke of Austria,
according to legend, Coeur de Lion slew the Duke's son and as punishment was given to a hungry lion. When the lion attacked him, he slew it
by thrusting his hand down its throat and tearing out its heart, which
he is supposed to have eaten.)　**268 perforce** forcibly

2.1 *Enter, before Angiers, Philip King of France,
Lewis [the] Dauphine, Austria, Constance,
Arthur, [and soldiers].*

KING PHILIP

Before Angiers well met, brave Austria.—
Arthur, that great forerunner of thy blood,   2
Richard, that robbed the lion of his heart
And fought the holy wars in Palestine,
By this brave duke came early to his grave;   5
And for amends to his posterity,
At our importance hither is he come   7
To spread his colors, boy, in thy behalf,   8
And to rebuke the usurpation   9
Of thy unnatural uncle, English John.
Embrace him, love him, give him welcome hither.

ARTHUR [*To Austria*]

God shall forgive you Coeur de Lion's death
The rather that you give his offspring life,
Shadowing their right under your wings of war.   14
I give you welcome with a powerless hand,
But with a heart full of unstainèd love.
Welcome before the gates of Angiers, Duke.

KING PHILIP

A noble boy! Who would not do thee right?

AUSTRIA [*Kissing Arthur*]

Upon thy cheek lay I this zealous kiss,
As seal to this indenture of my love: 20
That to my home I will no more return
Till Angiers and the right thou hast in France,

2.1. Location: France. Before Angiers. (The French and Austrian forces
enter from opposite sides before the "gates" of Angiers seen backstage.)
s.d. Austria (The Duke of Austria wears a lion skin that he supposedly
took from Coeur de Lion; see note 5 and l. 292.) **2 forerunner** ancestor.
(Richard was actually not a direct ancestor of Arthur, but his uncle.)
5 By . . . duke (A confusion of the Duke of Austria with Viscount Limoges, before whose castle Richard was mortally wounded. The roles of
the two were combined in *The Troublesome Reign of King John* as they
are in this play.) **7 importance** importunity **8 spread his colors** display his military colors, his battle ensigns **9 rebuke** put down
14 Shadowing sheltering **20 indenture** contract

Together with that pale, that white-faced shore,   23
Whose foot spurns back the ocean's roaring tides
And coops from other lands her islanders,   25
Even till that England, hedged in with the main,   26
That water-wallèd bulwark, still secure   27
And confident from foreign purposes,
Even till that utmost corner of the west
Salute thee for her king. Till then, fair boy,
Will I not think of home, but follow arms.

CONSTANCE
O, take his mother's thanks, a widow's thanks,
Till your strong hand shall help to give him strength
To make a more requital to your love!   34

AUSTRIA
The peace of heaven is theirs that lift their swords
In such a just and charitable war.

KING PHILIP
Well then, to work. Our cannon shall be bent   37
Against the brows of this resisting town.
Call for our chiefest men of discipline,   39
To cull the plots of best advantages.   40
We'll lay before this town our royal bones,
Wade to the marketplace in Frenchmen's blood,
But we will make it subject to this boy.   43

CONSTANCE
Stay for an answer to your embassy,
Lest unadvised you stain your swords with blood.   45
My Lord Chatillon may from England bring
That right in peace which here we urge in war,
And then we shall repent each drop of blood
That hot rash haste so indirectly shed.   49

    Enter Chatillon.

KING PHILIP
A wonder, lady! Lo, upon thy wish,
Our messenger Chatillon is arrived.—

---

23 pale . . . shore i.e., the chalk cliffs at Dover   **25 coops** encloses for
defense   **26 main** ocean   **27 still** perpetually   **34 more** greater
37 bent directed   **39 men of discipline** men trained in military strat-
egy   **40 To . . . advantages** to select positions that are most favorable for
attack   **43 But** unless   **45 unadvised** rashly   **49 indirectly** wrongfully,
misdirectedly

What England says, say briefly, gentle lord;   52
We coldly pause for thee. Chatillon, speak.   53

CHATILLON

Then turn your forces from this paltry siege
And stir them up against a mightier task.
England, impatient of your just demands,
Hath put himself in arms. The adverse winds,
Whose leisure I have stayed, have given him time   58
To land his legions all as soon as I.
His marches are expedient to this town,   60
His forces strong, his soldiers confident.
With him along is come the Mother-Queen,
An Ate, stirring him to blood and strife;   63
With her her niece, the Lady Blanche of Spain;   64
With them a bastard of the King's deceased.   65
And all th' unsettled humors of the land—   66
Rash, inconsiderate, fiery voluntaries,   67
With ladies' faces and fierce dragons' spleens—   68
Have sold their fortunes at their native homes,
Bearing their birthrights proudly on their backs,   70
To make a hazard of new fortunes here.
In brief, a braver choice of dauntless spirits   72
Than now the English bottoms have waft o'er   73
Did never float upon the swelling tide
To do offense and scathe in Christendom. *Drum beats.*   75
The interruption of their churlish drums   76
Cuts off more circumstance. They are at hand,   77
To parley or to fight. Therefore prepare.

KING PHILIP

How much unlooked-for is this expedition!   79

---

52 England the King of England (also in l. 56 and perhaps l. 46).
gentle noble **53 coldly** calmly **58 leisure** convenience. **stayed** waited
for **60 expedient** speedy **63 Ate** Greek goddess of discord **64 niece**
i.e., granddaughter **65 of . . . deceased** of the deceased King, i.e.,
Richard **66 unsettled humors** i.e., disgruntled individuals **67 inconsiderate** reckless, heedless. **voluntaries** volunteers **68 With ladies'
faces** i.e., beardless. **fierce dragons' spleens** i.e., utmost fierceness.
(The spleen was thought to be the seat of the passions.) **70 Bearing . . .
backs** i.e., having sold everything to obtain armor **72 choice** picked
company **73 bottoms** i.e., ships. **waft** wafted **75 scathe** harm
76 churlish uncouth, rude **77 circumstance** detailed reporting
79 expedition speed

AUSTRIA

By how much unexpected, by so much
We must awake endeavor for defense,
For courage mounteth with occasion.   82
Let them be welcome, then. We are prepared.

   Enter King [John] of England, Bastard, Queen
   [Eleanor], Blanche, Pembroke, and others.

KING JOHN

Peace be to France, if France in peace permit
Our just and lineal entrance to our own.   85
If not, bleed France, and peace ascend to heaven,
Whiles we, God's wrathful agent, do correct   87
Their proud contempt that beats His peace to heaven.

KING PHILIP

Peace be to England, if that war return
From France to England, there to live in peace.
England we love, and for that England's sake   91
With burden of our armor here we sweat.
This toil of ours should be a work of thine;   93
But thou from loving England art so far
That thou hast underwrought his lawful king,   95
Cut off the sequence of posterity,   96
Outfacèd infant state, and done a rape   97
Upon the maiden virtue of the crown.
Look here upon thy brother Geoffrey's face:
These eyes, these brows, were molded out of his;
This little abstract doth contain that large   101
Which died in Geoffrey, and the hand of time   102
Shall draw this brief into as huge a volume.   103
That Geoffrey was thy elder brother born,
And this his son. England was Geoffrey's right,
And this is Geoffrey's. In the name of God,   106

82 occasion emergency **85 lineal** by right of birth **87 correct** chastise **91 England's** i.e., Arthur's, whose claim to England the French King is supporting **93 This . . . thine** i.e., you should be supporting our cause also, since it is your duty **95 underwrought his** undermined its **96 sequence of posterity** lawful succession **97 Outfacèd infant state** defied the majesty of a boy king **101 little abstract** abridgment or epitome **101–102 doth . . . Geoffrey** contains that which, in its complete form, died in Geoffrey **103 draw this brief** enlarge this epitome **106 this** i.e., Arthur himself, or Angiers, or the English crown

How comes it then that thou art called a king,
When living blood doth in these temples beat
Which owe the crown that thou o'ermasterest?   109

KING JOHN
From whom hast thou this great commission, France,
To draw my answer from thy articles?   111

KING PHILIP
From that supernal judge that stirs good thoughts   112
In any breast of strong authority
To look into the blots and stains of right.
That judge hath made me guardian to this boy,
Under whose warrant I impeach thy wrong   116
And by whose help I mean to chastise it.

KING JOHN
Alack, thou dost usurp authority.

KING PHILIP
Excuse it is to beat usurping down.   119

ELEANOR
Who is it thou dost call usurper, France?

CONSTANCE
Let me make answer: thy usurping son.

ELEANOR
Out, insolent! Thy bastard shall be king,   122
That thou mayst be a queen and check the world!   123

CONSTANCE
My bed was ever to thy son as true
As thine was to thy husband, and this boy
Liker in feature to his father Geoffrey
Than thou and John in manners—being as like
As rain to water, or devil to his dam.   128
My boy a bastard? By my soul, I think

---

109 owe own   **111 draw . . . articles** i.e., claim the right to demand of
me an answer to the items in your indictment   **112 supernal** celestial,
supreme   **116 whose** i.e., the supreme judge's, God's.   **impeach** accuse   **119 Excuse . . . down** i.e., the excuse for what you call my usurping of authority is that I am in fact resisting and defeating usurpation
122 Out (An exclamation of remonstrance.)   **123 check** control
128 dam mother. (Constance says that Arthur is more like his father,
and therefore no bastard, than John is like his mother—a resemblance
that would not rule out bastardy, especially when the two are as alike
as the devil and his mother. Constance goes on to wonder if John's
brother Geoffrey might also be a bastard.)

His father never was so true begot.
It cannot be, an if thou wert his mother.   131

ELEANOR [*To Arthur*]
There's a good mother, boy, that blots thy father.   132

CONSTANCE [*To Arthur*]
There's a good grandam, boy, that would blot thee.   133

AUSTRIA
Peace!

BASTARD   Hear the crier!

AUSTRIA   What the devil art thou?   134

BASTARD
One that will play the devil, sir, with you,
An 'a may catch your hide and you alone.   136
You are the hare of whom the proverb goes,   137
Whose valor plucks dead lions by the beard.
I'll smoke your skin coat an I catch you right.   139
Sirrah, look to 't. I' faith I will, i' faith.

BLANCHE
O, well did he become that lion's robe   141
That did disrobe the lion of that robe!

BASTARD
It lies as sightly on the back of him   143
As great Alcides' shows upon an ass.   144
But, ass, I'll take that burden from your back,
Or lay on that shall make your shoulders crack.   146

AUSTRIA
What cracker is this same that deafs our ears   147
With this abundance of superfluous breath?
King Philip, determine what we shall do straight.   149

KING PHILIP
Women and fools, break off your conference.   150

---

131 an if if   **132 blots** slanders   **133 blot** (with a pun on "obliterate, efface")   **134 Hear the crier** (A mocking suggestion by the Bastard that Austria's call for silence likens him to the town crier.)   **136 An 'a** if he. **hide** i.e., the lion's skin Austria wears in celebration of his triumph over Richard Coeur de Lion   **137 the proverb** i.e., "even hares may insult the dead lion." (This proverb occurs in Erasmus's *Adages*.)
139 smoke thrash, beat. **your skin coat** your own skin   **141 he** i.e., Richard Coeur de Lion   **143 sightly** suitably. (Said ironically.) **him** i.e., the Duke of Austria   **144 Alcides** Hercules, who slew the Nemean lion as one of his twelve labors and thereafter wore its pelt   **146 lay on that** i.e., beat you with a club that   **147 cracker** i.e., boaster (with a play on *crack*, l. 146)   **149 straight** at once   **150 fools** children

King John, this is the very sum of all:
England and Ireland, Anjou, Touraine, Maine,
In right of Arthur do I claim of thee.
Wilt thou resign them and lay down thy arms?

KING JOHN
My life as soon. I do defy thee, France.
Arthur of Brittaine, yield thee to my hand,   156
And out of my dear love I'll give thee more
Than e'er the coward hand of France can win.
Submit thee, boy.

ELEANOR   Come to thy grandam, child.

CONSTANCE
Do, child, go to it grandam, child;   160
Give grandam kingdom, and it grandam will
Give it a plum, a cherry, and a fig.
There's a good grandam.

ARTHUR   Good my Mother, peace!
I would that I were low laid in my grave.
I am not worth this coil that's made for me.   165

[*He weeps.*]

ELEANOR
His mother shames him so, poor boy, he weeps.

CONSTANCE
Now shame upon you, whe'er she does or no!   167
His grandam's wrongs, and not his mother's shames,   168
Draws those heaven-moving pearls from his poor eyes,
Which heaven shall take in nature of a fee.   170
Ay, with these crystal beads heaven shall be bribed   171
To do him justice and revenge on you.

ELEANOR
Thou monstrous slanderer of heaven and earth!

CONSTANCE
Thou monstrous injurer of heaven and earth!
Call not me slanderer. Thou and thine usurp
The dominations, royalties, and rights   176

---

156 **Brittaine** Brittany   160 **Do . . . grandam** (Contemptuous baby
talk.)   **it** its (also in l. 161)   165 **coil** disturbance, fuss   167 **whe'er**
whether   168 **wrongs** wrongdoings.   **shames** insults   170 **a fee** i.e.,
the fee paid to heaven in return for pleading as Arthur's advocate
171 **beads** i.e., tears, here as gifts used to curry favor, or prayer beads
176 **dominations** dominions, sovereignties.   **royalties** royal prerogatives

Of this oppressèd boy. This is thy eldest son's son,   177
Infortunate in nothing but in thee.   178
Thy sins are visited in this poor child;   179
The canon of the law is laid on him,   180
Being but the second generation
Removèd from thy sin-conceiving womb.

KING JOHN
Bedlam, have done.

CONSTANCE   I have but this to say,   183
That he is not only plaguèd for her sin,   184
But God hath made her sin and her the plague   185
On this removèd issue, plagued for her   186
And with her plague; her sin his injury,   187
Her injury the beadle to her sin,   188
All punished in the person of this child,
And all for her. A plague upon her!

ELEANOR
Thou unadvisèd scold, I can produce   191
A will that bars the title of thy son.   192

CONSTANCE
Ay, who doubts that? A will, a wicked will,
A woman's will, a cankered grandam's will!

KING PHILIP
Peace, lady! Pause, or be more temperate.
It ill beseems this presence to cry aim   196
To these ill-tunèd repetitions.   197
Some trumpet summon hither to the walls   198

177 eldest son's son i.e., eldest grandchild, not son of the eldest son
178 Infortunate unfortunate   **179 visited** punished   **180 canon . . . law**
i.e., that the sins of parents shall be visited upon their children to the
third and fourth generation; see Exodus 20:5   **183 Bedlam** lunatic
184 he i.e., Arthur.   **her sin** i.e., Eleanor's alleged adultery when she
conceived John. (See ll. 124 ff.)   **185 her sin** i.e., John, the issue of her
sin   **186 removèd issue** distant descendant, i.e., Arthur.   **for her** on her
account   **187 with her plague** i.e., by the offspring, John, with whom
she was cursed.   **his injury** i.e., the wrong done to Arthur   **188 Her
injury** Eleanor's wrong deeds, which act as the officer (*beadle*) to incite
her son John (*her sin*) on to further wrongs   **191 unadvisèd** rash   **192 A
will** i.e., according to Holinshed and other chroniclers, the final testament of Richard Coeur de Lion naming John as his heir and disinherit-
ing Arthur who had been named heir in a previous will. (But Constance
deliberately takes *will* to mean "willfulness.")   **196 ill . . . presence** is
not proper in the presence of royalty   **196–197 cry aim To** encourage.
(An archery term.)   **198 trumpet** trumpeter

These men of Angiers. Let us hear them speak
Whose title they admit, Arthur's or John's.   200

> *Trumpet sounds. Enter citizens [one of them*
> *Hubert] upon the walls.*

HUBERT
Who is it that hath warned us to the walls?   201
KING PHILIP
'Tis France, for England.
KING JOHN   England, for itself.   202
You men of Angiers, and my loving subjects—
KING PHILIP
You loving men of Angiers, Arthur's subjects,
Our trumpet called you to this gentle parle—   205
KING JOHN
For our advantage; therefore hear us first.
These flags of France, that are advancèd here   207
Before the eye and prospect of your town,
Have hither marched to your endamagement.
The cannons have their bowels full of wrath,
And ready mounted are they to spit forth
Their iron indignation 'gainst your walls.
All preparation for a bloody siege
And merciless proceeding by these French
Confronts your city's eyes, your winking gates;   215
And but for our approach those sleeping stones,
That as a waist doth girdle you about,
By the compulsion of their ordinance   218
By this time from their fixèd beds of lime
Had been dishabited, and wide havoc made   220
For bloody power to rush upon your peace.
But on the sight of us your lawful king,
Who painfully, with much expedient march,   223
Have brought a countercheck before your gates

---

200 s.d. upon the walls i.e., in the upper gallery rearstage. (Throughout
this scene, the tiring house facade is visualized as the walls of Angiers.) **201 warned** summoned **202 'Tis France, for England** i.e., it is
the French King, on behalf of Arthur, true King of England **205 parle**
parley **207 advancèd** raised **215 winking** closed **218 their** i.e., *these*
French (l. 214). **ordinance** ordnance, artillery **220 dishabited** dis-
lodged **223 painfully** having taken great pains or care. **expedient**
swift

To save unscratched your city's threatened cheeks,
Behold, the French, amazed, vouchsafe a parle; 226
And now, instead of bullets wrapped in fire, 227
To make a shaking fever in your walls,
They shoot but calm words folded up in smoke 229
To make a faithless error in your ears. 230
Which trust accordingly, kind citizens, 231
And let us in, your king, whose labored spirits, 232
Forwearied in this action of swift speed, 233
Craves harborage within your city walls.

KING PHILIP
When I have said, make answer to us both. 235
Lo, in this right hand, whose protection 236
Is most divinely vowed upon the right 237
Of him it holds, stands young Plantagenet, 238
Son to the elder brother of this man,
And king o'er him and all that he enjoys. 240
For this downtrodden equity we tread 241
In warlike march these greens before your town,
Being no further enemy to you
Than the constraint of hospitable zeal 244
In the relief of this oppressèd child
Religiously provokes. Be pleasèd then
To pay that duty which you truly owe
To him that owes it, namely this young prince; 248
And then our arms, like to a muzzled bear,
Save in aspect, hath all offense sealed up. 250
Our cannons' malice vainly shall be spent
Against th' invulnerable clouds of heaven;
And with a blessèd and unvexed retire, 253
With unhacked swords and helmets all unbruised,
We will bear home that lusty blood again

226 **amazed** stunned   227 **bullets** cannonballs   229 **folded up in smoke**
i.e., deceptively concealed in rhetoric   230 **faithless error** perfidious
lie   231 **trust accordingly** trust as such lies deserve, i.e., not at all
232 **labored** oppressed with labor   233 **Forwearied in** exhausted by
235 **said** finished speaking   236–238 **in . . . holds** i.e., led by my right
hand, which hand is most sacredly committed to defend the right of the
person whose hand it now holds   240 **enjoys** possesses, rules over
241 **For** on behalf of.   **equity** justice, right   244 **constraint** necessity
248 **owes** owns, has a right to   250 **Save in aspect** except in appearance.   **hath . . . up** will see to it that all capacity for injury to you is
sealed up   253 **unvexed retire** unhindered withdrawal

Which here we came to spout against your town,
And leave your children, wives, and you in peace.
But if you fondly pass our proffered offer, 258
'Tis not the roundure of your old-faced walls 259
Can hide you from our messengers of war, 260
Though all these English and their discipline 261
Were harbored in their rude circumference. 262
Then tell us, shall your city call us lord
In that behalf which we have challenged it, 264
Or shall we give the signal to our rage
And stalk in blood to our possession?

HUBERT
In brief, we are the King of England's subjects.
For him, and in his right, we hold this town.

KING JOHN
Acknowledge then the King and let me in.

HUBERT
That can we not. But he that proves the King, 270
To him will we prove loyal. Till that time
Have we rammed up our gates against the world.

KING JOHN
Doth not the crown of England prove the King?
And if not that, I bring you witnesses,
Twice fifteen thousand hearts of England's breed—

BASTARD   Bastards, and else. 276

KING JOHN
To verify our title with their lives.

KING PHILIP
As many and as wellborn bloods as those— 278

BASTARD   Some bastards too.

KING PHILIP
Stand in his face to contradict his claim. 280

HUBERT
Till you compound whose right is worthiest, 281
We for the worthiest hold the right from both. 282

---

258 fondly pass foolishly pass up   **259 roundure** roundness, enclosure,
circumference   **260 messengers** i.e., cannonballs   **261 discipline** military skill   **262 rude** rough   **264 In . . . which** on behalf of him for
whom   **270 proves** i.e., proves himself, proves to be   **276 else** others,
suchlike   **278 bloods** men of mettle and of good breeding   **280 in his
face** opposite to him   **281 compound** settle, agree   **282 for** in the
interests of.   **hold** withhold

KING JOHN

  Then God forgive the sin of all those souls
  That to their everlasting residence,
  Before the dew of evening fall, shall fleet,   285
  In dreadful trial of our kingdom's king!   286

KING PHILIP

  Amen, amen! Mount, chevaliers! To arms!

BASTARD

  Saint George, that swinged the dragon, and e'er since   288
  Sits on 's horseback at mine hostess' door,   289
  Teach us some fence! [*To Austria.*] Sirrah, were I at
    home,   290
  At your den, sirrah, with your lioness,   291
  I would set an ox head to your lion's hide,   292
  And make a monster of you.

AUSTRIA   Peace! No more.

BASTARD

  O, tremble, for you hear the lion roar.

KING JOHN

  Up higher to the plain, where we'll set forth
  In best appointment all our regiments.   296

BASTARD

  Speed then, to take advantage of the field.   297

KING PHILIP

  It shall be so; and at the other hill
  Command the rest to stand. God and our right!   299
          Exeunt [*separately. The citizens remain
                       above, on the walls.*]

*Here after excursions, enter the Herald of France,
with trumpets, to the gates.*

FRENCH HERALD

  You men of Angiers, open wide your gates,

---

285 fleet fly, leave (their bodies)   **286 dreadful trial** fearful encounter,
contest (with a suggestion too of the soul's *dreadful trial* before God).
of . . . king to determine who is king of our kingdom   **288 swinged**
whipped, thrashed   **289 Sits . . . door** (One of the most common signs at
tavern doors was that of Saint George and the dragon.)   **290 fence** skill
in swordsmanship   **291 lioness** (with a suggestion of "whore")   **292 set
an ox head** i.e., give you the horns of a cuckold   **296 appointment** order,
readiness   **297 take . . . field** gain tactical position   **299 the rest** i.e.,
our reserve forces.   **s.d. excursions** skirmishes, sorties

And let young Arthur, Duke of Brittaine, in,
Who by the hand of France this day hath made   302
Much work for tears in many an English mother,   303
Whose sons lie scattered on the bleeding ground.
Many a widow's husband groveling lies,
Coldly embracing the discolored earth,
And victory, with little loss, doth play
Upon the dancing banners of the French,
Who are at hand, triumphantly displayed,   309
To enter conquerors and to proclaim
Arthur of Brittaine England's king and yours.   311

    Enter English Herald, with trumpet.

ENGLISH HERALD
Rejoice, you men of Angiers, ring your bells!
King John, your king and England's, doth approach,
Commander of this hot malicious day.   314
Their armors, that marched hence so silver bright,
Hither return all gilt with Frenchmen's blood.   316
There stuck no plume in any English crest   317
That is removèd by a staff of France.   318
Our colors do return in those same hands   319
That did display them when we first marched forth;   320
And like a jolly troop of huntsmen come
Our lusty English, all with purpled hands   322
Dyed in the dying slaughter of their foes.   323
Open your gates and give the victors way.
HUBERT
Heralds, from off our towers we might behold,
From first to last, the onset and retire   326

---

302 by . . . France with the aid of the French King   **303 work** cause
309 triumphantly displayed deployed or arranged for a triumphal
celebration   **311 s.d. trumpet** trumpeter   **314 Commander** victor.   **hot
malicious day** a day hotly and violently contested   **316 gilt** gilded in
red   **317–318 There . . . France** i.e., no English helmet was so dishon-
ored as to have the plume of its crest struck off by a French spear.
staff spear   **319–320 Our . . . forth** i.e., we have not been obliged to
strike our colors   **322 lusty** vigorous   **323 Dyed . . . foes** (Huntsmen
dipped their hands in the blood of a slain deer to celebrate the slaughter.)   **326 onset and retire** attack and retreat

Of both your armies, whose equality   327
By our best eyes cannot be censurèd.   328
Blood hath bought blood, and blows have answered
     blows,
Strength matched with strength, and power confronted
     power.
Both are alike, and both alike we like.
One must prove greatest. While they weigh so even,
We hold our town for neither, yet for both.   333

> *Enter the two Kings, with their powers, at several*
> *doors: [King John with Queen Eleanor, Blanche,*
> *the Bastard, and forces at one door, King Philip*
> *with Lewis, Austria, and forces at the other.]*

KING JOHN
France, hast thou yet more blood to cast away?
Say, shall the current of our right run on,
Whose passage, vexed with thy impediment,
Shall leave his native channel and o'erswell   337
With course disturbed even thy confining shores,   338
Unless thou let his silver water keep
A peaceful progress to the ocean?

KING PHILIP
England, thou hast not saved one drop of blood
In this hot trial more than we of France;
Rather, lost more. And by this hand I swear,
That sways the earth this climate overlooks,   344
Before we will lay down our just-borne arms,
We'll put thee down, 'gainst whom these arms we bear,
Or add a royal number to the dead,   347
Gracing the scroll that tells of this war's loss
With slaughter coupled to the name of kings.

327–328 whose . . . censurèd whose equality is such that our keenest
observations cannot determine any difference   **333 s.d. powers** armies.   **several** separate   **337 his native** its normal   **338 even . . . shores**
(John hints that his might, fully roused in defense of what he claims for
his own right, will spill over into French territory.)   **344 climate** portion
of the sky   **347 a royal number** i.e., a king's name. (King Philip will win
or die in the attempt, and perhaps take other kings with him.)

BASTARD

Ha, majesty! How high thy glory towers 350
When the rich blood of kings is set on fire!
O, now doth Death line his dead chaps with steel; 352
The swords of soldiers are his teeth, his fangs;
And now he feasts, mousing the flesh of men 354
In undetermined differences of kings. 355
Why stand these royal fronts amazèd thus? 356
Cry havoc, Kings! Back to the stainèd field, 357
You equal potents, fiery-kindled spirits! 358
Then let confusion of one part confirm 359
The other's peace. Till then, blows, blood, and death!

KING JOHN

Whose party do the townsmen yet admit? 361

KING PHILIP

Speak, citizens, for England. Who's your king?

HUBERT

The King of England, when we know the king.

KING PHILIP

Know him in us, that here hold up his right.

KING JOHN

In us, that are our own great deputy
And bear possession of our person here, 366
Lord of our presence, Angiers, and of you. 367

HUBERT

A greater power than we denies all this,
And, till it be undoubted, we do lock
Our former scruple in our strong-barred gates,
Kinged of our fear, until our fears, resolved, 371
Be by some certain king purged and deposed.

BASTARD

By heaven, these scroyles of Angiers flout you, Kings, 373
And stand securely on their battlements
As in a theater, whence they gape and point

350 **How . . . towers** to what height the glory-seeking spirit of majesty
soars. (An image from hawking.) **352 chaps** jaws **354 mousing** tearing,
gnawing **355 undetermined differences** unsettled quarrels **356 royal
fronts** i.e., faces of kings **357 Cry havoc** proclaim a general slaughter
with no taking of prisoners **358 potents** potentates **359 confusion**
destruction, overthrow. **part** faction, party **361 yet** now **366 bear . . .
person** embody the claims of sovereignty in my own person, needing no
deputy **367 Lord of our presence** my own master **371 Kinged of** ruled
by **373 scroyles** scoundrels

At your industrious scenes and acts of death.
Your royal presences be ruled by me: 377
Do like the mutines of Jerusalem,   378
Be friends awhile, and both conjointly bend   379
Your sharpest deeds of malice on this town.
By east and west let France and England mount
Their battering cannon chargèd to the mouths,   382
Till their soul-fearing clamors have brawled down   383
The flinty ribs of this contemptuous city.
I'd play incessantly upon these jades,   385
Even till unfencèd desolation   386
Leave them as naked as the vulgar air.   387
That done, dissever your united strengths
And part your mingled colors once again;
Turn face to face and bloody point to point.
Then, in a moment, Fortune shall cull forth
Out of one side her happy minion,   392
To whom in favor she shall give the day   393
And kiss him with a glorious victory.
How like you this wild counsel, mighty states?   395
Smacks it not something of the policy?   396

KING JOHN
Now, by the sky that hangs above our heads,
I like it well. France, shall we knit our powers
And lay this Angiers even with the ground,
Then after fight who shall be king of it?

BASTARD [*To King Philip*]
An if thou hast the mettle of a king,
Being wronged as we are by this peevish town,   402
Turn thou the mouth of thy artillery,
As we will ours, against these saucy walls;
And when that we have dashed them to the ground,   405

377 **Your royal presences** may Your Majesties   378 **mutines** muti-
neers.   **Jerusalem** (During the siege of Jerusalem by Titus, A.D. 70, two
rival Jewish factions united to resist the Romans.)   379 **conjointly bend**
together aim   382 **chargèd to the mouths** filled to the brim with shot
383 **soul-fearing** inspiring fear in the soul.   **brawled down** i.e., noisily
leveled   385 **play . . . jades** i.e., (1) fire cannon repeatedly upon these
wretches (2) torment these nags. (*Jades* are ill-conditioned horses.)
386 **unfencèd** defenseless   387 **vulgar** common   392 **minion** favorite
393 **give the day** award the victory   395 **states** kings   396 **something**
somewhat.   **the policy** the art of politics, a canny maneuver
402 **peevish** stubborn   405 **when that** when

Why, then defy each other, and pell-mell   406
Make work upon ourselves, for heaven or hell.

KING PHILIP
Let it be so. Say, where will you assault?

KING JOHN
We from the west will send destruction
Into this city's bosom.

AUSTRIA   I from the north.

KING PHILIP   Our thunder from the south
Shall rain their drift of bullets on this town.   413

BASTARD
O prudent discipline! From north to south   414
Austria and France shoot in each other's mouth.
I'll stir them to it.—Come, away, away!

                 [*The armies start to move.*]

HUBERT
Hear us, great kings! Vouchsafe awhile to stay,
And I shall show you peace and fair-faced league,
Win you this city without stroke or wound,
Rescue those breathing lives to die in beds
That here come sacrifices for the field.
Persever not, but hear me, mighty kings.   422

KING JOHN
Speak on with favor. We are bent to hear.   423

HUBERT
That daughter there of Spain, the Lady Blanche,
Is near to England. Look upon the years   425
Of Lewis the Dauphin and that lovely maid.
If lusty love should go in quest of beauty,
Where should he find it fairer than in Blanche?
If zealous love should go in search of virtue,   429
Where should he find it purer than in Blanche?
If love ambitious sought a match of birth,   431
Whose veins bound richer blood than Lady Blanche?   432
Such as she is, in beauty, virtue, birth,
Is the young Dauphin every way complete.   434

---

406 pell-mell headlong   **413 drift** shower.   **bullets** cannonballs
414 prudent discipline fine military skill. (Said sarcastically.)   **422 Persever** persevere   **423 favor** permission.   **bent** inclined   **425 near to England** a near relative of King John, i.e., his niece   **429 zealous** virtue-seeking   **431 of birth** i.e., of equal royal rank   **432 bound** contain **434 complete** accomplished, perfect in

If not complete of, say he is not she, 435
And she again wants nothing, to name want, 436
If want it be not that she is not he. 437
He is the half part of a blessèd man,
Left to be finishèd by such as she,
And she a fair divided excellence,
Whose fullness of perfection lies in him.
O, two such silver currents, when they join,
Do glorify the banks that bound them in;
And two such shores to two such streams made one,
Two such controlling bounds, shall you be, Kings,
To these two princes, if you marry them.
This union shall do more than battery can 447
To our fast-closèd gates; for at this match, 448
With swifter spleen than powder can enforce, 449
The mouth of passage shall we fling wide ope
And give you entrance. But without this match,
The sea enragèd is not half so deaf,
Lions more confident, mountains and rocks
More free from motion, no, not Death himself
In mortal fury half so peremptory, 455
As we to keep this city.
BASTARD   Here's a stay 456
That shakes the rotten carcass of old Death 457
Out of his rags! Here's a large mouth, indeed, 458
That spits forth Death and mountains, rocks and seas,
Talks as familiarly of roaring lions
As maids of thirteen do of puppy dogs.
What cannoneer begot this lusty blood? 462
He speaks plain cannon: fire and smoke and bounce. 463
He gives the bastinado with his tongue. 464
Our ears are cudgeled; not a word of his

435–437 If . . . he (The idea here appears to be that the two young
people lack only each other to be perfect in themselves.) **436 wants**
lacks **437 If . . . he** unless it is called a lack that she is not he **447 battery** artillery **448 match** (1) marriage (2) fire used to ignite gunpowder **449 spleen** i.e., eager violent energy **455 peremptory** determined **456–458 Here's . . . rags** i.e., here's a pause for consideration,
one that shakes things up so that the skeleton of Death itself is shaken
out of its rags and tatters. **stay** hindrance, obstacle **458 mouth** i.e.,
like the mouth of a cannon, but spewing forth rhetoric **462 lusty blood**
hot-blooded chap. (Said sardonically.) **463 bounce** i.e., the noise of the
cannon **464 bastinado** beating with a cudgel

But buffets better than a fist of France.
Zounds! I was never so bethumped with words   467
Since I first called my brother's father Dad.   468

                    [The French confer apart.]

ELEANOR *[To King John]*
Son, list to this conjunction; make this match.   469
Give with our niece a dowry large enough,
For by this knot thou shalt so surely tie
Thy now unsured assurance to the crown
That yon green boy shall have no sun to ripe   473
The bloom that promiseth a mighty fruit.
I see a yielding in the looks of France;
Mark how they whisper. Urge them while their souls
Are capable of this ambition,   477
Lest zeal, now melted by the windy breath   478
Of soft petitions, pity, and remorse,   479
Cool and congeal again to what it was.

HUBERT
Why answer not the double majesties
This friendly treaty of our threatened town?   482

KING PHILIP
Speak England first, that hath been forward first
To speak unto this city. What say you?

KING JOHN
If that the Dauphin there, thy princely son,   485
Can in this book of beauty read "I love,"   486
Her dowry shall weigh equal with a queen;
For Anjou and fair Touraine, Maine, Poitiers,
And all that we upon this side the sea—
Except this city now by us besieged—
Find liable to our crown and dignity,   491
Shall gild her bridal bed and make her rich

---

467 Zounds by God's (Christ's) wounds   **468 Since . . . Dad** i.e., since I
learned to speak. (Colloquial, but here with particular fitness to the
Bastard's illegitimacy.)   **469 list** listen   **473 green** youthful, hence
unripe.   **boy** i.e., Arthur   **477 capable of** susceptible to.   **ambition** i.e.,
scheme that might seem to their advantage   **478 zeal** i.e., the French
King's zeal in Arthur's behalf. (The metaphor is one of melting and
hardening wax.)   **479 remorse** compassion   **482 treaty** proposal   **485 If
that** if   **486 book . . . "I love"** (An allusion to William Lilly's famous
Latin grammar, in which the verb *amo*, "I love," was used as a para-
digm.)   **491 Find liable** regard as subject

In titles, honors, and promotions,   493
As she in beauty, education, blood,
Holds hand with any princess of the world.   495

KING PHILIP
What sayst thou, boy? Look in the lady's face.

LEWIS
I do, my lord, and in her eye I find
A wonder, or a wondrous miracle,
The shadow of myself formed in her eye,   499
Which, being but the shadow of your son,   500
Becomes a sun and makes your son a shadow.   501
I do protest I never loved myself
Till now infixèd I beheld myself
Drawn in the flattering table of her eye.   504
                              Whispers with Blanche.

BASTARD
Drawn in the flattering table of her eye!   505
   Hanged in the frowning wrinkle of her brow
And quartered in her heart! He doth espy   507
   Himself love's traitor. This is pity now,
That, hanged and drawn and quartered, there should be
In such a love so vile a lout as he.   510

BLANCHE [*To Lewis*]
My uncle's will in this respect is mine.
If he see aught in you that makes him like,
That anything he sees which moves his liking   513
I can with ease translate it to my will;   514
Or if you will, to speak more properly,   515
I will enforce it easily to my love.

---

493 promotions elevations, advancements in courtly degree   **495 Holds
hand with** equals   **499 shadow** image, reflection   **500 being** from
being.   **shadow** pale and substanceless imitation   **501 a shadow** i.e., a
mere shaded area contrasted with the sun's brightness. (The Dauphin
poetically describes a *miracle* in which his new self, formed in
Blanche's eye, casts into the shade his former self.)   **504 Drawn** pictured.   **table** tablet or flat surface on which the picture is painted
505 Drawn (with a pun on the meaning "disemboweled." The pun is
continued in the next two lines in *Hanged* and *quartered*; Elizabethan
punishment for traitors specified that they be *hanged*, taken down while
still alive, *drawn*, or disemboweled, and *quartered*, or cut up.)
507 quartered (with a pun on the meaning "lodged," and, in heraldry,
"placed quarterly on a shield or coat of arms")   **510 love** (1) profession
of love (2) lover   **513 That anything** whatever   **514 will** desire
515 properly exactly

Further I will not flatter you, my lord,
That all I see in you is worthy love,
Than this: that nothing do I see in you,
Though churlish thoughts themselves should be your
      judge,   52
That I can find should merit any hate.

KING JOHN
What say these young ones? What say you, my niece?

BLANCHE
That she is bound in honor still to do   52
What you in wisdom still vouchsafe to say.   52

KING JOHN
Speak then, Prince Dauphin. Can you love this lady?

LEWIS
Nay, ask me if I can refrain from love,
For I do love her most unfeignedly.

KING JOHN
Then do I give Volquessen, Touraine, Maine,
Poitiers, and Anjou, these five provinces,
With her to thee, and this addition more,
Full thirty thousand marks of English coin.   53
Philip of France, if thou be pleased withal,   53
Command thy son and daughter to join hands.   53

KING PHILIP
It likes us well. Young princes, close your hands.   53
      [*Lewis and Blanche exchange pledges of love.*]

AUSTRIA
And your lips too, for I am well assured
That I did so when I was first assured.   [*They kiss.*] 53

KING PHILIP
Now, citizens of Angiers, ope your gates.
Let in that amity which you have made,
For at Saint Mary's chapel presently   53
The rites of marriage shall be solemnized.
Is not the Lady Constance in this troop?
I know she is not, for this match made up   54

520 churlish sparing of praise   **523, 524 still** always   **531 marks** (A
mark was the equivalent of 13 shillings 4 pence.)   **532 withal** with
this   **533 daughter** i.e., future daughter-in-law   **534 likes** pleases.
close clasp   **536 assured** betrothed (with a play on *assured*, "certain,"
in l. 535)   **539 presently** at once   **542 made up** arranged, concluded

Her presence would have interrupted much.
Where is she and her son? Tell me, who knows.   544

LEWIS
She is sad and passionate at Your Highness' tent.   545

KING PHILIP
And, by my faith, this league that we have made
Will give her sadness very little cure.
Brother of England, how may we content
This widow lady? In her right we came,
Which we, God knows, have turned another way,
To our own vantage.

KING JOHN   We will heal up all,
For we'll create young Arthur Duke of Brittaine
And Earl of Richmond, and this rich, fair town
We make him lord of. Call the Lady Constance.
Some speedy messenger bid her repair   555
To our solemnity. I trust we shall,   556
If not fill up the measure of her will,   557
Yet in some measure satisfy her so   558
That we shall stop her exclamation.   559
Go we, as well as haste will suffer us,   560
To this unlooked-for, unprepared pomp.
                    Exeunt [all but the Bastard].

BASTARD
Mad world, mad kings, mad composition!   562
John, to stop Arthur's title in the whole,
Hath willingly departed with a part;   564
And France, whose armor conscience buckled on,
Whom zeal and charity brought to the field
As God's own soldier, rounded in the ear   567
With that same purpose-changer, that sly devil,   568
That broker that still breaks the pate of faith,   569
That daily break-vow, he that wins of all,   570
Of kings, of beggars, old men, young men, maids—
Who, having no external thing to lose   572

544 who whoever **545 passionate** filled with passionate sorrow
555 repair come **556 our solemnity** i.e., the wedding **557 the measure**
the full measure and extent **558 so** in such a way **559 exclamation**
complaint **560 suffer** allow **562 composition** agreement, compromise **564 departed with** given up **567 rounded** whispered to
568 With by **569 broker** go-between (with a pun on "one who
breaks"). **still . . . faith** continually knocks loyalty and truth over the
head **570 wins of** gets the better of **572 Who** i.e., the maids

But the word "maid," cheats the poor maid of that—   573
That smooth-faced gentleman, tickling Commodity,   574
Commodity, the bias of the world—   575
The world, who of itself is peisèd well,   576
Made to run even upon even ground,
Till this advantage, this vile-drawing bias,   578
This sway of motion, this Commodity,   579
Makes it take head from all indifferency,   580
From all direction, purpose, course, intent.
And this same bias, this Commodity,
This bawd, this broker, this all-changing word,   583
Clapped on the outward eye of fickle France,   584
Hath drawn him from his own determined aid,   585
From a resolved and honorable war,   586
To a most base and vile-concluded peace.
And why rail I on this Commodity?
But for because he hath not wooed me yet.   589
Not that I have the power to clutch my hand   590
When his fair angels would salute my palm,   591
But for my hand, as unattempted yet,   592
Like a poor beggar, raileth on the rich.
Well, whiles I am a beggar, I will rail
And say there is no sin but to be rich;
And being rich, my virtue then shall be
To say there is no vice but beggary.
Since kings break faith upon commodity,   598
Gain, be my lord, for I will worship thee.   *Exit.*

❖

573 cheats i.e., he, Commodity, cheats   **574 smooth-faced** bland, plausible.   **tickling Commodity** flattering self-interest   **575 bias** swaying
influence. (From the game of bowls, in which a weight in the side of a
bowl caused it to curve.)   **576 peisèd** balanced, in equilibrium   **578 advantage** advantage-seeking Commodity.   **vile-drawing** attracting to
evil   **579 sway of motion** swaying or controlling of motion from its
intended course   **580 take . . . indifferency** rush away from all balanced, equal motion   **583 all-changing** causing change in everything
584 Clapped on stuck on, presented to.   **outward eye** (1) eyeball (2) hole
in the bowling ball in which the lead creating the "bias" was in-
serted.   **France** i.e., the King of France. (Commodity, presented to King
Philip's eye in the guise of the marriage treaty, has acted like the bias in
a bowling ball to divert him from his former intention.)   **585 his . . . aid**
the aid he had determined to give Arthur   **586 resolved** resolved upon
589 But for merely   **590 clutch** clench (in a gesture of refusal)
591 angels coins bearing the figure of an angel, worth 10 shillings.
salute kiss (with a pun on the idea of an angelic salutation)   **592 unattempted** untempted   **598 upon** because of

3.1   *Enter Constance, Arthur, and Salisbury.*

CONSTANCE
  Gone to be married? Gone to swear a peace?
  False blood to false blood joined! Gone to be friends?
  Shall Lewis have Blanche, and Blanche those provinces?
  It is not so; thou hast misspoke, misheard.
  Be well advised; tell o'er thy tale again.   5
  It cannot be; thou dost but say 'tis so.
  I trust I may not trust thee, for thy word
  Is but the vain breath of a common man.   8
  Believe me, I do not believe thee, man;
  I have a king's oath to the contrary.
  Thou shalt be punished for thus frighting me,
  For I am sick and capable of fears,   12
  Oppressed with wrongs, and therefore full of fears,
  A widow, husbandless, subject to fears,
  A woman, naturally born to fears;
  And though thou now confess thou didst but jest,
  With my vexed spirits I cannot take a truce,   17
  But they will quake and tremble all this day.
  What dost thou mean by shaking of thy head?
  Why dost thou look so sadly on my son?
  What means that hand upon that breast of thine?
  Why holds thine eye that lamentable rheum,   22
  Like a proud river peering o'er his bounds?   23
  Be these sad signs confirmers of thy words?
  Then speak again—not all thy former tale,
  But this one word, whether thy tale be true.

SALISBURY
  As true as I believe you think them false   27
  That give you cause to prove my saying true.

CONSTANCE
  O, if thou teach me to believe this sorrow,
  Teach thou this sorrow how to make me die!
  And let belief and life encounter so
  As doth the fury of two desperate men

3.1. Location: France. The French King's quarters.
5 Be well advised be sure of what you are saying **8 a common man** i.e.,
a subject, not a king **12 capable of** susceptible to **17 take a truce**
make peace **22 lamentable rheum** sad moisture, i.e., tears **23 peering**
o'er his i.e., overflowing its **27 them** i.e., the French

Which in the very meeting fall and die.
Lewis marry Blanche? O boy, then where art thou?
France friend with England, what becomes of me?
[*To Salisbury.*] Fellow, begone! I cannot brook thy sight.   36
This news hath made thee a most ugly man.

SALISBURY
What other harm have I, good lady, done,
But spoke the harm that is by others done?

CONSTANCE
Which harm within itself so heinous is
As it makes harmful all that speak of it.

ARTHUR
I do beseech you, madam, be content.   42

CONSTANCE
If thou that bidd'st me be content wert grim,
Ugly, and slanderous to thy mother's womb,   44
Full of unpleasing blots and sightless stains,   45
Lame, foolish, crooked, swart, prodigious,   46
Patched with foul moles and eye-offending marks,   47
I would not care, I then would be content,
For then I should not love thee, no, nor thou
Become thy great birth nor deserve a crown.   50
But thou art fair, and at thy birth, dear boy,
Nature and Fortune joined to make thee great.
Of Nature's gifts thou mayst with lilies boast,
And with the half-blown rose. But Fortune, O,   54
She is corrupted, changed, and won from thee.
Sh' adulterates hourly with thine uncle John,   56
And with her golden hand hath plucked on France   57
To tread down fair respect of sovereignty,   58
And made his majesty the bawd to theirs.   59
France is a bawd to Fortune and King John,
That strumpet Fortune, that usurping John!

---

36 brook endure   **42 content** calm   **44 slanderous** disgraceful
45 sightless unsightly   **46 swart** swarthy.   **prodigious** monstrous, an
evil omen   **47 Patched** blotched   **50 Become** befit   **54 half-blown** only
partly opened, still young   **56 adulterates** commits adultery   **57 golden**
i.e., offering gold   **57–59 hath plucked on . . . theirs** i.e., she, Fortune,
has induced the King of France to tread underfoot Arthur's rights of
sovereignty, and has made the King of France the bawd between Fortune and King John

[*To Salisbury.*] Tell me, thou fellow, is not France
  forsworn?   62
Envenom him with words, or get thee gone   63
And leave those woes alone which I alone   64
Am bound to underbear.
SALISBURY   Pardon me, madam,   65
  I may not go without you to the kings.
CONSTANCE
  Thou mayst, thou shalt. I will not go with thee.
  I will instruct my sorrows to be proud,
  For grief is proud and makes his owner stoop.
                       [*She sits on the ground.*]
  To me and to the state of my great grief   70
  Let kings assemble, for my grief's so great
  That no supporter but the huge, firm earth
  Can hold it up. Here I and sorrows sit.
  Here is my throne; bid kings come bow to it.

    Enter King John, [King Philip of] France, [Lewis
    the] Dauphin, Blanche, Eleanor, Philip [the
    Bastard], Austria, [and attendants]. [The two
    kings are arm in arm.]

KING PHILIP
  'Tis true, fair daughter, and this blessèd day
  Ever in France shall be kept festival.
  To solemnize this day the glorious sun
  Stays in his course and plays the alchemist,   78
  Turning with splendor of his precious eye
  The meager cloddy earth to glittering gold.
  The yearly course that brings this day about
  Shall never see it but a holy day.
CONSTANCE [*Rising*]
  A wicked day, and not a holy day!
  What hath this day deserved? What hath it done,
  That it in golden letters should be set   85

62 **is not France forsworn** hasn't the French King broken his oath
63 **Envenom . . . words** i.e., curse him for being forsworn, as I do.
Envenom poison 64 **leave those woes alone** leave behind only those
woes 65 **underbear** endure 70 **state** majesty, as in a chair of state
78 **Stays in his course** stands still 85 **golden** i.e., red

Among the high tides in the calendar?   86
Nay, rather turn this day out of the week,
This day of shame, oppression, perjury.
Or if it must stand still, let wives with child   89
Pray that their burdens may not fall this day,
Lest that their hopes prodigiously be crossed.   91
But on this day let seamen fear no wreck;   92
No bargains break that are not this day made.   93
This day, all things begun come to ill end,
Yea, faith itself to hollow falsehood change!

KING PHILIP
By heaven, lady, you shall have no cause
To curse the fair proceedings of this day.
Have I not pawned to you my majesty?   98

CONSTANCE
You have beguiled me with a counterfeit
Resembling majesty, which, being touched and tried,   100
Proves valueless. You are forsworn, forsworn!
You came in arms to spill mine enemies' blood,   102
But now in arms you strengthen it with yours.   103
The grappling vigor and rough frown of war
Is cold in amity and painted peace,   105
And our oppression hath made up this league.   106
Arm, arm, you heavens, against these perjured kings!
A widow cries; be husband to me, heavens!   108
Let not the hours of this ungodly day
Wear out the day in peace, but ere sunset
Set armèd discord twixt these perjured kings!
Hear me, O, hear me!

AUSTRIA   Lady Constance, peace!

CONSTANCE
War, war, no peace! Peace is to me a war.
O Limoges, O Austria, thou dost shame   114

86 high tides i.e., great festivals   **89 stand still** remain   **91 prodigiously
be crossed** be thwarted by some monstrous birth defect   **92 But** except,
other than (since this is the most evil of days).   **wreck** shipwreck
93 No . . . made break only agreements made on this day   **98 pawned**
pledged.   **my majesty** i.e., my kingly word   **100 touched** tested (as one
tests gold by rubbing it on a touchstone)   **102 in arms** in armor   **103 in
arms** embracing.   **with yours** i.e., by uniting your enemies to your royal
house in marriage   **105 painted** specious, unreal   **106 our oppression**
our being oppressed   **108 A widow cries** it is a widow that cries
114 Limoges (Cf 2.1.5 note.)

That bloody spoil. Thou slave, thou wretch, thou
  coward!   115
Thou little valiant, great in villainy!
Thou ever strong upon the stronger side!
Thou Fortune's champion, that dost never fight
But when her humorous ladyship is by   119
To teach thee safety! Thou art perjured too,   120
And sooth'st up greatness. What a fool art thou,   121
A ramping fool, to brag and stamp and swear   122
Upon my party! Thou cold-blooded slave,   123
Hast thou not spoke like thunder on my side,
Been sworn my soldier, bidding me depend
Upon thy stars, thy fortune, and thy strength?
And dost thou now fall over to my foes?   127
Thou wear a lion's hide! Doff it for shame,
And hang a calfskin on those recreant limbs.   129

AUSTRIA
O, that a man should speak those words to me!

BASTARD
And hang a calfskin on those recreant limbs.

AUSTRIA
Thou dar'st not say so, villain, for thy life.

BASTARD
And hang a calfskin on those recreant limbs.

KING JOHN [*To Bastard*]
We like not this. Thou dost forget thyself.

        Enter Pandulph.

KING PHILIP
Here comes the holy legate of the Pope.

PANDULPH
Hail, you anointed deputies of heaven!
To thee, King John, my holy errand is.
I, Pandulph, of fair Milan cardinal,
And from Pope Innocent the legate here,
Do in his name religiously demand

---

115 spoil booty, i.e., the lion's pelt that Austria wears   **119 humorous**
capricious   **120 safety** i.e., how to choose the safe side   **121 sooth'st up
greatness** flatter the influential   **122 ramping** making a fierce show
123 Upon my party in my behalf   **127 fall over** go over, desert
129 calfskin (Customarily used to make coats for the fools kept to
amuse great families.)   **recreant** cowardly, having deserted his cause

Why thou against the Church, our holy mother,
So willfully dost spurn, and force perforce   142
Keep Stephen Langton, chosen Archbishop   143
Of Canterbury, from that Holy See.
This, in our foresaid Holy Father's name,
Pope Innocent, I do demand of thee.

KING JOHN
What earthy name to interrogatories   147
Can taste the free breath of a sacred king?   148
Thou canst not, Cardinal, devise a name
So slight, unworthy, and ridiculous,
To charge me to an answer, as the Pope.   151
Tell him this tale, and from the mouth of England
Add thus much more: that no Italian priest
Shall tithe or toll in our dominions;   154
But as we, under God, are supreme head,   155
So, under Him, that great supremacy
Where we do reign we will alone uphold
Without th' assistance of a mortal hand.
So tell the Pope, all reverence set apart
To him and his usurped authority.

KING PHILIP
Brother of England, you blaspheme in this.

KING JOHN
Though you and all the kings of Christendom
Are led so grossly by this meddling priest,   163
Dreading the curse that money may buy out,   164
And by the merit of vile gold, dross, dust,
Purchase corrupted pardon of a man

---

142 spurn oppose scornfully. (Literally, "kick.")   **force perforce** violently   **143 Stephen Langton** Pope Innocent's choice to be Archbishop
of Canterbury, whose rejection by King John led to a papal bull of
deposition and eventual resolution only after John had been forced
to pay tribute and acknowledge England to be a papal fiefdom
147–148 What . . . king what secular official can put the free breath of
a sacred king to the test by asking it so submit to formal questioning.
taste test. (Many editors emend to *task*.)   **151 charge . . . answer** command me to answer   **154 tithe** impose tithes, a tenth of one's income
given to the Church.   **toll** collect taxes   **155 supreme head** (The title
assumed by Henry VIII at the time of the Reformation.)   **163 led** led
astray.   **this meddling priest** i.e., the Pope   **164 the curse . . . out** i.e.,
excommunication, which a bribe to Rome can fix

Who in that sale sells pardon from himself,   167
Though you and all the rest, so grossly led,
This juggling witchcraft with revenue cherish,   169
Yet I alone, alone do me oppose
Against the Pope, and count his friends my foes.

PANDULPH
Then, by the lawful power that I have,
Thou shalt stand cursed and excommunicate;
And blessèd shall he be that doth revolt
From his allegiance to an heretic;
And meritorious shall that hand be called,
Canonizèd and worshiped as a saint,
That takes away by any secret course
Thy hateful life.

CONSTANCE   O, lawful let it be
That I have room with Rome to curse awhile!   180
Good father Cardinal, cry thou "Amen"
To my keen curses, for without my wrong   182
There is no tongue hath power to curse him right.

PANDULPH
There's law and warrant, lady, for my curse.

CONSTANCE
And for mine too. When law can do no right,   185
Let it be lawful that law bar no wrong.   186
Law cannot give my child his kingdom here,
For he that holds his kingdom holds the law;   188
Therefore, since law itself is perfect wrong,
How can the law forbid my tongue to curse?

PANDULPH
Philip of France, on peril of a curse,   191
Let go the hand of that arch-heretic,

---

167 Who . . . himself i.e., who, in selling indulgences, incurs his own damnation. (*From himself* may also suggest that the pardon stems only from him, not from God, and is therefore invalid.)   **169 juggling** cheating, deceiving.   **cherish** maintain   **180 room, Rome** (An obvious pun, pronounced alike in Elizabethan England.)   **182 without my wrong** i.e., (1) without recognition of the wrong done to me (2) without the motive of suffering wrongs as I have suffered   **185–186 When . . . wrong** i.e., when the law itself is powerless to remedy evils, people must be free to pursue wrongful remedies (such as cursing)   **188 holds the law** i.e., holds the law hostage   **191 a curse** excommunication

And raise the power of France upon his head
Unless he do submit himself to Rome.

ELEANOR
Look'st thou pale, France? Do not let go thy hand.

CONSTANCE [*To Eleanor*]
Look to it, devil, lest that France repent,   196
And by disjoining hands, hell lose a soul.

AUSTRIA
King Philip, listen to the Cardinal.

BASTARD
And hang a calfskin on his recreant limbs.

AUSTRIA
Well, ruffian, I must pocket up these wrongs,   200
Because—

BASTARD   Your breeches best may carry them.

KING JOHN
Philip, what sayst thou to the Cardinal?

CONSTANCE
What should he say, but as the Cardinal?   203

LEWIS
Bethink you, Father, for the difference   204
Is purchase of a heavy curse from Rome
Or the light loss of England for a friend.
Forgo the easier.

BLANCHE   That's the curse of Rome.

CONSTANCE
O Lewis, stand fast! The devil tempts thee here
In likeness of a new, untrimmèd bride.   209

BLANCHE
The Lady Constance speaks not from her faith
But from her need.

CONSTANCE [*To King Philip*] O, if thou grant my need,

---

196 Look to it see to it, take care.   **devil** i.e., Eleanor, or the devil
himself.   **lest that** lest   **200 pocket up** submit to. (But the Bastard
plays on the literal sense of putting in one's breeches pocket, perhaps
suggesting further that Austria will get a swift kick in the breeches.)
203 but as the Cardinal except what the Cardinal has already spoken
and as he would be expected to speak   **204 difference** choice   **209 untrimmèd** i.e., freshly married, unshorn (suggesting she is still a virgin).
(Alludes to the temptation of Saint Anthony by the devil in the form of a
naked woman.)

Which only lives but by the death of faith,   212
That need must needs infer this principle: 213
That faith would live again by death of need.   214
O, then tread down my need, and faith mounts up;   215
Keep my need up, and faith is trodden down!

KING JOHN
The King is moved, and answers not to this.

CONSTANCE [*To King Philip*]
O, be removed from him, and answer well!   218

AUSTRIA
Do so, King Philip. Hang no more in doubt.

BASTARD
Hang nothing but a calfskin, most sweet lout.   220

KING PHILIP
I am perplexed and know not what to say.

PANDULPH
What canst thou say but will perplex thee more,
If thou stand excommunicate and cursed?

KING PHILIP
Good Reverend Father, make my person yours,   224
And tell me how you would bestow yourself.   225
This royal hand and mine are newly knit,
And the conjunction of our inward souls
Married in league, coupled and linked together
With all religious strength of sacred vows.
The latest breath that gave the sound of words   230
Was deep-sworn faith, peace, amity, true love
Between our kingdoms and our royal selves;
And even before this truce, but new before,   233
No longer than we well could wash our hands
To clap this royal bargain up of peace,   235

212 Which . . . faith i.e., which need is so strong that I must put it ahead of matters of faith and promise-keeping **213 needs infer** necessarily imply **214 That . . . need** i.e., my faith will be rekindled once my prior and compelling necessity, Arthur's claim, has been satisfied **215 tread down** i.e., put down by satisfying, subdue **218 removed** separated (playing on *moved* in l. 217) **220 Hang** i.e., wear (playing on *Hang*, hesitate, in l. 219) **224 make . . . yours** put yourself in my place **225 bestow** conduct **230 latest** most recent **233 even before** just before. **but new** immediately **235 clap . . . up** i.e., conclude with a grasping of hands

Heaven knows, they were besmeared and overstained
With slaughter's pencil, where revenge did paint   237
The fearful difference of incensèd kings.   238
And shall these hands, so lately purged of blood,
So newly joined in love, so strong in both,   240
Unyoke this seizure and this kind regreet?   241
Play fast and loose with faith? So jest with heaven,
Make such unconstant children of ourselves,
As now again to snatch our palm from palm,
Unswear faith sworn, and on the marriage bed
Of smiling peace to march a bloody host
And make a riot on the gentle brow
Of true sincerity? O holy sir,
My Reverend Father, let it not be so!
Out of your grace, devise, ordain, impose
Some gentle order; and then we shall be blest
To do your pleasure and continue friends.

PANDULPH
All form is formless, order orderless,
Save what is opposite to England's love.
Therefore to arms! Be champion of our Church,
Or let the Church, our mother, breathe her curse,
A mother's curse, on her revolting son.   257
France, thou mayst hold a serpent by the tongue,
A chafèd lion by the mortal paw,   259
A fasting tiger safer by the tooth,
Than keep in peace that hand which thou dost hold.

KING PHILIP
I may disjoin my hand, but not my faith.

PANDULPH
So mak'st thou faith an enemy to faith,   263
And like a civil war sett'st oath to oath,
Thy tongue against thy tongue. O, let thy vow,
First made to heaven, first be to heaven performed,
That is, to be the champion of our Church!
What since thou swor'st is sworn against thyself   268

---

237 pencil paintbrush   **238 difference** dissension   **240 both** i.e., blood
and love   **241 Unyoke this seizure** disjoin this handclasp.   **regreet**
returned salutation, counterclasp   **257 revolting** rebellious   **259 mortal**
deadly   **263 So . . . to faith** i.e., you are trying to set your promise to
John against your religious vow to the Church   **268 since** since then

And may not be performèd by thyself,
For that which thou hast sworn to do amiss
Is not amiss when it is truly done;   271
And being not done where doing tends to ill,
The truth is then most done not doing it.
The better act of purposes mistook   274
Is to mistake again; though indirect,   275
Yet indirection thereby grows direct,
And falsehood falsehood cures, as fire cools fire   277
Within the scorchèd veins of one new-burned.   278
It is religion that doth make vows kept,
But thou hast sworn against religion;
By what thou swear'st against the thing thou swear'st,   281
And mak'st an oath the surety for thy truth
Against an oath. The truth thou art unsure   283
To swear, swears only not to be forsworn,   284
Else what a mockery should it be to swear!
But thou dost swear only to be forsworn,   286
And most forsworn to keep what thou dost swear.
Therefore thy later vows against thy first
Is in thyself rebellion to thyself;
And better conquest never canst thou make
Than arm thy constant and thy nobler parts
Against these giddy loose suggestions,   292
Upon which better part our prayers come in,   293
If thou vouchsafe them. But if not, then know   294
The peril of our curses light on thee
So heavy as thou shalt not shake them off,   296

271 truly done i.e., not done at all (since, as Pandulph explains two lines
later, an ill-considered vow is best performed by not performing it. This
is an example of equivocation, much deplored by many Elizabethans
and regarded as typical of Catholic duplicity.) **274–275 The better . . .
again** i.e., the best thing to do when one has made a wrong turn is to
turn again **277–278 as fire . . . new-burned** (Burns were commonly
treated with heat on the proverbial theory that one fire drives out
another.) **281 By . . . thing thou swearest** you swear against the very
thing by which you swear, i.e., by your oath of allegiance to John you
directly violate your prior vows given to the Church **283–284 The
truth . . . forsworn** i.e., your oath of allegiance to the true faith, which
you are now hesitant to affirm, is above all a promise not to break your
oath **286 But . . . forsworn** i.e., but you are now proposing an oath to
John in which you will indeed break your prior oath **292 suggestions**
temptations **293 Upon . . . part** in support of which better side
294 vouchsafe accept, agree to **296 as** that

But in despair die under their black weight.

AUSTRIA
Rebellion, flat rebellion!

BASTARD   Will 't not be?   298
Will not a calfskin stop that mouth of thine?

LEWIS
Father, to arms!

BLANCHE   Upon thy wedding day?
Against the blood that thou hast marrièd?   301
What, shall our feast be kept with slaughtered men?
Shall braying trumpets and loud churlish drums,
Clamors of hell, be measures to our pomp?   304
[Kneeling.] O husband, hear me! Ay, alack, how new
Is "husband" in my mouth! Even for that name,
Which till this time my tongue did ne'er pronounce,
Upon my knee I beg, go not to arms
Against mine uncle.

CONSTANCE [Kneeling]   O, upon my knee,
Made hard with kneeling, I do pray to thee,
Thou virtuous Dauphin, alter not the doom
Forethought by heaven!   312

BLANCHE [To Lewis]
Now shall I see thy love. What motive may
Be stronger with thee than the name of wife?

CONSTANCE
That which upholdeth him that thee upholds:
His honor. O, thine honor, Lewis, thine honor!

LEWIS
I muse Your Majesty doth seem so cold,   317
When such profound respects do pull you on.   318

PANDULPH
I will denounce a curse upon his head.   319

KING PHILIP [Letting go of King John's hand]
Thou shalt not need. England, I will fall from thee.

CONSTANCE [Rising]
O, fair return of banished majesty!

---

298 Will 't not be i.e., will nothing serve (to keep you quiet)   **301 blood**
(Blanche is related by blood to King John.)   **304 measures** musical
accompaniment.   **pomp** i.e., wedding ceremony   **312 Forethought**
destined   **317 muse** wonder   **318 respects** considerations
319 denounce proclaim, call down

ELEANOR
  O, foul revolt of French inconstancy!

KING JOHN
  France, thou shalt rue this hour within this hour.

BASTARD
  Old Time the clock setter, that bald sexton Time,
  Is it as he will? Well then, France shall rue.   325

BLANCHE [*Rising*]
  The sun's o'ercast with blood. Fair day, adieu!
  Which is the side that I must go withal?   327
  I am with both: each army hath a hand,
  And in their rage, I having hold of both,
  They whirl asunder and dismember me.
  Husband, I cannot pray that thou mayst win;
- Uncle, I needs must pray that thou mayst lose;
  Father, I may not wish the fortune thine;   333
  Grandam, I will not wish thy wishes thrive.
  Whoever wins, on that side shall I lose;
  Assurèd loss before the match be played.

LEWIS
  Lady, with me, with me thy fortune lies.

BLANCHE
  There where my fortune lives, there my life dies.

KING JOHN [*To the Bastard*]
  Cousin, go draw our puissance together.   339
                    [*Exit the Bastard.*]
  France, I am burned up with inflaming wrath,
  A rage whose heat hath this condition,
  That nothing can allay, nothing but blood—
  The blood, and dearest-valued blood, of France.

KING PHILIP
  Thy rage shall burn thee up, and thou shalt turn
  To ashes, ere our blood shall quench that fire.
  Look to thyself. Thou art in jeopardy.

KING JOHN
  No more than he that threats. To arms let's hie!   347
                    Exeunt [*separately*].

---

325 France shall rue i.e., if Time is to decide, France will rue sooner or later   **327 withal** with   **333 Father** i.e., father-in-law, King Philip   **339 Cousin** kinsman.   **puissance** armed force   **347 hie** hasten

3.2   *Alarums, excursions. Enter [the] Bastard, with
          Austria's head.*

BASTARD
　Now, by my life, this day grows wondrous hot.
　Some airy devil hovers in the sky   2
　And pours down mischief. Austria's head lie there,
　While Philip breathes.   [*He puts down the head.*] 4

　　Enter [King] John, Arthur, [and] Hubert.

KING JOHN
　Hubert, keep this boy. Philip, make up.   5
　My mother is assailèd in our tent,
　And ta'en, I fear.
BASTARD　　　　　　　　My lord, I rescued her;
　Her Highness is in safety, fear you not.
　But on, my liege! For very little pains
　Will bring this labor to an happy end.
　　　　　　　　　　　　　　Exeunt [with Austria's head].

3.3   *Alarums, excursions, retreat. Enter [King] John,
          Eleanor, Arthur, [the] Bastard, Hubert, [and]
          lords.*

KING JOHN [*To Eleanor*]
　So shall it be; Your Grace shall stay behind
　So strongly guarded. [*To Arthur.*] Cousin, look not sad. 2
　Thy grandam loves thee, and thy uncle will
　As dear be to thee as thy father was.
ARTHUR
　O, this will make my mother die with grief!

3.2. Location: France. Plains near Angiers. The battle is seen as following immediately upon the previous scene.
s.d. Alarums calls to arms.　**excursions** sorties　**2 airy devil** (Aerial
spirits or devils were thought to be the cause of tempests, thunder,
lightning, etc.)　**4 breathes** i.e., gets his breath　**5 make up** advance,
press on

3.3. Location: Scene continues on the plains near Angiers.
s.d. retreat signal for withdrawal of forces　**2 So** thus

KING JOHN [*To the Bastard*]
Cousin, away for England! Haste before,
And, ere our coming, see thou shake the bags
Of hoarding abbots; imprisoned angels   8
Set at liberty. The fat ribs of peace   9
Must by the hungry now be fed upon.
Use our commission in his utmost force.   11

BASTARD
Bell, book, and candle shall not drive me back   12
When gold and silver becks me to come on.   13
I leave Your Highness.—Grandam, I will pray,
If ever I remember to be holy,
For your fair safety. So I kiss your hand.

ELEANOR
Farewell, gentle cousin.

KING JOHN   Coz, farewell.   17
                                        [*Exit the Bastard.*]

ELEANOR
Come hither, little kinsman. Hark, a word.
                                        [*She takes Arthur aside.*]

KING JOHN
Come hither, Hubert. O my gentle Hubert,
We owe thee much! Within this wall of flesh   20
There is a soul counts thee her creditor   21
And with advantage means to pay thy love;   22
And, my good friend, thy voluntary oath   23
Lives in this bosom, dearly cherishèd.   24
Give me thy hand. I had a thing to say,
But I will fit it with some better tune.   26
By heaven, Hubert, I am almost ashamed
To say what good respect I have of thee.   28

HUBERT
I am much bounden to Your Majesty.   29

---

8 angels gold coins (with a common pun) **9 fat ribs of peace** (i.e., in contrast to the skeleton of war, the *bare-ribbed Death* of 5.2.177) **11 his** its **12 Bell, book, and candle** (Articles used in the office of excommunication.) **13 becks** beckon **17 Coz** cousin, i.e., kinsman **20 Within . . . flesh** i.e., within me **21 counts** that counts **22 advantage** interest **23 thy voluntary oath** your freely given allegiance **24 Lives in this bosom** is vividly felt in my heart **26 some better tune** i.e., better words, and some better reward **28 respect** opinion **29 bounden** obligated

KING JOHN
  Good friend, thou hast no cause to say so yet,
  But thou shalt have; and, creep time ne'er so slow,
  Yet it shall come for me to do thee good.
  I had a thing to say—but let it go.
  The sun is in the heaven, and the proud day,
  Attended with the pleasures of the world,
  Is all too wanton and too full of gauds   36
  To give me audience. If the midnight bell   37
  Did with his iron tongue and brazen mouth
  Sound on into the drowsy race of night;   39
  If this same were a churchyard where we stand,
  And thou possessèd with a thousand wrongs;   41
  Or if that surly spirit, melancholy,
  Had baked thy blood and made it heavy, thick,
  Which else runs tickling up and down the veins,
  Making that idiot, laughter, keep men's eyes   45
  And strain their cheeks to idle merriment,   46
  A passion hateful to my purposes;   47
  Or if that thou couldst see me without eyes,
  Hear me without thine ears, and make reply
  Without a tongue, using conceit alone,   50
  Without eyes, ears, and harmful sound of words—   51
  Then, in despite of brooded watchful day,   52
  I would into thy bosom pour my thoughts.
  But, ah, I will not! Yet I love thee well,
  And, by my troth, I think thou lov'st me well.

HUBERT
  So well that what you bid me undertake,   56
  Though that my death were adjunct to my act,   57
  By heaven, I would do it.

KING JOHN   Do not I know thou wouldst?
  Good Hubert, Hubert, Hubert, throw thine eye
  On yon young boy. I'll tell thee what, my friend,

---

36 gauds showy ornaments, trifles   **37 To give me audience** i.e., for you
to hearken to my words   **39 race** running, course. (*Face* and *ear* have
been suggested as emendations.)   **41 possessèd with** obsessed by
45 idiot jester   **46 strain** stretch (in laughter)   **47 passion** emotion
50 conceit the mental faculty   **51 harmful** (because it is dangerous to
speak of such matters)   **52 brooded** brooding (and hence vigilant in
defense of its young)   **56 what** whatever   **57 adjunct to** consequent
upon

He is a very serpent in my way,
And wheresoe'er this foot of mine doth tread
He lies before me. Dost thou understand me?
Thou art his keeper.

HUBERT   And I'll keep him so
That he shall not offend Your Majesty.

KING JOHN   Death.

HUBERT
My lord?

KING JOHN A grave.

HUBERT   He shall not live.

KING JOHN   Enough.
I could be merry now. Hubert, I love thee.
Well, I'll not say what I intend for thee.
Remember.—Madam, fare you well.
I'll send those powers o'er to Your Majesty.   70

ELEANOR
My blessing go with thee!

KING JOHN   For England, cousin, go.   71
Hubert shall be your man, attend on you
With all true duty.—On toward Calais, ho!   *Exeunt.*

*

3.4   *Enter [King Philip of] France, [Lewis the]
        Dauphin, Pandulph, [and] attendants.*

KING PHILIP
So, by a roaring tempest on the flood,   1
A whole armada of convicted sail   2
Is scattered and disjoined from fellowship.

PANDULPH
Courage and comfort! All shall yet go well.

KING PHILIP
What can go well when we have run so ill?
Are we not beaten? Is not Angiers lost?
Arthur ta'en prisoner? Divers dear friends slain?

---

70 powers troops **71 cousin** i.e., Arthur

3.4. Location: France. The French King's quarters.
1 flood seas **2 convicted** doomed

And bloody England into England gone,   8
O'erbearing interruption, spite of France?   9

LEWIS
What he hath won, that hath he fortified.
So hot a speed, with such advice disposed,   11
Such temperate order in so fierce a cause,
Doth want example. Who hath read or heard   13
Of any kindred action like to this?   14

KING PHILIP
Well could I bear that England had this praise,
So we could find some pattern of our shame.   16

Enter Constance, [*with her hair about her ears*].

Look who comes here! A grave unto a soul,   17
Holding th' eternal spirit, against her will,
In the vile prison of afflicted breath.—   19
I prithee, lady, go away with me.

CONSTANCE
Lo, now! Now see the issue of your peace.   21

KING PHILIP
Patience, good lady. Comfort, gentle Constance.

CONSTANCE
No, I defy all counsel, all redress,   23
But that which ends all counsel, true redress:
Death. Death, O amiable, lovely Death!
Thou odoriferous stench! Sound rottenness!   26
Arise forth from the couch of lasting night,
Thou hate and terror to prosperity,
And I will kiss thy detestable bones,
And put my eyeballs in thy vaulty brows,   30
And ring these fingers with thy household worms,   31
And stop this gap of breath with fulsome dust,   32

---

8 bloody England the bloodstained King of England   **9 O'erbearing
interruption** overcoming all resistance.   **spite** in spite   **11 with . . .
disposed** directed with such judgment   **13 Doth want example** lacks
parallel instance   **14 kindred** comparable   **16 So** provided.   **pattern**
precedent   **17 A grave . . . soul** i.e., a mere shell of a body without the
will to live   **19 prison . . . breath** (The soul was thought to leave the
body from the mouth with the last expiring breath.)   **21 issue** outcome   **23 defy** reject.   **redress** comfort   **26 odoriferous** sweet-
smelling.   **Sound** wholesome   **30 vaulty** arched and hollow   **31 thy
household worms** the worms of your retinue   **32 this gap of breath** i.e.,
my mouth.   **fulsome** loathsome

And be a carrion monster like thyself.
Come, grin on me, and I will think thou smil'st,
And buss thee as thy wife. Misery's love,　　　35
O, come to me!
KING PHILIP　　　　O fair affliction, peace!　　36
CONSTANCE
No, no, I will not, having breath to cry.　　37
O, that my tongue were in the thunder's mouth!
Then with a passion would I shake the world,
And rouse from sleep that fell anatomy　　　40
Which cannot hear a lady's feeble voice,
Which scorns a modern invocation.　　　42
PANDULPH
Lady, you utter madness, and not sorrow.
CONSTANCE
Thou art not holy to belie me so.
I am not mad. This hair I tear is mine;
My name is Constance; I was Geoffrey's wife;
Young Arthur is my son, and he is lost.
I am not mad; I would to heaven I were,
For then 'tis like I should forget myself!　　49
O, if I could, what grief should I forget?
Preach some philosophy to make me mad,
And thou shalt be canonized, Cardinal;
For, being not mad but sensible of grief,　　53
My reasonable part produces reason　　54
How I may be delivered of these woes,　　55
And teaches me to kill or hang myself.
If I were mad, I should forget my son,
Or madly think a babe of clouts were he.　　58
I am not mad. Too well, too well I feel
The different plague of each calamity.　　60
KING PHILIP
Bind up those tresses. O, what love I note

---

35 buss kiss. **Misery's love** you whom those in misery love (as a way of ending their misery) **36 affliction** afflicted one **37 having** as long as I have **40 fell anatomy** cruel skeleton (the usual figure of Death in pictorial representations) **42 modern** everyday, commonplace. **invocation** entreaty **49 like** likely **53 sensible of** capable of feeling **54 reasonable part** i.e., brain **55 delivered of** (1) freed from (2) delivered of, as in childbirth **58 babe of clouts** rag doll **60 different plague** distinct affliction

In the fair multitude of those her hairs!
Where but by chance a silver drop hath fallen, 63
Even to that drop ten thousand wiry friends 64
Do glue themselves in sociable grief, 65
Like true, inseparable, faithful loves,
Sticking together in calamity.

CONSTANCE
To England, if you will.

KING PHILIP   Bind up your hairs. 68

CONSTANCE
Yes, that I will. And wherefore will I do it?
I tore them from their bonds and cried aloud,
"O, that these hands could so redeem my son, 71
As they have given these hairs their liberty!"
But now I envy at their liberty,
And will again commit them to their bonds,
Because my poor child is a prisoner.

                      [*She binds up her hair.*]

And, father Cardinal, I have heard you say
That we shall see and know our friends in heaven.
If that be true, I shall see my boy again;
For since the birth of Cain, the first male child,
To him that did but yesterday suspire, 80
There was not such a gracious creature born.
But now will canker sorrow eat my bud 82
And chase the native beauty from his cheek, 83
And he will look as hollow as a ghost,
As dim and meager as an ague's fit,
And so he'll die; and, rising so again, 86
When I shall meet him in the court of heaven
I shall not know him. Therefore never, never
Must I behold my pretty Arthur more.

PANDULPH
You hold too heinous a respect of grief. 90

---

63 silver drop i.e., tear **64 wiry friends** i.e., hairs **65 Do . . . grief** i.e., cling together in sympathy of grief, bound to one another by the tears falling on them **68 To England** (Perhaps an answer to Philip's invitation at l. 20; perhaps evidence of textual revision.) **71 redeem** free from imprisonment **80 suspire** breathe his first breath **82 canker** like a cankerworm, feeding on buds **83 native** natural **86 so . . . so** thus . . . thus **90 heinous a respect** terrible an opinion

CONSTANCE
　He talks to me that never had a son.

KING PHILIP
　You are as fond of grief as of your child.　　　　　92

CONSTANCE
　Grief fills the room up of my absent child,　　　　93
　Lies in his bed, walks up and down with me,
　Puts on his pretty looks, repeats his words,
　Remembers me of all his gracious parts,　　　　　96
　Stuffs out his vacant garments with his form;
　Then, have I reason to be fond of grief?
　Fare you well! Had you such a loss as I,
　I could give better comfort than you do.
　　　　　　　　[*She unbinds her hair again.*]
　I will not keep this form upon my head　　　　　101
　When there is such disorder in my wit.　　　　　102
　O Lord! My boy, my Arthur, my fair son!
　My life, my joy, my food, my all the world!
　My widow-comfort, and my sorrows' cure!　　*Exit.*

KING PHILIP
　I fear some outrage, and I'll follow her. *Exit* [*attended*].　106

LEWIS
　There's nothing in this world can make me joy.
　Life is as tedious as a twice-told tale
　Vexing the dull ear of a drowsy man;　　　　　109
　And bitter shame hath spoiled the sweet world's taste,
　That it yields naught but shame and bitterness.　　111

PANDULPH
　Before the curing of a strong disease,
　Even in the instant of repair and health,
　The fit is strongest. Evils that take leave,　　　114
　On their departure most of all show evil.
　What have you lost by losing of this day?　　　116

LEWIS
　All days of glory, joy, and happiness.

92 fond of foolishly doting on　**93 room** place　**96 Remembers** re-
minds　**101 form** coiffure (with idea of order, contrasted with *disorder*
in l. 102)　**102 wit** i.e., brain　**106 outrage** i.e., outrage upon herself,
suicide　**109 dull** inattentive　**111 That** so that　**114 fit** bout of illness
116 this day this day's battle. (But the Dauphin replies bitterly, using
day in the more common meaning.)

PANDULPH
  If you had won it, certainly you had.
  No, no. When Fortune means to men most good,   119
  She looks upon them with a threatening eye.
  'Tis strange to think how much King John hath lost
  In this which he accounts so clearly won.
  Are not you grieved that Arthur is his prisoner?

LEWIS
  As heartily as he is glad he hath him.

PANDULPH
  Your mind is all as youthful as your blood.
  Now hear me speak with a prophetic spirit;
  For even the breath of what I mean to speak
  Shall blow each dust, each straw, each little rub,   128
  Out of the path which shall directly lead
  Thy foot to England's throne. And therefore mark.
  John hath seized Arthur, and it cannot be
  That, whiles warm life plays in that infant's veins,   132
  The misplaced John should entertain an hour,   133
  One minute, nay, one quiet breath of rest.
  A scepter snatched with an unruly hand   135
  Must be as boisterously maintained as gained;   136
  And he that stands upon a slippery place
  Makes nice of no vile hold to stay him up.   138
  That John may stand, then Arthur needs must fall;
  So be it, for it cannot be but so.

LEWIS
  But what shall I gain by young Arthur's fall?

PANDULPH
  You, in the right of Lady Blanche your wife,
  May then make all the claim that Arthur did.

LEWIS
  And lose it, life and all, as Arthur did.

PANDULPH
  How green you are and fresh in this old world!
  John lays you plots; the times conspire with you,   146

---

119 means intends   **128 rub** obstacle. (From the game of bowls.)
132 whiles while.   **warm life** i.e., blood   **133 misplaced** i.e., usurping
135 unruly violating proper rule   **136 boisterously** violently
138 Makes nice of no is not scrupulous about any   **146 lays you plots**
i.e., makes plots by which you may profit

For he that steeps his safety in true blood   147
Shall find but bloody safety, and untrue.   148
This act so evilly borne shall cool the hearts   149
Of all his people and freeze up their zeal,
That none so small advantage shall step forth   151
To check his reign but they will cherish it;
No natural exhalation in the sky,   153
No scope of nature, no distempered day,   154
No common wind, no customèd event,   155
But they will pluck away his natural cause   156
And call them meteors, prodigies, and signs,
Abortives, presages, and tongues of heaven,   158
Plainly denouncing vengeance upon John.   159

LEWIS
Maybe he will not touch young Arthur's life,
But hold himself safe in his prisonment.   161

PANDULPH
O, sir, when he shall hear of your approach,
If that young Arthur be not gone already,
Even at that news he dies; and then the hearts
Of all his people shall revolt from him,   165
And kiss the lips of unacquainted change,   166
And pick strong matter of revolt and wrath   167
Out of the bloody fingers' ends of John.   168
Methinks I see this hurly all on foot;   169
And, O, what better matter breeds for you   170
Than I have named! The bastard Faulconbridge
Is now in England, ransacking the Church,
Offending charity. If but a dozen French
Were there in arms, they would be as a call   174

---

147 true blood blood of a true prince   **148 untrue** uncertain, insecure
149 borne carried out   **151 none . . . advantage** no opportunity, however
small   **153 exhalation** meteor   **154 scope of nature** i.e., one of those
prodigious phenomena within nature's power.   **distempered** stormy
155 customèd customary   **156 pluck away his** discard its.   **cause**
explanation   **158 Abortives** untimely or monstrous births
159 denouncing calling down   **161 But . . . prisonment** but regard
himself as safe so long as Arthur is imprisoned   **165 him** i.e., John
166 kiss . . . change i.e., welcome any change.   **unacquainted** unfamiliar   **167 pick strong matter of** find compelling reason for   **168 Out . . .
John** i.e., out of John's bloody-handed deeds   **169 hurly** commotion.
on foot in motion   **170 breeds** is ripening   **174 call** (1) decoy (2) call to
arms

To train ten thousand English to their side,   175
Or as a little snow, tumbled about,
Anon becomes a mountain. O noble Dauphin,
Go with me to the King. 'Tis wonderful
What may be wrought out of their discontent,
Now that their souls are topful of offense.   180
For England go. I will whet on the King.

LEWIS
Strong reasons make strange actions. Let us go.
If you say ay, the King will not say no.   *Exeunt.*

❖

175 train attract   **180 topful of offense** brimful of grievance and sated with John's offenses

4.1   *Enter Hubert and Executioners [with irons and rope].*

HUBERT
  Heat me these irons hot, and look thou stand   1
  Within the arras. When I strike my foot   2
  Upon the bosom of the ground, rush forth
  And bind the boy which you shall find with me
  Fast to the chair. Be heedful. Hence, and watch.

FIRST EXECUTIONER
  I hope your warrant will bear out the deed.   6

HUBERT
  Uncleanly scruples! Fear not you. Look to 't.   7
                    [The Executioners withdraw.]
  Young lad, come forth. I have to say with you.   8

        Enter Arthur.

ARTHUR
  Good morrow, Hubert.

HUBERT   Good morrow, little prince.

ARTHUR
  As little prince, having so great a title   10
  To be more prince, as may be. You are sad.   11

HUBERT
  Indeed, I have been merrier.

ARTHUR   Mercy on me!
  Methinks nobody should be sad but I.
  Yet I remember, when I was in France,
  Young gentlemen would be as sad as night,
  Only for wantonness. By my christendom,   16
  So I were out of prison and kept sheep,   17
  I should be as merry as the day is long;

4.1. Location: England. A room in a castle. A chair is provided.
1 look take care   **2 Within the arras** behind the wall hangings. (Evidently the Executioners go out as though to heat their irons and then conceal themselves behind the arras, ready at l. 71 to come forth.)
6 bear out provide sufficient authority for   **7 Uncleanly** improper, unbecoming   **8 to say** something to speak about   **10–11 As . . . be** i.e., I am as little a prince, despite my being entitled to be greater, as is possible   **16 for wantonness** out of affected behavior.   **By my christendom** as I am a Christian   **17 So** provided

And so I would be here, but that I doubt   19
My uncle practices more harm to me.   20
He is afraid of me and I of him.
Is it my fault that I was Geoffrey's son?
No, indeed, is 't not; and I would to heaven
I were your son, so you would love me, Hubert.   24

HUBERT [*Aside*]
If I talk to him, with his innocent prate   25
He will awake my mercy, which lies dead.
Therefore I will be sudden, and dispatch.

ARTHUR
Are you sick, Hubert? You look pale today.
In sooth, I would you were a little sick,   29
That I might sit all night and watch with you.   30
I warrant I love you more than you do me.

HUBERT [*Aside*]
His words do take possession of my bosom.—
Read here, young Arthur.   [*Showing a paper.*]
                [*Aside.*] How now, foolish rheum?   33
Turning dispiteous torture out of door?   34
I must be brief, lest resolution drop
Out at mine eyes in tender womanish tears.—
Can you not read it? Is it not fair writ?   37

ARTHUR
Too fairly, Hubert, for so foul effect.   38
Must you with hot irons burn out both mine eyes?

HUBERT
Young boy, I must.

ARTHUR   And will you?

HUBERT   And I will.

ARTHUR
Have you the heart? When your head did but ache,
I knit my handkerchief about your brows—   42
The best I had, a princess wrought it me—   43
And I did never ask it you again;   44

---

19 would be would like to be. **but** except. **doubt** fear   **20 practices**
plots   **24 so** provided   **25 prate** prattle   **29 sooth** truth   **30 watch with**
stay awake tending to   **33 rheum** i.e., tears. (Literally, a fluid discharge.)   **34 Turning . . . door** i.e., banishing pitiless torture   **37 fair**
handsomely, legibly   **38 effect** purpose, meaning   **42 knit** bound
43 wrought i.e., embroidered.   **me** for me   **44 did . . . you** never asked
for it back from you

And with my hand at midnight held your head,
And like the watchful minutes to the hour   46
Still and anon cheered up the heavy time,   47
Saying, "What lack you?" and "Where lies your grief?"
Or "What good love may I perform for you?"   49
Many a poor man's son would have lain still
And ne'er have spoke a loving word to you,
But you at your sick service had a prince.   52
Nay, you may think my love was crafty love,
And call it cunning. Do, an if you will.
If heaven be pleased that you must use me ill,
Why then you must. Will you put out mine eyes?
These eyes that never did nor never shall
So much as frown on you?
HUBERT   I have sworn to do it,
And with hot irons must I burn them out.

ARTHUR
Ah, none but in this iron age would do it!   60
The iron of itself, though heat red-hot,   61
Approaching near these eyes, would drink my tears
And quench his fiery indignation   63
Even in the matter of mine innocence;   64
Nay, after that, consume away in rust,
But for containing fire to harm mine eye.   66
Are you more stubborn-hard than hammered iron?
An if an angel should have come to me   68
And told me Hubert should put out mine eyes,
I would not have believed him—no tongue but Hubert's.
HUBERT   Come forth!   [*He stamps his foot.*
        Executioners come forth, with a cord, irons, etc.]

                Do as I bid you do.

ARTHUR
O, save me, Hubert, save me! My eyes are out
Even with the fierce looks of these bloody men.

---

46 watchful . . . hour minutes that mark the progress of the hour
47 Still and anon continually   **49 love** loving assistance   **52 at your
sick service** to serve you in your sickness   **60 iron age** degenerate time
(with play on *hot irons*)   **61 heat** heated   **63 his** its   **64 matter . . .
innocence** substance betokening my innocence, i.e., my tears   **66 But
for containing** merely because it had contained   **68 An if** if.   **should
have** had

HUBERT
    Give me the iron, I say, and bind him here.
               [*They start to bind Arthur to a chair.*]

ARTHUR
    Alas, what need you be so boisterous-rough?   75
    I will not struggle; I will stand stone-still.
    For heaven's sake, Hubert, let me not be bound!
    Nay, hear me, Hubert: drive these men away,
    And I will sit as quiet as a lamb;
    I will not stir, nor wince, nor speak a word,
    Nor look upon the iron angerly.   81
    Thrust but these men away, and I'll forgive you,
    Whatever torment you do put me to.

HUBERT
    Go stand within. Let me alone with him.

FIRST EXECUTIONER
    I am best pleased to be from such a deed.   85
                 [*Exeunt Executioners.*]

ARTHUR
    Alas, I then have chid away my friend!
    He hath a stern look, but a gentle heart.
    Let him come back, that his compassion may
    Give life to yours.

HUBERT   Come, boy, prepare yourself.

ARTHUR
    Is there no remedy?

HUBERT   None but to lose your eyes.

ARTHUR
    O heaven, that there were but a mote in yours,   91
    A grain, a dust, a gnat, a wandering hair,
    Any annoyance in that precious sense!   93
    Then feeling what small things are boisterous there,   94
    Your vile intent must needs seem horrible.

HUBERT
    Is this your promise? Go to, hold your tongue.   96

ARTHUR
    Hubert, the utterance of a brace of tongues   97

---

75 what why   **81 angerly** angrily, complainingly   **85 from** away from
91 mote minute particle of anything   **93 precious sense** i.e., sight
94 boisterous painful, irritating   **96 Go to** (An exclamation of remonstrance.)   **97 of a brace** of even a pair

Must needs want pleading for a pair of eyes. 98

Let me not hold my tongue. Let me not, Hubert! 99

Or, Hubert, if you will, cut out my tongue,

So I may keep mine eyes. O, spare mine eyes, 101

Though to no use but still to look on you! 102

Lo, by my troth, the instrument is cold 103

And would not harm me.

HUBERT   I can heat it, boy.

ARTHUR

No, in good sooth. The fire is dead with grief, 105

Being create for comfort, to be used 106

In undeserved extremes. See else yourself. 107

There is no malice in this burning coal;

The breath of heaven hath blown his spirit out

And strewed repentant ashes on his head. 110

HUBERT

But with my breath I can revive it, boy.

ARTHUR

An if you do, you will but make it blush

And glow with shame of your proceedings, Hubert.

Nay, it perchance will sparkle in your eyes, 114

And, like a dog that is compelled to fight,

Snatch at his master that doth tarre him on. 116

All things that you should use to do me wrong

Deny their office. Only you do lack 118

That mercy which fierce fire and iron extends, 119

Creatures of note for mercy-lacking uses. 120

HUBERT

Well, see to live. I will not touch thine eye 121

For all the treasure that thine uncle owes. 122

Yet am I sworn, and I did purpose, boy,

With this same very iron to burn them out.

---

98 Must . . . pleading must be inadequate to plead sufficiently   **99 Let me not** don't make me, don't hold me to my promise to   **101 So** provided, if thereby   **102 still** always   **103 troth** faith   **105 in good sooth** certainly   **106 create** created   **107 extremes** i.e., extreme cruelties. **See else yourself** see for yourself if it isn't true   **110 on his head** i.e., like a penitent sinner heaping ashes on his head   **114 sparkle in** scatter sparks into   **116 Snatch** snap.   **tarre** provoke, incite   **118 Deny** refuse to do.   **office** function   **119 extends** proffer   **120 Creatures . . . uses** things (i.e., fire and iron) noted as instruments of torture   **121 see to live** i.e., live, and continue to see   **122 owes** owns

ARTHUR
  O, now you look like Hubert! All this while
  You were disguisèd.

HUBERT   Peace! No more. Adieu.
  Your uncle must not know but you are dead.   127
  I'll fill these doggèd spies with false reports.   128
  And, pretty child, sleep doubtless and secure   129
  That Hubert, for the wealth of all the world,
  Will not offend thee.

ARTHUR   O heaven! I thank you, Hubert.   131

HUBERT
  Silence! No more. Go closely in with me.   132
  Much danger do I undergo for thee.   *Exeunt.*

❖

4.2   *Enter [King] John, Pembroke, Salisbury, and*
      other lords. [The King sits on his throne.]

KING JOHN
  Here once again we sit, once again crowned,
  And looked upon, I hope, with cheerful eyes.

PEMBROKE
  This "once again," but that Your Highness pleased,
  Was once superfluous. You were crowned before,
  And that high royalty was ne'er plucked off,
  The faiths of men ne'er stainèd with revolt.
  Fresh expectation troubled not the land
  With any longed-for change or better state.

SALISBURY
  Therefore, to be possessed with double pomp,   9
  To guard a title that was rich before,   10
  To gild refinèd gold, to paint the lily,
  To throw a perfume on the violet,
  To smooth the ice, or add another hue
  Unto the rainbow, or with taper light

---

127 but other than that   **128 doggèd** fierce, malicious   **129 doubtless**
fearless   **131 offend** harm   **132 closely** secretly

4.2. Location: England. The court of King John.
9 be possessed with have possession of (the crown)   **10 guard** trim,
ornament; also, protect

To seek the beauteous eye of heaven to garnish,   15
Is wasteful and ridiculous excess.

PEMBROKE
But that your royal pleasure must be done,
This act is as an ancient tale new told,
And in the last repeating troublesome,
Being urgèd at a time unseasonable.

SALISBURY
In this the antique and well-noted face   21
Of plain old form is much disfigurèd;   22
And, like a shifted wind unto a sail,   23
It makes the course of thoughts to fetch about,   24
Startles and frights consideration,   25
Makes sound opinion sick and truth suspected,   26
For putting on so new a fashioned robe.   27

PEMBROKE
When workmen strive to do better than well,
They do confound their skill in covetousness;   29
And oftentimes excusing of a fault
Doth make the fault the worse by th' excuse,
As patches set upon a little breach   32
Discredit more in hiding of the fault
Than did the fault before it was so patched.

SALISBURY
To this effect, before you were new-crowned,
We breathed our counsel. But it pleased Your Highness 36
To overbear it, and we are all well pleased,   37
Since all and every part of what we would
Doth make a stand at what Your Highness will.   39

KING JOHN
Some reasons of this double coronation

15 **eye of heaven** i.e., the sun (much too fair and bright to be enhanced
by a *taper light* or candle) 21 **well-noted** familiar 22 **form** custom
23 **a shifted wind** a wind that shifts direction 24 **fetch about** change
direction, tack 25 **frights consideration** i.e., frightens everyone into
anxious reflection 26–27 **Makes . . . robe** i.e., leads to the weakening of
sound loyalty and to suspicions about the truth of John's dynastic
claims, in that the English throne has dressed itself in this strange new
ceremony 29 **confound** destroy, disrupt. **in covetousness** i.e., by their
greedy desire to do better 32 **breach** hole 36 **breathed** spoke
37 **overbear** overrule 39 **Doth . . . will** may go no further than what
Your Highness desires

I have possessed you with, and think them strong;   41
And more, more strong, when lesser is my fear   42
I shall endue you with. Meantime but ask   43
What you would have reformed that is not well,
And well shall you perceive how willingly
I will both hear and grant you your requests.

PEMBROKE

Then I, as one that am the tongue of these   47
To sound the purposes of all their hearts,   48
Both for myself and them—but chief of all
Your safety, for the which myself and them   50
Bend their best studies—heartily request   51
Th' enfranchisement of Arthur, whose restraint   52
Doth move the murmuring lips of discontent
To break into this dangerous argument:
If what in rest you have in right you hold,   55
Why then your fears—which, as they say, attend   56
The steps of wrong—should move you to mew up   57
Your tender kinsman, and to choke his days
With barbarous ignorance and deny his youth
The rich advantage of good exercise.   60
That the time's enemies may not have this   61
To grace occasions, let it be our suit   62
That you have bid us ask his liberty,   63
Which for our goods we do no further ask   64
Than whereupon our weal, on you depending,   65
Counts it your weal he have his liberty.   66

41 **possessed you with** informed you of   42–43 **And . . . with** i.e., and I
shall provide you with even more and stronger reasons, strong in proportion as my fear (in Arthur) grows less   47 **tongue** spokesman   48 **sound**
express   50 **them** i.e., they   51 **Bend** direct.   **studies** efforts   52 **enfranchisement** freeing from imprisonment   55 **If . . . hold** if in fact you hold by
right of law what you now possess in peace.   **in rest** in security, peaceably,
or, possibly, in arrest (referring to Arthur)   56 **Why then** i.e., why is it,
then, that   56–57 **attend . . . wrong** i.e., are evidence of wrongdoing, follow
in the train of wrongdoing   57 **mew up** shut up. (A falconing term.)
60 **exercise** i.e., exercise in arms and other gentlemanly accomplishments
61 **the time's enemies** enemies of the present state of affairs   62 **grace
occasions** i.e., suit their purposes, lend credence to their criticisms
62–63 **let . . . liberty** let the petition that you invited us to present (ll. 43–46)
be Arthur's liberty   64 **our goods** our personal benefit   65 **whereupon** to
the extent that.   **weal** welfare   66 **Counts . . . liberty** i.e., considers that it
will be good for your welfare to have Arthur at liberty, and therefore for
ours too, since we depend on you

Enter Hubert.

KING JOHN
Let it be so. I do commit his youth
To your direction.—Hubert, what news with you?
                              [*He takes Hubert aside.*]

PEMBROKE
This is the man should do the bloody deed;
He showed his warrant to a friend of mine.
The image of a wicked heinous fault
Lives in his eye; that close aspect of his   72
Doth show the mood of a much troubled breast,
And I do fearfully believe 'tis done,
What we so feared he had a charge to do.   75

SALISBURY
The color of the King doth come and go
Between his purpose and his conscience,
Like heralds twixt two dreadful battles set.   78
His passion is so ripe it needs must break.   79

PEMBROKE
And when it breaks, I fear will issue thence
The foul corruption of a sweet child's death.

KING JOHN [*Coming forward*]
We cannot hold mortality's strong hand.
Good lords, although my will to give is living,
The suit which you demand is gone and dead.
He tells us Arthur is deceased tonight.   85

SALISBURY
Indeed we feared his sickness was past cure.

PEMBROKE
Indeed we heard how near his death he was
Before the child himself felt he was sick.
This must be answered, either here or hence.   89

KING JOHN
Why do you bend such solemn brows on me?
Think you I bear the shears of destiny?
Have I commandment on the pulse of life?

---

72 close aspect furtive appearance   **75 charge** commission   **78 battles**
armies in battle order   **79 ripe** (like a boil full of pus, the *foul corruption* of l. 81)   **85 tonight** last night   **89 answered** atoned for.   **hence** i.e.,
in heaven, or perhaps on the field of battle

SALISBURY

It is apparent foul play, and 'tis shame   93
That greatness should so grossly offer it.   94
So thrive it in your game! And so, farewell.   95

PEMBROKE

Stay yet, Lord Salisbury. I'll go with thee,
And find th' inheritance of this poor child,
His little kingdom of a forcèd grave.   98
That blood which owed the breadth of all this isle,   99
Three foot of it doth hold; bad world the while!   100
This must not be thus borne. This will break out
To all our sorrows, and ere long, I doubt.   102

                              Exeunt [*lords*].

KING JOHN

They burn in indignation. I repent.
There is no sure foundation set on blood,
No certain life achieved by others' death.

          Enter Messenger.

A fearful eye thou hast. Where is that blood   106
That I have seen inhabit in those cheeks?
So foul a sky clears not without a storm.
Pour down thy weather: how goes all in France?   109

MESSENGER

From France to England. Never such a power
For any foreign preparation   111
Was levied in the body of a land.   112
The copy of your speed is learned by them;   113
For when you should be told they do prepare,
The tidings comes that they are all arrived.

KING JOHN

O, where hath our intelligence been drunk?   116

93 apparent evident, blatant   **94 That . . . it** i.e., that a king should
flaunt foul play so flagrantly   **95 So . . . game** may your schemes lead
to the same (bad) end   **98 forcèd** imposed by violence   **99 owed**
owned   **100 the while** while such things occur   **102 doubt** fear
106 fearful full of fear, and prompting fear in others   **109 weather**
storm, tempest.   **goes all** is it all going. (But the Messenger replies
literally in the sense that everything is physically going from France to
England in an invasion.)   **111 preparation** expedition   **112 body** i.e.,
length and breadth   **113 copy** example.   **your speed** (as when John
proceeded to Angiers; see 2.1.56 ff.)   **116 our intelligence** our spies, spy
network

Where hath it slept? Where is my mother's care,
That such an army could be drawn in France   118
And she not hear of it?

MESSENGER   My liege, her ear
Is stopped with dust. The first of April died
Your noble mother; and, as I hear, my lord,
The Lady Constance in a frenzy died
Three days before. But this from rumor's tongue
I idly heard; if true or false I know not.   124

KING JOHN
Withhold thy speed, dreadful Occasion!   125
O, make a league with me till I have pleased
My discontented peers! What, Mother dead?
How wildly then walks my estate in France!   128
Under whose conduct came those powers of France   129
That thou for truth giv'st out are landed here?   130

MESSENGER
Under the Dauphin.

    Enter [the] Bastard and Peter of Pomfret.

KING JOHN   Thou hast made me giddy
With these ill tidings. [*To the Bastard.*] Now, what
    says the world
To your proceedings? Do not seek to stuff   133
My head with more ill news, for it is full.

BASTARD
But if you be afeard to hear the worst,   135
Then let the worst unheard fall on your head.   136

KING JOHN
Bear with me, cousin, for I was amazed   137
Under the tide; but now I breathe again
Aloft the flood, and can give audience   139
To any tongue, speak it of what it will.

BASTARD
How I have sped among the clergymen,   141

---

118 drawn mustered, assembled   **124 idly** by chance   **125 Occasion**
course of events   **128 estate** power   **129 conduct** command   **130 for
truth giv'st out** claim to be true   **133 proceedings** i.e., mission against
the monasteries; see 3.3.6 ff.   **135–136 But . . . head** but if you are
afraid to listen to bad news, misfortune will come upon you unawares
(and be much more dangerous)   **137 amazed** bewildered   **139 Aloft the
flood** riding on the sea's surface (continuing the metaphor of *tide*,
l. 138)   **141 sped** succeeded

The sums I have collected shall express.
But as I traveled hither through the land,
I find the people strangely fantasied,   144
Possessed with rumors, full of idle dreams,
Not knowing what they fear, but full of fear.
And here's a prophet that I brought with me
From forth the streets of Pomfret, whom I found   148
With many hundreds treading on his heels,
To whom he sung, in rude harsh-sounding rhymes,
That ere the next Ascension Day at noon   151
Your Highness should deliver up your crown.

KING JOHN
Thou idle dreamer, wherefore didst thou so?

PETER
Foreknowing that the truth will fall out so.

KING JOHN
Hubert, away with him! Imprison him,
And on that day at noon, whereon he says
I shall yield up my crown, let him be hanged.
Deliver him to safety and return,   158
For I must use thee. [*Exit Hubert with Peter of Pomfret.*]
        O my gentle cousin,   159
Hear'st thou the news abroad, who are arrived?

BASTARD
The French, my lord. Men's mouths are full of it.
Besides, I met Lord Bigot and Lord Salisbury,
With eyes as red as new-enkindled fire,
And others more, going to seek the grave
Of Arthur, whom they say is killed tonight   165
On your suggestion.

KING JOHN   Gentle kinsman, go,   166
And thrust thyself into their companies.
I have a way to win their loves again.
Bring them before me.

BASTARD   I will seek them out.

KING JOHN
Nay, but make haste, the better foot before.   170

---

144 **strangely fantasied** full of strange fancies   148 **Pomfret** Pontefract, in Yorkshire   151 **Ascension Day** the Thursday forty days after Easter celebrating the ascent of Christ into heaven   158 **safety** safekeeping   159 **gentle** noble   165 **is killed tonight** was killed last night   166 **suggestion** instigation   170 **the better foot before** i.e., as quickly as you can

O, let me have no subject enemies
When adverse foreigners affright my towns   172
With dreadful pomp of stout invasion!   173
Be Mercury, set feathers to thy heels,   174
And fly like thought from them to me again.   175

BASTARD
  The spirit of the time shall teach me speed.   *Exit.*

KING JOHN
  Spoke like a sprightful noble gentleman!   177
  [*To the Messenger.*] Go after him, for he perhaps shall
      need
  Some messenger betwixt me and the peers;
  And be thou he.

MESSENGER   With all my heart, my liege.   [*Exit.*]

KING JOHN   My mother dead!

      Enter Hubert.

HUBERT
  My lord, they say five moons were seen tonight:
  Four fixèd, and the fifth did whirl about
  The other four in wondrous motion.

KING JOHN
  Five moons!

HUBERT   Old men and beldams in the streets   186
  Do prophesy upon it dangerously.   187
  Young Arthur's death is common in their mouths,
  And, when they talk of him, they shake their heads
  And whisper one another in the ear;
  And he that speaks doth grip the hearer's wrist,
  Whilst he that hears makes fearful action,   192
  With wrinkled brows, with nods, with rolling eyes.
  I saw a smith stand with his hammer, thus,
  The whilst his iron did on the anvil cool,
  With open mouth swallowing a tailor's news;
  Who, with his shears and measure in his hand,
  Standing on slippers, which his nimble haste

172 adverse hostile   **173 stout** bold   **174 feathers** (Mercury, messenger of the gods, had winged sandals.)   **175 like thought** as swift as thought **177 sprightful** spirited   **186 beldams** old women   **187 prophesy upon it** make predictions from it, expound its meaning for the future.   **dangerously** in terms of future danger, or threateningly to public order **192 action** gestures

Had falsely thrust upon contrary feet,   199
Told of a many thousand warlike French   200
That were embattlèd and ranked in Kent.   201
Another lean unwashed artificer   202
Cuts off his tale and talks of Arthur's death.

KING JOHN
Why seek'st thou to possess me with these fears?   204
Why urgest thou so oft young Arthur's death?
Thy hand hath murdered him. I had a mighty cause
To wish him dead, but thou hadst none to kill him.

HUBERT
No had, my lord? Why, did you not provoke me?   208

KING JOHN
It is the curse of kings to be attended
By slaves that take their humors for a warrant   210
To break within the bloody house of life,   211
And on the winking of authority   212
To understand a law, to know the meaning   213
Of dangerous majesty, when perchance it frowns
More upon humor than advised respect.   215

HUBERT [Showing his warrant]
Here is your hand and seal for what I did.

KING JOHN
O, when the last account twixt heaven and earth
Is to be made, then shall this hand and seal
Witness against us to damnation!
How oft the sight of means to do ill deeds   220
Make deeds ill done! Hadst not thou been by,   221
A fellow by the hand of nature marked,
Quoted, and signed to do a deed of shame,   223
This murder had not come into my mind.

199 upon contrary feet the left slipper on the right foot and vice versa
200 a many thousand many thousands of   **201 embattlèd** drawn up in
battle array   **202 artificer** artisan   **204 possess . . . fears** give me these
fearful tidings   **208 No had** had I not.   **provoke** incite   **210 humors**
whims   **211 the bloody . . . life** the body, animated by life blood and
made bloody by murder   **212 winking** closing the eyes (i.e., when the
person in authority closes his eyes to the law, or gives the merest hint of
approving illegality)   **213 understand a law** i.e., infer what is being
commanded   **215 upon humor** through whim.   **advised respect** careful
consideration   **220–221 How . . . done** how often seeing a way to do ill
deeds prompts us to go ahead   **223 Quoted, and signed** particularly
designated and marked out

But, taking note of thy abhorred aspect,
Finding thee fit for bloody villainy,
Apt, liable to be employed in danger,   227
I faintly broke with thee of Arthur's death,   228
And thou, to be endearèd to a king,
Made it no conscience to destroy a prince.   230

HUBERT My lord—

KING JOHN
Hadst thou but shook thy head or made a pause
When I spake darkly what I purposèd,   233
Or turned an eye of doubt upon my face,
As bid me tell my tale in express words,   235
Deep shame had struck me dumb, made me break off,
And those thy fears might have wrought fears in me.
But thou didst understand me by my signs
And didst in signs again parley with sin,
Yea, without stop didst let thy heart consent,
And consequently thy rude hand to act
The deed which both our tongues held vile to name.
Out of my sight, and never see me more!
My nobles leave me, and my state is braved,   244
Even at my gates, with ranks of foreign powers.
Nay, in the body of this fleshly land,   246
This kingdom, this confine of blood and breath,   247
Hostility and civil tumult reigns
Between my conscience and my cousin's death.

HUBERT
Arm you against your other enemies;
I'll make a peace between your soul and you.
Young Arthur is alive. This hand of mine
Is yet a maiden and an innocent hand,
Not painted with the crimson spots of blood.
Within this bosom never entered yet
The dreadful motion of a murderous thought;   256

227 liable suitable.   danger something dangerous to the victim
228 faintly broke with hesitatingly broached the subject with   230 conscience matter of conscience   233 darkly indirectly   235 As as though
to.   express explicit   244 my state is braved my authority is challenged   246 body . . . land i.e., John's own body. (Uses the figure of
the microcosm, in which man is conceived as the epitome of the uni-
verse.)   247 confine (1) territorial limit (2) prison   256 motion impulse

And you have slandered nature in my form,   257
Which, howsoever rude exteriorly,   258
Is yet the cover of a fairer mind
Than to be butcher of an innocent child.

KING JOHN
Doth Arthur live? O, haste thee to the peers!
Throw this report on their incensèd rage,   262
And make them tame to their obedience.
Forgive the comment that my passion made
Upon thy feature, for my rage was blind,   265
And foul imaginary eyes of blood   266
Presented thee more hideous than thou art.
O, answer not, but to my closet bring   268
The angry lords with all expedient haste.
I conjure thee but slowly; run more fast!   270

                    Exeunt [*separately*].

❖

4.3   *Enter Arthur, on the walls,* [*disguised as a
            shipboy*].

ARTHUR
The wall is high, and yet will I leap down.
Good ground, be pitiful and hurt me not!
There's few or none do know me; if they did,
This shipboy's semblance hath disguised me quite.   4
I am afraid, and yet I'll venture it.
If I get down, and do not break my limbs,
I'll find a thousand shifts to get away.   7
As good to die and go as die and stay. [*He leaps down.*]

---

257 slandered . . . form i.e., slandered my nature by judging me harshly
in terms of my unattractive appearance; or, slandered human nature in
my person   **258 rude** rough   **262 Throw . . . rage** i.e., tell them this
news as though throwing water on their burning rage   **265 feature**
outward appearance   **266 imaginary . . . blood** your eyes, which I
imagined to be bloody in thought, or, more probably, my eyes made
bloodshot with rage at imagined wrong   **268 closet** private chamber
270 conjure adjure, urge

4.3. Location: England. Before the walls of a castle.
s.d. on the walls in the gallery rearstage, above the doors   **4 semblance**
disguise   **7 shifts** (1) stratagems (2) changes of costume

O me! My uncle's spirit is in these stones.
Heaven take my soul, and England keep my bones!

                                  Dies.

    Enter Pembroke, Salisbury [with a letter], and
    Bigot.

SALISBURY
Lords, I will meet him at Saint Edmundsbury.   11
It is our safety, and we must embrace   12
This gentle offer of the perilous time.

PEMBROKE
Who brought that letter from the Cardinal?

SALISBURY
The Count Melun, a noble lord of France,
Whose private with me of the Dauphin's love   16
Is much more general than these lines import.   17

BIGOT
Tomorrow morning let us meet him, then.

SALISBURY
Or rather then set forward, for 'twill be
Two long days' journey, lords, or ere we meet.   20

    Enter [the] Bastard.

BASTARD
Once more today well met, distempered lords!   21
The King by me requests your presence straight.   22

SALISBURY
The King hath dispossessed himself of us.
We will not line his thin bestainèd cloak
With our pure honors, nor attend the foot   25
That leaves the print of blood where'er it walks.
Return and tell him so. We know the worst.

BASTARD
Whate'er you think, good words, I think, were best.

SALISBURY
Our griefs, and not our manners, reason now.   29

---

11 him i.e., the Dauphin. **Saint Edmundsbury** Bury St. Edmunds, in
Suffolk   **12 our safety** our only means of safety   **16 private** private
communication   **17 general** all-embracing   **20 or ere** before   **21 distempered** disaffected   **22 straight** at once   **25 attend the foot** follow in
the footsteps of one, serve one   **29 griefs** grievances. **reason** speak.
(But the Bastard answers in the sense of "rationality," l. 30, and "common sense," l. 31.)

BASTARD

But there is little reason in your grief.
Therefore 'twere reason you had manners now.

PEMBROKE

Sir, sir, impatience hath his privilege.　　　　　　32

BASTARD

'Tis true—to hurt his master, no man else.　　　　33

SALISBURY

This is the prison. [*He sees Arthur's body.*] What is he lies
here?

PEMBROKE

O death, made proud with pure and princely beauty!
The earth had not a hole to hide this deed.

SALISBURY

Murder, as hating what himself hath done,　　　　37
Doth lay it open to urge on revenge.

BIGOT

Or, when he doomed this beauty to a grave,　　　　39
Found it too precious-princely for a grave.

SALISBURY [*To the Bastard*]

Sir Richard, what think you? You have beheld.　　41
Or have you read or heard, or could you think,　　42
Or do you almost think, although you see,　　　　43
That you do see? Could thought, without this object,　44
Form such another? This is the very top,　　　　45
The height, the crest, or crest unto the crest,
Of murder's arms. This is the bloodiest shame,　　47
The wildest savagery, the vilest stroke
That ever walleyed wrath or staring rage　　　　49
Presented to the tears of soft remorse.　　　　50

PEMBROKE

All murders past do stand excused in this;　　　51
And this, so sole and so unmatchable,　　　　52

32, 33 his its　**33 'Tis . . . else** i.e., perhaps anger must be allowed to
speak, as you say, but it is apt to hurt the speaker more than his listen-
ers. You'll be sorry for what you say.　**37 as** as if　**39 he** i.e., murder
41 Sir Richard i.e., the Bastard　**42 Or . . . think** have you either read
or heard (of anything like this) or could you believe　**43 almost** even
44 That that which　**44–45 Could . . . another** could you possibly imagine another sight like this without its actually being set before you
47 arms coat of arms. (This deed is the crest on top of the crest of
murder's coat of arms.)　**49 walleyed** glaring fiercely　**50 remorse**
pity　**51 in this** in comparison to this　**52 sole** unique

Shall give a holiness, a purity,
To the yet unbegotten sin of times,   54
And prove a deadly bloodshed but a jest,   55
Exampled by this heinous spectacle.   56

BASTARD
It is a damnèd and a bloody work,
The graceless action of a heavy hand—   58
If that it be the work of any hand.

SALISBURY
If that it be the work of any hand?
We had a kind of light what would ensue.   61
It is the shameful work of Hubert's hand,
The practice and the purpose of the King,   63
From whose obedience I forbid my soul,
Kneeling before this ruin of sweet life,   [*He kneels*]
And breathing to his breathless excellence
The incense of a vow, a holy vow,   67
Never to taste the pleasures of the world,
Never to be infected with delight,   69
Nor conversant with ease and idleness,
Till I have set a glory to this hand   71
By giving it the worship of revenge.   72

PEMBROKE, BIGOT [*Kneeling*]
Our souls religiously confirm thy words.   [*All rise.*]
    Enter Hubert.

HUBERT
Lords, I am hot with haste in seeking you.
Arthur doth live. The King hath sent for you.

SALISBURY
O, he is bold and blushes not at death.
Avaunt, thou hateful villain! Get thee gone!   77

HUBERT
I am no villain.

SALISBURY [*Drawing his sword*]   Must I rob the law?   78

---

54 times i.e., future times **55 but** to be only **56 Exampled by** compared with **58 graceless** unholy. **heavy** wicked **61 light** premonition **63 practice** plot, treachery **67 The incense of a vow** i.e., a vow that ascends to heaven, like incense **69 infected** tainted, imbued **71 this hand** i.e., either Arthur's hand, or Salisbury's own hand, which he raises in taking an oath **72 worship** honor **77 Avaunt** begone **78 Must . . . law** must I deprive the law of its intended victim by killing you myself

BASTARD
    Your sword is bright, sir. Put it up again.   79

SALISBURY
    Not till I sheathe it in a murderer's skin.

HUBERT [*Drawing*]
    Stand back, Lord Salisbury, stand back, I say!
    By heaven, I think my sword's as sharp as yours.
    I would not have you, lord, forget yourself,
    Nor tempt the danger of my true defense,   84
    Lest I, by marking of your rage, forget   85
    Your worth, your greatness, and nobility.

BIGOT
    Out, dunghill! Dar'st thou brave a nobleman?   87

HUBERT
    Not for my life. But yet I dare defend
    My innocent life against an emperor.

SALISBURY
    Thou art a murderer.

HUBERT   Do not prove me so;   90
    Yet I am none. Whose tongue soe'er speaks false,
    Not truly speaks; who speaks not truly, lies.

PEMBROKE
    Cut him to pieces!

BASTARD [*Drawing*]   Keep the peace, I say!

SALISBURY
    Stand by, or I shall gall you, Faulconbridge.   94

BASTARD
    Thou wert better gall the devil, Salisbury.
    If thou but frown on me, or stir thy foot,
    Or teach thy hasty spleen to do me shame,   97
    I'll strike thee dead. Put up thy sword betimes,   98
    Or I'll so maul you and your toasting iron   99
    That you shall think the devil is come from hell.

BIGOT
    What wilt thou do, renownèd Faulconbridge?
    Second a villain and a murderer?

---

79 bright i.e., unused   **84 tempt** risk, test   **85 by marking of your rage**
paying attention only to your wrath   **87 brave** insult   **90 prove me so**
i.e., make me a murderer by tempting me to kill you   **94 Stand by** stand
aside.   **gall** wound   **97 spleen** i.e., wrath   **98 betimes** promptly
99 toasting iron sword. (Used contemptuously.)

HUBERT
  Lord Bigot, I am none.
BIGOT   Who killed this prince?
HUBERT
  'Tis not an hour since I left him well.
  I honored him, I loved him, and will weep
  My date of life out for his sweet life's loss. [*He weeps.*] 106
SALISBURY
  Trust not those cunning waters of his eyes,
  For villainy is not without such rheum, 108
  And he, long traded in it, makes it seem 109
  Like rivers of remorse and innocency.
  Away with me, all you whose souls abhor
  Th' uncleanly savors of a slaughterhouse! 112
  For I am stifled with this smell of sin.
BIGOT
  Away toward Bury, to the Dauphin there!
PEMBROKE
  There, tell the King, he may inquire us out.
                           Exeunt lords.
BASTARD
  Here's a good world! Knew you of this fair work?
  Beyond the infinite and boundless reach
  Of mercy, if thou didst this deed of death,
  Art thou damned, Hubert.
HUBERT   Do but hear me, sir.
BASTARD Ha! I'll tell thee what;
  Thou'rt damned as black—nay, nothing is so black;
  Thou art more deep damned than Prince Lucifer.
  There is not yet so ugly a fiend of hell
  As thou shalt be, if thou didst kill this child.
HUBERT
  Upon my soul—
BASTARD   If thou didst but consent
  To this most cruel act, do but despair;
  And if thou want'st a cord, the smallest thread
  That ever spider twisted from her womb
  Will serve to strangle thee; a rush will be a beam 129
  To hang thee on; or wouldst thou drown thyself,

---

106 date duration   **108 rheum** watery discharge, i.e., tears   **109 traded**
experienced   **112 savors** odors   **129 rush** reed

Put but a little water in a spoon
And it shall be as all the ocean,
Enough to stifle such a villain up.
I do suspect thee very grievously.

HUBERT
If I in act, consent, or sin of thought
Be guilty of the stealing that sweet breath
Which was embounded in this beauteous clay,   137
Let hell want pains enough to torture me.   138
I left him well.

BASTARD   Go, bear him in thine arms.
I am amazed, methinks, and lose my way   140
Among the thorns and dangers of this world.

         [Hubert picks up Arthur.]

How easy dost thou take all England up!
From forth this morsel of dead royalty,
The life, the right, and truth of all this realm
Is fled to heaven; and England now is left
To tug and scamble and to part by th' teeth   146
The unowed interest of proud-swelling state.   147
Now for the bare-picked bone of majesty
Doth doggèd war bristle his angry crest,   149
And snarleth in the gentle eyes of peace.
Now powers from home and discontents at home   151
Meet in one line; and vast confusion waits,   152
As doth a raven on a sick-fall'n beast,
The imminent decay of wrested pomp.   154
Now happy he whose cloak and cincture can   155
Hold out this tempest! Bear away that child
And follow me with speed. I'll to the King.
A thousand businesses are brief in hand,   158
And heaven itself doth frown upon the land.

             Exeunt.

137 clay i.e., Arthur's body   **138 want** lack   **140 amazed** stunned
146 scamble scramble.   **part by th' teeth** tear apart by the teeth, as a
ravenous animal would do   **147 unowed interest** disputed ownership or
control   **149 doggèd** fierce. (War is viewed as a pack of dogs fighting
over a bone and bristling their hackles, continuing the metaphor of
l. 146.)   **151 powers from home** foreign armies   **152 in one line** in
united purpose.   **vast confusion waits** limitless chaos awaits
154 wrested pomp usurped majesty   **155 cincture** belt   **158 are brief in
hand** demand immediate action

5.1   *Enter King John and Pandulph, [with] attendants.*

KING JOHN [*Giving Pandulph the crown*]
  Thus have I yielded up into your hand
  The circle of my glory.
PANDULPH [*Giving back the crown*]   Take again
  From this my hand, as holding of the Pope,
  Your sovereign greatness and authority.
KING JOHN
  Now keep your holy word. Go meet the French,
  And from His Holiness use all your power
  To stop their marches 'fore we are inflamed.
  Our discontented counties do revolt;   8
  Our people quarrel with obedience,
  Swearing allegiance and the love of soul   10
  To stranger blood, to foreign royalty.   11
  This inundation of mistempered humor   12
  Rests by you only to be qualified.   13
  Then pause not, for the present time's so sick
  That present med'cine must be ministered,   15
  Or overthrow incurable ensues.
PANDULPH
  It was my breath that blew this tempest up,
  Upon your stubborn usage of the Pope;   18
  But since you are a gentle convertite,   19
  My tongue shall hush again this storm of war
  And make fair weather in your blustering land.
  On this Ascension Day, remember well,
  Upon your oath of service to the Pope,
  Go I to make the French lay down their arms.
                                    Exit [with attendants].
KING JOHN
  Is this Ascension Day? Did not the prophet
  Say that before Ascension Day at noon

5.1. Location: England. The court of King John.
8 counties shires; possibly, nobles   **10 love of soul** most sincere love
11 stranger foreign   **12–13 This . . . qualified** this erratic behavior
(thought to be caused by the excess of one of the bodily humors) can be
reduced to its right proportion only by you   **15 present** prompt
18 Upon following   **19 convertite** convert

My crown I should give off? Even so I have.
I did suppose it should be on constraint;
But, heaven be thanked, it is but voluntary.

Enter [the] Bastard.

BASTARD
All Kent hath yielded. Nothing there holds out
But Dover Castle. London hath received,
Like a kind host, the Dauphin and his powers.   32
Your nobles will not hear you, but are gone
To offer service to your enemy,
And wild amazement hurries up and down
The little number of your doubtful friends.   36

KING JOHN
Would not my lords return to me again
After they heard young Arthur was alive?

BASTARD
They found him dead and cast into the streets,
An empty casket, where the jewel of life
By some damned hand was robbed and ta'en away.

KING JOHN
That villain Hubert told me he did live.

BASTARD
So, on my soul, he did, for aught he knew.
But wherefore do you droop? Why look you sad?
Be great in act, as you have been in thought.
Let not the world see fear and sad distrust   46
Govern the motion of a kingly eye.
Be stirring as the time; be fire with fire;   48
Threaten the threatener, and outface the brow
Of bragging horror. So shall inferior eyes,
That borrow their behaviors from the great,
Grow great by your example and put on
The dauntless spirit of resolution.
Away, and glister like the god of war   55
When he intendeth to become the field!
Show boldness and aspiring confidence.

32 powers army   **36 doubtful** not to be relied on; fearful   **46 distrust**
lack of confidence, fainting courage   **48 as the time** as the state of
affairs demands   **55 become** grace, adorn

What, shall they seek the lion in his den,
And fright him there? And make him tremble there?
O, let it not be said! Forage, and run   59
To meet displeasure farther from the doors,
And grapple with him ere he come so nigh.

KING JOHN
The legate of the Pope hath been with me,
And I have made a happy peace with him;
And he hath promised to dismiss the powers
Led by the Dauphin.

BASTARD   O inglorious league!
Shall we, upon the footing of our land,   66
Send fair-play orders and make compromise,   67
Insinuation, parley, and base truce
To arms invasive? Shall a beardless boy,   69
A cockered silken wanton, brave our fields   70
And flesh his spirit in a warlike soil,   71
Mocking the air with colors idly spread,   72
And find no check? Let us, my liege, to arms!   73
Perchance the Cardinal cannot make your peace;
Or if he do, let it at least be said
They saw we had a purpose of defense.   76

KING JOHN
Have thou the ordering of this present time.

BASTARD
Away, then, with good courage! Yet, I know,   78
Our party may well meet a prouder foe.   *Exeunt.*   79

✤

59 Forage seek out the enemy as prey   **66 upon . . . land** standing on
our native soil   **67 fair-play orders** chivalric conditions   **69 invasive**
invading   **70 cockered . . . wanton** spoiled, dandified youngster.   **brave**
(1) arrogantly display his splendor in (2) defy   **71 flesh** initiate in bloodshed or inure to bloodshed   **72 idly** carelessly, insolently   **73 check**
restraint   **76 of defense** to defend ourselves   **78–79 Yet . . . foe** i.e., yet
this call for courage is scarcely necessary, since our side is ready to
take on a more spirited and fierce foe than this one. (Or he could mean,
to himself, that he fears the enemy will prove too much for them.)

5.2   *Enter, in arms, [Lewis the] Dauphin, Salisbury,*
        Melun, Pembroke, Bigot, soldiers.

LEWIS

My Lord Melun, let this be copied out,   1
And keep it safe for our remembrance.

                 [He gives a document.]

Return the precedent to these lords again,   3
That, having our fair order written down,   4
Both they and we, perusing o'er these notes,
May know wherefore we took the Sacrament,   6
And keep our faiths firm and inviolable.

SALISBURY

Upon our sides it never shall be broken.
And, noble Dauphin, albeit we swear
A voluntary zeal and an unurged faith   10
To your proceedings, yet believe me, Prince,
I am not glad that such a sore of time   12
Should seek a plaster by contemned revolt,   13
And heal the inveterate canker of one wound   14
By making many. O, it grieves my soul
That I must draw this metal from my side   16
To be a widow maker! O, and there
Where honorable rescue and defense
Cries out upon the name of Salisbury!   19
But such is the infection of the time
That, for the health and physic of our right,   21
We cannot deal but with the very hand   22
Of stern injustice and confusèd wrong.
And is 't not pity, O my grievèd friends,

5.2. Location: England. The Dauphin's camp at St. Edmundsbury.
1 this i.e., the agreement with the English lords. (See ll. 33–34 of the
preceding scene.)   **3 precedent** original document, first draft   **4 order**
proposal   **6 took the Sacrament** i.e., received communion to confirm
the sacredness of our vows   **10 unurged** uncompelled   **12–13 that . . .
revolt** i.e., that the ills of this troublesome time should seek out the
despised remedy of rebellion.   **plaster** dressing for a wound.   **contemned** reviled   **14 inveterate canker** chronic and deep-seated ulcer
16 metal i.e., sword   **19 Cries out upon** appeal to, or, exclaim against
21 physic medical cure   **22 We . . . hand** i.e., we are obliged to use the
very means (which we otherwise deplore). The nobles must fight fire
with fire.

That we, the sons and children of this isle,
Were born to see so sad an hour as this,
Wherein we step after a stranger, march   27
Upon her gentle bosom, and fill up
Her enemies' ranks—I must withdraw and weep
Upon the spot of this enforcèd cause—   30
To grace the gentry of a land remote,   31
And follow unacquainted colors here?   [*He weeps.*] 32
What, here? O nation, that thou couldst remove! 33
That Neptune's arms, who clippeth thee about,   34
Would bear thee from the knowledge of thyself,
And grapple thee unto a pagan shore,
Where these two Christian armies might combine   37
The blood of malice in a vein of league,   38
And not to spend it so unneighborly!

LEWIS
A noble temper dost thou show in this,
And great affections wrestling in thy bosom   41
Doth make an earthquake of nobility.   42
O, what a noble combat hast thou fought
Between compulsion and a brave respect!   44
Let me wipe off this honorable dew,
That silverly doth progress on thy cheeks.
                    [*He wipes Salisbury's eyes.*]
My heart hath melted at a lady's tears,
Being an ordinary inundation;
But this effusion of such manly drops,
This shower, blown up by tempest of the soul,
Startles mine eyes, and makes me more amazed
Than had I seen the vaulty top of heaven   52
Figured quite o'er with burning meteors.   53

27 step after follow (as in a march). **stranger** foreign (leader) **30 spot**
(1) stain (2) place. **enforcèd cause** i.e., cause into which I am forced
31 grace honor **32 unacquainted colors** i.e., the banners of a foreign
power **33 remove** depart, change location, i.e., go from this scene of
civil carnage to a crusade against pagan enemies **34 clippeth** embraces **37–38 combine . . . league** i.e., unite the malice they now ex-
pend on one another in a league of hostility, a crusade, against a pagan
foe **41 affections** passions **42 Doth . . . nobility** i.e., produces tumult
in your noble nature **44 compulsion** what you are compelled to do (by
the hard necessities of the times). **brave respect** gallant consideration
(of your country's need) **52 had I seen** if I had seen **53 Figured**
adorned

Lift up thy brow, renownèd Salisbury,
And with a great heart heave away this storm.
Commend these waters to those baby eyes   56
That never saw the giant world enraged,
Nor met with fortune other than at feasts,
Full warm of blood, of mirth, of gossiping.
Come, come, for thou shalt thrust thy hand as deep
Into the purse of rich prosperity
As Lewis himself. So, nobles, shall you all,
That knit your sinews to the strength of mine.

    Enter Pandulph.

And even there, methinks, an angel spake.   64
Look where the holy legate comes apace,
To give us warrant from the hand of heaven,
And on our actions set the name of right
With holy breath.

PANDULPH   Hail, noble prince of France!
The next is this: King John hath reconciled
Himself to Rome. His spirit is come in   70
That so stood out against the holy Church,
The great metropolis and See of Rome.
Therefore thy threatening colors now wind up,   73
And tame the savage spirit of wild war,
That, like a lion fostered up at hand,   75
It may lie gently at the foot of peace
And be no further harmful than in show.

LEWIS
Your Grace shall pardon me; I will not back.   78
I am too highborn to be propertied,   79
To be a secondary at control,   80
Or useful servingman and instrument
To any sovereign state throughout the world.
Your breath first kindled the dead coal of wars

---

56 Commend entrust, bequeath. (Leave tears to babies, says the Dauphin, that have never known the fury of the world at large and have had no worse fortune than to be well fed and entertained.) **64 an angel spake** (1) i.e., Pandulph comes with warrant from "the hand of heaven" (2) a pun on *angel* meaning a coin, in "the purse of rich prosperity." A trumpet may sound at this point.   **70 is come in** has submitted **73 wind up** furl   **75 at hand** by hand (and hence tame) **78 shall** must.   **back** go back   **79 propertied** made a tool of   **80 secondary at control** subordinate under someone else's command

Between this chastised kingdom and myself,
And brought in matter that should feed this fire;   85
And now 'tis far too huge to be blown out
With that same weak wind which enkindled it.
You taught me how to know the face of right,   88
Acquainted me with interest to this land,   89
Yea, thrust this enterprise into my heart.
And come ye now to tell me John hath made
His peace with Rome? What is that peace to me?
I, by the honor of my marriage bed,   93
After young Arthur, claim this land for mine;
And, now it is half conquered, must I back
Because that John hath made his peace with Rome?
Am I Rome's slave? What penny hath Rome borne,
What men provided, what munition sent,
To underprop this action? Is 't not I   99
That undergo this charge? Who else but I,   100
And such as to my claim are liable,   101
Sweat in this business and maintain this war?
Have I not heard these islanders shout out
"Vive le roi!" as I have banked their towns?   104
Have I not here the best cards for the game
To win this easy match played for a crown?   106
And shall I now give o'er the yielded set?   107
No, no, on my soul, it never shall be said.

PANDULPH
You look but on the outside of this work.

LEWIS
Outside or inside, I will not return
Till my attempt so much be glorified
As to my ample hope was promisèd
Before I drew this gallant head of war,   113
And culled these fiery spirits from the world

---

85 matter i.e., fuel   **88 right** my true claim   **89 interest** title, right
93 by the . . . bed i.e., in the name of Blanche, my wife   **99 underprop**
support   **100 charge** expense   **101 liable** subject   **104 Vive le roi** long
live the king. (Also a term in card playing; the metaphor continues in
banked, won by putting in the bank, *game, match, crown,* a five-shilling
stake, *set,* round in a game, etc.)   **banked** coasted, skirted   **106 crown**
(1) symbol of monarchy (2) stake in a game   **107 give o'er** abandon.
the yielded set the round or rubber already won   **113 drew** assembled.   **head of war** army

To outlook conquest and to win renown　　　　　　　115
Even in the jaws of danger and of death.

　　　　　　　　　　　　[A trumpet sounds.]

What lusty trumpet thus doth summon us?　　　　　　117

　　　Enter [the] Bastard.

BASTARD
According to the fair play of the world,　　　　　　118
Let me have audience. I am sent to speak.
My holy lord of Milan, from the King
I come, to learn how you have dealt for him;
And, as you answer, I do know the scope
And warrant limited unto my tongue.

PANDULPH
The Dauphin is too willful-opposite,　　　　　　124
And will not temporize with my entreaties.　　　　　　125
He flatly says he'll not lay down his arms.

BASTARD
By all the blood that ever fury breathed,　　　　　　127
The youth says well. Now hear our English king,
For thus his royalty doth speak in me.
He is prepared, and reason too he should.　　　　　　130
This apish and unmannerly approach,
This harnessed masque and unadvisèd revel,　　　　　　132
This unhaired sauciness and boyish troops,　　　　　　133
The King doth smile at, and is well prepared
To whip this dwarfish war, these pygmy arms,
From out the circle of his territories.
That hand which had the strength, even at your door,
To cudgel you and make you take the hatch,　　　　　　138
To dive like buckets in concealèd wells,　　　　　　139
To crouch in litter of your stable planks,　　　　　　140
To lie like pawns locked up in chests and trunks,　　　　　　141

---

115 outlook stare down　**117 lusty** vigorous　**118 fair play** i.e., rules of
chivalry　**124 willful-opposite** stubbornly opposed　**125 temporize**
come to an agreement　**127 blood** bold warriors　**130 reason . . . should**
with good reason　**132 harnessed** in armor.　**unadvisèd revel** ill-
considered entertainment　**133 unhaired** beardless, youthful　**138 take
the hatch** leap over the lower half door; i.e., make a hasty and undigni-
fied retreat　**139 concealèd wells** wells offering a place to hide
140 crouch i.e., hide.　**litter** straw bedding for animals.　**planks**
floors　**141 pawns** articles in pawn

To hug with swine, to seek sweet safety out   142
In vaults and prisons, and to thrill and shake   143
Even at the crying of your nation's crow,   144
Thinking his voice an armèd Englishman—
Shall that victorious hand be feebled here
That in your chambers gave you chastisement?   147
No! Know the gallant monarch is in arms,
And like an eagle o'er his aerie towers,   149
To souse annoyance that comes near his nest.   150
And you degenerate, you ingrate revolts,   151
You bloody Neroes, ripping up the womb   152
Of your dear mother England, blush for shame!
For your own ladies and pale-visaged maids
Like Amazons come tripping after drums;   155
Their thimbles into armèd gauntlets change,   156
Their needles to lances, and their gentle hearts
To fierce and bloody inclination.

LEWIS
There end thy brave, and turn thy face in peace.   159
We grant thou canst outscold us. Fare thee well.
We hold our time too precious to be spent
With such a brabbler.

PANDULPH   Give me leave to speak.   162
BASTARD
No, I will speak.
LEWIS   We will attend to neither.   163
Strike up the drums, and let the tongue of war
Plead for our interest and our being here.
BASTARD
Indeed, your drums, being beaten, will cry out;
And so shall you, being beaten. Do but start
An echo with the clamor of thy drum,

142 **hug** i.e., bed down   143 **thrill** shiver   144 **crying . . . crow** i.e.,
crowing of the rooster, a French national symbol   147 **your chambers**
i.e., your own terrain   149 **aerie** nest. **towers** soars   150 **souse** swoop
down upon   151 **revolts** rebels   152 **Neroes** (The Roman emperor Nero
allegedly ripped open the womb of his mother after having murdered
her.)   155 **Amazons** female warriors of ancient mythology   156 **armèd
gauntlets** steel-plated gloves worn as part of the armor   159 **brave**
defiant boast.   **turn thy face** go back where you came from
162 **brabbler** noisy, quarrelsome person   163 **attend to** (1) listen to
(2) wait for

And even at hand a drum is ready braced   169
That shall reverberate all as loud as thine.
Sound but another, and another shall,
As loud as thine, rattle the welkin's ear   172
And mock the deep-mouthed thunder. For at hand—
Not trusting to this halting legate here,
Whom he hath used rather for sport than need—
Is warlike John; and in his forehead sits
A bare-ribbed Death, whose office is this day   177
To feast upon whole thousands of the French.

LEWIS
Strike up our drums, to find this danger out.

BASTARD
And thou shalt find it, Dauphin, do not doubt.
                    [*Drums beat.*] *Exeunt* [*separately*].

5.3   *Alarums. Enter* [*King*] *John and Hubert.*

KING JOHN
How goes the day with us? O, tell me, Hubert.

HUBERT
Badly, I fear. How fares Your Majesty?

KING JOHN
This fever that hath troubled me so long
Lies heavy on me. O, my heart is sick!

   Enter a Messenger.

MESSENGER
My lord, your valiant kinsman, Faulconbridge,
Desires Your Majesty to leave the field
And send him word by me which way you go.

KING JOHN
Tell him, toward Swinestead, to the abbey there.   8

MESSENGER
Be of good comfort, for the great supply   9

---

169 ready braced i.e., tightened, ready to be struck   **172 welkin's**
heaven's, sky's   **177 bare-ribbed Death** i.e., Death envisaged as a skeleton.   **office** function

5.3. Location: England. The field of battle.
8 Swinestead (in Lincolnshire)   **9 supply** reinforcement

That was expected by the Dauphin here
Are wrecked three nights ago on Goodwin Sands.   11
This news was brought to Richard but even now.   12
The French fight coldly, and retire themselves.   13

KING JOHN
Ay me, this tyrant fever burns me up,
And will not let me welcome this good news.
Set on toward Swinestead. To my litter straight;
Weakness possesseth me, and I am faint.   *Exeunt.*

5.4   *Enter Salisbury, Pembroke, and Bigot.*

SALISBURY
I did not think the King so stored with friends.

PEMBROKE
Up once again! Put spirit in the French.
If they miscarry, we miscarry too.

SALISBURY
That misbegotten devil, Faulconbridge,
In spite of spite, alone upholds the day.   5

PEMBROKE
They say King John, sore sick, hath left the field.

Enter Melun, wounded, [led by a soldier].

MELUN
Lead me to the revolts of England here.   7

SALISBURY
When we were happy we had other names.

PEMBROKE
It is the Count Melun.

SALISBURY   Wounded to death.

MELUN
Fly, noble English, you are bought and sold!   10
Unthread the rude eye of rebellion   11

---

11 Goodwin Sands dangerous shoals off Kent   **12 Richard** i.e., the
Bastard   **13 retire themselves** retreat

5.4. Location: The field of battle, as before.
5 In spite of spite i.e., despite anything we do   **7 revolts** rebels
10 bought and sold i.e., betrayed   **11 Unthread . . . eye** i.e., withdraw
from the hazardous undertaking in which you are engaged, just as you
would withdraw thread from a needle's eye

And welcome home again discarded faith.
Seek out King John and fall before his feet;
For if the French be lords of this loud day,
He means to recompense the pains you take   15
By cutting off your heads. Thus hath he sworn,
And I with him, and many more with me,
Upon the altar at Saint Edmundsbury,
Even on that altar where we swore to you
Dear amity and everlasting love.

SALISBURY
May this be possible? May this be true?

MELUN
Have I not hideous death within my view,
Retaining but a quantity of life,   23
Which bleeds away, even as a form of wax
Resolveth from his figure 'gainst the fire?   25
What in the world should make me now deceive,
Since I must lose the use of all deceit?   27
Why should I then be false, since it is true
That I must die here and live hence by truth?   29
I say again, if Lewis do win the day,
He is forsworn if e'er those eyes of yours
Behold another daybreak in the east.
But even this night, whose black contagious breath   33
Already smokes about the burning crest   34
Of the old, feeble, and day-wearied sun,
Even this ill night, your breathing shall expire,
Paying the fine of rated treachery   37
Even with a treacherous fine of all your lives,   38
If Lewis by your assistance win the day.
Commend me to one Hubert with your king;
The love of him, and this respect besides,   41
For that my grandsire was an Englishman,   42
Awakes my conscience to confess all this.
In lieu whereof, I pray you, bear me hence   44

---

15 He i.e., the French Dauphin   **23 quantity** small quantity
25 Resolveth from his figure melts and loses its shape   **27 use** profit
29 hence i.e., in heaven   **33 contagious** (Night air was thought to be
noxious.)   **34 smokes** becomes misty   **37 fine** penalty.   **rated**
(1) assessed, evaluated (2) rebuked, chided   **38 fine** end (with a pun on
fine of the previous line)   **41 respect** consideration   **42 For that** because, in that   **44 In lieu whereof** in payment for which (information)

From forth the noise and rumor of the field,   45
Where I may think the remnant of my thoughts
In peace, and part this body and my soul
With contemplation and devout desires.

SALISBURY
We do believe thee, and beshrew my soul   49
But I do love the favor and the form   50
Of this most fair occasion, by the which
We will untread the steps of damnèd flight,   52
And like a bated and retirèd flood,   53
Leaving our rankness and irregular course,   54
Stoop low within those bounds we have o'erlooked   55
And calmly run on in obedience
Even to our ocean, to our great King John.
My arm shall give thee help to bear thee hence,
For I do see the cruel pangs of death
Right in thine eye. Away, my friends! New flight,   60
And happy newness, that intends old right!   61

Exeunt [leading off Melun].

❖

5.5   *Enter [Lewis the] Dauphin and his train.*

LEWIS
The sun of heaven, methought, was loath to set,
But stayed and made the western welkin blush,
When English measure backward their own ground   3
In faint retire. O, bravely came we off,   4
When with a volley of our needless shot,   5

---

45 rumor noise   **49 beshrew** curse   **50 But** unless.   **favor . . . form** i.e., outward appearance   **52 untread** retrace.   **damnèd flight** cursed breaking away from proper obedience   **53 bated** checked, abated. **retirèd** having receded.   **flood** river   **54 rankness** overgrowth, i.e., flooding, exceeding of proper bounds   **55 Stoop low** (1) subside, like a river (2) kneel.   **o'erlooked** (1) overflowed (2) disregarded   **60 Right** unmistakably.   **New flight** i.e., another breaking away (see l. 52) **61 happy newness** a change for the better.   **intends old right** intends to reestablish an ancient right or just cause

5.5. Location: England. The French camp.
3 measure traverse   **4 faint retire** fainthearted retreat.   **bravely . . . off** we left the field of battle in fine fettle   **5 needless** i.e., fired toward a disappearing enemy that needed no encouragement to flee

After such bloody toil, we bid good night,
And wound our tattering colors clearly up,   7
Last in the field, and almost lords of it!

Enter a Messenger.

MESSENGER
Where is my prince, the Dauphin?
LEWIS   Here. What news?
MESSENGER
The Count Melun is slain. The English lords
By his persuasion are again fall'n off,   11
And your supply, which you have wished so long,
Are cast away and sunk on Goodwin Sands.
LEWIS
Ah, foul shrewd news! Beshrew thy very heart!   14
I did not think to be so sad tonight
As this hath made me. Who was he that said
King John did fly an hour or two before
The stumbling night did part our weary powers?   18
MESSENGER
Whoever spoke it, it is true, my lord.
LEWIS
Well, keep good quarter and good care tonight.   20
The day shall not be up so soon as I,
To try the fair adventure of tomorrow.   *Exeunt.*

❖

5.6   *Enter [the] Bastard and Hubert, severally.*

HUBERT
Who's there? Speak, ho! Speak quickly, or I shoot.
BASTARD
A friend. What art thou?
HUBERT   Of the part of England.   2

---

7 tattering flying in tatters (because of the day's fierce engagement).
clearly free from entanglement, without enemy interference   **11 are
again fall'n off** have withdrawn allegiance once again   **14 shrewd** of
evil import   **18 stumbling** causing to stumble   **20 quarter** watch

**5.6. Location: England. An open place in the neighborhood of Swine-
stead Abbey.**
s.d. severally at separate doors   **2 Of the part** on the side

BASTARD
Whither dost thou go?
HUBERT   What's that to thee?
Why may not I demand of thine affairs
As well as thou of mine?
BASTARD   Hubert, I think?
HUBERT   Thou hast a perfect thought.   7
I will upon all hazards well believe   8
Thou art my friend, that know'st my tongue so well.
Who art thou?
BASTARD   Who thou wilt. And if thou please,
Thou mayst befriend me so much as to think
I come one way of the Plantagenets.
HUBERT
Unkind remembrance! Thou and eyeless night   13
Have done me shame. Brave soldier, pardon me,
That any accent breaking from thy tongue   15
Should scape the true acquaintance of mine ear.
BASTARD
Come, come; sans compliment, what news abroad?   17
HUBERT
Why, here walk I in the black brow of night,
To find you out.
BASTARD   Brief, then; and what's the news?
HUBERT
O, my sweet sir, news fitting to the night,
Black, fearful, comfortless, and horrible.
BASTARD
Show me the very wound of this ill news.
I am no woman; I'll not swoon at it.
HUBERT
The King, I fear, is poisoned by a monk.
I left him almost speechless, and broke out   25
To acquaint you with this evil, that you might
The better arm you to the sudden time   27
Than if you had at leisure known of this.   28

---

7 perfect correct   **8 upon all hazards** against any odds   **13 Unkind
remembrance** (Hubert chides his own faulty memory.)   **Thou** i.e., my
memory   **15 accent** speech   **17 sans compliment** without the usual
civilities   **25 out** away   **27 to the sudden time** for this emergency
28 at leisure i.e., later, because of a leisurely report

BASTARD
  How did he take it? Who did taste to him?   29

HUBERT
  A monk, I tell you, a resolvèd villain,
  Whose bowels suddenly burst out. The King
  Yet speaks, and peradventure may recover.

BASTARD
  Who didst thou leave to tend His Majesty?

HUBERT
  Why, know you not? The lords are all come back,
  And brought Prince Henry in their company,   35
  At whose request the King hath pardoned them,
  And they are all about His Majesty.

BASTARD
  Withhold thine indignation, mighty heaven,
  And tempt us not to bear above our power!   39
  I'll tell thee, Hubert, half my power this night,   40
  Passing these flats, are taken by the tide;   41
  These Lincoln Washes have devourèd them.
  Myself, well mounted, hardly have escaped.
  Away before! Conduct me to the King.
  I doubt he will be dead or ere I come.   *Exeunt.* 45

❖

5.7   *Enter Prince Henry, Salisbury, and Bigot.*

PRINCE HENRY
  It is too late. The life of all his blood   1
  Is touched corruptibly, and his pure brain,   2

---

29 it i.e., the poison. **Who did taste to him** (A "taster" was supposed to eat a portion of everything the King was to eat in order to protect him from poisoning. The monk who did so here took the poison knowingly— as a *resolvèd villain*—to ensure the King's death.) **35 Prince Henry** i.e., John's son, the future Henry III **39 tempt . . . power** don't try us beyond our power of endurance **40 power** army **41 Passing** traversing. **flats** tidal flatlands in the large inlet called the Wash, between Lincolnshire and Norfolk **45 doubt** fear. **or ere** before

5.7. Location: England. The orchard of Swinestead Abbey.
1 life essence **2 touched** infected. **corruptibly** leading to corruption and death. **pure** clear

Which some suppose the soul's frail dwelling-house,
Doth by the idle comments that it makes   4
Foretell the ending of mortality.   5

Enter Pembroke.

PEMBROKE
His Highness yet doth speak, and holds belief
That, being brought into the open air,
It would allay the burning quality
Of that fell poison which assaileth him.   9

PRINCE HENRY
Let him be brought into the orchard here.

[Exit Bigot.]

Doth he still rage?

PEMBROKE   He is more patient
Than when you left him. Even now he sung.

PRINCE HENRY
O vanity of sickness! Fierce extremes   13
In their continuance will not feel themselves.   14
Death, having preyed upon the outward parts,
Leaves them invisible, and his siege is now   16
Against the mind, the which he pricks and wounds
With many legions of strange fantasies,   18
Which, in their throng and press to that last hold,   19
Confound themselves. 'Tis strange that Death should
   sing.   20
I am the cygnet to this pale faint swan,   21
Who chants a doleful hymn to his own death,
And from the organ pipe of frailty sings
His soul and body to their lasting rest.

SALISBURY
Be of good comfort, Prince, for you are born

---

4 idle comments babble **5 mortality** life **9 fell** cruel **13 vanity**
absurdity **14 In . . . themselves** i.e., by the very intensity of their
continuation produce a loss of sensation **16 invisible** imperceptibly (?),
insensate (?) **his** its, Death's **18 legions** (1) vast numbers (2) armies
19 hold stronghold (the mind) **20 Confound** destroy, i.e., make incoher-
ent and senseless **21 cygnet** young swan. (It was a popular belief
that the swan sang only once in its life, just before it died, as its spirit
attempted to pass through its long neck, the *organ pipe of frailty*
of l. 23.)

To set a form upon that indigest   26
Which he hath left so shapeless and so rude.   27

    [*King*] *John brought in* [*in a chair, attended by Bigot*].

KING JOHN
  Ay, marry, now my soul hath elbowroom;
  It would not out at windows nor at doors.
  There is so hot a summer in my bosom
  That all my bowels crumble up to dust.
  I am a scribbled form, drawn with a pen
  Upon a parchment, and against this fire
  Do I shrink up.
PRINCE HENRY   How fares Your Majesty?
KING JOHN
  Poisoned—ill fare! Dead, forsook, cast off;   35
  And none of you will bid the winter come
  To thrust his icy fingers in my maw,
  Nor let my kingdom's rivers take their course
  Through my burned bosom, nor entreat the north
  To make his bleak winds kiss my parchèd lips
  And comfort me with cold. I do not ask you much—
  I beg cold comfort; and you are so strait   42
  And so ingrateful, you deny me that.
PRINCE HENRY
  O, that there were some virtue in my tears   44
  That might relieve you!
KING JOHN   The salt in them is hot.
  Within me is a hell, and there the poison
  Is as a fiend confined to tyrannize
  On unreprievable condemnèd blood.

    Enter [*the*] *Bastard.*

BASTARD
  O, I am scalded with my violent motion
  And spleen of speed to see Your Majesty!   50

26 indigest shapeless mass, i.e., the confused state **27 rude** shapeless, crude **35 fare** (1) food (2) fortune **42 cold comfort** (1) the comfort of cold to my burning (2) empty consolation (since real consolation is no longer possible). **strait** niggardly **44 virtue** power **50 spleen** i.e., eagerness

KING JOHN

O cousin, thou art come to set mine eye.   51
The tackle of my heart is cracked and burnt,   52
And all the shrouds wherewith my life should sail   53
Are turnèd to one thread, one little hair.
My heart hath one poor string to stay it by,   55
Which holds but till thy news be utterèd,
And then all this thou seest is but a clod
And module of confounded royalty.   58

BASTARD

The Dauphin is preparing hitherward,   59
Where God He knows how we shall answer him!   60
For in a night the best part of my power,   61
As I upon advantage did remove,   62
Were in the Washes all unwarily
Devourèd by the unexpected flood.   [*The King dies.*] 64

SALISBURY

You breathe these dead news in as dead an ear.—
My liege! My lord!—But now a king, now thus.

PRINCE HENRY

Even so must I run on, and even so stop.
What surety of the world, what hope, what stay,   68
When this was now a king and now is clay?

BASTARD [*To the King*]

Art thou gone so? I do but stay behind
To do the office for thee of revenge,
And then my soul shall wait on thee to heaven,   72
As it on earth hath been thy servant still.—   73
Now, now, you stars that move in your right spheres,   74
Where be your powers? Show now your mended faiths,   75
And instantly return with me again
To push destruction and perpetual shame

---

51 set mine eye close my eyes (in death)   **52 tackle** rigging of a ship
53 shrouds ropes giving support to masts (with a suggestion also of
burial garments)   **55 string** (1) heartstring (2) rope, as in ll. 53–54.   **stay
it** support itself   **58 module** counterfeit, mere image.   **confounded**
destroyed   **59 preparing** repairing, coming   **60 answer** encounter
61 in a night during the night.   **power** army   **62 upon advantage** to
gain, or taking, favorable opportunity.   **remove** shift position   **64 flood**
i.e., tide   **68 stay** support   **72 wait on** attend   **73 still** always   **74 stars**
i.e., nobles.   **right spheres** proper orbits (around the throne, like heavenly bodies around the earth)   **75 faiths** loyalties (to the crown)

Out of the weak door of our fainting land.
Straight let us seek, or straight we shall be sought;   79
The Dauphin rages at our very heels.

SALISBURY
It seems you know not, then, so much as we.
The Cardinal Pandulph is within at rest,
Who half an hour since came from the Dauphin,
And brings from him such offers of our peace
As we with honor and respect may take,   85
With purpose presently to leave this war.

BASTARD
He will the rather do it when he sees
Ourselves well sinewèd to our defense.   88

SALISBURY
Nay, 'tis in a manner done already,
For many carriages he hath dispatched   90
To the seaside, and put his cause and quarrel
To the disposing of the Cardinal,
With whom yourself, myself, and other lords,
If you think meet, this afternoon will post   94
To consummate this business happily.

BASTARD
Let it be so. And you, my noble Prince,
With other princes that may best be spared,
Shall wait upon your father's funeral.   98

PRINCE HENRY
At Worcester must his body be interred,
For so he willed it.

BASTARD   Thither shall it, then.
And happily may your sweet self put on   101
The lineal state and glory of the land,   102
To whom, with all submission, on my knee
I do bequeath my faithful services   104
And true subjection everlastingly.   *[He kneels.]*

SALISBURY
And the like tender of our love we make,   106

---

79 Straight at once **85 respect** self-respect **88 well sinewèd to our**
well strengthened in our own **90 carriages** baggage vehicles **94 post**
hasten **98 wait upon** act as escorts and pallbearers in **101 happily**
propitiously **102 lineal state** crown by right of succession
104 bequeath give **106 tender** offer

To rest without a spot for evermore.   107

      [All kneel to Prince Henry, and then rise.]

PRINCE HENRY
  I have a kind soul that would give you thanks
  And knows not how to do it but with tears.

BASTARD
  O, let us pay the time but needful woe,   110
  Since it hath been beforehand with our griefs.
  This England never did, nor never shall,
  Lie at the proud foot of a conqueror
  But when it first did help to wound itself.
  Now these her princes are come home again,   115
  Come the three corners of the world in arms   116
  And we shall shock them. Naught shall make us rue,   117
  If England to itself do rest but true.

        Exeunt [with the King's body].

---

107 rest remain. **spot** stain **110 but needful woe** no more weeping
than necessary **115 home** i.e., back to true faith and allegiance
116 three . . . world i.e., all the world except England, the fourth corner **117 shock** meet with force

Date and Text

The Life and Death of King John, as it is called in the original text, first appeared in the First Folio of 1623. That text appears to have been set up from Shakespeare's foul papers as copied by two scribes with a view to future theatrical use, although the manuscript does not show signs of having been actually employed as a promptbook. Apart from Francis Meres's listing of the play (in his *Palladis Tamia: Wit's Treasury,* 1598, a slender volume on contemporary literature and art, valuable because it lists most of Shakespeare's plays that existed at that time), dating clues are scarce. Editors have suggested dates ranging from 1590 to 1598, and have proposed topical allusions to bolster their various arguments. The consensus today is that *King John* was probably written shortly before or after *Richard II* in about 1594–1595, or 1596. Many editors assume that Shakespeare would have preferred to write this historically independent play in the interim between his two four-play series (*Henry VI* through *Richard III* and *Richard II* through *Henry V*), rather than interrupt the flow of composition on either of those series. This suggestion is scarcely provable, however. In any case, the link between *Richard II* and *1 Henry IV* is not so close as to preclude interruption.

A major critic of the consensus view is E. A. J. Honigmann, editor of the Arden *King John* (1954), who argues for a date in 1590 preceding the publication in 1591 of *The Troublesome Reign of King John* (which he regards as a bad quarto). Honigmann is joined by Robert Smallwood in his New Penguin edition of *King John* (1974). This argument has aroused controversy but little acceptance.

Textual Notes

These textual notes are not a historical collation, either of the early folios or of more recent editions; they are simply a record of departures in this edition from the copy text. The reading adopted in this edition appears in boldface, followed by the rejected reading from the copy text, i.e., the First Folio. Only major alterations in punctuation are noted. Changes in lineation are not indicated, nor are some minor and obvious typographical errors.

Abbreviations used:
F the First Folio
s.d. stage direction
s.p. speech prefix

Copy text: the First Folio.

1.1. 30 s.d. Exeunt Exit **49 s.d. Enter . . . Philip** [after "What men are you?" in F] **50 s.p. [and elsewhere] Bastard** Philip **75 whe'er** where [also at 2.1.167] **147 I** It **188 too** two **189 conversion. Now** conuersion, now **208 smack** smoake **219 s.d.** [at l. 221 in F] **237 he get** get **me! Sir** me sir **257 Thou** That

2.1 [here F reads "Scaena Secunda"] **1 s.p. King Philip** Lewis [also at l. 18] **63 Ate** Ace **75 s.d. Drum beats** [at l. 77 in F] **89 s.p. [and elsewhere] King Philip** Fran **106 Geoffrey's. In** Geffreyes in **113 breast** beast **120 s.p. [and elsewhere] Eleanor** Queen **144 shows** shooes **149 Philip** Lewis **150 s.p. King Philip** Lew **152 Anjou** Angiers **166 s.p. Eleanor** Qu. Mo **187 plague; her sin** plague her sinne, **200 s.d. citizens** a Citizen **201 s.p. Hubert** Cit [and so until l. 325] **215 Confronts your** Comfort yours **252 invulnerable** involuerable **259 roundure** rounder **335 run** rome **368 s.p. Hubert** Fra **371 Kinged** Kings **463 cannon: fire** Cannon fire, **469 s.p. Eleanor** Old Qu **488 Anjou** Angiers **497 s.p. [and elsewhere] Lewis** Dol

3.1 [here F reads "Actus Secundus"] **74** [following this line, F reads "Actus Tertius, Scaena prima"] **s.d. Austria** Austria, Constance **110 day** daies **155 God** heauen **196 it** that **259 chafèd** cased **283 oath. The** oath the **317 s.p. [and elsewhere] Lewis** Dolph **323 s.p. King John** Eng

3.2. 4 s.d. Enter . . . Hubert [at l. 3 in F] **10 s.d. Exeunt** Exit

3.4 [here F reads "Scaena Tertia"] **2 armada** Armado **44 not holy** holy **64 friends** fiends **110 world's** words **182 make** makes

4.1. 6 s.p. First Executioner Exec [also at l. 85] **50 lain** lyen **63 his** this **80 wince** winch **91 mote** moth **120 mercy-lacking** mercy, lacking

4.2. 1 again crowned against crown'd **42 when** then **73 Doth** Do **105 s.d. Enter Messenger** [at l. 103 in F] **143 traveled** trauail'd **247 blood and breath,** blood, and breathe **261 haste** hast [also at l. 269]

4.3. 33 man mans **155 cincture** center **159 s.d. Exeunt** Exit

5.2. 16 metal mettle **26 Were** Was **36 grapple** cripple **43 hast thou** hast **133 unhaired** vn-heard **135 these** this **145 his** this

5.4. 27 lose loose

5.5. 7 wound woon'd

5.6. 13 eyeless endles

5.7. 17 mind winde   **21 cygnet** Symet   **60 God** heauen   **108 give you** giue

Shakespeare's Sources

To understand Shakespeare's use of sources in *King John*, we must first understand the play's relationship to the anonymous play *The Troublesome Reign of King John*, published in 1591. According to E.A.J. Honigmann (in his Arden edition of *King John*, 1954), *Troublesome Reign* is a bad quarto pirated from Shakespeare's text rather than a source for it. *Troublesome Reign* does indeed show features of a bad quarto. Moreover, a 1611 reprint of this play is attributed to "W. Sh.," and another in 1622 to "W. Shakespeare." The Folio editors did not register *King John* for publication in 1623, as though assuming it had already been published in some form. Nevertheless, most scholars still hold to the view that *Troublesome Reign* is a source. Its early date, by 1591, would mean a still earlier date for a play on which it was based. Honingmann's argument for dating *King John* in 1590 has not won acceptance.

If, on the other hand, we accept the argument that Shakespeare was substantially rewriting an earlier play on King John, the pattern of his indebtedness becomes clear on two points: (1) *Troublesome Reign* was his main though not his only source, and (2) Shakespeare consciously toned down the earlier play's anti-Catholic excesses and scurrilous humor. His characters are more thoughtful and complex, the paradoxes of kingship more disturbing. Shakespeare's alteration of a crude and chauvinistic source play into a subtle exploration of political rule anticipates his similar transformation of the irrepressible *Famous Victories of Henry V* (c. 1586–1587) into the *Henry IV* plays and *Henry V*.

Briefly, some differences between *Troublesome Reign* and *King John* are as follows. In *Troublesome Reign*, as the following excerpt suggests, John is a hero and a martyr for his defiance of Rome. His claim to the English throne is unquestioned. The barons who rise against him are loyal to Rome. Vice is rampant in monasteries and other ecclesiastical institutions. An abbot is discovered to be hiding a nun in his treasure chest. John is poisoned by a monk who is in league with the abbot and who receives absolution for his deed. The Bastard, John's loyal supporter, is an invincible

foe of ecclesiastical corruption and treason against the
state. In Shakespeare, on the other hand, John's claim to
the throne is dynastically questionable, and his treatment
of his nephew Arthur is reprehensible. The barons' opposition to him is prompted by a genuine moral revulsion.
Although they learn belatedly that rebellion is more de-
structive than the evil it seeks to correct, since rebellion
provides a fatal opportunity for foreign opportunists such
as the French Dauphin, the barons are not simply tools of
the Papacy. The Bastard struggles too with his conscience
over John's treatment of Arthur. The Church is often guilty
of political duplicity, as are virtually all the kings and political leaders in the play, but the Church shows no signs of
moral decadence. John is poisoned by a monk, but without
evidence of conspiracy.

These contrasting estimates of King John reflect the two
views of him held concurrently in Tudor England. One, the
older and more critical, is that of medieval historians generally and Polydore Vergil in particular. The other, a more
favorable estimate, is essentially a Protestant defense of
John, a rewriting of history in order to view him (despite his
failures) as a martyr of Catholic oppression and hence a
forerunner of the Reformation. William Tyndale began this
revisionist view of John in his *The Obedience of a Christian
Man* (1528). The case was vividly expounded by John Bale in
his *King Johan*, a play begun before 1536 and rewritten in
1538 and 1561. Whether the author of *Troublesome Reign*,
or Shakespeare, consulted Bale is uncertain, but the author
of *Troublesome Reign* was certainly heir to the Protestant
tradition. A major repository of the Protestant view, in any
event, was John Foxe's *Acts and Monuments* (1583 edition),
known as the *Book of Martyrs;* more copies of this work
were to be found in English households than of any other
book except the Bible, and its influence on Shakespeare
must have been considerable. (A brief selection follows.)
Richard Grafton and Raphael Holinshed took the Protestant line in their chronicles, and thus passed on the tradition to *Troublesome Reign*.

Shakespeare's play, though based primarily for its materials on *Troublesome Reign*, allows for expression of the
more critical attitude toward John of the older non-
Protestant line. Honigmann argues that Shakespeare also

consulted the *Historia Maior* of Matthew Paris (published 1571) and perhaps the Latin manuscript *Wakefield Chronicle*, but scholarly opinion on this point is divided.

The Troublesome Reign of King John

[The historical narrative in *Troublesome Reign* is generally close to that of Shakespeare's *King John*. This selection begins with King John receiving his crown again from the Pope's Legate, and corresponds to the whole of Act 5 in Shakespeare's play.]

PART 2

2.4   *Enter King John, Bastard, Pandulph, and a many priests with them.*

PANDULPH [*Returning the crown to John*]
　Thus, John, thou art absolved from all thy sins
　And freed by order from our father's curse.   2
　Receive thy crown again with this proviso:
　That thou remain true liegeman to the Pope
　And carry arms in right of holy Rome.
JOHN
　I hold the same as tenant to the Pope,
　And thank Your Holiness for your kindness shown.
BASTARD
　A proper jest, when kings must stoop to friars!   8
　Need hath no law when friars must be kings.   9

　　Enter a Messenger.

MESSENGER
　Please it Your Majesty, the Prince of France,
　With all the nobles of Your Grace's land,
　Are marching hitherward in good array.
　Where'er they set their foot, all places yield.

2.4. Location: The royal court of England.
s.d. a many many   **2 our father's** i.e., the Pope's   **8 proper** fine. (Said ironically.)   **9 Need hath no law** i.e., law bows to sheer political might

Thy land is theirs, and not a foot holds out
But Dover Castle, which is hard besieged.

PANDULPH
Fear not, King John. Thy kingdom is the Pope's,
And they shall know His Holiness hath power
To beat them soon from whence he hath to do.   18

> *Drums and trumpets. Enter Lewis, Melun,*
> *Salisbury, Essex, Pembroke, and all the nobles*
> *from France and England.*

LEWIS
Pandulph, as gave His Holiness in charge,   19
So hath the Dauphin mustered up his troops
And won the greatest part of all this land.
But ill becomes Your Grace, Lord Cardinal,
Thus to converse with John, that is accurst.   23

PANDULPH
Lewis of France, victorious conqueror,
Whose sword hath made this island quake for fear,
Thy forwardness to fight for holy Rome   26
Shall be remunerated to the full.
But know, my lord, King John is now absolved.
The Pope is pleased, the land is blest again,
And thou hast brought each thing to good effect.
It resteth then that thou withdraw thy powers   31
And quietly return to France again,
For all is done the Pope would wish thee do.

LEWIS
But all's not done that Lewis came to do.
Why Pandulph, hath King Philip sent his son
And been at such excessive charge in wars   36
To be dismissed with words? King John shall know
England is mine, and he usurps my right.

PANDULPH
Lewis, I charge thee and thy complices,   39
Upon the pain of Pandulph's holy curse,

---

18 from whence ... do from wherever his authority extends   **19 as ...
in charge** as His Holiness commanded   **23 accurst** excommunicated
26 forwardness eagerness   **31 It resteth** it remains only   **36 And ...
charge** and been put to such considerable expense   **39 complices**
accomplices

That thou withdraw thy powers to France again
And yield up London and the neighbor towns
That thou hast ta'en in England by the sword.

MELUN

Lord Cardinal, by Lewis' princely leave,   44
It can be naught but usurpation
In thee, the Pope, and all the Church of Rome
Thus to insult on kings of Christendom—   47
Now with a word to make them carry arms,
Then with a word to make them leave their arms.
This must not be. Prince Lewis, keep thine own!
Let Pope and popelings curse their bellies full.

BASTARD

My lord of Melun, what title had the Prince
To England and the crown of Albion   53
But such a title as the Pope confirmed?
The prelate now lets fall his feignèd claim;
Lewis is but the agent for the Pope;
Then must the Dauphin cease, sith he hath ceased.   57
But cease or no it greatly matters not,
If you, my lords and barons of the land,
Will leave the French and cleave unto your King.
For shame, ye peers of England! Suffer not
Yourselves, your honors, and your land to fall,
But with resolvèd thoughts beat back the French
And free the land from yoke of servitude.

SALISBURY

Philip, not so. Lord Lewis is our king   65
And we will follow him unto the death.

PANDULPH

Then in the name of Innocent the Pope
I curse the Prince and all that take his part,
And excommunicate the rebel peers
As traitors to the King and to the Pope.

LEWIS

Pandulph, our swords shall bless ourselves again.   71

---

44 by . . . leave if Prince Lewis will allow me to speak   **47 insult on**
triumph contemptuously over   **53 Albion** England   **57 sith he** i.e., since
Pandulph (representing the Pope)   **65 Philip** i.e., the Bastard   **71 bless
ourselves** i.e., undo the excommunication

Prepare thee, John! Lords, follow me your king.

Exeunt [Lewis and the English lords].

JOHN

Accursèd John! The devil owes thee shame.   73

Resisting Rome or yielding to the Pope, all's one.   74

The devil take the Pope, the peers, and France!

Shame be my share for yielding to the priest.

PANDULPH

Comfort thyself, King John. The Cardinal goes

Upon his curse to make them leave their arms.   *Exit.* 78

BASTARD

Comfort, my lord, and curse the Cardinal!

Betake yourself to arms. My troops are prest   80

To answer Lewis with a lusty shock.   81

The English archers have their quivers full;

Their bows are bent, the pikes are prest to push.

Good cheer, my lord! King Richard's fortune hangs   84

Upon the plume of warlike Philip's helm.

Then let them know his brother and his son

Are leaders of the Englishmen in arms.

JOHN

Philip, I know not how to answer thee.

But let us hence to answer Lewis' pride.   [*Exeunt.*]

2.5   *Excursions. Enter Melun with English lords.*

MELUN

O, I am slain! Nobles, Salisbury, Pembroke,

My soul is charged. Here me, for what I say   2

Concerns the peers of England and their state.

---

73 owes thee shame is ashamed of you   **74 Resisting . . . one** (John
bitterly complains that he is caught between the supporters of the hated
Papacy and those who would take away his kingdom by force, both of
them intolerable.)   **78 Upon his curse** on pain of excommunication
80 prest ready   **81 lusty** vigorous   **84 Richard** i.e., Richard I, Coeur de
Lion, father of the Bastard and brother of John

**2.5. Location: The field of battle. The scene is essentially continuous
with the previous; excursions would start onstage as the actors of
scene 4 leave.**
2 charged burdened with sin

Listen, brave lords, a fearful mourning tale
To be delivered by a man of death.
Behold these scars, the dole of bloody Mars,
Are harbingers from nature's common foe,   7
Citing this trunk to Tellus' prison house.   8
Life's charter, lordings, lasteth not an hour,
And fearful thoughts, forerunners of my end,
Bids me give physic to a sickly soul.   11
O peers of England, know you what you do?
There's but a hair that sunders you from harm.   13
The hook is baited and the train is made,   14
And simply you run doting to your deaths.   15
But, lest I die and leave my tale untold,
With silence slaughtering so brave a crew,
This I aver: if Lewis win the day,
There's not an Englishman that lifts his hand
Against King John to plant the heir of France   20
But is already damned to cruel death.
I heard it vowed! Myself amongst the rest
Swore on the later aid to this edict.
Two causes, lords, makes me display this drift:
The greatest for the freedom of my soul,
That longs to leave this mansion free from guilt;   26
The other on a natural instinct,
For that my grandsire was an Englishman.   28
Misdoubt not, lords, the truth of my discourse.
No frenzy, nor no brainsick idle fit,
But well advised and wotting what I say   31
Pronounce I here before the face of heaven
That nothing is discovered but a truth.
'Tis time to fly. Submit yourselves to John.
The smiles of France shade in the frowns of death.   35
Lift up your swords! Turn face against the French;
Expel the yoke that's framèd for your necks.
Back, war-men, back! Imbowel not the clime,   38

---

7 **nature's common foe** i.e., death 8 **Citing** summoning. **trunk** body.
Tellus' earth's 11 **physic** medicine 13 **sunders** separates 14 **train**
trap 15 **doting** foolishly, infatuatedly 20 **plant** i.e., plant as king in
England 26 **mansion** i.e., body 28 **For that** because 31 **wotting**
knowing 35 **shade in** conceal as in a shadow 38 **Imbowel not the
clime** do not disembowel your realm

Your seat, your nurse, your birthday's breathing place, 39
That bred you, bears you, brought you up in arms.
Ah, be not so ingrate to dig your mother's grave!
Preserve your lambs and beat away the wolf.
My soul hath said. Contrition's penitence   43
Lays hold on man's redemption for my sin.
Farewell, my lords!
Witness my faith when we are met in heaven,
And, for my kindness, give me grave room here.   47
My soul doth fleet. World's vanities, farewell! [*He dies.*]

SALISBURY
Now, joy betide thy soul, well-meaning man!
How now, my lords, what cooling card is this?   50
A greater grief grows now than erst hath been.   51
What counsel give you? Shall we stay and die,
Or shall we home and kneel unto the King?

PEMBROKE
My heart misgave this sad accursèd news.   54
What have we done? Fie, lords, what frenzy moved
Our hearts to yield unto the pride of France?
If we persever, we are sure to die;
If we desist, small hope again of life.

SALISBURY
Bear hence the body of this wretched man,
That made us wretched with his dying tale,
And stand not wailing on our present harms,
As women wont, but seek our harm's redress.   62
As for myself, I will in haste be gone
And kneel for pardon to our sovereign John.

PEMBROKE
Ay, there's the way. Let's rather kneel to him
Than to the French, that would confound us all.
                                        Exeunt.

❖

39 Your . . . place the place where you were born and first drew breath
43 said spoken   **47 give me grave room** provide me a grave, bury me
50 cooling card something that cools one's enthusiasm. (A metaphor
from card playing.)   **51 erst** formerly   **54 misgave** had a foreboding of
62 wont are accustomed to do

2.6   *Enter King John, carried between two lords.*

JOHN

    Set down, set down the load not worth your pain,
    For done I am with deadly wounding grief,
    Sickly and succorless, hopeless of any good.
    The world hath wearied me, and I have wearied it.
    It loaths I live; I live and loath myself.
    Who pities me? To whom have I been kind?
    But to a few; a few will pity me.
    Why die I not? Death scorns so vile a prey.
    Why live I not? Life hates so sad a prize.
    I sue to both to be retained of either,
    But both are deaf; I can be heard of neither.
    Nor death nor life, yet life and ne'er the near,   12
    Ymixed with death, biding I wot not where.

    [Enter the Bastard.]

BASTARD

    How fares my lord, that he is carried thus?
    Not all the awkward fortunes yet befall'n
    Made such impression of lament in me.
    Nor ever did my eye attaint my heart   17
    With any object moving more remorse
    Than now beholding of a mighty king
    Borne by his lords in such distressèd state.

JOHN

    What news with thee? If bad, report it straight;
    If good, be mute. It doth but flatter me.   22

BASTARD

    Such as it is, and heavy though it be   23
    To glut the world with tragic elegies,
    Once will I breathe, to aggravate the rest,   25
    Another moan to make the measure full.   26
    The bravest bowman had not yet sent forth
    Two arrows from the quiver at his side

2.6. Location: Near Swinestead Abbey.
12 ne'er the near never the nearer (to life or death)   **17 attaint** strike,
affect   **22 flatter me** i.e., beguile me with a false sense of hope
23 heavy sad   **25–26 Once . . . full** (The Bastard will punctuate his
gloomy report with sighs.)

But that a rumor went throughout our camp
That John was fled, the King had left the field.
At last the rumor scaled these ears of mine,   31
Who rather chose as sacrifice for Mars   32
Than ignominious scandal by retire.   33
I cheered the troops as did the Prince of Troy   34
His weary followers 'gainst the Myrmidons,   35
Crying aloud, "Saint George! The day is ours!"
But fear had captivated courage quite,
And, like the lamb before the greedy wolf,
So, heartless, fled our war-men from the field.   39
Short tale to make, myself amongst the rest
Was fain to fly before the eager foe.   41
By this time night had shadowed all the earth
With sable curtains of the blackest hue,
And fenced us from the fury of the French,
As Io from the jealous Juno's eye.   45
When in the morning our troops did gather head,   46
Passing the Washes with our carriages,   47
The impartial tide, deadly and inexorable,
Came raging in with billows threatening death
And swallowed up the most of all our men.
Myself upon a Galloway right free, well paced,   51
Outstripped the floods that followed, wave by wave.
I so escaped to tell this tragic tale.

JOHN
Grief upon grief, yet none so great a grief
To end this life and thereby rid my grief.
Was ever any so infortunate,
The right idea of a cursèd man,   57
As I, poor I, a triumph for despite?   58
My fever grows. What ague shakes me so?

---

31 scaled attacked, as if scaling a fortified wall   **32–33 Who . . . retire**
i.e., I who chose defeat and death if necessary rather than retreat
34 Prince of Troy i.e., Hector   **35 Myrmidons** followers of Achilles
39 heartless dispirited, having lost courage   **41 eager** fierce   **45 Io**
beloved of Jove and transformed into a heifer to conceal her from the
jealous eyes of Juno   **46 gather head** assemble in strength   **47 the
Washes** the Wash, a low area by the sea in Lincolnshire and Norfolk,
often flooded   **51 a Galloway . . . paced** a small-sized riding horse,
easily managed and of good gait   **57 right idea** exact portrait, epitome
58 a triumph for despite an object of scorn

How far to Swinestead, tell me, do you know?
Present unto the Abbot word of my repair. 61
My sickness rages, to tyrannize upon me.
I cannot live unless this fever leave me.

BASTARD

Good cheer, my lord. The abbey is at hand.
Behold, my lord, the churchmen come to meet you.

Enter the Abbot and certain Monks.

ABBOT

All health and happiness to our sovereign lord the King!

JOHN

Nor health nor happiness hath John at all.
Say, Abbot, am I welcome to thy house?

ABBOT

Such welcome as our abbey can afford
Your Majesty shall be assurèd of.

BASTARD

The King, thou seest, is weak and very faint.
What victuals hast thou to refresh His Grace?

ABBOT

Good store, my lord. Of that you need not fear,
For Lincolnshire and these our abbey grounds
Were never fatter nor in better plight. 75

JOHN

Philip, thou never need'st to doubt of cates. 76
Nor king nor lord is seated half so well
As are the abbeys throughout all the land.
If any plot of ground do pass another, 79
The friars fasten on it straight. 80
But let us in, to taste of their repast.
It goes against my heart to feed with them,
Or be beholding to such abbey grooms. 83

Exeunt. Manet the Monk.

MONK

Is this the King that never loved a friar?
Is this the man that doth contemn the Pope? 85

---

61 my repair my imminent arrival **75 plight** condition **76 doubt of cates** fear lack of delicacies **79 pass another** surpass others (in fertility) **80 straight** straightway **83 beholding** beholden. **grooms** i.e., rascals **s.d. Manet** he remains onstage **85 contemn** scorn

Is this the man that robbed the holy Church
And yet will fly unto a friary?
Is this the King that aims at abbey's lands?
Is this the man whom all the world abhors
And yet will fly unto a friary?
Accurst be Swinestead Abbey, abbot, friars,
Monks, nuns, and clerks, and all that dwells therein,   92
If wicked John escape alive away!
Now, if that thou wilt look to merit heaven
And be canonized for a holy saint,
To please the world with a deserving work
Be thou the man to set thy country free
And murder him that seeks to murder thee.

    Enter the Abbot.

ABBOT
Why are not you within to cheer the King?
He now begins to mend, and will to meat.   100
MONK [*To himself, not seeing the Abbot*]
What if I 'say to strangle him in his sleep?   101
ABBOT
What, at thy *mumpsimus*? Away,   102
And seek some means for to pastime the King.   103
MONK [*To himself*]
I'll set a dudgeon dagger at his heart   104
And with a mallet knock him on the head.
ABBOT
Alas, what means this monk, to murder me?
Dare lay my life he'll kill me for my place.   107
MONK [*To himself*]
I'll poison him, and it shall ne'er be known,
And then I'll be the chiefest of my house.
ABBOT
If I were dead, indeed he is the next.   110
But I'll away, forwhy the monk is mad,   111
And in his madness he will murder me.

---

92 clerk clerics   **100 meat** food   **101 'say** essay   **102 mumpsimus**
(Literally, bigoted opposition to reform; here, a vague term of contempt,
ironically appropriate to the speech of an abbot.)   **103 for to pastime** to
entertain   **104 dudgeon dagger** dagger with a hilt made of dudgeon, a
special kind of wood   **107 Dare lay** I dare wager   **110 the next** i.e., next
in line to be abbot   **111 forwhy** because

MONK

    My lord, I cry your lordship mercy! I saw you not.   113

ABBOT

    Alas, good Thomas, do not murder me!

    And thou shalt have my place with thousand thanks.

MONK

    I murder you? God shield from such a thought!

ABBOT

    If thou wilt needs, yet let me say my prayers.   117

MONK

    I will not hurt your lordship, good my lord.

    But, if you please, I will impart a thing

    That shall be beneficial to us all.

ABBOT

    Wilt thou not hurt me, holy monk, say on.   121

MONK

    You know, my lord, the King is in our house.

ABBOT   True.

MONK

    You know likewise the King abhors a friar.

ABBOT   True.

MONK

    And he that loves not a friar is our enemy.

ABBOT   Thou say'st true.

MONK   Then the King is our enemy.

ABBOT   True.

MONK

    Why then should we not kill our enemy?

    And, the King being our enemy,

    Why then should we not kill the King?

ABBOT

    O blessèd monk! I see God moves thy mind

    To free this land from tyrant's slavery.

    But who dare venture for to do this deed?   135

MONK

    Who dare? Why I, my lord, dare do the deed.

    I'll free my country and the Church from foes

    And merit heaven by killing of a king.

113 I cry . . . mercy I beg your lordship's pardon **117 wilt needs** must
121 Wilt thou not if you won't **135 for to do** to do

ABBOT
    Thomas, kneel down. [*The Monk kneels.*] And if thou
      art resolved,
    I will absolve thee here from all thy sins,
    Forwhy the deed is meritorious.   141
    Forward! And fear not, man, for every month
    Our friars shall sing a Mass for Thomas' soul.

MONK
    God and Saint Francis prosper my attempt!
    For now, my lord, I go about my work.   *Exeunt.*

2.7   *Enter Lewis and his army.*

LEWIS
    Thus victory, in bloody laurel clad,
    Follows the fortune of young Lodowick.   2
    The Englishmen, as daunted at our sight,   3
    Fall as the fowl before the eagle's eyes.
    Only two crosses of contrary change   5
    Do nip my heart and vex me with unrest:
    Lord Melun's death, the one part of my soul;
    A braver man did never live in France.
    The other grief—ay, that's a gall indeed—   9
    To think that Dover Castle should hold out
    'Gainst all assaults, and rest impregnable.   11
    Ye warlike race of Francus, Hector's son,   12
    Triumph in conquest of that tyrant John!
    The better half of England is our own,
    And towards the conquest of the other part
    We have the face of all the English lords.   16
    What then remains but overrun the land?

---

141 Forwhy because

**2.7. Location: With Lewis the Dauphin in the field, in the east of En-
gland.**
2 Lodowick i.e., Lewis the Dauphin. (See also l. 44.) **3 at our sight** at
the sight of us **5 crosses of contrary change** thwartings, changes for
the worse **9 gall** irritation **11 rest** remain **12 race of Francus, Hector's son** i.e., the Franci, the Franks or French, mythologically regarded
as descended from Hector of Troy **16 face** countenance, support

Be resolute, my warlike followers,
And, if good fortune serve as she begins,
The poorest peasant of the realm of France
Shall be a master o'er an English lord.

    Enter a Messenger.

Fellow, what news?

FIRST MESSENGER
Pleaseth Your Grace, the Earl of Salisbury,
Pembroke, Essex, Clare, and Arundel,
With all the barons that did fight for thee,
Are on a sudden fled with all their powers
To join with John, to drive thee back again.

    Enter another Messenger.

SECOND MESSENGER
Lewis, my lord, why standst thou in a maze?   28
Gather thy troops; hope not of help from France!
For all thy forces, being fifty sail,
Containing twenty thousand soldiers,
With victual and munition for the war,
Putting from Calais in unlucky time,   33
Did cross the seas, and on the Goodwin Sands   34
The men, munition, and the ships are lost.

    Enter another Messenger.

LEWIS   More news? Say on.

THIRD MESSENGER
John, my lord, with all his scattered troops,
Flying the fury of your conquering sword,
As Pharaoh erst within the bloody sea,   39
So he and his, environed with the tide,
On Lincoln Washes all were overwhelmed;
The barons fled, our forces cast away.   42

---

28 maze state of bewilderment   **33 Putting** putting forth   **34 Goodwin Sands** a treacherous place for ships off Kent   **39 Pharaoh** (when crossing the Red Sea, Exodus 14).   **erst** formerly, of yore   **42 The barons ... away** (The Messenger reports, along with the good news of John's army being drowned in the Wash, the bad news that the English barons have deserted Lewis and that the French reinforcements have been *cast away* or lost as already reported at ll. 30–35; see also l. 47.)

LEWIS
  Was ever heard such unexpected news?
THIRD MESSENGER
  Yet, Lodowick, revive thy dying heart.
  King John and all his forces are consumed;
  The less thou needst the aid of English earls,
  The less thou needst to grieve thy navy's wreck,
  And follow time's advantage with success.   48
LEWIS
  Brave Frenchmen, armed with magnanimity,   49
  March after Lewis, who will lead you on
  To chase the barons' power that wants a head!   51
  For John is drowned, and I am England's king.
  Though our munition and our men be lost,
  Philip of France will send us fresh supplies.   *Exeunt.*

❖

2.8   *Enter two Friars, laying a cloth.*

FIRST FRIAR   Dispatch, dispatch! The King desires to eat.
  Would 'a might eat his last, for the love he bears to   2
  churchmen.
SECOND FRIAR   I am of thy mind, too, and so it should be,
  an we might be our own carvers. I marvel why they dine   5
  here in the orchard.
FIRST FRIAR   I know not, nor I care not. The King comes.

    [*Enter King John, the Bastard, the Abbot, and
    the Monk.*]

JOHN   Come on, Lord Abbot, shall we sit together?
ABBOT   Pleaseth Your Grace, sit down.   [*The King sits.*]
JOHN   Take your places, sirs. No pomp in penury; all beg-

---

48 And . . . success i.e., and so it is time to follow up your advantages
with further successes   **49 magnanimity** lofty courage and fortitude
51 wants a head lacks an army

2.8. Location: Swinestead Abbey.
2 'a he   **5 an** if

gars and friends may come. Where necessity keeps the house, courtesy is barred the table. Sit down, Philip.

BASTARD   My lord, I am loath to allude so much to the proverb, "Honors change manners." A king is a king, 14 though fortune do her worst, and we as dutiful, in despite of her frown, as if Your Highness were now in the highest type of dignity. 17

JOHN   Come, no more ado. An you tell me much of dignity, 18 you'll mar my appetite in a surfeit of sorrow. What cheer, Lord Abbot? Methinks you frown like an host that knows his guest hath no money to pay the reckoning.

ABBOT   No, my liege, if I frown at all it is for I fear this cheer too homely to entertain so mighty a guest as Your Majesty.

BASTARD   I think rather, my Lord Abbot, you remember my last being here, when I went in progress for pouches; [To John] and the rancor of his heart breaks out 27 in his countenance to show he hath not forgot me.

ABBOT   Not so, my lord. You, and the meanest follower of 29 His Majesty, are heartily welcome to me.

MONK   Wassail, my liege! And, as a poor monk may say, welcome to Swinestead.

JOHN   Begin, monk, and report hereafter thou was taster to a king.

MONK   As much health to Your Highness as to my own heart! 35
                    [The Monk drinks to the King.]

JOHN [Drinking]   I pledge thee, kind monk.

MONK   The merriest draft that ever was drunk in England! Am I not too bold with Your Highness?

JOHN   Not a whit. All friends and fellows for a time.

MONK [Aside]   If the inwards of a toad be a compound of 40 any proof, why, so, it works!   Exit. 41

---

14 Honors change manners i.e., a change in station or fortune will lead to a change in the way people behave toward one; here, a king lowered in fortune might expect to be less ceremoniously treated   **17 type** image, epitome   **18 An** if   **27 pouches** money pouches   **29 meanest** most humble   **35 As much . . . heart** (With ironic hidden meaning: may you be as healthy as I am, I who have just poisoned us both.)   **40 toad** (Thought to be poisonous.)   **41 proof** potency

JOHN

   Stay, Philip! Where's the monk?

BASTARD   He is dead, my lord.   42

JOHN

   Then drink not, Philip, for a world of wealth!

BASTARD

   What cheer, my liege? Your color 'gins to change.

JOHN

   So doth my life. O Philip, I am poisoned!
   The monk? The devil! The poison 'gins to rage.
   It will depose myself, a king, from reign.

BASTARD

   This abbot hath an interest in this act.
   At all adventures, take thou that from me!   49

                     [He kills the Abbot.]

   There lie the Abbot, abbey, lubber, devil!
   March with the monk unto the gates of hell.
   How fares my lord?

JOHN

   Philip, some drink! O, for the frozen Alps
   To tumble on and cool this inward heat
   That rageth as the furnace, sevenfold hot,
   To burn the holy three in Babylon!   56
   Power after power forsake their proper power;   57
   Only the heart impugns with faint resist   58
   The fierce invade of him that conquers kings.   59
   Help, God! O, pain! Die, John! O plague
   Inflicted on thee for thy grievous sins!
   Philip, a chair, and by and by a grave.   62
   My legs disdain the carriage of a king.   63

               [The King is helped into a chair.]

42 Where's the monk (In John Foxe's *Acts and Monuments*, the monk, once he has drunk the poison drink and has seen John do so also, goes out to the farmery, or farm area, of the abbey and there dies; probably he leaves the stage in this scene, although somehow the Bastard must know immediately that he is dead.) **49 At all adventures** in any event
56 the holy three in Babylon i.e., Shadrach, Meshach, and Abednego, delivered from the burning fiery furnace by Daniel. (See Daniel 3.)
57 Power . . . power i.e., my faculties, one by one, forsake their strength
58 impugns fights against. **resist** resistance **59 invade** invasion. **him** i.e., death **62 a chair** i.e., get me a sick chair or litter **63 the carriage of** to uphold or sustain

BASTARD
    Ah, good my liege, with patience conquer grief
    And bear this pain with kingly fortitude.

JOHN
    Methinks I see a catalogue of sin,
    Wrote by a fiend in marble characters—   67
    The least enough to lose my part in heaven.
    Methinks the devil whispers in mine ears
    And tells me 'tis in vain to hope for grace;
    I must be damned for Arthur's sudden death.
    I see, I see a thousand thousand men
    Come to accuse me for my wrong on earth,
    And there is none so merciful a God
    That will forgive the number of my sins.
    How have I lived but by another's loss?
    What have I loved but wrack of others' weal?   77
    When have I vowed and not infringed mine oath?
    Where have I done a deed deserving well?
    How, what, when, and where have I bestowed a day
    That tended not to some notorious ill?
    My life, replete with rage and tyranny,
    Craves little pity for so strange a death.
    Or who will say that John deceased too soon?
    Who will not say he rather lived too long?
    Dishonor did attaint me in my life
    And shame attendeth John unto his death.
    Why did I scape the fury of the French
    And died not by the temper of their swords?
    Shameless my life, and shamefully it ends,
    Scorned by my foes, disdainèd of my friends.

BASTARD
    Forgive the world and all your earthly foes
    And call on Christ, who is your latest friend.   93

JOHN
    My tongue doth falter. Philip, I tell thee, man,
    Since John did yield unto the priest of Rome,
    Nor he nor his have prospered on the earth.
    Curst are his blessings, and his curse is bliss.   97

---

67 in marble characters i.e., carved in stone   **77 wrack . . . weal** the
destruction of others' well-being   **93 latest** last   **97 Curst . . . bliss** i.e.,
those he blesses are cursed, and those he curses are blessed

But in the spirit I cry unto my God,
As did the kingly prophet David cry,
Whose hands, as mine, with murder were attaint.   100
I am not he shall build the Lord a house,
Or root these locusts from the face of earth;   102
But, if my dying heart deceive me not,
From out these loins shall spring a kingly branch   104
Whose arms shall reach unto the gates of Rome,
And with his feet tread down the strumpet's pride   106
That sits upon the chair of Babylon.
Philip, my heartstrings break. The poison's flame
Hath overcome in me weak nature's power,
And, in the faith of Jesu, John doth die.

BASTARD
See how he strives for life, unhappy lord,
Whose bowels are divided in themselves!   112
This is the fruit of popery, when true kings
Are slain and shouldered out by monks and friars.

Enter a Messenger.

MESSENGER
Please it Your Grace, the barons of the land,
Which all this while bare arms against the King,
Conducted by the Legate of the Pope,   117
Together with the Prince His Highness' son,   118
Do crave to be admitted to the presence of the King.

BASTARD
Your son, my lord, young Henry, craves to see   120
Your Majesty, and brings with him besides
The barons that revolted from Your Grace.—   122
O, piercing sight! He fumbleth in the mouth.   123

---

100 attaint attainted, convicted **102 these locusts** i.e., the Catholic
prelates **104 kingly branch** i.e., Henry VIII, father of Queen Elizabeth
106 the strumpet's i.e., the Whore of Babylon's, the Pope's **112 bowels
are divided** (John Foxe reports in his *Acts and Monuments* that a monk
named Simon prepared a poisoned cup of wine from "a most venomous
toad" with which he toasted the King and was toasted in return, whereupon the monk died, "his guts gushing out of his belly," and thereafter
"had continually from thenceforth three monks to sing Mass for his
soul.") **117 Conducted** led here. **Legate** i.e., Pandulph **118 Prince . . .
son** i.e., Prince Henry, John's son **120–122 Your . . . Grace** (The Bastard repeats the Messenger's news in the ears of the King, who is
rapidly failing.) **123 fumbleth** mumbles

His speech doth fail.—Lift up yourself, my lord,
And see the Prince to comfort you in death.

*Enter Pandulph, young Henry, [and] Barons with
daggers in their hands, [and kneel].*

PRINCE
  O, let me see my Father ere he die!
  O uncle, were you here and suffered him   127
  To be thus poisoned by a damnèd monk?
  Ah, he is dead! Father, sweet Father, speak!
BASTARD
  His speech doth fail. He hasteth to his end.
PANDULPH
  Lords, give me leave to joy the dying king
  With sight of these his nobles kneeling here
  With daggers in their hands, who offer up
  Their lives for ransom of their foul offense.
  Then, good my lord, if you forgive them all,
  Lift up your hand in token you forgive.
                          [*The King makes a sign.*]
SALISBURY
  We humbly thank Your royal Majesty,
  And vow to fight for England and her King.
  And, in the sight of John, our sovereign lord,
  In spite of Lewis and the power of France,
  Who hitherward are marching in all haste,
  We crown young Henry in his father's stead.
PRINCE
  Help, help, he dies! Ah, Father, look on me!
PANDULPH
  King John, farewell. In token of thy faith,
  And sign thou diest the servant of the Lord,
  Lift up thy hand, that we may witness here
  Thou diest the servant of our Savior Christ.
                  [*The King makes a sign, and dies.*]
  Now, joy betide thy soul! [*A noise within.*] What noise is
  this?

      Enter a Messenger.

127 uncle i.e., the Bastard

MESSENGER
  Help, lords! The Dauphin maketh hitherward
  With ensigns of defiance in the wind,
  And all our army standeth at a gaze,   151
  Expecting what their leaders will command.   152

BASTARD
  Let's arm ourselves in young King Henry's right,
  And beat the power of France to sea again.

PANDULPH
  Philip, not so. But I will to the Prince   155
  And bring him face to face to parle with you.   156

BASTARD
  Lord Salisbury, yourself shall march with me;
  So shall we bring these troubles to an end.

KING HENRY
  Sweet uncle, if thou love thy sovereign,
  Let not a stone of Swinestead Abbey stand,
  But pull the house about the friars' ears,
  For they have killed my father and my king.

                        *Exeunt [with the Abbot's body. King
                        Henry III and the dead body of King
                                John remain onstage.]*

2.9   *A parle sounded. [Enter] Lewis, Pandulph,
           Salisbury, etc., [to young King Henry III and the
           body of the dead King John].*

PANDULPH
  Lewis of France, young Henry, England's king,
  Requires to know the reason of the claim
  That thou canst make to anything of his.
  King John, that did offend, is dead and gone.

---

151 at a gaze bewildered   **152 Expecting** awaiting   **155 the Prince** i.e.,
Lewis   **156 parle** parley, negotiate

**2.9. Location: Near Swinestead Abbey. The scene appears to occur soon
after 2.8 and to be essentially continuous; Pandulph must go meet the
Dauphin while the Bastard and Salisbury prepare to fight, but
Henry III and the dead King John may remain onstage.**
s.d. parle trumpet call for a parley, negotiation under a truce

See where his breathless trunk in presence lies,
And he as heir apparent to the crown
Is now succeeded to his father's room.

KING HENRY
  Lewis, what law of arms doth lead thee thus
  To keep possession of my lawful right?
  Answer in fine if thou wilt take a peace   10
  And make surrender of my right again,
  Or try thy title with the dint of sword.
  I tell thee, Dauphin, Henry fears thee not.
  For now the barons cleave unto their king,
  And, what thou hast in England, they did get.

LEWIS
  Henry of England, now that John is dead,
  That was the chiefest enemy to France,
  I may the rather be induced to peace.
  But Salisbury, and you barons of the realm,
  This strange revolt agrees not with the oath
  That you on Bury altar lately sware.   21

SALISBURY
  Nor did the oath Your Highness there did take
  Agree with honor of the Prince of France.

BASTARD
  My lord, what answer make you to the King?

LEWIS
  Faith, Philip, this I say: It boots not me   25
  Nor any prince nor power of Christendom
  To seek to win this island Albion
  Unless he have a party in the realm   28
  By treason for to help him in his wars.
  The peers which were the party on my side
  Are fled from me. Then boots me not to fight.
  But on conditions, as mine honor wills,
  I am contented to depart the realm.

KING HENRY
  On what conditions will Your Highness yield?

LEWIS
  That shall we think upon by more advice.   35

---

10 in fine in conclusion   **21 Bury** Bury St. Edmunds   **25 boots** avails
28 party faction   **35 by more advice** on more consideration

BASTARD

    Then, kings and princes, let these broils have end,   36
    And at more leisure talk upon the league.   37
    Meanwhile, to Worcester let us bear the King
    And there inter his body, as beseems.   39
    But first, in sight of Lewis, heir of France,
    Lords, take the crown and set it on his head
    That by succession is our lawful king.
                       They crown young Henry.
    Thus England's peace begins in Henry's reign,
    And bloody wars are closed with happy league.
    Let England live but true within itself
    And all the world can never wrong her state.
    Lewis, thou shalt be bravely shipped to France,
    For never Frenchman got of English ground
    The twentieth part that thou hast conquerèd.
    Dauphin, thy hand. To Worcester we will march.
    Lords, all lay hands to bear your sovereign
    With obsequies of honor to his grave.
    If England's peers and people join in one,
    Nor pope, nor France, nor Spain can do them wrong.
           [Exeunt, ceremoniously bearing off the body
                             of King John.]

Text based on *The Troublesome Reign of John, King of England, with the Discovery of King Richard Coeur de Lion's Base Son, Vulgarly Named the Bastard Faulconbridge; Also the Death of King John at Swinestead Abbey. . . 1591.* On dating, see Sources headnote. Speech prefixes have been silently regularized.

In the following, departures from the original text appear in boldface; original readings are in roman.

2.4.84 Good God   **2.7.29 not out**   **2.8.56 three** tree   **106 tread** treads

---

36 broils conflicts, squabbles   **37 talk upon the league** discuss terms of peace   **39 beseems** is fitting

Acts and Monuments of Martyrs (1583 edition)
By John Foxe

[Among the events of King John's reign providing material for Foxe's anti-Catholic polemicism is that of Peter the false prophet. The year is 1212.]

The next year, the French King began his attempt in hope of the crown of England, being well manned with the bishops, monks, prelates, and priests, and their servants to maintain the same, bragging of the letters which they had received from the great men there. But behold the work of God: the English navy took three hundred of the French King's ships, well loaden[1] with wheat, wine, meal, flesh,[2] armor, and such other like meet[3] for the war, and an hundred they brent[4] within the haven, taking the spoil[5] with them. In the meantime, the priests within England had provided them a certain false counterfeit prophet called Peter Wakefield of Poiz, who was an idle gadder-about and a prattling merchant.[6] This Peter they made to prophesy lies, rumoring his prophecies abroad[7] to bring the King out of all credit with his people. . . .

This counterfeit soothsayer prophecied of King John that he should reign no longer than Ascension Day[8] within the year of Our Lord 1213, which was the fourteenth year from his coronation, and this, he said, he had by revelation. Then was it of him demanded whether he[9] should be slain or be expelled, or should of himself[10] give over the crown. He answered that he could not tell. But of this he was sure, he said: that neither he[11] nor any of his stock or lineage should reign, that day once finished.

The King, hearing of this, laughed much at it and made but a scoff thereof. "Tush," saith he, "it is but an idiot knave and such a one as lacketh his right wits." But when

---

1 **loaden** laden 2 **flesh** meat 3 **meet** suitable 4 **brent** burned 5 **spoil** plunder 6 **prattling merchant** i.e., dealer in gossip 7 **abroad** far and wide 8 **Ascension Day** the day of Christ's ascension into heaven, forty days after his resurrection 9 **demanded whether he** asked whether he, i.e., King John 10 **of himself** of his own initiative 11 **he** i.e., King John

this foolish prophet had so escaped the danger of the King's displeasure and that he made no more of it, he gat him abroad[12] and prated thereof at large (as he was a very idle vagabond) and used to tattle and talk more than enough. So that they which loved the King caused him anon after[13] to be apprehended as a malefactor and to be thrown in prison, the King not yet knowing thereof.

Anon after, the fame of this fantastical prophet went all the realm over, and his name was known everywhere—as foolishness is much regarded of[14] people where wisdom is not in place. Specially because he was then imprisoned for the matter, the rumor was the larger, their wonderings[15] were the wantoner,[16] their practicing[17] the foolisher, their busy talks and other idle occupying[18] the greater. Continually from thence, as the rude manner of people is, old gossips' tales went abroad, new tales were invented, fables were added to fables, and lies grew upon lies. So that every day new slanders were raised on[19] the King, and not one of them true. Rumors arose, blasphemies were spread, the enemies rejoiced, and treasons by the priests were maintained, and what[20] likewise was surmised or other subtlety practiced, all was then fathered upon this foolish prophet. As, "thus saith Peter Wakefield," "thus hath he prophesied," and "this shall come to pass"—yea, many times when he thought nothing less.

When the Ascension Day was come which was prophesied of afore,[21] King John commanded his regal tent to be spread abroad in the open field, passing that day with his noble Council and men of honor in the greatest solemnity[22] that ever he did afore, solacing himself with musical instruments and songs, most in sight amongst his trusty friends. When that day was past in all prosperity and mirth, his enemies, being confused, turned all to an allegorical understanding to make the prophecy good, and said: "He is no longer king, for the Pope reigneth and not he." Yet reigned he still, and his son after him, to prove that prophet a liar.

---

12 gat him abroad went about   13 anon after soon afterward   14 of by
15 wonderings speculations   16 wantoner more ungoverned, irresponsible   17 practicing devising (of speculations)   18 occupying passing of the time   19 on about   20 what whatever   21 prophesied of afore prophesied earlier   22 solemnity ceremonial magnificence

Then was the King by his Council persuaded that this
false prophet had troubled all the realm, perverted the
hearts of the people, and raised the commons against him.
For his words went over the sea by the help of his prelates
and came to the French King's ear and gave unto him a
great encouragement to invade the land; he had not else[23]
done it so suddenly.[24] But he was most foully deceived, as
all they are and shall be that put their trust in such dark
drowsy dreams of hypocrites. The King therefore commanded that he[25] should be drawn[26] and hanged like a traitor.

[Foxe's account of the submission of King John to the Pope
dwells in detail on the horrors of such a betrayal of English
interests and rights to the Papacy.]

Then sent the Pope again into England his legate, Pandulph, with other ambassadors; the King, also at Canterbury (by letters, as it should seem, certified from[27] his
own ambassadors), waited their coming. Where, the thirteenth
day of May, the King received them, making unto them an
oath that, of and for all things wherein he stood accursed,[28]
he would make ample restitution and satisfaction. Unto
whom also all the lords and barons of England—so many as
there were with the King attending the legate's coming—
sware[29] in like manner, and that, if the King would not accomplish in everything the oath which he had taken, that
then they would cause him to hold and confirm the same
whether that he would or not. . . .
Then submitted the King himself unto the court of Rome
and to the Pope, and, resigning, gave up his dominions and
realms of England and Ireland from him and from his heirs
for evermore that should come of him,[30] with this condition:
that the King and his heirs should take again these two dominions[31] of the Pope to farm,[32]* paying yearly therefor to

---

23 else otherwise   24 suddenly quickly   25 he i.e., Peter   26 drawn
disemboweled   27 as it should seem, certified from as it appears,
informed by   28 accursed excommunicated   29 sware swore   30 come
of him be descended from him   31 these two dominions i.e., England
and Ireland   32 to farm on terms of rental. (The Pope remains the
feudal landlord.) Or perhaps to ferm, to establish or make firm.

the court of Rome a thousand marks of silver. Then took the King the crown from his head, kneeling upon his knees in the presence of all his lords and barons of England to Pandulph, the Pope's chief legate, saying in this wise: "Here I resign up the crown of the realm of England to the Pope's hands, Innocent the Third, and put me wholly in his mercy and ordinance." Then took Pandulph the crown of King John and kept it five days as a possession and seisin,[33] taking of these two realms of England and Ireland. Confirming also all things promised by his charter obligatory. . . .

Upon this obligation, the King was discharged the second day of July from that tyrannical interdiction under which he continued[34] six years and three months.

[Foxe's account of the death of King John leaves no doubt as to the murderous perfidy of the assassin at Swinestead Abbey: the King was "most traitorously poisoned by a monk of that abbey, of the sect of the Cistercians or Saint Bernard's brethren, called Simon of Swinestead." Foxe's chief source is the *Chronicle* of William Caxton, Book 7.]

The foresaid monk Simon, being much offended with certain talk that the King had at his table concerning Lodowick, the French King's son, which then had entered and usurped upon him,[35] did cast in his wicked heart how he most speedily might bring him to his end. And first of all he counseled with his abbot, showing[36] him the whole matter and what he was minded to do. He alleged for himself the prophecy of Caiaphas, John 11, saying, "It is better that one man die than all the people should perish. I am well contented," saith he, "to lose my life and so become a martyr, that I may utterly destroy this tyrant." With that the abbot did weep for gladness and much commended his fervent zeal, as he took it.

The monk, then being absolved of his abbot for doing this act aforehand,[37] went secretly into a garden upon the back side and, finding there a most venomous toad, he so pricked

---

33 seisin possession as of a freehold **34 continued** had continued
35 which . . . upon him who had at that time invaded England and usurped power. (*Lodowick*, i.e., Lewis the Dauphin; see *Troublesome Reign*, 2.7, note 2.) **36 showing** revealing **37 absolved . . . aforehand** absolved ahead of time by the abbot for doing this deed

him and pressed him with his penknife that he made him vomit all the poison that was within him. This done, he conveyed it into a cup of wine and, with a smiling and flattering countenance, he said thus to the King: "If it shall like Your princely Majesty, here is such a cup of wine as ye never drunk a better before in all your lifetime. I trust this wassail shall make all England glad." And with that he drank a great draft thereof, the King pledging[38] him. The monk anon after went to the farmery[39] and there died, his guts gushing out of his belly, and had continually from thenceforth three monks to sing Mass for his soul, confirmed by their general chapter.[40] What became after that of King John ye shall know right well in the process[41] following. I would ye did mark well the wholesome proceedings of these holy votaries, how virtuously they obey their kings whom God hath appointed, and how religiously they bestow their confessions, absolutions, and Masses.

The King, within a short space after feeling great grief in his body, asked for Simon the monk, and answer was made that he was departed this life. "Then God have mercy upon me," said he, "I suspected as much after he had said that all England should thereof be glad; he meant now, I perceive then, of his own generation."[42] With that he commanded his chariot to be prepared, for he was not able to ride. So went he from thence to Slaford Castle and from thence to Newark upon Trent, and there, within less than three days, he died.

––––––––––

Text based on John Foxe, *Acts and Monuments of Matters Most Special and Memorable Happening in the Church . . . against the True Martyrs of Christ. . . . Newly revised and recognized, partly also augmented, and now the fourth time again published . . . by . . . John Foxe. . . . An. 1583. . . . Printed by John Day . . . 1583,* pp. 252–256. The first edition of this work appeared in 1563.

In the following, the departures from the original text appears in boldface; the original reading is in roman.

p. 151 *farm forme

––––––––––

38 pledging toasting   **39 farmery** buildings and yards belonging to the abbey farm   **40 chapter** assembly of members of the monastic order
41 process narrative   **42 generation** sect

Further Reading

Blanpied, John W. "Stalking 'Strong Possession' in *King John.*" *Time and the Artist in Shakespeare's English Histories.* Newark, Del.: Univ. of Delaware Press, 1983. Blanpied focuses on Shakespeare's treatment of the political struggles in his nine history plays, exploring the dramatist's effort to impose form upon the intransigent materials of history. In *King John*, Blanpied argues, the formlessness of history ultimately overwhelms the desire to order it; political power in the play is split between John's de facto authority and the Bastard's theatrical energy, which John needs in order to transform his possession into effective rule.

Bonjour, Adrien. "The Road to Swinstead Abbey: A Study of the Sense and Structure of *King John.*" *ELH* 18 (1951): 253–274. Bonjour is perhaps the first critic to argue for the play's artistic unity. The play, he finds, articulates the falling curve of John's career and the rising curve of the Bastard's. Their linked, unfolding destinies determine the fate of the nation and demonstrate the necessity of personal integrity for the maintenance of England's strength.

Burckhardt, Sigurd. "*King John:* The Ordering of this Present Time." *ELH* 33 (1966): 133–153. Rpt. in *Shakespearean Meanings.* Princeton, N.J.: Princeton Univ. Press, 1968. Beginning with the single line *King John* shares with its source, the anonymous *The Troublesome Reign of King John*, Burckhardt shows how Shakespeare's play refuses the orthodox moral and political logic of the earlier play. Shakespeare's *King John*, in Burckhardt's suggestive account, reveals the inadequacy of the Tudor doctrines of obedience, demonstrating that the bonds of community rather than the operations of providence solve the problems of authority posed by the play.

Calderwood, James L. "Commodity and Honour in *King John.*" *University of Toronto Quarterly* 29 (1960): 341–356. Rpt. in *Shakespeare, The Histories: A Collection of Critical Essays*, ed. Eugene M. Waith. Englewood Cliffs,

N.J.: Prentice Hall, 1965. For Calderwood, *King John* is structured around two opposing value systems: one based on commodity and the other on honor. Characters are continually presented with choices that pit self-interest against more public, generous loyalties; in their decisions Calderwood discovers the play's political implications and its unity.

Campbell, Lily B. "The Troublesome Reign of King John." *Shakespeare's "Histories": Mirrors of Elizabethan Policy.* San Marino, Calif.: Huntington Library, 1947. Campbell explores how Shakespeare shapes the play's presentation of the conflicts between John and the Catholic Church to mirror political issues of Elizabeth's reign raised by the imprisonment and death of Mary Stuart: the monarch's right to the throne, the relationship of papal and civil authority, the duty of obedience, and the accountability of royalty.

Champion, Larry S. "The Maturity of Perspective: *King John, 1, 2 Henry IV, Henry V.*" *Perspective in Shakespeare's English Histories.* Athens, Ga.: Univ. of Georgia Press, 1980. Champion's book examines how Shakespeare's dramaturgy manipulates and modifies his audience's responses to the characters and events of the history plays. In *King John* Champion finds that the organization and arrangement of scenes require the audience to view characters from divergent public and private angles, provoking the play's complex ambiguity and shifting sympathies.

Elliott, John R., Jr. "Shakespeare and the Double Image of King John." *Shakespeare Studies* 1 (1965): 64–84. Elliott discovers two antithetical images of King John in Shakespeare's sources: one, a villainous usurper; the other, a proto-Protestant martyr. In *King John,* he argues, Shakespeare draws material from both traditions, producing a play sensitive to the ironies of history, resisting the simplifications of Tudor political doctrine.

Hibbard, G. R. "From Dialectical Rhetoric to Metaphorical Thinking: *King John.*" *The Making of Shakespeare's Dramatic Poetry.* Toronto: Univ. of Toronto Press, 1981. Hibbard finds in *King John*'s variety of rhetorical styles evidence of Shakespeare's interest in reassessing old techniques and testing new ones. The familiar rhetoric of argument, well-suited to the claims and counterclaims of the combatants, gives way at moments to a more dramatic rhetorical mode that anticipates the achievement of the great tragedies, where language is not merely the medium of speech but a way of apprehending reality.

Jones, Emrys. "*King John:* The Self and the World." *The Origins of Shakespeare.* Oxford: Clarendon Press, 1977. Emphasizing the uniqueness of *King John*'s tone and vision, Jones sees its theme as the encounter of innocence with worldliness. The play's political action is dominated by self-interest and self-deception, and reveals the insufficiency of human will to control events. In the Bastard, Jones contends, Shakespeare creates a character initiated into full moral awareness, who registers both his skepticism about, and his hope for, a loyal and unified England.

Jones, Robert C. "Truth in *King John.*" *Studies in English Literature, 1500–1900* 25 (1985): 397–417. Focusing primarily on the Bastard as a fictional character in the midst of historical action, Jones explores *King John*'s relation to the truth it putatively claims to represent. History, as Jones finds it dramatized, continually reveals disturbing gaps between the realities of power and the orthodox notions of legitimate rule, resisting the discovery of the "right and true" except in the construction of clarifying fictions.

Matchett, William H. "Richard's Divided Heritage in *King John.*" *Essays in Criticism* 12 (1962): 231–253. Rpt. in *Shakespeare's Histories: An Anthology of Modern Criticism,* ed. William A. Armstrong. Baltimore: Penguin, 1972. Finding the play's central concern to be the question of who should rule England, Matchett explores the respective claims of John, Arthur, and the Bastard, who divide the necessities for rule between them: possession, right, and character. Matchett finds that the play's thematic focus deepens in the final scene to consider the question of true honor, embodied in the Bastard as he kneels to Henry III and relinquishes personal ambition for his loyalty to England.

Pierce, Robert B. "*King John.*" *Shakespeare's History Plays: The Family and the State.* Columbus, Ohio: Ohio State Univ. Press, 1971. *King John,* for Pierce, represents

Shakespeare's movement beyond the rigid pattern of retribution and moral polarities in his first tetralogy of history plays. Pierce sees John as a villain-king finally defeated and replaced by a monarch who reestablishes order and right, but he argues that the moral urgency of the conflict is subordinated in the play to a sense of the flawed humanity of the characters.

Reese, M. M. *"King John." The Cease of Majesty: A Study of Shakespeare's History Plays.* New York: St. Martin's Press, 1961. Seeing *King John* as a bridge between Shakespeare's two historical tetralogies, Reese argues that the play marks a significant transition in Shakespeare's understanding of political morality. The play's sober patriotism affirms the duty of obedience to a de facto king, but it reveals also that the public good may best be served by commitments to principles at odds with the ethics of private life.

Saccio, Peter. "John: The Legitimacy of the King." *Shakespeare's English Kings: History, Chronicle, and Drama.* New York: Oxford Univ. Press, 1977. Saccio examines the difference between the historians' accounts of John's reign and Shakespeare's dramatic version of it. Shakespeare compresses the events of John's seventeen-year rule so that the ecclesiastical and baronial conflicts appear related to the dynastic struggle between John and Arthur, and unlike his sources, he presents John unequivocally as a usurper, as part of the play's thematic exploration of illegitimacy.

Sprague, Arthur Colby. *"King John." Shakespeare's Histories: Plays for the Stage.* London: The Society for Theatre Research, 1964. Tracing the history of *King John* on the stage, Sprague considers what performance reveals about the play's thematic concerns and dramatic appeal.

Tillyard, E. M. W. *"King John." Shakespeare's History Plays,* 1944. Rpt., New York: Barnes and Noble, 1964. For Tillyard, *King John* marks a new direction for Shakespeare's histories with its innovations of language and character. Turning away from the retributive pattern of history discovered in the first tetralogy and the metaphysical language that expressed it, Shakespeare moves toward a new realism and vitality, especially in his creation of the Bastard, who serves to focus the play's two main concerns: the ethics of rebellion and the character of the true king.

Waith, Eugene M. "*King John* and the Drama of History." *Shakespeare Quarterly* 29 (1978): 192–211. Examining the traditions of acting, costuming, and set design during the period of the play's great theatrical popularity from 1745 to the end of the nineteenth century, Waith claims that the principal interest of the play lay not in its political concerns but in its emotional effects, and that the play's insistence upon its own historicity was viewed primarily as a means of encouraging an audience's emotional response through the intensified impression of reality.

HENRY VIII

Introduction

However much we may like to think of *The Tempest* (c. 1610–1611) as Shakespeare's farewell to his art, celebrating his retirement to Stratford in 1611 or 1612, his career was in fact not quite finished. He probably wrote *The Famous History of the Life of King Henry the Eighth* in 1613, and he evidently collaborated with the playwright John Fletcher (and possibly Francis Beaumont) in *The Two Noble Kinsmen* (1613–1616). *Henry VIII* was performed by the King's men, Shakespeare's acting company, at the Globe playhouse on June 29, 1613, as a "new" play, though perhaps it had also been performed earlier that spring at the indoors Blackfriars playhouse. During the Globe performance, small cannon (called chambers) were discharged to welcome Henry VIII and his fellow masquers to Cardinal Wolsey's house (1.4.64 ff.), accidentally setting fire to the thatch roof and burning the Globe to the ground in less than an hour. (The theater was subsequently rebuilt.) The letter reporting this incident refers to the play by the title *All Is True*, but its identification with the extant play of *Henry VIII* is virtually certain.

Not everyone has always agreed that the entire play is by Shakespeare, although doubts did not arise until the nineteenth century. Alfred Lord Tennyson was the first to suspect that much of the play is metrically non-Shakespearean. His friend James Spedding took up the suggestion in his study *Who Wrote Shakespeare's Henry VIII?* His conclusions, based on the assumption that Fletcher's mannered blank verse is generally end-stopped and much given to double or "feminine" endings, assigned only 1.1–2, 2.3–4, 3.2 (through line 204), and 5.1 to Shakespeare, attributing all the rest to Fletcher. These metrical tests have been bolstered by subsequent researchers and augmented by other methods of statistical analysis. The result is perhaps a more elaborate case for joint authorship than for most other plays of doubtful attribution. Some of the stylistic shifts noted by Tennyson are indeed discernible, as for example in the movement from the dense, elliptical grammar and compact images of the first two scenes to the conversational fluency of scenes 3 and 4.

Against these arguments, however, the case for Shakespeare's sole authorship is impressive. Although Shakespeare did apparently collaborate with Fletcher in *The Two Noble Kinsmen* during his last years, that play was excluded from the 1623 Folio, whereas *Henry VIII* was included as Shakespeare's final history play. Spedding's hypothesis of joint authorship would rob from Shakespeare several of the play's most famous scenes, such as the farewell speeches of the Duke of Buckingham, Cardinal Wolsey, and Queen Katharine, and conversely would credit Fletcher with a dramatic power not shown elsewhere. The "Fletcherian" style may well have been the result of Shakespeare's having known the work of the younger man, who became Shakespeare's heir as chief writer for the King's men. Unquestionably, Shakespeare's style did change in his later years under the influence of a sophisticated courtly audience at the indoors Blackfriars theater; the Prologue to *Henry VIII* suggests that the play was written with the more exclusive audience of Blackfriars ("The first and happiest hearers of the town") particularly in mind. Even if *Henry VIII* is a different sort of history play from *I Henry IV*, it is stylistically close to Shakespeare's late romances. The shift in texture from scenes 1 and 2 to scenes 3 and 4 makes good sense dramatically; scene 4, for example, dramatizing an evening party, is suitably conversational, whereas the dense first scene is largely expository. Neither external evidence nor tradition during Shakespeare's day links the play with Fletcher. Scholarly efforts to assign portions of the text to other authors date only from the nineteenth century, where they should be seen as part of a broader effort to reassign various parts of many other plays and thereby rescue Shakespeare from scenes presumed unworthy of his genius. The tendency to regard *Henry VIII* as defective and lacking in unity may well have been caused in part by eighteenth- and nineteenth-century productions of the play, which, although frequent and popular, treated the play as a vehicle for famous actors and actresses in the parts of Wolsey and Katharine (Thomas Betterton, John Philip Kemble, Sarah Siddons, Charles Kean, and, more recently, Sybil Thorndike, Charles Laughton, Flora Robson), and accordingly cut Act 5 and sometimes much of Act 4 along with other "extraneous" parts. Productions and criticism during the last thirty years, on the other hand, have shown *Henry VIII* to possess an impressive cohesion and to be an integral product of the late years in which Shakespeare centered his attention on romance and tragicomedy. We are safest in assuming that nineteenth-century efforts to deny Shakespeare sole authorship are now happily out of fashion, and that the Folio editors knew what they were doing when they included *Henry VIII*.

What was Shakespeare's purpose in this unexpected return to the English history play? He had set it aside fourteen years earlier, in 1599, bringing to completion in *Henry V* a series of eight plays on England's civil wars of the fifteenth century and another on the reign of King John. Why turn in 1613 to a historical subject so separated in time from that of Shakespeare's earlier interest and potentially so controversial because of its relation to the religious battle between Catholics and Protestants? Earlier generations of critics and playgoers, as we have seen, generally regarded parts of *Henry VIII* as belonging to another author or as the product of Shakespeare's presumed dotage, especially the fifth act with its apparent anticlimax following the deaths of the play's central characters, Wolsey and Katharine. More recent efforts to understand the whole of *Henry VIII* regard it as an experimental work, blending conventional genres (history, tragedy, and romance) and stressing masquelike stage effects in the opulent manner of court entertainment. Since its thematic focus is also one of courtly celebration, expressing gratitude for Queen Elizabeth's Protestant rule and wary hopes that her successor James will follow suit, the play may best be seen as a reworking of the English history play to meet the new mood of 1613. This return to a type of drama long since abandoned by Shakespeare resembles his similar fascination during his late years with the once-forgotten genre of romance.

In some ways, *Henry VIII* is deliberately unlike Shakespeare's earlier history plays and so should not be judged by their standards. The Prologue is at pains to stress that the play will contain no merriment or bawdry, no "fellow / In a long motley coat." And indeed the play is unusually lacking in a comic subplot devoted to the endearing antics of a tavern crew. To be sure, the views of the citizens are not ignored, for Queen Katharine champions their hatred of Wolsey's taxes. In the fifth act the people put in a brief appearance, crowding bumptiously forward at the christening of the Princess Elizabeth (5.4). Even here, however, the tone is one of condescending amusement at their childish eagerness to see their future queen. The common people do not provide choric commentary, as they do in *Richard III* or *Richard II*.

These factors may well reflect the increasing influence of the court on Shakespeare and the King's men. Ever since they had become the King's men in 1603, when James I came to the throne, Shakespeare's company had enjoyed a closer relationship with the throne than before. *Measure for Measure* and *Macbeth*, among other of Shakespeare's plays, seem to contain flattering allusions to the new monarch. Moreover, faced with increasing competition from the boys' acting companies, which, since reopening in 1599 after a hiatus of nearly a decade, had attracted a courtly and sophisticated clientele, Shakespeare's company acquired the lease of Blackfriars in 1608 and henceforth used this "private" theater as their winter playhouse. Shakespeare's late plays are staged with public, private, and courtly conditions of performance in mind. The late romances show the influence of Inigo Jones's lavish designs for court masques, as in *Cymbeline*'s use of machinery for celestial ascents and descents. *Henry VIII* reflects similar conditions of staging in its masquing scene (1.4), in the pageantlike trial of Katharine and the baptism of Elizabeth, and in the vision of white-robed figures dancing before the dying Katharine (4.2). This affinity to courtly entertainment should not be overstressed, for Shakespeare's company remained a public company throughout his career, and its stage was always fluidly bare of scenery when compared with Jones's ingenious devices and use of scenic perspective. Nonetheless, *Henry VIII* should be viewed as a history play for a somewhat more select audience than that of his earlier histories. The play's ornate compliments to Elizabeth have a courtly flavor. The year 1613 saw the politically important marriage of the Elector Palatine to James's daughter Elizabeth, who was often flatteringly compared with her namesake

Queen Elizabeth; and, although *Henry VIII* is not among the plays known to have been performed for this occasion, the marriage itself would have given added significance to the play.

Shakespeare's earlier histories also honor as well as examine critically the institution of monarchy, but even here *Henry VIII* provides a different emphasis. Shakespeare's earlier histories had focused on such issues as the education of a prince and on the dilemmas of power a ruler faces. *Henry VIII* is less a study of kingship and more a dramatic expression of gratitude. *Henry VIII* is not a patriotic play in a broadly popular sense. It lacks battles and triumphant oratory. It voices thanksgiving for a particular ruling family. *Henry VIII* is above all the remarkable story of Queen Elizabeth's birth. The story is certainly not without its ironies, for providence works in mysterious ways, and Elizabeth's parents were complex persons. Shakespeare's play reveals an increasing psychological interest in analysis of motive, as do other later history plays, such as John Ford's *Perkin Warbeck*. Yet the unifying impulse of the play remains the celebration of the birth of Elizabeth.

This rising action in the play is counterpointed by a series of tragic falls, which indeed seem at first to be the play's chief concern. These falls proceed in remorseless succession—Buckingham, Katharine, Wolsey. In the edifying manner of that staple of medieval tragedy, the "Fall of Princes," these deaths offer useful lessons on statecraft and personal conduct. All these characters stoically exemplify the art of holy dying. One after another, they forgive their enemies and regret such sins as they have committed, and yet they also prophesy that God's retribution will light on offenders' heads. The prevailing mood in the falls of Buckingham and Katharine is one of pity, for both are victims of the ruthless Wolsey.

Cardinal Wolsey is the most interesting character of the three and best illustrates another convention of medieval tragedy, the Wheel of Fortune. Even as he topples one victim after another, dispatching Surrey to Ireland, wheedling his way into the King's favor, reversing England's foreign policy with bewildering speed from pro-French to pro-Empire and back again, all the while amassing a vast personal fortune and negotiating for supreme power within the

Roman Church, we sense that he is preparing his own catas-
trophe. Fortune raises insolent worldly persons of this sort,
but an overseeing power is at work and will manifest itself
through the King. Wolsey, in a nobly contrite farewell, sees
the moral of his fall: had he served God zealously, God
would not "Have left me naked to mine enemies" (3.2.458).
Wolsey knows he has ventured beyond his depth in scheming, "Like little wanton boys that swim on bladders" (l. 360).
Shakespeare's appraisal of this controversial man is mixed,
partly because his chief source, Raphael Holinshed's
Chronicles (1578), incorporated both anti-Wolseyan dia-
tribes and George Cavendish's appreciative account of Wolsey's last days. Still, the portraiture remains consistent
throughout, for Wolsey is always intelligent and munificent
(as in his founding of Cardinal College, later Christ Church,
at Oxford) even though he employs his talents for worldly
ends. His chief wrongdoing is his meddling on behalf of
Rome, his finagling to gain the papacy, and, most of all, his
sending of England's wealth overseas for reasons of private
gain. Yet even this corrupt behavior has a function in the
rising action of the story, for, had not Wolsey schemed
against Queen Katharine in his plot to marry King Henry to
the French Duchess of Alençon, Katharine might never have
fallen to make way for Anne Bullen; and had not Wolsey
given a sumptuous party to impress the court with his magnificence (1.4), Henry might never have met Queen Elizabeth's mother. Wolsey's fate is to introduce Henry to the
woman whose rise will mean Wolsey's fall and the birth of a
future queen. An overriding cosmic irony converts the
worst intents of schemers to beneficent ends.

King Henry and Anne Bullen, who as Elizabeth's parents
play the roles essential to England's bright future, are
largely unaware of the great destiny they are performing.
Henry especially, like Wolsey, is examined with some skepticism. His pious insistence that "conscience" alone ban-
ishes him from Katharine's bed elicits a wry observation,
sotto voce, from the Duke of Suffolk: "No, his conscience /
Has crept too near another lady" (2.2.17–18). As Henry ne-
glectfully condones Wolsey's abuse of authority and credu-
lously accepts perjured testimony against Buckingham, we
catch glimpses of the whimsical tyrant whom history has
revealed to us. These criticisms are muted, however, for

Henry is after all Elizabeth's father. He is not only exoner-
ated from most wrongdoing but steps boldly forward at the
play's end as champion of religious reform. Anne too is am-
bivalently treated. In her scene with the Old Lady (2.3), we
are reminded of the all-too-apparent reasons there are for
suspecting that Anne is a schemer, a high-class auctioneer
of her beauty who knows that Henry will pay handsomely.
An Elizabethan audience would be bound to recall her grim
fate at the hands of the public executioner. Yet in her own
person Anne resists these ironies. All the characters of the
play, whether they stand to profit or lose by Anne's marriage, speak admiringly of her beauty and honor. Although
her speeches are few, her appearances are sumptuously
staged with Anne at the center of a meaningful pageant.

The religious issue is presented with a similar tact and
ambiguity, for it too is both controversial and of significance to England's future. Our sympathies are charitably
disposed toward Katharine, whose innocent fall is a sad
price for England's larger happiness. Shakespeare refuses
to associate her with the decaying order of Catholicism, as
he might have done. On the other hand, Bishop Gardiner,
the villain of Act 5, is undeniably a Catholic and persecutor
of heretics, a dangerous man whose overthrow by Henry
and the Protestant Cranmer signals the beginning of a new
era in religion. Though Shakespeare tactfully omits the relationship between Katharine's divorce and the Reformation, his audience would have had little difficulty making
the connection in Act 5 between Cranmer's Protestant victory and the birth of Elizabeth. These two rising actions co-
alesce and give perspective to the pitiable falls from
greatness that have necessarily contributed to a happy and
even miraculous conclusion. History and tragicomic romance fulfill a common purpose in *Henry VIII*.

Act 5 is thus central to the play's thematic concerns, despite the poor opinion in which it was held in the nineteenth
century, and despite the apparently episodic way in which
it introduces new characters (notably Archbishop Cranmer)
and new issues. The ending confirms a pattern seen earlier
in the sad stories of Buckingham and especially Wolsey, in
which we mortals "outrun / By violent swiftness that which
we run at, / And lose by overrunning" (1.1.141–143). Vain
human striving after fame overreaches itself and brings it-

self down. The process is, in *Henry VIII*, not primarily a punishment for villainy, for there are no real villains here, but a curative process by which frail proud men ascend on Fortune's wheel only to discover how illusory are her rewards and how comforting are Fortune's losses that bring us to ourselves. Not a moment of ease does Wolsey enjoy until he is ruined in worldly terms. He assures Thomas Cromwell, at the moment of his fall, that "I know myself now, and I feel within me / A peace above all earthly dignities" (3.2.379–380). His fall is thus a happy fall, an instructive one for himself and others: "Mark but my fall, and that that ruined me" (l. 440). Even Katharine and her gentleman usher, Griffin, perceive a happiness in Wolsey's decline, not because it satisfies a desire for vengeance but because it offers a comforting precedent of self-discovery through suffering: "His overthrow heaped happiness upon him; / For then, and not till then, he felt himself" (4.2.64–65). To know oneself in these terms, *nosce teipsum*, is to enjoy the inestimable gift of penance and the laying aside of worldly striving. Cranmer is a suitable protagonist in Act 5 and substitute for Wolsey as the King's adviser because he cares so little for himself in a worldly sense. He is the instrument of a higher power that, having imposed various trials on members of the court for their individual and collective betterment, at last reveals a meaning in that suffering and a future happiness arising out of man's imperfect attempts to know himself. As Buckingham says earlier (2.1.124), "Heaven has an end in all."

The play when staged offers a visual contrast between ceremonial pomp and worldly loss leading to renunciation and death. The processions and public events, conveyed by unusually full stage directions, celebrate the ordered arrangement of a hierarchical society. Yet among the most powerful scenes are those of Wolsey bidding farewell to his wealth and power, and of Katharine in her isolation and approaching death. The Prologue promises to give us noble scenes, "Sad, high, and working, full of state and woe," and in this we are not disappointed. The Prologue also promises that the audience "May here find truth too"; and, despite the necessary omission of much bloodshed (we are never told directly what will become of Anne Bullen and Sir

Thomas More), the play does give a vivid account of
Henry VIII's time. We "see / The very persons of our noble
story / As they were living." Our impression is of great political and religious change, of splendor and richness,
above all of the insecurity of worldly felicity under such a
king. Theatrically the play is sumptuous, pageantlike;
though it chooses not to amuse us with comedy and es-
chews battle scenes, it abounds in personages from history.
In *Henry VIII* Shakespeare adapts the history play to his
late world of romance.

Henry VIII
in Performance

During a performance of *Henry VIII* on June 29, 1613, the Globe Theatre burned to the ground. The Jacobean diplomat Sir Henry Wooton, noting in a letter the play's "many extraordinary circumstances of pomp and majesty," reported that the theater was destroyed "within less than an hour" of the roof thatch catching fire from a shot fired as part of the ceremony in Act 1, scene 4. The play was performed at the rebuilt Globe in 1628 and presumably at other times before the theaters were closed by act of Parliament in 1642.

On the Restoration stage the play was unquestionably popular. The diarist Samuel Pepys judged it "a rare play" when Thomas Betterton, in the role of Henry, returned it to the stage in 1663. Pepys saw *Henry VIII* again in 1664, though he was "mightily dissatisfied," and once more in 1668, when he was "mightily pleased with the history and shows of it." In 1691, the theater historian Gerard Langbaine reported that the play "frequently appears on the present stage." It continued to be revived throughout the eighteenth century, with Barton Booth and then James Quin succeeding Betterton in the role of Henry. Booth played the King in 1727 in the spectacular version at the Theatre Royal, Drury Lane, produced to celebrate the coronation of George II. In 1744, Hannah Pritchard first played Katharine, opposite Quin as Henry in a production at the Theatre Royal, Covent Garden, and Peg Woffington took the part at Covent Garden in 1749 and again in 1751. In November of 1788 John Philip Kemble produced the play at Drury Lane, with his sister, Sarah Siddons, originating her much-admired acting of Katharine. Kemble played a minor role, a composite of Griffith and Cromwell, concentrating as director and manager on the play's scenic effects.

Largely because of the opportunities for theatrical splendor and the star roles it provides, the play became a great favorite on the nineteenth-century stage. Kemble regularly revived the play after he moved to Covent Garden in 1803, most spectacularly in 1811 in a production hailed by *The Times* as "the most dazzling stage exhibition that we have ever seen." William Charles Macready produced the play in 1837 and 1838 at Covent Garden, followed by Samuel Phelps at the Sadler's Wells Theatre in 1845, both in the usual elaborate nineteenth-century manner and with a three-act text that ended with the fall of Wolsey. In 1848, as his final appearance before he left for an American tour, Macready staged the first three acts of Shakespeare's play in a command performance for Queen Victoria and Prince Albert at Drury Lane, with Charlotte Cushman as Katharine and Phelps playing Henry. In 1848, in a revival at Sadler's Wells, Phelps restored much of the text of the play. Unquestionably the most significant production of the middle years of the century, however, was Charles Kean's magnificent *Henry VIII* at the Princess's Theatre in 1855. Splendidly emphasizing the play's pageantry and processions and with, as Kean boasted, "scrupulous attendance to historical truth in costume, architecture, and the multiplied details of action," *Henry VIII* played for one hundred nearly consecutive nights. Kean's text cut many lines to allow time for his elaborate staging, but, like Phelps, Kean performed all of Shakespeare's scenes and in their Shakespearean order.

In America the play was also successful, from the first attracting star actors to its rich parts. Lewis Hallam played Henry in New York in 1799 at the Park Theatre. In 1810 two ambitious theater managers, Thomas Cooper and Stephen Price, lured George Frederick Cooke to America, and the following year he played Cardinal Wolsey at the Park Theatre. Fanny Kemble and her father Charles played *Henry VIII* in New York while touring in 1834. Charlotte Cushman had great success as Katharine in a number of productions in the years between 1848 and her retirement from the stage in 1874; in her search for testing roles, she also acted Wolsey in 1849. Edwin Booth was a more natural Wolsey, acting the part in 1876 at the Arch Street Theatre in Philadelphia, and then to great acclaim in January 1878, in an opulent production at Booth's Theatre in New York. Helena Modjeska, opposite Otis Skinner's Henry, played Katharine "with exquisite pathos," as one reviewer remarked, at New York's Garden Theater in 1892, emerging as a worthy rival of Ellen Terry in the role.

On both sides of the Atlantic, productions exploited the opportunities the play provides for spectacular staging with large, impressive sets somewhat in the manner of grand opera. Nowhere was this potential for theatrical splendor better realized than in Henry Irving's lavish production in 1892 at the Lyceum Theatre in London, the most magnificent Shakespearean performance ever attempted by that grand master of large-scale theatrical effects. The scene at Wolsey's York Place in Act 1, scene 5, in which King Henry first meets Anne Bullen, featured an opulent banquet and then a sequence of dances, one dignified and stately, another performed in a wild manner by strangely costumed men whirling lighted torches. The first scene of Act 2 revealed the Duke of Buckingham (Johnston Forbes-Robertson), passing on his way to execution, against a beautifully detailed set of "the King's Stairs, Westminster." Katharine (Ellen Terry), at her trial, was surrounded by her maids and the sumptuously garbed supporters of her cause, while King Henry sat on his throne and listened to the advice of Cardinals Wolsey and Campeius, all amidst the Tudor Gothic magnificence of "a hall in Blackfriars." Even these scenic triumphs paled before the spectacle of Anne Bullen's coronation (4.1) in an authentic reproduction of "a street in Westminster" of the Tudor era, replete with three-storied wooden-beamed houses. At every casement appeared citizens and their wives, while below on the street (according to the journal *Dramatic Notes*) were "prentices indulging in horseplay, beggars, and street-players, the halberdiers and men-at-arms clearing the way for the attendants on Anne Boleyn [i.e., Bullen] going to her coronation." And so it went, through to the celestial vision appearing to the dying Queen Katharine, and a finale in Grey Friars Church at Greenwich, faithfully redone in the theater with ancient stained glass windows and timeworn stairs.

Staging of this kind made heavy demands on the playscript. As in opera, the sets were expensive and difficult to shift, so that scenes not fitting into the designer's decor had to be sacrificed or rearranged. The script as a whole needed to be heavily cut in order to make allowance for the ponderous and time-consuming scene changes. In any case, these alterations fit well with Irving's intentions; like most of the Victorian actor-managers, he was mainly interested in the central roles of Henry VIII, Wolsey, Katharine, and Buckingham. Performance focused on moments of high seriousness and pathos: Buckingham's farewell to the world, Wolsey's reflections on the passing of his glory, Katharine's defense at her trial and her celestial vision, and, when it was included, the play's concluding prophecy of Queen Elizabeth's reign. The eloquent speeches of these scenes were well suited to the histrionic talents of actors trained in oratorical delivery and accustomed to prominence onstage at the expense of the supporting cast.

At His Majesty's Theatre in 1910, Herbert Beerbohm Tree produced one of the last of the spectacular productions of *Henry VIII*, with a text cutting all of Act 5 and ending with a lavish ceremony of Anne's coronation. A silent film was made of five scenes from Tree's production and publicly released to wide acclaim in 1911. In 1916 he took the play to America, where it drew large and enthusiastic crowds and was praised by most reviewers for its magnificent staging. The *New York Evening Mail* headline, however, termed the evening "A Worn Echo of Another Day," and indeed a movement away from the elaborate scenic emphasis of Victorian Shakespearean production had already begun.

In 1902 Frank Benson had directed the play at Stratford-upon-Avon, with Ellen Terry as Katharine, in a production that eschewed spectacle for sentiment. Instead of emphasizing the play's pomp and processions, Benson focused on its tragic rhythms. The elegiac mode was intensified for the cast by the knowledge that Frank Rodney, playing Buckingham, was almost literally in "the last hour / Of [his] weary life," soon to die of throat cancer. Ben Greet, in 1916, directed a fast-paced production on a simple set at the Old Vic, with his usual confidence in the text to move an audience. Eight years later, the Old Vic again saw a *Henry VIII* markedly different from the slow and massive play of nineteenth-century production. Robert Atkins, a disciple of William Poel and equally committed to recovering the principles of Elizabethan staging, produced an energetic and intelligent version with a set composed of black velvet curtains and gilt arches. The most striking visual effect was the shadow of a cross thrown onto the backcloth.

Though Lewis Casson's *Henry VIII* at London's Empire Theatre in 1925, starring Sybil Thorndike as Katharine (and with a young man named Laurence Olivier as the assistant stage manager and playing a servant), attractively recalled the old scenic traditions, Terence Gray at the Cambridge Festival Theatre in 1931 energetically anticipated more modern ones. On a shiny aluminum ramp curving up to the top of the stage, characters dressed like playing-card kings and queens acted out what Gray called "a masque in the modern manner." Cardboard cutouts were used to stand in for the minor roles, and their lines were spoken by actors from the sides of the stage. In the christening scene, the set began to revolve and the baby Elizabeth, obviously a toy, was thrown into the audience.

Productions at Stratford-upon-Avon in 1949 by Tyrone Guthrie and in 1983 by Howard Davies similarly sought to undercut the pageantry, though less startlingly than Gray. Guthrie's production was marked by deliberately distracting stage business, diverting attention from the official spectacle. A duchess sneezed during Cranmer's prophecy, and, though this effect was subsequently cut, other discordant business remained. When the production was revived at the Old Vic in 1953, the year of Elizabeth II's coronation, Guthrie reduced the dislocating effects, allowing what was left to humanize rather than undermine the pageantry. Davies's 1983 production was a Brechtian political drama using a grating score by Ilona Sekacz to highlight an ironic treatment of Tudor history. The coronation procession included tailor's dummies and spoken stage directions. Set against Hayden Griffin's stage design, consisting of cutout flats, the patriotic pageantry emerged as an exercise in political legitimation unable to obscure the reality of realpolitik and human suffering.

While continuing the movement away from the scenic elaboration of the nineteenth century, other modern productions have focused more on the human drama than on the alienated politics of Davies's *Henry VIII*. In 1958 at the Old Vic, Michael Benthall directed John Gielgud as Wolsey and Edith Evans as Katharine in an often moving production that strove to preserve, as critic J. C. Trewin noted, "a balance between the personal play and the processional drama." At Stratford-upon-Avon in 1969, Trevor Nunn sought a different balance. Donald Sinden's virile Henry had an odd mixture of hard-nosed political savvy and self-deceived romanticism; Peggy Ashcroft's Katharine was at once passionate and dignified. Processions wound through the theater, but they seemed purposefully irrelevant to a production that began and ended with Henry staring out into the darkness. Kevin Billington's BBC television production (1979), with Claire Bloom superbly cast as Queen Katharine, opted for an intimate and virtually uncut performance that focused, in ways wonderfully appropriate for television's small screen, on the individual experience of loss. In 1986 the play was performed at Stratford, Ontario, in a production by Brian Rintoul that emphasized the supervisory presence of a king who was visibly trying to control the forces of history through vigilance and will. This fine production, always aware of the lines of political force and yet sensitively tracing the emotional connections between characters, found an energy and integrity in avoiding the extremes of paranoia or pageantry.

A refusal to privilege the play's visual elements and a largely ironic or disillusioned presentation of its reading of Tudor history characterize most of the all-too-infrequent productions on the modern stage. Still, it is possible that the nineteenth century perceived something vital about *Henry VIII* that we have lost. The play is in fact Shakespeare's most spectacular historical drama. The original production must have gone to extraordinary lengths to vividly enact the many processions and ceremonials in which the play abounds. No other play by Shakespeare can approach *Henry VIII* in the elaboration of stage directions asking for thrones and chairs of state, banquets, masques, ceremonial last speeches, trials, visions, council meetings, and above all rich costumes. An important irony, of course, surrounds these effects, for the splendor of worldly achievement leads inevitably to falls from power, and it is only by the enigmatic workings of providence that courtly pageantry and intrigue ultimately combine to produce a great future for England. Nevertheless, costuming and properties are essential parts of the play's complex effect. The Prologue promises matters "full of state and woe, / Such noble scenes as draw the eye to flow," and the play does not disappoint these expectations.

One staging sequence demonstrates with particular vividness the flexibility of the Shakespearean stage for which

the play was originally written. In Act 5, scene 2, Thomas
Cranmer, the Archbishop of Canterbury, is summoned before the King's Privy Council on charges of heresy. The
King is aware of Cranmer's danger, however, and determines to witness the proceedings from *"a window above"*—
i.e., the gallery at the rear of the stage in the Elizabethan
playhouse, above the main acting platform. From that upper vantage, the King beholds the way Cranmer is humili-
ated by being kept waiting at the door, and accordingly the
King conceals himself behind a curtain to observe what follows. In what is conventionally marked as scene 3 of Act 5, a
council table is brought in, the councillors seat themselves,
and Cranmer is called into the room. He has not in fact exited and reentered, however; he stands at the door while the
scene imaginatively changes from an anteroom to the council chamber itself. Cranmer thereupon steps forward as
though entering. There is no break in the action, and the
King's presence all this while in the curtained space
"above" confirms the theatrical continuity. Lack of scenery
allows the Elizabethan stage to shift from outside to inside
through an appeal to the audience's imagination; the convention is as clear and understandable to an audience as is
the use of movable scenery. The swiftness and continuity of
this sequence is something that the nineteenth century,
with its passion for verisimilar stage effects, could not have
achieved, a flexibility that is possible on the more open
stage of the modern theater; but the play itself offers such a
range of possibilities that we can only begin to see into its
complexity when we perceive how different are the ways in
which it has been offered to appreciative audiences.

HENRY VIII

[Dramatis Personae

KING HENRY THE EIGHTH

DUKE OF BUCKINGHAM
DUKE OF NORFOLK
DUKE OF SUFFOLK
EARL OF SURREY
LORD ABERGAVENNY
LORD SANDS (*Sir Walter Sands*)
LORD CHAMBERLAIN
LORD CHANCELLOR
SIR HENRY GUILDFORD
SIR THOMAS LOVELL
SIR ANTHONY DENNY
SIR NICHOLAS VAUX

CARDINAL WOLSEY
THOMAS CROMWELL, *Wolsey's aide, later in King Henry's service*
SECRETARY *of Wolsey*
SERVANT *of Wolsey*
CARDINAL CAMPEIUS
CAPUCHIUS, *Ambassador from the Emperor Charles the Fifth*
GARDINER, *King Henry's secretary, later Bishop of Winchester*
PAGE *to Gardiner*
THOMAS CRANMER, *Archbishop of Canterbury*
BISHOP OF LINCOLN

QUEEN KATHARINE, *King Henry's wife, later divorced*
PATIENCE, *her attendant*
GRIFFITH, *her gentleman usher*
GENTLEWOMAN, } *attending*
GENTLEMAN,   } *Queen Katharine*

ANNE BULLEN, *Queen Katharine's Maid of Honor, later Queen*
OLD LADY, *friend of Anne Bullen*

BRANDON
SERGEANT AT ARMS
SURVEYOR *to the Duke of Buckingham*

Three GENTLEMEN
CRIER
SCRIBE
MESSENGER *to Queen Katharine*
DOCTOR BUTTS
KEEPER *of the Council Chamber*
PORTER
Porter's MAN
GARTER KING AT ARMS

Speaker of the PROLOGUE *and* EPILOGUE

Lords, Ladies, Gentlemen, Judges, Bishops, Priests, Vergers, Lord Mayor of London and Aldermen, Common People, Attendants, Guards, Tipstaves, Halberdiers, Scribes, Secretaries, Officers, Pursuivants, Pages, Guards, Queen Katharine's Women, Musicians, Choristers, and Dancers as spirits

SCENE: *London; Westminster; Kimbolton*]

Prologue   [*Enter Prologue.*]

PROLOGUE

I come no more to make you laugh. Things now
That bear a weighty and a serious brow,
Sad, high, and working, full of state and woe,   3
Such noble scenes as draw the eye to flow,
We now present. Those that can pity here
May, if they think it well, let fall a tear;
The subject will deserve it. Such as give
Their money out of hope they may believe
May here find truth too. Those that come to see
Only a show or two, and so agree   10
The play may pass, if they be still and willing,
I'll undertake may see away their shilling
Richly in two short hours. Only they   13
That come to hear a merry, bawdy play,
A noise of targets, or to see a fellow   15
In a long motley coat guarded with yellow,   16
Will be deceived. For, gentle hearers, know   17
To rank our chosen truth with such a show
As fool and fight is, besides forfeiting
Our own brains and the opinion that we bring   20
To make that only true we now intend,   21
Will leave us never an understanding friend.
Therefore, for goodness' sake, and as you are known
The first and happiest hearers of the town,   24
Be sad, as we would make ye. Think ye see   25
The very persons of our noble story
As they were living. Think you see them great,   27
And followed with the general throng and sweat
Of thousand friends; then, in a moment, see
How soon this mightiness meets misery.

Prologue.
3 Sad . . . working serious, lofty, and exciting the emotions.   **state** dignity   **10 show** spectacle   **13 two short hours** (A conventional period of time for a play.)   **15 targets** shields   **16 motley coat** pied costume of the fool.   **guarded** trimmed   **17 deceived** disappointed.   **know** i.e., it must be acknowledged that   **20 Our own brains** i.e., the labor of our brains   **20–21 the opinion . . . intend** the reputation we have for presenting truthfully what we intend to play   **24 first** foremost.   **happiest hearers** best-qualified audience   **25 sad** serious   **27 great** in high position

And if you can be merry then, I'll say
A man may weep upon his wedding day.   [*Exit.*]

✣

1.1   *Enter the Duke of Norfolk at one door; at the
other, the Duke of Buckingham and the Lord
Abergavenny.*

BUCKINGHAM
  Good morrow, and well met. How have ye done
  Since last we saw in France?
NORFOLK   I thank Your Grace,   2
  Healthful, and ever since a fresh admirer   3
  Of what I saw there.
BUCKINGHAM   An untimely ague   4
  Stayed me a prisoner in my chamber when   5
  Those suns of glory, those two lights of men,
  Met in the vale of Andren.
NORFOLK   Twixt Guînes and Ardres.   7
  I was then present, saw them salute on horseback,
  Beheld them when they lighted, how they clung   9
  In their embracement, as they grew together;   10
  Which had they, what four throned ones could have
      weighed   11
  Such a compounded one?
BUCKINGHAM   All the whole time
  I was my chamber's prisoner.
NORFOLK   Then you lost
  The view of earthly glory. Men might say
  Till this time pomp was single, but now married
  To one above itself. Each following day   16
  Became the next day's master, till the last   17
  Made former wonders its. Today the French,   18
  All clinquant, all in gold, like heathen gods,   19
  Shone down the English; and tomorrow they   20
  Made Britain India—every man that stood   21

1.1. Location: London. The royal court.
2 saw i.e., saw each other **3 fresh** untired **4 what I saw there** (Norfolk's description is of the famous meeting of Henry VIII and Francis I of France in 1520. It was near Calais, at the Field of the Cloth of Gold, so called because of the magnificence of the display.) **ague** fever
5 Stayed kept **7 vale of Andren** (The name, more properly *Ardres*, appears as *Andren* in Holinshed.) **9 lighted** alighted, dismounted
10 as as if **11 Which had they** i.e., if they had grown together.
weighed equaled in weight **16 following** succeeding **17 master** teacher, model **18 its** its own **19 clinquant** glittering **20 they** i.e., the English **21 India** i.e., seem as wealthy as the West Indies

Showed like a mine. Their dwarfish pages were
As cherubins, all gilt. The madams too,   23
Not used to toil, did almost sweat to bear
The pride upon them, that their very labor   25
Was to them as a painting. Now this masque   26
Was cried incomparable; and th' ensuing night   27
Made it a fool and beggar. The two kings,
Equal in luster, were now best, now worst,
As presence did present them; him in eye   30
Still him in praise; and being present both,   31
'Twas said they saw but one, and no discerner   32
Durst wag his tongue in censure. When these suns—   33
For so they phrase 'em—by their heralds challenged
The noble spirits to arms, they did perform
Beyond thought's compass, that former fabulous story,   36
Being now seen possible enough, got credit,   37
That _Bevis_ was believed.

BUCKINGHAM   O, you go far.   38

NORFOLK
As I belong to worship and affect   39
In honor honesty, the tract of everything   40
Would by a good discourser lose some life
Which action's self was tongue to. All was royal;   42
To the disposing of it naught rebelled.   43
Order gave each thing view; the office did   44
Distinctly his full function.

BUCKINGHAM   Who did guide—   45
I mean, who set the body and the limbs
Of this great sport together, as you guess?   47

23 **gilt** (Carved statues of cherubim in churches were often gilded.)
madams ladies   25 **pride** finery.   **that** so that   26 **Was . . . painting** i.e.,
flushed them as though with cosmetics   27 **cried** declared   30 **As . . .
them** i.e., when they appeared   30–31 **him . . . praise** i.e., the one in
view at the moment received the praise   32 **discerner** beholder
33 **Durst** dared.   **censure** judgment (of one above the other)   36 **that . . .
story** so that stories previously thought fabulous   37 **got credit** gained
credibility   38 **Bevis** the fourteenth-century romance _Bevis of Hamp-
ton_   39 **belong to worship** am of noble rank   39–40 **affect . . . honesty**
i.e., love truth with honorable regard   40 **tract** telling; course
42 **Which . . . to** i.e., which would be best described by the event itself
43 **rebelled** jarred   44–45 **Order . . . function** everything appeared in its
proper place, and every official performed his function without confusion   47 **sport** entertainment

NORFOLK
One, certes, that promises no element   48
In such a business.

BUCKINGHAM   I pray you, who, my lord?   49

NORFOLK
All this was ordered by the good discretion
Of the right reverend Cardinal of York.   51

BUCKINGHAM
The devil speed him! No man's pie is freed   52
From his ambitious finger. What had he
To do in these fierce vanities? I wonder   54
That such a keech can with his very bulk   55
Take up the rays o' the beneficial sun   56
And keep it from the earth.

NORFOLK   Surely, sir,
There's in him stuff that puts him to these ends;   58
For being not propped by ancestry, whose grace
Chalks successors their way, nor called upon   60
For high feats done to the crown, neither allied   61
To eminent assistants, but spiderlike,   62
Out of his self-drawing web, 'a gives us note   63
The force of his own merit makes his way—
A gift that heaven gives for him which buys
A place next to the King.

ABERGAVENNY   I cannot tell
What heaven hath given him—let some graver eye
Pierce into that—but I can see his pride
Peep through each part of him. Whence has he that?
If not from hell, the devil is a niggard,
Or has given all before, and he begins   71
A new hell in himself.

BUCKINGHAM   Why the devil,

48–49 One . . . business i.e., one whose lowly origin would indicate that
he lacked the capacity required for managing business of such a regal
nature. **certes** certainly   **51 Cardinal of York** i.e., Cardinal Wolsey
52 speed prosper   **54 fierce** extravagant   **55 keech** (Literally, fat of a
slaughtered animal rolled into a lump; applied to Wolsey, who was
reputed to be a butcher's son.)   **56 sun** i.e., King Henry   **58 stuff . . .
him** traits that whet him on   **60 Chalks . . . way** indicates the path
noble descendants are to follow   **61 high feats** great deeds.   **to** for
62 assistants high officials of the crown   **63 self-drawing** spun out of
his own entrails.   **'a . . . note** he lets us know   **71 he** i.e., Wolsey

Upon this French going out, took he upon him,   73
Without the privity o' the King, t' appoint   74
Who should attend on him? He makes up the file   75
Of all the gentry, for the most part such
To whom as great a charge as little honor   77
He meant to lay upon; and his own letter,   78
The honorable board of council out,   79
Must fetch him in he papers.

ABERGAVENNY   I do know   80
  Kinsmen of mine, three at the least, that have
  By this so sickened their estates that never   82
  They shall abound as formerly.

BUCKINGHAM   O, many   83
  Have broke their backs with laying manors on 'em   84
  For this great journey. What did this vanity   85
  But minister communication of   86
  A most poor issue?

NORFOLK   Grievingly I think   87
  The peace between the French and us not values   88
  The cost that did conclude it.

BUCKINGHAM   Every man,
  After the hideous storm that followed, was   90
  A thing inspired, and, not consulting, broke   91
  Into a general prophecy: that this tempest,   92
  Dashing the garment of this peace, aboded   93
  The sudden breach on 't.

NORFOLK   Which is budded out;   94
  For France hath flawed the league and hath attached   95
  Our merchants' goods at Bordeaux.

73 **going out** expedition, display 74 **Without . . . King** without the
King's being privy (to his plan) 75 **file** list 77–78 **To . . . upon** (i.e., the
Cardinal imposed charges for defraying the expenses of the costly
interview on those noblemen to whom he gave places of little honor)
78 **letter** i.e., summons 79 **out** not consulted 80 **Must . . . papers**
compels the cooperation of every person he cites. **he papers** whomever
he lists 82 **sickened** i.e., depleted 83 **abound** thrive 84 **laying . . .
'em** i.e., pawning estates for wardrobes 85 **What . . . vanity** i.e., what
did this extravagance accomplish 86–87 **minister . . . issue** provide
occasion for a conference that had little value, poor results 88 **not
values** is not worth 90 **hideous storm** (Holinshed reports such a storm
that interrupted the festivities and was taken as a prognostication.)
91 **consulting** i.e., each other 92 **general** common to all 93 **aboded**
foretold 94 **on 't** of it. **is budded out** i.e., has come to pass 95 **flawed**
broken. **attached** seized

ABERGAVENNY   Is it therefore
Th' ambassador is silenced?
NORFOLK   Marry, is 't.   97
ABERGAVENNY
  A proper title of a peace, and purchased   98
  At a superfluous rate!
BUCKINGHAM   Why, all this business   99
  Our reverend cardinal carried.
NORFOLK   Like it Your Grace,   100
  The state takes notice of the private difference
  Betwixt you and the Cardinal. I advise you—
  And take it from a heart that wishes towards you
  Honor and plenteous safety—that you read   104
  The Cardinal's malice and his potency
  Together; to consider further that   106
  What his high hatred would effect wants not   107
  A minister in his power. You know his nature,   108
  That he's revengeful, and I know his sword
  Hath a sharp edge; it's long, and 't may be said
  It reaches far, and where 'twill not extend,
  Thither he darts it. Bosom up my counsel;   112
  You'll find it wholesome. Lo, where comes that rock   113
  That I advise your shunning.   114

> *Enter Cardinal Wolsey, the purse borne before
> him, certain of the guard, and two Secretaries
> with papers. The Cardinal in his passage fixeth
> his eye on Buckingham, and Buckingham on
> him, both full of disdain.*

WOLSEY [*To a Secretary*]
  The Duke of Buckingham's surveyor, ha?   115
  Where's his examination?
SECRETARY   Here, so please you.   116
                     [*He gives a paper.*]

97 Marry (An oath, originally "by the Virgin Mary.")   **98 A proper . . .
peace** i.e., a fine business to give the name of peace to   **99 superfluous
rate** excessive price   **100 carried** supervised.   **Like it** may it please
  104 read interpret   **106 Together** i.e., as equally strong   **107–108 wants
. . . power** is not without means under his control   **112 Bosom up** take
to heart and shut up in your bosom   **113 wholesome** beneficial
114 s.d. purse i.e., containing the great seal, pertaining to Wolsey as
Lord Chancellor   **115 surveyor** overseer of a household or estate
116 examination deposition

WOLSEY
  Is he in person ready?

SECRETARY   Ay, please Your Grace.

WOLSEY
  Well, we shall then know more, and Buckingham
  Shall lessen this big look.   119

              Exeunt Cardinal and his train.

BUCKINGHAM
  This butcher's cur is venom-mouthed, and I   120
  Have not the power to muzzle him; therefore best
  Not wake him in his slumber. A beggar's book   122
  Outworths a noble's blood.

NORFOLK   What, are you chafed?   123
  Ask God for temperance; that's th' appliance only   124
  Which your disease requires.

BUCKINGHAM   I read in 's looks
  Matter against me, and his eye reviled   126
  Me as his abject object. At this instant   127
  He bores me with some trick. He's gone to the King;   128
  I'll follow and outstare him.

NORFOLK   Stay, my lord,
  And let your reason with your choler question   130
  What 'tis you go about. To climb steep hills   131
  Requires slow pace at first. Anger is like
  A full hot horse who, being allowed his way,   133
  Self-mettle tires him. Not a man in England   134
  Can advise me like you. Be to yourself
  As you would to your friend.

BUCKINGHAM   I'll to the King,
  And from a mouth of honor quite cry down   137
  This Ipswich fellow's insolence, or proclaim   138
  There's difference in no persons.

NORFOLK   Be advised;   139
  Heat not a furnace for your foe so hot

---

119 big haughty   **120 butcher's cur** (Another dig at Wolsey's reputed lowly origin.)   **122 book** book learning   **123 blood** noble descent. **chafed** angry   **124 appliance only** only remedy   **126 Matter against** quarrel with   **127 abject** cast-off, rejected   **128 bores** undermines, cheats   **130 question** debate, discuss   **131 go about** intend   **133 full hot** high-spirited   **134 Self-mettle** his own ardent spirits   **137 of honor** i.e., of a gentleman   **138 Ipswich** (Wolsey's birthplace)   **139 difference** distinctions in rank.   **Be advised** take care

That it do singe yourself. We may outrun
By violent swiftness that which we run at,
And lose by overrunning. Know you not
The fire that mounts the liquor till 't run o'er   144
In seeming to augment it wastes it? Be advised.
I say again there is no English soul
More stronger to direct you than yourself,
If with the sap of reason you would quench
Or but allay the fire of passion.

BUCKINGHAM   Sir,   149
I am thankful to you, and I'll go along
By your prescription. But this top-proud fellow,   151
Whom from the flow of gall I name not, but   152
From sincere motions, by intelligence,   153
And proofs as clear as founts in July when   154
We see each grain of gravel, I do know
To be corrupt and treasonous.

NORFOLK   Say not "treasonous."

BUCKINGHAM
To th' King I'll say 't, and make my vouch as strong   157
As shore of rock. Attend. This holy fox,
Or wolf, or both—for he is equal ravenous   159
As he is subtle, and as prone to mischief
As able to perform 't—his mind and place   161
Infecting one another, yea, reciprocally,
Only to show his pomp as well in France
As here at home, suggests the King our master   164
To this last costly treaty, th' interview   165
That swallowed so much treasure and like a glass
Did break i' the wrenching.

NORFOLK   Faith, and so it did.   167

BUCKINGHAM
Pray, give me favor, sir. This cunning cardinal   168
The articles o' the combination drew   169

144 **mounts** causes (by boiling) to rise   149 **allay** temper, moderate
151 **top-proud** supremely proud   152 **from . . . gall** i.e., from promptings
of anger   153 **motions** motives.   **intelligence** secret information
154 **founts** springs   157 **vouch** assertion, allegation   159 **equal**
equally   161 **place** office, rank   164 **suggests** incites   165 **last** latest,
recent.   **interview** i.e., Field of the Cloth of Gold   167 **wrenching** rough
handling, rinsing   168 **favor** attention   169 **articles o' the combination**
terms of the peace treaty

As himself pleased; and they were ratified
As he cried "Thus let be," to as much end   171
As give a crutch to the dead. But our count-cardinal   172
Has done this, and 'tis well; for worthy Wolsey,
Who cannot err, he did it. Now this follows,
Which, as I take it, is a kind of puppy
To th' old dam, treason: Charles the Emperor,   176
Under pretense to see the Queen his aunt—
For 'twas indeed his color, but he came   178
To whisper Wolsey—here makes visitation;   179
His fears were that the interview betwixt
England and France might through their amity
Breed him some prejudice, for from this league
Peeped harms that menaced him; privily   183
Deals with our cardinal, and, as I trow—   184
Which I do well, for I am sure the Emperor
Paid ere he promised, whereby his suit was granted
Ere it was asked—but when the way was made
And paved with gold, the Emperor thus desired
That he would please to alter the King's course   189
And break the foresaid peace. Let the King know,
As soon he shall by me, that thus the Cardinal
Does buy and sell his honor as he pleases,
And for his own advantage.

NORFOLK   I am sorry
To hear this of him, and could wish he were
Something mistaken in 't.

BUCKINGHAM   No, not a syllable.   195
I do pronounce him in that very shape
He shall appear in proof.   197

          Enter Brandon, a Sergeant at Arms before him,
          and two or three of the guard.

BRANDON
Your office, Sergeant: execute it.

---

171 end purpose   **172 count-cardinal** i.e., cardinal putting on the airs of
an aristocrat   **176 dam** mother (used especially of animals).   **Charles**
i.e., Charles V, Holy Roman Emperor, nephew of Queen Katharine, who
had much to fear from an English-French alliance   **178 color** pretext
179 whisper whisper to   **183 privily** secretly   **184 trow** believe   **189 he**
i.e., Wolsey   **195 Something mistaken** somewhat misunderstood
197 He . . . proof experience shall prove him

SERGEANT   Sir,
  My lord the Duke of Buckingham, and Earl
  Of Hereford, Stafford, and Northampton, I
  Arrest thee of high treason, in the name
  Of our most sovereign king.
BUCKINGHAM   Lo, you, my lord,
  The net has fall'n upon me! I shall perish
  Under device and practice.
BRANDON   I am sorry   204
  To see you ta'en from liberty, to look on   205
  The business present. 'Tis His Highness' pleasure
  You shall to the Tower.
BUCKINGHAM   It will help me nothing   207
  To plead mine innocence, for that dye is on me
  Which makes my whit'st part black. The will of heaven
  Be done in this and all things! I obey.
  O my Lord Aberga'nny, fare you well.
BRANDON
  Nay, he must bear you company. [*To Abergavenny.*] The
    King
  Is pleased you shall to the Tower, till you know
  How he determines further.
ABERGAVENNY   As the Duke said,
  The will of heaven be done and the King's pleasure
  By me obeyed!
BRANDON   Here is a warrant from
  The King t' attach Lord Montacute and the bodies   217
  Of the Duke's confessor, John de la Car,   218
  One Gilbert Perk, his chancellor—
BUCKINGHAM   So, so;   219
  These are the limbs o' the plot. No more, I hope?
BRANDON
  A monk o' the Chartreux.
BUCKINGHAM   O, Nicholas Hopkins?
BRANDON   He.   221

---

204 device and practice stratagems and plots   **205 to look on** i.e., and
sorry to look on   **207 nothing** not at all   **217 attach** arrest   **218, 219 John
de la Car, Gilbert Perk** (The names are from Holinshed's account: "Master
John de la Car alias de la Court, the Duke's confessor, and Sir Gilbert
Perke, priest, the Duke's chancellor.")   **221 Chartreux** Carthusian order

BUCKINGHAM
My surveyor is false. The o'ergreat Cardinal
Hath showed him gold; my life is spanned already.   223
I am the shadow of poor Buckingham,   224
Whose figure even this instant cloud puts on,   225
By darkening my clear sun. My lord, farewell.   226
                                          Exeunt.

                        ❖

1.2   *Cornets. Enter King Henry, leaning on the*
          Cardinal's shoulder, the nobles, and Sir
          Thomas Lovell. The Cardinal places himself
          under the King's feet on his right side. [The
          Cardinal's Secretary attends him.]

KING
My life itself, and the best heart of it,   1
Thanks you for this great care. I stood i' the level   2
Of a full-charged confederacy, and give thanks   3
To you that choked it. Let be called before us
That gentleman of Buckingham's. In person   5
I'll hear him his confessions justify,   6
And point by point the treasons of his master
He shall again relate.   8

          A noise within, crying "Room for the Queen!"
          Enter the Queen [Katharine], ushered by the
          Duke of Norfolk and [the Duke of] Suffolk. She
          kneels. [The] King riseth from his state, takes her
          up, kisses and placeth her by him.

KATHARINE
Nay, we must longer kneel. I am a suitor.

223 spanned measured   **224–226 I am . . . sun** i.e., I am the mere semblance of my former self, whose form and future hopes are obscured in
this sudden cloud of affliction by the darkening of my king's favor

1.2. Location: London. The council chamber.
s.d. under . . . feet i.e., at the foot of the royal dais   **1 best heart** most
essential part   **2 level** aim   **3 full-charged confederacy** fully prepared
conspiracy   **5 That . . . Buckingham's** i.e., Buckingham's surveyor
(1.1.115), whom Wolsey has induced to testify against his master
6 justify prove, confirm   **8 s.d. state** chair of state, raised seat with a
canopy

KING
Arise, and take place by us. Half your suit
Never name to us; you have half our power.
The other moiety ere you ask is given.   12
Repeat your will and take it.

KATHARINE   Thank Your Majesty.   13
That you would love yourself, and in that love
Not unconsidered leave your honor nor
The dignity of your office, is the point
Of my petition.

KING   Lady mine, proceed.

KATHARINE
I am solicited, not by a few,
And those of true condition, that your subjects   19
Are in great grievance. There have been commissions   20
Sent down among 'em which hath flawed the heart   21
Of all their loyalties; wherein, although,
My good lord Cardinal, they vent reproaches
Most bitterly on you, as putter-on   24
Of these exactions, yet the King our master—
Whose honor heaven shield from soil!—even he escapes
    not
Language unmannerly, yea, such which breaks
The sides of loyalty and almost appears
In loud rebellion.

NORFOLK   Not "almost appears,"
It doth appear; for, upon these taxations,
The clothiers all, not able to maintain
The many to them 'longing, have put off   32
The spinsters, carders, fullers, weavers, who,   33
Unfit for other life, compelled by hunger
And lack of other means, in desperate manner
Daring th' event to th' teeth, are all in uproar,   36
And danger serves among them.

KING   Taxation?   37

---

12 moiety half   **13 Repeat your will** express your desire   **19 condition**
disposition (to loyalty)   **20 grievance** distress.   **commissions** i.e., writs
authorizing a tax levy, and the agents to carry them out   **21 flawed**
damaged, cracked   **24 putter-on** instigator   **32 to them 'longing** in their
employ.   **put off** laid off   **33 spinsters** spinners.   **carders** those who
comb wool for impurities.   **fullers** those who beat wool to clean it
36 Daring . . . teeth defiantly challenging the outcome   **37 danger . . .
them** danger is rife among them

Wherein? And what taxation? My lord Cardinal,
You that are blamed for it alike with us,
Know you of this taxation?

WOLSEY   Please you, sir,
I know but of a single part in aught   41
Pertains to the state, and front but in that file   42
Where others tell steps with me.

KATHARINE   No, my lord?   43
You know no more than others? But you frame   44
Things that are known alike, which are not wholesome   45
To those which would not know them and yet must   46
Perforce be their acquaintance. These exactions,   47
Whereof my sovereign would have note, they are   48
Most pestilent to the hearing, and to bear 'em
The back is sacrifice to the load. They say   50
They are devised by you, or else you suffer
Too hard an exclamation.   Still exaction!   52

KING
The nature of it? In what kind, let's know,
Is this exaction?

KATHARINE   I am much too venturous
In tempting of your patience, but am boldened   55
Under your promised pardon. The subjects' grief   56
Comes through commissions, which compels from each
The sixth part of his substance, to be levied   58
Without delay; and the pretense for this   59
Is named your wars in France. This makes bold mouths;
Tongues spit their duties out, and cold hearts freeze
Allegiance in them. Their curses now
Live where their prayers did, and it's come to pass
This tractable obedience is a slave   64
To each incensèd will. I would Your Highness   65

41 **a single part** one individual's share   42–43 **front . . . me** take my place
merely in the front rank with others who share the responsibility.   **tell
steps** keep step, march   44–46 **You know . . . them** i.e., in a sense you
know no more than others; but you devise measures known to all (the
Council) which are so evil that men would rather not know   47 **their
acquaintance** i.e., known to them   48 **note** knowledge   50 **is sacrifice to**
i.e., is bowed down under   52 **exclamation** reproach   55 **boldened** made
bold   56 **grief** grievance   58 **substance** wealth   59 **pretense** pretext
64 **tractable** i.e., once docile   64–65 **is . . . will** i.e., gives way to angry
defiance

Would give it quick consideration, for
There is no primer business.

KING   By my life,   67
This is against our pleasure.

WOLSEY   And for me,
I have no further gone in this than by   69
A single voice, and that not passed me but   70
By learnèd approbation of the judges. If I am   71
Traduced by ignorant tongues, which neither know   72
My faculties nor person, yet will be   73
The chronicles of my doing, let me say
'Tis but the fate of place, and the rough brake   75
That virtue must go through. We must not stint   76
Our necessary actions in the fear
To cope malicious censurers, which ever,   78
As ravenous fishes, do a vessel follow
That is new trimmed, but benefit no further   80
Than vainly longing. What we oft do best,
By sick interpreters, once weak ones, is   82
Not ours, or not allowed; what worst, as oft   83
Hitting a grosser quality, is cried up   84
For our best act. If we shall stand still,
In fear our motion will be mocked or carped at,   86
We should take root here where we sit,
Or sit state-statues only.

KING   Things done well,   88
And with a care, exempt themselves from fear;
Things done without example, in their issue   90
Are to be feared. Have you a precedent
Of this commission? I believe, not any.   92
We must not rend our subjects from our laws   93

---

67 primer more urgent   **69–70 I have . . . voice** i.e., my part in this was
only to cast one vote in the Council   **71 approbation** approval
72 Traduced defamed   **73 faculties** qualities   **75 place** high office.
brake thicket   **76 stint** stop   **78 To cope** of encountering.   **ever** always
80 new trimmed newly fitted out   **82 sick interpreters** i.e., those who
explain our conduct out of malicious envy.   **once** at one time or another.   **weak** weak-witted   **83 Not . . . allowed** either not credited to us,
or disapproved of   **84 Hitting . . . quality** being understood, or appreciated, by more vulgar natures. (The indiscriminate praise achievements
less fine because their grosser minds understand them.)   **86 In fear** for
fear that   **88 state-statues** statues of statesmen   **90 example** precedent.   **issue** consequences   **92 Of** for   **93 rend** tear

And stick them in our will. Sixth part of each?   94
A trembling contribution! Why, we take   95
From every tree lop, bark, and part o' the timber,   96
And though we leave it with a root, thus hacked,
The air will drink the sap. To every county
Where this is questioned send our letters with   99
Free pardon to each man that has denied
The force of this commission. Pray look to 't;   101
I put it to your care.
WOLSEY [*Aside to his Secretary*]   A word with you.
Let there be letters writ to every shire
Of the King's grace and pardon. The grieved commons 104
Hardly conceive of me; let it be noised   105
That through our intercession this revokement
And pardon comes. I shall anon advise you   107
Further in the proceeding.   *Exit Secretary.*

    Enter Surveyor.

KATHARINE [*To the King*]
I am sorry that the Duke of Buckingham
Is run in your displeasure.
KING   It grieves many.   110
The gentleman is learned, and a most rare speaker,
To nature none more bound; his training such   112
That he may furnish and instruct great teachers
And never seek for aid out of himself. Yet see,   114
When these so noble benefits shall prove
Not well disposed, the mind growing once corrupt,   116
They turn to vicious forms ten times more ugly
Than ever they were fair. This man so complete,   118
Who was enrolled 'mongst wonders, and when we,
Almost with ravished listening, could not find
His hour of speech a minute—he, my lady,
Hath into monstrous habits put the graces   122
That once were his, and is become as black

---

94 stick . . . will make them the victims of our caprice   **95 trembling**
causing to tremble   **96 lop** branches   **99 questioned** disputed   **101 force**
validity   **104 grace** mercy.   **grieved** aggrieved   **105 Hardly conceive** have
a bad opinion.   **noised** reported, rumored   **107 anon** soon   **110 Is run in**
has incurred   **112 To . . . bound** none more indebted to nature for talents   **114 out of** beyond   **116 disposed** applied   **118 complete** accomplished   **122 habits** garments, i.e., shapes

As if besmeared in hell. Sit by us. You shall hear—
This was his gentleman in trust—of him
Things to strike honor sad.—Bid him recount
The fore-recited practices, whereof   127
We cannot feel too little, hear too much.

WOLSEY
Stand forth, and with bold spirit relate what you,
Most like a careful subject, have collected   130
Out of the Duke of Buckingham.

KING   Speak freely.

SURVEYOR
First, it was usual with him—every day
It would infect his speech—that if the King
Should without issue die, he'll carry it so   134
To make the scepter his. These very words
I've heard him utter to his son-in-law,
Lord Aberga'nny, to whom by oath he menaced
Revenge upon the Cardinal.

WOLSEY   Please Your Highness, note
This dangerous conception in this point.
Not friended by his wish to your high person,   140
His will is most malignant, and it stretches
Beyond you to your friends.

KATHARINE   My learned lord Cardinal,
Deliver all with charity.

KING   Speak on.   143
How grounded he his title to the crown
Upon our fail? To this point hast thou heard him   145
At any time speak aught?

SURVEYOR   He was brought to this
By a vain prophecy of Nicholas Henton.   147

KING
What was that Henton?

SURVEYOR   Sir, a Chartreux friar,
His confessor, who fed him every minute
With words of sovereignty.

KING   How know'st thou this?

127 practices intrigues   **130 collected** i.e., learned by spying   **134 issue**
offspring.   **carry it so** manage affairs so as   **140 Not . . . wish** his wish
(that the King die childless) being ungratified   **143 Deliver** tell   **145 fail**
i.e., dying without an heir   **147 Henton** (According to Holinshed, an alias
for Nicholas Hopkins; see 1.1.221.)

SURVEYOR
Not long before Your Highness sped to France,
The Duke being at the Rose, within the parish   152
Saint Lawrence Poultney, did of me demand
What was the speech among the Londoners   154
Concerning the French journey. I replied,
Men feared the French would prove perfidious,
To the King's danger. Presently the Duke   157
Said, 'twas the fear indeed, and that he doubted   158
'Twould prove the verity of certain words
Spoke by a holy monk, "that oft," says he,
"Hath sent to me, wishing me to permit
John de la Car, my chaplain, a choice hour
To hear from him a matter of some moment;   163
Whom after under the confession's seal
He solemnly had sworn that what he spoke
My chaplain to no creature living but
To me should utter, with demure confidence   167
This pausingly ensued: 'Neither the King nor 's heirs,
Tell you the Duke, shall prosper. Bid him strive
To gain the love o' the commonalty; the Duke
Shall govern England.'"
KATHARINE   If I know you well,
You were the Duke's surveyor, and lost your office
On the complaint o' the tenants. Take good heed
You charge not in your spleen a noble person   174
And spoil your nobler soul. I say, take heed;
Yes, heartily beseech you.
KING   Let him on.—   176
Go forward.
SURVEYOR   On my soul, I'll speak but truth.
I told my lord the Duke, by the devil's illusions
The monk might be deceived, and that 'twas dangerous
For him to ruminate on this so far until
It forged him some design, which, being believed,   181

---

152 the Rose (A manor house belonging to Buckingham.)   **154 speech**
talk   **157 Presently** immediately   **158 doubted** feared, suspected
163 moment importance   **167 demure** grave, solemn   **174 spleen** malice   **176 on** go on   **181 forged him** caused him to fashion.   **being believed** i.e., if the Duke put faith in what the monk was telling him

It was much like to do. He answered, "Tush,   182
It can do me no damage," adding further
That, had the King in his last sickness failed,   184
The Cardinal's and Sir Thomas Lovell's heads
Should have gone off.

KING   Ha? What, so rank? Aha,
There's mischief in this man.—Canst thou say further?

SURVEYOR
I can, my liege.

KING   Proceed.

SURVEYOR   Being at Greenwich,
After Your Highness had reproved the Duke
About Sir William Bulmer—

KING   I remember
Of such a time. Being my sworn servant,
The Duke retained him his. But on; what hence?   192

SURVEYOR
"If," quoth he, "I for this had been committed,
As to the Tower, I thought, I would have played
The part my father meant to act upon   195
Th' usurper Richard, who, being at Salisbury,
Made suit to come in 's presence, which if granted,
As he made semblance of his duty, would   198
Have put his knife into him."

KING   A giant traitor!

WOLSEY
Now, madam, may His Highness live in freedom,   200
And this man out of prison?

KATHARINE   God mend all!

KING
There's something more would out of thee. What sayst?

SURVEYOR
After "the Duke his father," with "the knife,"
He stretched him, and, with one hand on his dagger,   204
Another spread on 's breast, mounting his eyes,   205
He did discharge a horrible oath, whose tenor

---

182 much like very likely   **184 failed** died   **192 his** as his own   **195 my
father** i.e., the Duke of Buckingham of Richard III's time   **198 semblance** pretense.   **duty** i.e., kneeling   **200 may** can   **204 stretched him**
i.e., raised himself to his full height   **205 mounting** raising

Was, were he evil used, he would outgo   207
His father by as much as a performance
Does an irresolute purpose.
KING   There's his period,   209
  To sheathe his knife in us. He is attached;   210
  Call him to present trial. If he may   211
  Find mercy in the law, 'tis his; if none,
  Let him not seek 't of us. By day and night,
  He's a traitor to the height.   *Exeunt.* 214

❖

1.3 *Enter Lord Chamberlain and Lord Sands.*

CHAMBERLAIN
  Is 't possible the spells of France should juggle   1
  Men into such strange mysteries?
SANDS   New customs,   2
  Though they be never so ridiculous,
  Nay, let 'em be unmanly, yet are followed.
CHAMBERLAIN
  As far as I see, all the good our English
  Have got by the late voyage is but merely   6
  A fit or two o' the face; but they are shrewd ones,   7
  For when they hold 'em, you would swear directly   8
  Their very noses had been counselors
  To Pepin or Clotharius, they keep state so.   10
SANDS
  They have all new legs, and lame ones. One would take it, 11
  That never see 'em pace before, the spavin   12

---

207 evil used badly treated   **209 irresolute** unaccomplished.   **period**
aim, goal   **210 attached** arrested   **211 present** immediate   **214 to the
height** in the highest degree

1.3. Location: London. The royal court.
1 juggle beguile, bewitch   **2 mysteries** artificial fashions   **6 the late
voyage** i.e., to the Field of the Cloth of Gold   **7 fit . . . face** affected ways
of screwing up the face into a grimace   **8 hold 'em** i.e., maintain the
grimaces   **10 Pepin, Clotharius** kings of ancient France in the sixth and
seventh centuries.   **keep state** i.e., behave with an affected dignity
11 legs mannerisms of walking and making obeisances   **12 see** saw.
pace walk.   **spavin** disease of horses causing swelling of joints and
lameness

Or springhalt reigned among 'em.
CHAMBERLAIN   Death, my lord!   13
   Their clothes are after such a pagan cut to 't   14
   That sure they've worn out Christendom.

    Enter Sir Thomas Lovell.

                     How now?   15
What news, Sir Thomas Lovell?
LOVELL   Faith, my lord,
   I hear of none but the new proclamation
   That's clapped upon the court gate.
CHAMBERLAIN   What is 't for?   18
LOVELL
   The reformation of our traveled gallants,
   That fill the court with quarrels, talk, and tailors.
CHAMBERLAIN
   I'm glad 'tis there. Now I would pray our monsieurs
   To think an English courtier may be wise
   And never see the Louvre.
LOVELL   They must either—   23
   For so run the conditions—leave those remnants
   Of fool and feather that they got in France,   25
   With all their honorable points of ignorance   26
   Pertaining thereunto, as fights and fireworks,   27
   Abusing better men than they can be
   Out of a foreign wisdom, renouncing clean
   The faith they have in tennis and tall stockings,
   Short blistered breeches, and those types of travel,   31
   And understand again like honest men,
   Or pack to their old playfellows. There, I take it,   33
   They may, *cum privilegio, "oui"* away   34
   The lag end of their lewdness and be laughed at.   35

---

13 springhalt nervous twitching in a horse's hind legs   **14 to 't** moreover, besides   **15 they've . . . Christendom** they have exhausted the repertory of Christian fashions   **18 clapped** placed   **23 Louvre** royal palace in France, seat of the French court   **25 fool and feather** i.e., folly and fashion   **26 honorable . . . ignorance** i.e., what they ignorantly assume to be honorable   **27 as** such as.   **fireworks** i.e., whores   **31 blistered** puffed.   **types** emblems   **33 pack** be off   **34 cum privilegio** with exclusive right, immunity   **34–35 oui . . . lewdness** i.e., in French manner pass the last days of their worthless lives

SANDS
  'Tis time to give 'em physic, their diseases   36
  Are grown so catching.
CHAMBERLAIN   What a loss our ladies
  Will have of these trim vanities!
LOVELL   Ay, marry,   38
  There will be woe indeed, lords. The sly whoresons
  Have got a speeding trick to lay down ladies;   40
  A French song and a fiddle has no fellow.   41
SANDS
  The devil fiddle 'em! I am glad they are going,
  For sure there's no converting of 'em. Now
  An honest country lord, as I am, beaten
  A long time out of play, may bring his plainsong   45
  And have an hour of hearing, and, by 'r Lady,
  Held current music too.
CHAMBERLAIN   Well said, Lord Sands.   47
  Your colt's tooth is not cast yet?
SANDS   No, my lord,   48
  Nor shall not while I have a stump.
CHAMBERLAIN   Sir Thomas,   49
  Whither were you a-going?
LOVELL   To the Cardinal's.
  Your lordship is a guest too.
CHAMBERLAIN   O, 'tis true.
  This night he makes a supper, and a great one,   52
  To many lords and ladies. There will be
  The beauty of this kingdom, I'll assure you.
LOVELL
  That churchman bears a bounteous mind indeed,
  A hand as fruitful as the land that feeds us;   56
  His dews fall everywhere.
CHAMBERLAIN   No doubt he's noble;
  He had a black mouth that said other of him.   58

---

36 physic medicine **38 trim vanities** finely dressed but worthless
dandies **40 speeding** successful. **lay down** seduce **41 fellow** equal
45 play i.e., playing love games. **plainsong** simple chant or air
47 Held current regarded as fashionable **48 colt's tooth** i.e., lecherous-
ness of youth. **cast** given up **49 stump** i.e., of a tooth (with a bawdy
pun) **52 makes** gives **56 fruitful** generous **58 He . . . mouth** a person
must have an evil habit of speech

SANDS

    He may, my lord. H'as wherewithal: in him   59
    Sparing would show a worse sin than ill doctrine.   60
    Men of his way should be most liberal;   61
    They are set here for examples.

CHAMBERLAIN   True, they are so;
    But few now give so great ones. My barge stays;   63
    Your lordship shall along. Come, good Sir Thomas,
    We shall be late else, which I would not be,   65
    For I was spoke to, with Sir Henry Guildford,   66
    This night to be comptrollers.

SANDS   I am your lordship's.   67

                             Exeunt.

�֍

1.4   *Hautboys. A small table under a state for the*
        Cardinal, a longer table for the guests. Then
        enter Anne Bullen and divers other ladies and
        gentlemen as guests, at one door; at another
        door enter Sir Henry Guildford.

GUILDFORD

    Ladies, a general welcome from His Grace
    Salutes ye all. This night he dedicates
    To fair content and you. None here, he hopes,
    In all this noble bevy, has brought with her   4
    One care abroad. He would have all as merry
    As, first, good company, good wine, good welcome
    Can make good people.

        Enter Lord Chamberlain, Lord Sands, and |Sir
        Thomas] Lovell.

                 O my lord, you're tardy.
    The very thought of this fair company
    Clapped wings to me.

CHAMBERLAIN   You are young, Sir Harry Guildford.

---

59 H'as he has. **wherewithal** necessary means **60 Sparing** frugality.
show appear. **ill doctrine** heresy **61 way** way of life **63 stays** waits
for me **65 else** otherwise **66 spoke to** asked **67 comptrollers** masters
of ceremonies

1.4. Location: Westminster. A hall in York Place.
s.d. Hautboys reed instruments related to the modern oboe. **state**
canopy **4 bevy** company

SANDS

  Sir Thomas Lovell, had the Cardinal
  But half my lay thoughts in him, some of these   11
  Should find a running banquet ere they rested,   12
  I think would better please 'em. By my life,   13
  They are a sweet society of fair ones.

LOVELL

  O, that your lordship were but now confessor
  To one or two of these!

SANDS   I would I were;
  They should find easy penance.

LOVELL   Faith, how easy?

SANDS

  As easy as a down bed would afford it.

CHAMBERLAIN

  Sweet ladies, will it please you sit? Sir Harry,
  Place you that side; I'll take the charge of this.   20
                     [*The guests are shown their*
                              places at table.]
  His Grace is entering. Nay, you must not freeze;
  Two women placed together makes cold weather.
  My Lord Sands, you are one will keep 'em waking;   23
  Pray, sit between these ladies.

SANDS   By my faith,
  And thank your lordship. By your leave, sweet ladies.
                [*He takes a place between Anne Bullen*
                            and another lady.]
  If I chance to talk a little wild, forgive me;
  I had it from my father.

ANNE   Was he mad, sir?

SANDS

  O, very mad, exceeding mad, in love too.
  But he would bite none; just as I do now,
  He would kiss you twenty with a breath.   30
                         [*He kisses her.*]

CHAMBERLAIN   Well said, my lord.   31

---

11 lay secular   **12 running banquet** hasty meal (with bawdy double meaning, found also perhaps in *lay*, l. 11, *confessor, easy penance*, etc.) **13 I think** i.e., which I think   **20 Place you** assign places on   **23 waking** i.e., lively   **30 kiss you** kiss. (*You* is used colloquially to acknowledge the person addressed.)   **twenty** i.e., twenty women.   **with a breath** at one breath   **31 said** done

So, now you're fairly seated. Gentlemen,
The penance lies on you if these fair ladies
Pass away frowning.
SANDS   For my little cure,   34
Let me alone.   35

    Hautboys. Enter Cardinal Wolsey and takes his
    state.

WOLSEY
You're welcome, my fair guests. That noble lady
Or gentleman that is not freely merry
Is not my friend. This, to confirm my welcome;
And to you all, good health!   [*He drinks.*]
SANDS   Your Grace is noble.
Let me have such a bowl may hold my thanks   40
And save me so much talking.
WOLSEY   My Lord Sands,
I am beholding to you; cheer your neighbors.   42
Ladies, you are not merry. Gentlemen,
Whose fault is this?
SANDS   The red wine first must rise
In their fair cheeks, my lord; then we shall have 'em
Talk us to silence.
ANNE   You are a merry gamester,   46
My Lord Sands.
SANDS   Yes, if I make my play.   47
Here's to your ladyship; and pledge it, madam,   48
For 'tis to such a thing—
ANNE   You cannot show me.   49
SANDS [*To Wolsey*]
I told Your Grace they would talk anon.
    Drum and trumpet. Chambers discharged.
WOLSEY   What's that?   50

34 cure (1) remedy (2) cure of souls (continuing the ecclesiastical metaphor of l. 15) **35 s.d. state** chair of state **40 may** as may **42 beholding** beholden. **cheer** entertain **46 gamester** sportful, frolicsome
person. (But Sands, in his reply, plays on the sense of "gambler.")
47 make my play win my game (of love) **48 pledge it** drink in response
to my toast **49 'tis . . . thing** (Sands proposes his toast in an unfinished
sentence that is erotically suggestive.) **You . . . me** i.e., you can't teach
me a lesson in how to drink a toast. (Anne parries the erotic suggestion
of Sands by drinking to him.) **50 s.d. Chambers** small pieces of cannon
(the firing of which in 1613 probably started the fire that burned down
the Globe playhouse)

CHAMBERLAIN
　　Look out there, some of ye.　　　　[*Exit a Servant.*]
WOLSEY　　　　　　　　　　What warlike voice,
　　And to what end, is this? Nay, ladies, fear not;
　　By all the laws of war you're privileged.　　　　53

　　　　Enter a Servant.

CHAMBERLAIN
　　How now? What is 't?
SERVANT　　　　　　　　A noble troop of strangers,　　54
　　For so they seem. They've left their barge and landed,
　　And hither make, as great ambassadors　　　　56
　　From foreign princes.
WOLSEY　　　　　　　　Good Lord Chamberlain,
　　Go, give 'em welcome; you can speak the French tongue;
　　And, pray, receive 'em nobly and conduct 'em
　　Into our presence, where this heaven of beauty
　　Shall shine at full upon them. Some attend him.
　　　　　　　　　[*Exit Chamberlain, attended.*]
　　　　　　　　　　All rise, and tables removed.
　　You have now a broken banquet, but we'll mend it.
　　A good digestion to you all! And once more
　　I shower a welcome on ye. Welcome all!

　　　　*Hautboys. Enter King and others, as maskers,
　　　　habited like shepherds, ushered by the Lord
　　　　Chamberlain. They pass directly before the
　　　　Cardinal and gracefully salute him.*

　　A noble company! What are their pleasures?
CHAMBERLAIN
　　Because they speak no English, thus they prayed
　　To tell Your Grace that, having heard by fame　　67
　　Of this so noble and so fair assembly
　　This night to meet here, they could do no less,
　　Out of the great respect they bear to beauty,
　　But leave their flocks and, under your fair conduct,　　71
　　Crave leave to view these ladies and entreat

---

53 privileged i.e., entitled to immunity in the event of conflict
54 strangers foreigners　**56 make** come　**67 fame** report　**71 fair
conduct** kind permission

An hour of revels with 'em.

WOLSEY   Say, Lord Chamberlain,
They have done my poor house grace, for which I
     pay 'em
A thousand thanks, and pray 'em take their pleasures.
               Choose ladies; King and Anne Bullen.

KING
The fairest hand I ever touched! O beauty,
Till now I never knew thee!   *Music. Dance.*

WOLSEY
My lord!

CHAMBERLAIN   Your Grace?

WOLSEY   Pray, tell 'em thus much from me:
There should be one amongst 'em, by his person,
More worthy this place than myself, to whom,   80
If I but knew him, with my love and duty
I would surrender it.

CHAMBERLAIN   I will, my lord.
                    Whisper [with the maskers].

WOLSEY
What say they?

CHAMBERLAIN   Such a one, they all confess,
There is indeed, which they would have Your Grace
Find out, and he will take it.

WOLSEY   Let me see, then.   85
          [He comes from his chair of state.]
By all your good leaves, gentlemen; here I'll make
My royal choice.   *[He bows before the King.]*

KING *[Unmasking]* Ye have found him, Cardinal.
You hold a fair assembly; you do well, lord.
You are a churchman, or I'll tell you, Cardinal,
I should judge now unhappily.

WOLSEY   I am glad   90
Your Grace is grown so pleasant.

KING   My Lord Chamberlain, 91
Prithee, come hither. What fair lady's that?

---

80 this place i.e., this chair of state   **85 it** i.e., the chair of state
90 unhappily unfavorably   **91 pleasant** merry

CHAMBERLAIN
  An 't please Your Grace, Sir Thomas Bullen's
    daughter—   93
  The Viscount Rochford—one of Her Highness' women.
KING
  By heaven, she is a dainty one.—Sweetheart,
  I were unmannerly to take you out   96
  And not to kiss you. [*He kisses Anne.*] A health,
    gentlemen!   97
  Let it go round.   [*He offers a toast.*]
WOLSEY
  Sir Thomas Lovell, is the banquet ready
  I' the privy chamber?
LOVELL   Yes, my lord.
WOLSEY [*To the King*]   Your Grace,
  I fear, with dancing is a little heated.
KING
  I fear, too much.
WOLSEY   There's fresher air, my lord,
  In the next chamber.
KING
  Lead in your ladies every one.—Sweet partner,
  I must not yet forsake you.—Let's be merry,
  Good my lord Cardinal. I have half a dozen healths
  To drink to these fair ladies, and a measure   107
  To lead 'em once again; and then let's dream
  Who's best in favor. Let the music knock it.   109
                              Exeunt, with trumpets.

❖

93 An 't if it   **96 take you out** lead you out for a dance   **97 health**
toast   **107 measure** stately dance   **109 best in favor** handsomest.
knock it strike up

2.1 *Enter two Gentlemen, at several doors.*

FIRST GENTLEMAN
Whither away so fast?

SECOND GENTLEMAN   O, God save ye!
Ev'n to the hall, to hear what shall become   2
Of the great Duke of Buckingham.

FIRST GENTLEMAN   I'll save you
That labor, sir. All's now done but the ceremony
Of bringing back the prisoner.

SECOND GENTLEMAN   Were you there?

FIRST GENTLEMAN
Yes, indeed was I.

SECOND GENTLEMAN   Pray, speak what has happened.

FIRST GENTLEMAN
You may guess quickly what.

SECOND GENTLEMAN   Is he found guilty?

FIRST GENTLEMAN
Yes, truly is he, and condemned upon 't.

SECOND GENTLEMAN
I am sorry for 't.

FIRST GENTLEMAN   So are a number more.

SECOND GENTLEMAN   But pray, how passed it?   10

FIRST GENTLEMAN
I'll tell you in a little. The great Duke   11
Came to the bar, where to his accusations
He pleaded still not guilty and alleged   13
Many sharp reasons to defeat the law.   14
The King's attorney on the contrary
Urged on the examinations, proofs, confessions   16
Of divers witnesses, which the Duke desired
To have brought viva voce to his face;   18
At which appeared against him his surveyor,
Sir Gilbert Perk his chancellor, and John Car,
Confessor to him, with that devil monk,
Hopkins, that made this mischief.

2.1. Location: Westminster. A street.
s.d. several separate   **2 the hall** i.e., Westminster Hall, where the trial
was held   **10 passed it** did it proceed   **11 in a little** in brief   **13 alleged**
brought forward   **14 law** i.e., case against him   **16 examinations** depositions   **18 viva voce** so that their voices could be heard

SECOND GENTLEMAN   That was he
  That fed him with his prophecies?
FIRST GENTLEMAN   The same.
  All these accused him strongly, which he fain   24
  Would have flung from him, but indeed he could not;
  And so his peers, upon this evidence,
  Have found him guilty of high treason. Much
  He spoke, and learnedly, for life; but all
  Was either pitied in him or forgotten.   29
SECOND GENTLEMAN
  After all this, how did he bear himself?
FIRST GENTLEMAN
  When he was brought again to th' bar, to hear
  His knell rung out, his judgment, he was stirred   32
  With such an agony he sweat extremely,
  And something spoke in choler, ill and hasty.   34
  But he fell to himself again, and sweetly   35
  In all the rest showed a most noble patience.
SECOND GENTLEMAN
  I do not think he fears death.
FIRST GENTLEMAN   Sure he does not;
  He never was so womanish. The cause
  He may a little grieve at.
SECOND GENTLEMAN   Certainly
  The Cardinal is the end of this.
FIRST GENTLEMAN   'Tis likely,   40
  By all conjectures; first, Kildare's attainder,   41
  Then deputy of Ireland, who removed,   42
  Earl Surrey was sent thither, and in haste too,
  Lest he should help his father.
SECOND GENTLEMAN   That trick of state 44
  Was a deep envious one.
FIRST GENTLEMAN   At his return   45

24 which i.e., which accusations. **fain** gladly **29 Was . . . forgotten**
either produced no effect or produced only ineffectual pity
32 judgment sentence **34 choler** anger. **ill** malevolent **35 fell to**
recovered **40 end** cause **41 Kildare's attainder** i.e., the confiscation of
estates and sentencing to death of the Earl of Kildare, Lord Lieutenant
of Ireland (whom Wolsey, according to Holinshed, removed to make
room for Thomas Howard, Earl of Surrey, son-in-law to Buckingham,
and thereby keep Surrey in effective exile) **42 who removed** i.e., Kildare having been removed **44 father** i.e., father-in-law. **trick of state**
political stratagem **45 envious** malicious

No doubt he will requite it. This is noted,   46
And generally: whoever the King favors,   47
The Cardinal instantly will find employment,
And far enough from court too.

SECOND GENTLEMAN   All the commons
Hate him perniciously and, o' my conscience,   50
Wish him ten fathom deep. This duke as much
They love and dote on, call him bounteous Buckingham,
The mirror of all courtesy—   53

Enter Buckingham from his arraignment,
tipstaves before him, the ax with the edge
towards him, halberds on each side, accompanied
with Sir Thomas Lovell, Sir Nicholas Vaux, Sir
Walter Sands, and common people, etc.

FIRST GENTLEMAN   Stay there, sir,
And see the noble ruined man you speak of.

SECOND GENTLEMAN
Let's stand close and behold him.

BUCKINGHAM   All good people,
You that thus far have come to pity me,
Hear what I say, and then go home and lose me.   57
I have this day received a traitor's judgment,
And by that name must die. Yet, heaven bear witness,
And if I have a conscience, let it sink me,   60
Even as the ax falls, if I be not faithful!
The law I bear no malice for my death;
'T has done, upon the premises, but justice;   63
But those that sought it I could wish more Christians.   64
Be what they will, I heartily forgive 'em.
Yet let 'em look they glory not in mischief,
Nor build their evils on the graves of great men,   67
For then my guiltless blood must cry against 'em.
For further life in this world I ne'er hope,
Nor will I sue, although the King have mercies
More than I dare make faults. You few that loved me

---

46 requite repay   **47 generally** by everybody   **50 perniciously** with deadly hatred   **53 mirror** i.e., paragon   **s.d. tipstaves** bailiffs.   **halberds** halberdiers, with long-handled weapons.   **Walter** ("William" in Holinshed.)   **57 lose** forget   **60 sink** ruin   **63 premises** evidence   **64 more** better   **67 Nor . . . men** i.e., nor extend their own evil careers by extinguishing the lives of noblemen. (*Evils* may suggest "hovels" or "privies.")

And dare be bold to weep for Buckingham,
His noble friends and fellows, whom to leave   73
Is only bitter to him, only dying,   74
Go with me like good angels to my end,
And, as the long divorce of steel falls on me,   76
Make of your prayers one sweet sacrifice,   77
And lift my soul to heaven.—Lead on, i' God's name!

LOVELL
I do beseech Your Grace, for charity,
If ever any malice in your heart
Were hid against me, now to forgive me frankly.

BUCKINGHAM
Sir Thomas Lovell, I as free forgive you
As I would be forgiven. I forgive all.
There cannot be those numberless offenses
'Gainst me that I cannot take peace with; no black envy   85
Shall mark my grave. Commend me to His Grace,
And if he speak of Buckingham, pray tell him
You met him half in heaven. My vows and prayers
Yet are the King's and, till my soul forsake,   89
Shall cry for blessings on him. May he live
Longer than I have time to tell his years!   91
Ever beloved and loving may his rule be!
And when old Time shall lead him to his end,   93
Goodness and he fill up one monument!   94

LOVELL
To th' waterside I must conduct Your Grace,
Then give my charge up to Sir Nicholas Vaux,
Who undertakes you to your end.

VAUX   Prepare there;   97
The Duke is coming. See the barge be ready,
And fit it with such furniture as suits   99
The greatness of his person.

BUCKINGHAM   Nay, Sir Nicholas,
Let it alone; my state now will but mock me.   101
When I came hither, I was Lord High Constable

73–74 whom . . . him i.e., the loss of whose dear company is the only
cause of bitterness in death   **76 divorce of steel** i.e., separation of body
and soul effected by the executioner's ax   **77 sacrifice** offering   **85 take**
make.   **envy** malice   **89 Yet** still.   **forsake** leave my body   **91 tell**
count   **93 Time** age   **94 monument** tomb   **97 undertakes** takes charge
of   **99 furniture** equipment   **101 state** rank

And Duke of Buckingham; now, poor Edward Bohun.　103
Yet I am richer than my base accusers,
That never knew what truth meant. I now seal it,　105
And with that blood will make 'em one day groan for 't.
My noble father, Henry of Buckingham,
Who first raised head against usurping Richard,　108
Flying for succor to his servant Banister,
Being distressed, was by that wretch betrayed,
And without trial fell; God's peace be with him!
Henry the Seventh succeeding, truly pitying
My father's loss, like a most royal prince
Restored me to my honors, and out of ruins
Made my name once more noble. Now his son,
Henry the Eighth, life, honor, name, and all
That made me happy, at one stroke has taken
Forever from the world. I had my trial,
And must needs say a noble one; which makes me
A little happier than my wretched father.
Yet thus far we are one in fortunes: both
Fell by our servants, by those men we loved most—
A most unnatural and faithless service!
Heaven has an end in all. Yet, you that hear me,　124
This from a dying man receive as certain:
Where you are liberal of your loves and counsels
Be sure you be not loose; for those you make friends　127
And give your hearts to, when they once perceive
The least rub in your fortunes, fall away　129
Like water from ye, never found again
But where they mean to sink ye. All good people,
Pray for me! I must now forsake ye. The last hour
Of my long weary life is come upon me.
Farewell! And when you would say something that
　　is sad,
Speak how I fell. I have done; and God forgive me!
　　　　　　　　　　　Exeunt Duke and train.
FIRST GENTLEMAN
　O, this is full of pity! Sir, it calls,

103 Bohun (The Duke's family name was actually Stafford; Shakespeare
follows the error in Holinshed.)　**105 seal** ratify, attest to the truth of
108 raised head gathered an army　**124 end** aim　**127 loose** wanting in
restraint, careless　**129 rub** impediment. (A term from bowls.)

I fear, too many curses on their heads
That were the authors.
SECOND GENTLEMAN   If the Duke be guiltless,
'Tis full of woe. Yet I can give you inkling
Of an ensuing evil, if it fall,
Greater than this.
FIRST GENTLEMAN   Good angels keep it from us!
What may it be? You do not doubt my faith, sir?   142
SECOND GENTLEMAN
This secret is so weighty, 'twill require
A strong faith to conceal it.
FIRST GENTLEMAN   Let me have it;
I do not talk much.
SECOND GENTLEMAN   I am confident;   145
You shall, sir. Did you not of late days hear   146
A buzzing of a separation   147
Between the King and Katharine?
FIRST GENTLEMAN   Yes, but it held not;   148
For when the King once heard it, out of anger
He sent command to the Lord Mayor straight
To stop the rumor and allay those tongues   151
That durst disperse it.
SECOND GENTLEMAN   But that slander, sir,
Is found a truth now, for it grows again
Fresher than e'er it was, and held for certain
The King will venture at it. Either the Cardinal,
Or some about him near, have, out of malice   156
To the good Queen, possessed him with a scruple   157
That will undo her. To confirm this too,
Cardinal Campeius is arrived, and lately,   159
As all think, for this business.
FIRST GENTLEMAN   'Tis the Cardinal;

---

142 faith i.e., ability to keep a secret   **145 am confident** i.e., trust your
discretion   **146 shall** i.e., shall hear it.   **late** recent   **147 buzzing** rumor   **148 held not** ceased; or perhaps was not believed   **151 allay**
restrain   **156 about him near** close to him   **157 possessed . . . scruple**
put into his mind a doubt. (Katharine had been married to Henry's
older brother, Prince Arthur, who died, still in his early teens, a year
after the marriage. Such a precontract would normally invalidate a
subsequent marriage with any close relative of Arthur's, but Henry's
marriage to Katharine had been made possible by a papal dispensa-
tion.)   **159 Cardinal Campeius** i.e., Cardinal Lorenzo Campeggio, sent
from Rome to confer on the legality of the King's marriage

And merely to revenge him on the Emperor 161
For not bestowing on him at his asking
The archbishopric of Toledo, this is purposed. 163

SECOND GENTLEMAN
I think you have hit the mark. But is 't not cruel
That she should feel the smart of this? The Cardinal 165
Will have his will, and she must fall.

FIRST GENTLEMAN   'Tis woeful.
We are too open here to argue this; 167
Let's think in private more.   *Exeunt.*

❖

2.2   *Enter Lord Chamberlain, reading this letter.*

CHAMBERLAIN   "My lord, the horses your lordship sent
for, with all the care I had, I saw well chosen, ridden, 2
and furnished. They were young and handsome, and 3
of the best breed in the north. When they were ready
to set out for London, a man of my lord Cardinal's,
by commission and main power, took 'em from me 6
with this reason: his master would be served before a
subject, if not before the King; which stopped our
mouths, sir."
I fear he will indeed. Well, let him have them.
He will have all, I think.

    *Enter to the Lord Chamberlain the Dukes of
    Norfolk and Suffolk.*

NORFOLK   Well met, my Lord Chamberlain.
CHAMBERLAIN   Good day to both Your Graces.
SUFFOLK
How is the King employed?
CHAMBERLAIN   I left him private, 14
Full of sad thoughts and troubles.
NORFOLK   What's the cause? 15

---

161 Emperor (The Queen was the aunt of Charles V, Holy Roman Emperor and King of Spain; see 1.1.176 and note.)   **163 purposed** intended   **165 smart** pain   **167 open** public

2.2. Location: London. The royal court.
2 ridden broken in, trained   **3 furnished** equipped   **6 commission** warrant.   **main** great   **14 private** alone   **15 sad** serious

CHAMBERLAIN
It seems the marriage with his brother's wife
Has crept too near his conscience.

SUFFOLK   No, his conscience
Has crept too near another lady.

NORFOLK   'Tis so.
This is the Cardinal's doing. The king-cardinal,
That blind priest, like the eldest son of Fortune,   20
Turns what he list. The King will know him one day.   21

SUFFOLK
Pray God he do! He'll never know himself else.

NORFOLK
How holily he works in all his business!   23
And with what zeal! For, now he has cracked the league
Between us and the Emperor, the Queen's great-nephew,
He dives into the King's soul and there scatters
Dangers, doubts, wringing of the conscience,
Fears, and despairs, and all these for his marriage.
And out of all these to restore the King,
He counsels a divorce, a loss of her
That, like a jewel, has hung twenty years
About his neck, yet never lost her luster;
Of her that loves him with that excellence
That angels love good men with; even of her
That, when the greatest stroke of fortune falls,
Will bless the King. And is not this course pious?

CHAMBERLAIN
Heaven keep me from such counsel! 'Tis most true
These news are everywhere; every tongue speaks 'em,   38
And every true heart weeps for 't. All that dare
Look into these affairs see this main end,
The French king's sister. Heaven will one day open   41
The King's eyes, that so long have slept upon   42
This bold bad man.

SUFFOLK   And free us from his slavery.

NORFOLK   We had need pray,
And heartily, for our deliverance,

20–21 blind . . . list (Alludes to Fortune, conventionally depicted as blind
and turning her wheel.)   **21 list** wishes   **23 he** i.e., Wolsey   **38 news are**
(*News* was commonly considered a plural noun.)   **41 The . . . sister** i.e.,
the Duchess of Alençon; see 3.2.85–86   **42 slept upon** been blind to

Or this imperious man will work us all
From princes into pages. All men's honors   47
Lie like one lump before him, to be fashioned   48
Into what pitch he please.

SUFFOLK   For me, my lords,   49
I love him not, nor fear him; there's my creed.
As I am made without him, so I'll stand,   51
If the King please. His curses and his blessings
Touch me alike; they're breath I not believe in.
I knew him, and I know him; so I leave him
To him that made him proud, the Pope.

NORFOLK   Let's in,
And with some other business put the King
From these sad thoughts that work too much upon him.
My lord, you'll bear us company?

CHAMBERLAIN   Excuse me;
The King has sent me otherwhere. Besides,   59
You'll find a most unfit time to disturb him.
Health to your lordships.

NORFOLK   Thanks, my good Lord Chamberlain.   61
      Exit Lord Chamberlain; and the King draws
          the curtain and sits reading pensively.

SUFFOLK
How sad he looks! Sure he is much afflicted.   62

KING
Who's there, ha?

NORFOLK   Pray God he be not angry.

KING
Who's there, I say? How dare you thrust yourselves
Into my private meditations?
Who am I? Ha?

NORFOLK
A gracious king that pardons all offenses

---

47 pages attendants   **48 lump** i.e., lump of clay   **49 pitch** height (literally, of a falcon's flight), i.e., degree of dignity. (In a mixed metaphor, the Cardinal is likened to one who reduces all men of rank to one lump, which he will refashion into creatures of whatever stature he pleases.)
51 As . . . stand i.e., inasmuch as my rank was conferred on me by the King, not by Wolsey, I'll stand firm   **59 otherwhere** elsewhere   **61 s.d. curtain** (The King is probably in a "discovery space" rear stage.)
62 afflicted troubled

Malice ne'er meant. Our breach of duty this way   68
Is business of estate, in which we come   69
To know your royal pleasure.
KING   Ye are too bold.
Go to! I'll make ye know your times of business.
Is this an hour for temporal affairs, ha?

    Enter Wolsey and Campeius, with a commission.

Who's there? My good lord Cardinal? O my Wolsey,
The quiet of my wounded conscience,
Thou art a cure fit for a king. [*To Campeius.*] You're
  welcome,
Most learnèd reverend sir, into our kingdom.
Use us and it. [*To Wolsey.*] My good lord, have great care
I be not found a talker.
WOLSEY   Sir, you cannot.   78
I would Your Grace would give us but an hour
Of private conference.
KING [*To Norfolk and Suffolk*] We are busy; go.
NORFOLK [*Aside to Suffolk*]
This priest has no pride in him?
SUFFOLK [*Aside to Norfolk*]   Not to speak of.
I would not be so sick, though, for his place.   82
But this cannot continue.
NORFOLK [*Aside to Suffolk*] If it do,
I'll venture one have-at-him.
SUFFOLK [*Aside to Norfolk*]   I another.   84
    Exeunt Norfolk and Suffolk.
WOLSEY
Your Grace has given a precedent of wisdom   85
Above all princes, in committing freely
Your scruple to the voice of Christendom.   87
Who can be angry now? What envy reach you?   88

---

68 this way in this respect   **69 estate** public weal   **78 I . . . talker** i.e.,
lest my offer of hospitality be only talk, not deeds   **82 sick** i.e., sick
with pride.   **for his place** even to gain his high office   **84 have-at-him**
i.e., thrust at him (Wolsey) in fencing   **85 precedent** example
87 scruple doubt.   **voice of Christendom** i.e., the Pope, through his
representative Campeius, and the clerics and scholars of various conti-
nental universities to whom Henry submitted his problem of "conscience"   **88 envy** malice

The Spaniard, tied by blood and favor to her,   89
Must now confess, if they have any goodness,   90
The trial just and noble. All the clerks—   91
I mean the learnèd ones in Christian kingdoms—
Have their free voices. Rome, the nurse of judgment,   93
Invited by your noble self, hath sent
One general tongue unto us, this good man,   95
This just and learnèd priest, Card'nal Campeius,
Whom once more I present unto Your Highness.

KING [*Embracing Campeius*]
And once more in mine arms I bid him welcome,
And thank the holy conclave for their loves.   99
They have sent me such a man I would have wished for.

CAMPEIUS
Your Grace must needs deserve all strangers' loves,   101
You are so noble. To Your Highness' hand
I tender my commission, by whose virtue,
The court of Rome commanding, you, my lord
Cardinal of York, are joined with me their servant
In the unpartial judging of this business.
                    [*He gives the King a document.*]

KING
Two equal men. The Queen shall be acquainted   107
Forthwith for what you come. Where's Gardiner?   108

WOLSEY
I know Your Majesty has always loved her
So dear in heart not to deny her that   110
A woman of less place might ask by law: 111
Scholars allowed freely to argue for her.

KING
Ay, and the best she shall have, and my favor
To him that does best; God forbid else. Cardinal,
Prithee, call Gardiner to me, my new secretary.
I find him a fit fellow.   [*Wolsey goes to the door.*] 116

        Enter Gardiner.

89 **The Spaniard** i.e., Charles V and his court   90 **confess** concede
91 **clerks** clerics, scholars   93 **voices** votes   95 **One general tongue** i.e.,
a spokesman   99 **conclave** College of Cardinals   101 **needs** necessarily.   **strangers'** foreigners'   107 **equal** impartial.   **acquainted** informed   108 **Gardiner** i.e., Stephen Gardiner, Wolsey's secretary; he
later becomes one of the most influential members of the King's Council   110 **that** that which   111 **less place** lower rank   116 **fit** suitable

WOLSEY [*Aside to Gardiner*]
  Give me your hand. Much joy and favor to you;
  You are the King's now.
GARDINER [*Aside to Wolsey*]   But to be commanded
  Forever by Your Grace, whose hand has raised me.
KING   Come hither, Gardiner.   *Walks and whispers.*
CAMPEIUS
  My lord of York, was not one Doctor Pace   121
  In this man's place before him?
WOLSEY   Yes, he was.
CAMPEIUS
  Was he not held a learnèd man?
WOLSEY   Yes, surely.
CAMPEIUS
  Believe me, there's an ill opinion spread, then,
  Even of yourself, Lord Cardinal.
WOLSEY   How? Of me?
CAMPEIUS
  They will not stick to say you envied him,   126
  And, fearing he would rise, he was so virtuous,
  Kept him a foreign man still, which so grieved him   128
  That he ran mad and died.
WOLSEY   Heaven's peace be with him!   129
  That's Christian care enough. For living murmurers   130
  There's places of rebuke. He was a fool,
  For he would needs be virtuous. That good fellow,
                      [*Indicating Gardiner*]
  If I command him, follows my appointment;   133
  I will have none so near else. Learn this, brother: 134
  We live not to be gripped by meaner persons.   135
KING [*To Gardiner*]
  Deliver this with modesty to the Queen.   136
                      Exit Gardiner.
  The most convenient place that I can think of

---

121 Doctor Pace i.e., Richard Pace, Dean of Saint Paul's and Secretary of
State, who served King Henry and Wolsey on diplomatic missions
126 stick hesitate. **envied him** i.e., were hostile toward Pace **128 Kept
. . . still** kept him constantly abroad on diplomatic missions **129 died**
(Pace actually died in 1536, six years after Wolsey's death.)
130 murmurers grumblers, troublemakers **133 appointment** bidding
134 none . . . else i.e., no one besides him so close to the King
135 gripped clutched at **136 Deliver . . . modesty** make this known gently

For such receipt of learning is Blackfriars;   138
There ye shall meet about this weighty business.
My Wolsey, see it furnished. O my lord,
Would it not grieve an able man to leave   141
So sweet a bedfellow? But conscience, conscience!
O, 'tis a tender place, and I must leave her.   *Exeunt.*

❖

2.3   *Enter Anne Bullen and an Old Lady.*

ANNE
  Not for that neither. Here's the pang that pinches:
  His Highness having lived so long with her, and she
  So good a lady that no tongue could ever
  Pronounce dishonor of her—by my life,   4
  She never knew harm-doing—O, now, after
  So many courses of the sun enthroned,
  Still growing in a majesty and pomp, the which   7
  To leave a thousandfold more bitter than
  'Tis sweet at first t' acquire—after this process,   9
  To give her the avaunt! It is a pity   10
  Would move a monster.
OLD LADY   Hearts of most hard temper
  Melt and lament for her.
ANNE   O, God's will, much better
  She ne'er had known pomp. Though 't be temporal,   13
  Yet, if that quarrel, Fortune, do divorce   14
  It from the bearer, 'tis a sufferance panging   15
  As soul and body's severing.
OLD LADY   Alas, poor lady!
  She's a stranger now again.
ANNE   So much the more   17
  Must pity drop upon her. Verily,

138 **such . . . learning** giving a proper reception to such learned men.
Blackfriars convent buildings in London surrendered to the crown in
Henry VIII's time   141 **able** vigorous

2.3. Location: London. The Queen's apartments.
4 **Pronounce** speak   7 **Still** always   9 **process** course of events   10 **give
. . . avaunt** bid her begone.   **pity** pitiful situation   13 **temporal** merely
worldly prosperity, not heavenly   14 **quarrel** quarreler, troublemaker
15 **sufferance panging** suffering as painful   17 **stranger** foreigner

I swear, 'tis better to be lowly born,
And range with humble livers in content,   20
Than to be perked up in a glistering grief   21
And wear a golden sorrow.

OLD LADY   Our content
Is our best having.

ANNE   By my troth and maidenhead,   23
I would not be a queen.

OLD LADY   Beshrew me, I would,
And venture maidenhead for 't; and so would you,   25
For all this spice of your hypocrisy.   26
You that have so fair parts of woman on you   27
Have too a woman's heart, which ever yet   28
Affected eminence, wealth, sovereignty;   29
Which, to say sooth, are blessings; and which gifts,   30
Saving your mincing, the capacity   31
Of your soft cheveril conscience would receive   32
If you might please to stretch it.

ANNE   Nay, good troth.

OLD LADY
Yes, troth, and troth. You would not be a queen?

ANNE
No, not for all the riches under heaven.

OLD LADY
'Tis strange. A threepence bowed would hire me,   36
Old as I am, to queen it. But, I pray you,
What think you of a duchess? Have you limbs
To bear that load of title?

ANNE   No, in truth.

OLD LADY
Then you are weakly made. Pluck off a little;   40
I would not be a young count in your way   41
For more than blushing comes to. If your back

20 **range** rank. **livers** persons 21 **perked up** trimmed out 23 **having** possession. **troth** good faith 25 **venture** risk 26 **For all** in spite of. **spice** dash, touch 27 **parts** qualities 28 **ever yet** always 29 **Affected** loved 30 **sooth** truth 31 **Saving your mincing** i.e., your affected coyness notwithstanding 32 **cheveril** kid leather. (Used as a type of flexibility.) 36 **bowed** crooked and therefore worthless; with sexual pun on "bawd," continued in *queen* (quean, whore), *bear, count* (female pudenda), *way, emballing* 40 **Pluck off** come lower 41 **count** (A rank below that of duke.)

Cannot vouchsafe this burden, 'tis too weak   43
Ever to get a boy.

ANNE   How you do talk!
I swear again, I would not be a queen
For all the world.

OLD LADY   In faith, for little England
You'd venture an emballing. I myself   47
Would for Caernarvonshire, although there 'longed   48
No more to the crown but that. Lo, who comes here?

  Enter Lord Chamberlain.

CHAMBERLAIN
Good morrow, ladies. What were 't worth to know
The secret of your conference?

ANNE   My good lord,   51
Not your demand; it values not your asking.   52
Our mistress' sorrows we were pitying.

CHAMBERLAIN
It was a gentle business, and becoming
The action of good women. There is hope
All will be well.

ANNE   Now I pray God, amen!

CHAMBERLAIN
You bear a gentle mind, and heavenly blessings
Follow such creatures. That you may, fair lady,
Perceive I speak sincerely, and high note's
Ta'en of your many virtues, the King's Majesty
Commends his good opinion of you, and   61
Does purpose honor to you no less flowing   62
Than Marchioness of Pembroke; to which title
A thousand pound a year annual support
Out of his grace he adds.

ANNE   I do not know   65
What kind of my obedience I should tender.
More than my all is nothing; nor my prayers

---

43 vouchsafe this burden i.e., accept this load of honors (with sexual
suggestion of bearing a man)   **47 emballing** investiture with the ball as
a royal emblem (with sexual suggestion)   **48 Caernarvonshire** an especially impoverished and barren Welsh county.   **'longed** belonged
51 conference conversation   **52 Not your demand** i.e., it is not even
worth your demand.   **values not** is not worth   **61 Commends** ex-
presses   **62 purpose** intend.   **flowing** abundant   **65 grace** favor

Are not words duly hallowed, nor my wishes
More worth than empty vanities; yet prayers and wishes
Are all I can return. Beseech your lordship,
Vouchsafe to speak my thanks and my obedience,   71
As from a blushing handmaid, to His Highness,
Whose health and royalty I pray for.

CHAMBERLAIN   Lady,
I shall not fail t' approve the fair conceit   74
The King hath of you. [*Aside.*] I have perused her well;
Beauty and honor in her are so mingled
That they have caught the King. And who knows yet
But from this lady may proceed a gem
To lighten all this isle? [*To Anne.*] I'll to the King, 79
And say I spoke with you.

ANNE   My honored lord!   *Exit Lord Chamberlain.*

OLD LADY   Why, this it is! See, see,
I have been begging sixteen years in court,
Am yet a courtier beggarly, nor could   84
Come pat betwixt too early and too late   85
For any suit of pounds; and you—O fate!—   86
A very fresh fish here—fie, fie, fie upon
This compelled fortune!—have your mouth filled up   88
Before you open it.

ANNE   This is strange to me.

OLD LADY
How tastes it? Is it bitter? Forty pence, no.   90
There was a lady once—'tis an old story—
That would not be a queen, that would she not,
For all the mud in Egypt. Have you heard it?   93

ANNE
Come, you are pleasant.

OLD LADY   With your theme, I could 94
O'ermount the lark. The Marchioness of Pembroke?
A thousand pounds a year for pure respect?   96
No other obligation? By my life,

---

71 Vouchsafe be so kind as   **74 approve . . . conceit** confirm the good
opinion   **79 lighten** give light to. (Refers to Queen Elizabeth.)
84 beggarly i.e., still in need   **85 pat** precisely at the opportune time
86 suit of pounds request for money   **88 compelled** unsought, forced
upon one   **90 Forty pence, no** i.e., I'll venture a small sum that it isn't
bitter to you   **93 the mud in Egypt** i.e., the wealth of Egypt resulting
from its fecund land   **94 pleasant** merry   **96 pure** mere

That promises more thousands. Honor's train   98
Is longer than his foreskirt. By this time   99
I know your back will bear a duchess. Say,
Are you not stronger than you were?

ANNE   Good lady,
Make yourself mirth with your particular fancy,
And leave me out on 't. Would I had no being,   102
If this salute my blood a jot! It faints me   104
To think what follows.
The Queen is comfortless, and we forgetful
In our long absence. Pray, do not deliver   107
What here you've heard to her.

OLD LADY   What do you think me? *Exeunt.*

2.4   *Trumpets, sennet, and cornets. Enter two*
Vergers, with short silver wands; next them two
Scribes, in the habit of doctors; after them the
[Arch] bishop of Canterbury alone; after him
the Bishops of Lincoln, Ely, Rochester, and
Saint Asaph; next them, with some small
distance, follows a Gentleman bearing the
purse, with the great seal, and a cardinal's hat;
then two Priests, bearing each a silver cross;
then [Griffith,] a Gentleman Usher, bareheaded,
accompanied with a Sergeant at Arms bearing
a silver mace; then two Gentlemen bearing two
great silver pillars; after them, side by side, the
two Cardinals; two Noblemen with the sword
and mace. The King takes place under the
cloth of state; the two Cardinals sit under him
as judges. The Queen takes place some distance

98–99 Honor's . . . foreskirt i.e., honors to come will exceed this present gift, just as an elongated robe trailing behind is longer than the front of a skirt   **102 your . . . fancy** your own private imaginings   **104 salute** act upon, excite.   **faints me** makes me faint   **107 deliver** report

2.4. Location: London. A hall in Blackfriars.
s.d. sennet trumpet call announcing a procession.   **Vergers** those who carry the verge or emblem of office; particularly, attendants on a church dignitary.   **habit of doctors** i.e., furred black gowns and flat caps worn by doctors of law.   **cloth of state** canopy.

from the King. The Bishops place themselves
on each side the court, in manner of a
consistory; below them the Scribes. The Lords
sit next the Bishops. The rest of the attendants
stand in convenient order about the stage.

WOLSEY
  Whilst our commission from Rome is read,
  Let silence be commanded.
KING   What's the need?
  It hath already publicly been read,
  And on all sides th' authority allowed;   4
  You may then spare that time.
WOLSEY   Be 't so. Proceed.
SCRIBE
  Say, "Henry, King of England, come into the court."
CRIER
  Henry, King of England, come into the court.
KING   Here.
SCRIBE
  Say, "Katharine, Queen of England, come into the
    court."
CRIER
  Katharine, Queen of England, come into the court.
            The Queen makes no answer, rises out
      of her chair, goes about the court, comes to the
            King, and kneels at his feet; then speaks.
KATHARINE
  Sir, I desire you do me right and justice,
  And to bestow your pity on me; for
  I am a most poor woman, and a stranger,
  Born out of your dominions, having here
  No judge indifferent, nor no more assurance   15
  Of equal friendship and proceeding. Alas, sir,   16
  In what have I offended you? What cause
  Hath my behavior given to your displeasure
  That thus you should proceed to put me off   19
  And take your good grace from me? Heaven witness;

---

consistory college of cardinals **4 allowed** conceded **15 indifferent**
impartial **16 equal** fair **19 put me off** discard me

I have been to you a true and humble wife,
At all times to your will conformable,
Ever in fear to kindle your dislike,   23
Yea, subject to your countenance—glad or sorry
As I saw it inclined. When was the hour
I ever contradicted your desire,
Or made it not mine too? Or which of your friends
Have I not strove to love, although I knew
He were mine enemy? What friend of mine
That had to him derived your anger did I   30
Continue in my liking, nay, gave notice
He was from thence discharged? Sir, call to mind
That I have been your wife in this obedience
Upward of twenty years, and have been blessed
With many children by you. If, in the course   35
And process of this time, you can report,
And prove it too, against mine honor aught—   37
My bond to wedlock, or my love and duty
Against your sacred person—in God's name   39
Turn me away, and let the foul'st contempt
Shut door upon me, and so give me up
To the sharp'st kind of justice. Please you, sir,
The King your father was reputed for
A prince most prudent, of an excellent
And unmatched wit and judgment. Ferdinand   45
My father, King of Spain, was reckoned one   46
The wisest prince that there had reigned by many   47
A year before. It is not to be questioned
That they had gathered a wise council to them
Of every realm, that did debate this business,
Who deemed our marriage lawful. Wherefore I humbly
Beseech you, sir, to spare me till I may
Be by my friends in Spain advised, whose counsel
I will implore. If not, i' the name of God,
Your pleasure be fulfilled!
WOLSEY   You have here, lady,
And of your choice, these reverend fathers, men

---

23 dislike displeasure   **30 derived** drawn   **35 many children** (The
Queen gave birth to five children, only one of whom, later Queen Mary,
survived infancy.)   **37 aught** anything   **39 Against** toward   **45 wit**
intelligence   **46–47 one The wisest** the very wisest

Of singular integrity and learning,
Yea, the elect o' the land, who are assembled
To plead your cause. It shall be therefore bootless   59
That longer you desire the court, as well   60
For your own quiet as to rectify   61
What is unsettled in the King.

CAMPEIUS   His Grace
Hath spoken well and justly. Therefore, madam,
It's fit this royal session do proceed,   64
And that without delay their arguments
Be now produced and heard.

KATHARINE   Lord Cardinal,
To you I speak.

WOLSEY   Your pleasure, madam?

KATHARINE   Sir,
I am about to weep; but, thinking that
We are a queen, or long have dreamed so, certain   69
The daughter of a king, my drops of tears
I'll turn to sparks of fire.

WOLSEY   Be patient yet.

KATHARINE
I will, when you are humble; nay, before,   72
Or God will punish me. I do believe,
Induced by potent circumstances, that   74
You are mine enemy, and make my challenge   75
You shall not be my judge. For it is you
Have blown this coal betwixt my lord and me—   77
Which God's dew quench! Therefore I say again,
I utterly abhor, yea, from my soul   79
Refuse you for my judge, whom yet once more
I hold my most malicious foe, and think not
At all a friend to truth.

WOLSEY   I do profess
You speak not like yourself, who ever yet   83
Have stood to charity and displayed th' effects   84
Of disposition gentle and of wisdom

59 **bootless** profitless   60 **That . . . court** that you entreat the court to
postpone its work   61 **quiet** peace of mind   64 **fit** appropriate
69 **certain** certainly   72 **before** i.e., sooner than that (which will never
be)   74 **Induced** persuaded   75 **make my challenge** I raise my formal
objection (that)   77 **blown this coal** i.e., stirred up this trouble
79 **abhor** protest against. (A technical term of canon law.)   83 **ever yet**
always   84 **stood to** upheld

O'ertopping woman's pow'r. Madam, you do me wrong.
I have no spleen against you, nor injustice   87
For you or any. How far I have proceeded,
Or how far further shall, is warranted   89
By a commission from the consistory,
Yea, the whole consistory of Rome. You charge me
That I have blown this coal. I do deny it.
The King is present. If it be known to him
That I gainsay my deed, how may he wound,   94
And worthily, my falsehood, yea, as much   95
As you have done my truth! If he know
That I am free of your report, he knows   97
I am not of your wrong. Therefore in him   98
It lies to cure me, and the cure is to
Remove these thoughts from you; the which before
His Highness shall speak in, I do beseech   101
You, gracious madam, to unthink your speaking
And to say so no more.

KATHARINE   My lord, my lord,
I am a simple woman, much too weak
T' oppose your cunning. You're meek and humble-
  mouthed;
You sign your place and calling, in full seeming,   106
With meekness and humility; but your heart
Is crammed with arrogancy, spleen, and pride.
You have, by fortune and His Highness' favors,
Gone slightly o'er low steps and now are mounted   110
Where powers are your retainers, and your words,   111
Domestics to you, serve your will as 't please   112
Yourself pronounce their office. I must tell you,   113
You tender more your person's honor than   114
Your high profession spiritual, that again
I do refuse you for my judge, and here
Before you all appeal unto the Pope,

87 spleen malice **89 warranted** justified **94 gainsay my deed** deny my
acts **95 worthily** deservedly **97 report** adverse report, accusation
98 am . . . wrong am innocent of having wronged you **101 in** regarding **106 sign** signify, show marks of. **in full seeming** to all appearances **110 slightly** easily **111 powers . . . retainers** i.e., you command
the service of people of rank **111–113 your words . . . office** i.e., your
clever speeches serve your ends in any way you choose; or, your very
words are immediately acted upon **114 tender more** are more con-
cerned for

To bring my whole cause 'fore His Holiness
And to be judged by him.
>   *She curtsies to the King, and offers to depart.*

CAMPEIUS   The Queen is obstinate,
Stubborn to justice, apt to accuse it, and   120
Disdainful to be tried by 't. 'Tis not well.
She's going away.

KING   Call her again.

CRIER
Katharine, Queen of England, come into the court.

GRIFFITH   Madam, you are called back.

KATHARINE
What need you note it? Pray you, keep your way;   126
When you are called, return. Now, the Lord help!
They vex me past my patience. Pray you, pass on.
I will not tarry; no, nor ever more
Upon this business my appearance make
In any of their courts.
>   *Exeunt Queen and her attendants.*

KING   Go thy ways, Kate.
That man i' the world who shall report he has
A better wife, let him in naught be trusted
For speaking false in that. Thou art alone—
If thy rare qualities, sweet gentleness,
Thy meekness saintlike, wifelike government,   136
Obeying in commanding, and thy parts   137
Sovereign and pious else, could speak thee out—   138
The queen of earthly queens.—She's noble born,
And like her true nobility she has
Carried herself towards me.

WOLSEY   Most gracious sir,   141
In humblest manner I require Your Highness   142
That it shall please you to declare, in hearing
Of all these ears—for where I am robbed and bound,
There must I be unloosed, although not there
At once and fully satisfied—whether ever I   146

---

120 **Stubborn** resistant   126 **What** why.   **keep your way** move on
136 **government** self-control, behavior   137 **Obeying in commanding**
i.e., combining the qualities of obedient wife and regal queen.   **parts**
qualities   138 **else** besides.   **speak thee out** declare you as you are
141 **Carried** borne, behaved   142 **require** request   146 **At . . . satisfied**
given full restitution

Did broach this business to Your Highness, or
Laid any scruple in your way, which might
Induce you to the question on 't? Or ever
Have to you, but with thanks to God for such
A royal lady, spake one the least word that might   151
Be to the prejudice of her present state,
Or touch of her good person?

KING   My lord Cardinal,   153
I do excuse you; yea, upon mine honor,   154
I free you from 't. You are not to be taught   155
That you have many enemies that know not
Why they are so, but, like to village curs,
Bark when their fellows do. By some of these
The Queen is put in anger. You're excused.
But will you be more justified? You ever   160
Have wished the sleeping of this business, never desired
It to be stirred, but oft have hindered, oft,
The passages made toward it. On my honor,   163
I speak my good lord Cardinal to this point,   164
And thus far clear him. Now, what moved me to 't,
I will be bold with time and your attention;
Then mark th' inducement. Thus it came; give heed to 't:
My conscience first received a tenderness,
Scruple, and prick, on certain speeches uttered
By th' Bishop of Bayonne, then French ambassador,
Who had been hither sent on the debating
A marriage twixt the Duke of Orleans and
Our daughter Mary. I' the progress of this business,
Ere a determinate resolution, he—   174
I mean the Bishop—did require a respite,   175
Wherein he might the King his lord advertise   176
Whether our daughter were legitimate,
Respecting this our marriage with the dowager,   178
Sometime our brother's wife. This respite shook   179
The bosom of my conscience, entered me,
Yea, with a spitting power, and made to tremble   181
The region of my breast, which forced such way

151 **one the least** a single   153 **touch** sullying   154 **excuse** exonerate
155 **are not** do not need   160 **justified** vindicated   163 **passages** proceedings   164 **speak** describe   174 **determinate resolution** final decision
175 **require** request   176 **advertise** inform, confer with   178 **dowager**
widow   179 **Sometime** formerly   181 **spitting** piercing

That many mazed considerings did throng   183
And pressed in with this caution. First, methought   184
I stood not in the smile of heaven, who had   185
Commanded nature that my lady's womb,
If it conceived a male child by me, should
Do no more offices of life to 't than   188
The grave does to the dead; for her male issue
Or died where they were made, or shortly after   190
This world had aired them. Hence I took a thought   191
This was a judgment on me that my kingdom,
Well worthy the best heir o' the world, should not
Be gladded in 't by me. Then follows that   194
I weighed the danger which my realms stood in
By this my issue's fail, and that gave to me   196
Many a groaning throe. Thus hulling in   197
The wild sea of my conscience, I did steer
Toward this remedy, whereupon we are
Now present here together; that's to say,
I meant to rectify my conscience—which
I then did feel full sick, and yet not well—   202
By all the reverend fathers of the land
And doctors learned. First I began in private
With you, my lord of Lincoln. You remember
How under my oppression I did reek   206
When I first moved you.

LINCOLN   Very well, my liege.   207
KING
I have spoke long. Be pleased yourself to say
How far you satisfied me.

LINCOLN   So please Your Highness,
The question did at first so stagger me—
Bearing a state of mighty moment in 't,   211
And consequence of dread—that I committed   212
The daring'st counsel which I had to doubt   213

---

183 mazed considerings conflicting and confused thoughts   **184 caution**
warning   **185 smile** i.e., favor   **188 offices** services   **190 Or** either
191 aired given air to   **194 gladded** made happy   **196 By . . . fail** by my
lacking a son   **197 throe** pang, pain.   **hulling** drifting with sails
furled   **202 yet** still, even now   **206 oppression** distress.   **reek** sweat
207 moved mentioned the business to   **211–212 Bearing . . . dread**
relating to matters of the greatest consequence to the state and outcome
fearful to contemplate   **212–213 I committed . . . doubt** i.e., I hesitantly
and with foreboding offered the best advice I could give

And did entreat Your Highness to this course
Which you are running here.
KING [*To Canterbury*]   I then moved you,
My lord of Canterbury, and got your leave
To make this present summons. Unsolicited
I left no reverend person in this court,
But by particular consent proceeded
Under your hands and seals. Therefore, go on,   220
For no dislike i' the world against the person
Of the good Queen, but the sharp thorny points
Of my allegèd reasons, drives this forward.
Prove but our marriage lawful, by my life
And kingly dignity, we are contented
To wear our mortal state to come with her,   226
Katharine our queen, before the primest creature   227
That's paragoned o' the world.
CAMPEIUS   So please Your Highness,   228
The Queen being absent, 'tis a needful fitness   229
That we adjourn this court till further day.   230
Meanwhile must be an earnest motion   231
Made to the Queen to call back her appeal
She intends unto His Holiness.
KING [*Aside*]   I may perceive
These cardinals trifle with me. I abhor
This dilatory sloth and tricks of Rome.
My learned and well-belovèd servant, Cranmer,
Prithee, return. With thy approach, I know,   237
My comfort comes along.—Break up the court!
I say, set on.   *Exeunt in manner as they entered.*   239

❖

220 **Under . . . seals** i.e., with your signed agreement   226 **wear . . . her**
(1) share the state of human existence with her till we die (2) share royal
pomp with her   227 **primest** most excellent   228 **paragoned** set forth
as a perfect model   229 **needful fitness** necessary and proper action
230 **further** future   231 **motion** appeal, request   237 **Prithee, return**
(Henry apostrophizes the Protestant churchman, Thomas Cranmer, who
at this time, though the play doesn't say so directly, is on the Continent
collecting opinions on the King's marriage question. His return is
mentioned at 3.2.401.)   239 **set on** do it, proceed

3.1   *Enter Queen and her women, as at work.*

KATHARINE
  Take thy lute, wench. My soul grows sad with troubles;
  Sing, and disperse 'em if thou canst. Leave working.   2
GENTLEWOMAN [*Sings*]
      Orpheus with his lute made trees,   3
    And the mountain tops that freeze,
      Bow themselves when he did sing.
    To his music plants and flowers
    Ever sprung, as sun and showers   7
      There had made a lasting spring.

    Everything that heard him play,
    Even the billows of the sea,
      Hung their heads, and then lay by.   11
    In sweet music is such art,
    Killing care and grief of heart   13
      Fall asleep, or hearing, die.

Enter a Gentleman.

KATHARINE   How now?
GENTLEMAN
  An 't please Your Grace, the two great cardinals   16
  Wait in the presence.
KATHARINE   Would they speak with me?   17
GENTLEMAN
  They willed me say so, madam.
KATHARINE   Pray Their Graces   18
  To come near. [*Gentleman goes to the door.*] What can
    be their business
  With me, a poor weak woman, fall'n from favor?
  I do not like their coming. Now I think on 't,
  They should be good men, their affairs as righteous.   22
  But all hoods make not monks.

Enter the two cardinals, Wolsey and Campeius.

3.1. Location: London. The Queen's apartments.
2 Leave stop   **3 Orpheus** legendary musician in Greek mythology.
made trees i.e., caused trees to bow   **7 as** as if   **11 lay by** subsided
13 Killing care (so that) care that kills   **16 An 't** if it   **17 presence**
reception room   **18 willed** bade   **22 their . . . righteous** i.e., the business
they come on should be, like themselves, good

WOLSEY   Peace to Your Highness!
KATHARINE
  Your Graces find me here part of a huswife—   24
  I would be all—against the worst may happen.   25
  What are your pleasures with me, reverend lords?
WOLSEY
  May it please you, noble madam, to withdraw
  Into your private chamber, we shall give you
  The full cause of our coming.
KATHARINE   Speak it here.
  There's nothing I have done yet, o' my conscience,
  Deserves a corner. Would all other women   31
  Could speak this with as free a soul as I do!   32
  My lords, I care not, so much I am happy   33
  Above a number, if my actions   34
  Were tried by ev'ry tongue, ev'ry eye saw 'em,
  Envy and base opinion set against 'em,   36
  I know my life so even. If your business   37
  Seek me out, and that way I am wife in,   38
  Out with it boldly. Truth loves open dealing.
WOLSEY *Tanta est erga te mentis integritas, regina ser-* 40
enissima—   41
KATHARINE O, good my lord, no Latin!
  I am not such a truant since my coming
  As not to know the language I have lived in.
  A strange tongue makes my cause more strange,
    suspicious;   45
  Pray, speak in English. Here are some will thank you,
  If you speak truth, for their poor mistress' sake.
  Believe me, she has had much wrong. Lord Cardinal,
  The willing'st sin I ever yet committed   49
  May be absolved in English.
WOLSEY   Noble lady,
  I am sorry my integrity should breed—

---

24 part of a huswife i.e., partially tending to household duties **25 I . . .
all** i.e., I wish to be a complete housewife, in case I am divorced and
forced to live alone. **against** in anticipation of **31 a corner** i.e., secrecy **32 free** innocent **33 happy** fortunate (in virtue) **34 a number**
many **36 Envy** malice. **opinion** rumor **37 even** constant, upright
38 Seek . . . in concerns me regarding my conduct as a wife
40–41 Tanta . . . serenissima so innocent are our intentions toward you,
most serene queen **45 strange** foreign **49 willing'st** most deliberate

And service to His Majesty and you—
So deep suspicion, where all faith was meant.
We come not by the way of accusation,   54
To taint that honor every good tongue blesses,
Nor to betray you any way to sorrow—
You have too much, good lady—but to know
How you stand minded in the weighty difference   58
Between the King and you, and to deliver,   59
Like free and honest men, our just opinions   60
And comforts to your cause.

CAMPEIUS   Most honored madam,
My lord of York, out of his noble nature,
Zeal, and obedience he still bore Your Grace,   63
Forgetting, like a good man, your late censure
Both of his truth and him—which was too far—   65
Offers, as I do, in a sign of peace,   66
His service and his counsel.

KATHARINE [*Aside*]   To betray me.—
My lords, I thank you both for your good wills.
Ye speak like honest men; pray God ye prove so!
But how to make ye suddenly an answer
In such a point of weight, so near mine honor—
More near my life, I fear—with my weak wit,   72
And to such men of gravity and learning,
In truth, I know not. I was set at work   74
Among my maids, full little, God knows, looking
Either for such men or such business.
For her sake that I have been—for I feel   77
The last fit of my greatness—good Your Graces,   78
Let me have time and counsel for my cause.
Alas, I am a woman, friendless, hopeless!

WOLSEY
Madam, you wrong the King's love with these fears.
Your hopes and friends are infinite.

KATHARINE   In England
But little for my profit. Can you think, lords,   83

___

54 by the way for the purpose   **58 minded** inclined, disposed.   **difference** quarrel   **59 deliver** declare   **60 free** frank   **63 still bore** has always borne   **65 far** severe   **66 in** as   **72 wit** understanding   **74 set** seated   **77 For . . . been** for the sake of the queenly person I once was   **78 fit** brief space, short spell   **83 profit** benefit

That any Englishman dare give me counsel,
Or be a known friend, 'gainst His Highness' pleasure,
Though he be grown so desperate to be honest,   86
And live a subject? Nay, forsooth, my friends,
They that must weigh out my afflictions,   88
They that my trust must grow to, live not here.
They are, as all my other comforts, far hence
In mine own country, lords.

CAMPEIUS   I would Your Grace
Would leave your griefs and take my counsel.

KATHARINE   How, sir?

CAMPEIUS
Put your main cause into the King's protection;
He's loving and most gracious. 'Twill be much
Both for your honor better and your cause;
For if the trial of the law o'ertake ye,
You'll part away disgraced.

WOLSEY   He tells you rightly.   97

KATHARINE
Ye tell me what ye wish for both—my ruin.
Is this your Christian counsel? Out upon ye!
Heaven is above all yet; there sits a judge
That no king can corrupt.

CAMPEIUS   Your rage mistakes us.   101

KATHARINE
The more shame for ye! Holy men I thought ye,
Upon my soul, two reverend cardinal virtues;   103
But cardinal sins and hollow hearts I fear ye.   104
Mend 'em, for shame, my lords. Is this your comfort?
The cordial that ye bring a wretched lady,   106
A woman lost among ye, laughed at, scorned?
I will not wish ye half my miseries;
I have more charity. But say I warned ye;
Take heed, for heaven's sake take heed, lest at once   110
The burden of my sorrows fall upon ye.

---

86 so desperate i.e., reckless enough as **88 weigh out** compensate for
97 part away depart **101 mistakes** misjudges **103 cardinal virtues** i.e.,
justice, temperance, fortitude, and prudence, constituting four of the
seven virtues opposing the seven Deadly Sins **104 cardinal sins** i.e., the
seven Deadly Sins **106 cordial** restorative medicine **110 at once** all at
once

WOLSEY

  Madam, this is a mere distraction.   112

  You turn the good we offer into envy.   113

KATHARINE

  Ye turn me into nothing. Woe upon ye

  And all such false professors! Would you have me—

  If you have any justice, any pity,

  If ye be anything but churchmen's habits—   117

  Put my sick cause into his hands that hates me?

  Alas, he's banished me his bed already,

  His love too long ago! I am old, my lords,

  And all the fellowship I hold now with him

  Is only my obedience. What can happen

  To me above this wretchedness? All your studies   123

  Make me a curse like this!

CAMPEIUS   Your fears are worse.   124

KATHARINE

  Have I lived thus long—let me speak myself,   125

  Since virtue finds no friends—a wife, a true one?

  A woman, I dare say without vainglory,

  Never yet branded with suspicion?

  Have I with all my full affections

  Still met the King, loved him next heaven, obeyed him, 130

  Been, out of fondness, superstitious to him,   131

  Almost forgot my prayers to content him,

  And am I thus rewarded? 'Tis not well, lords.

  Bring me a constant woman to her husband,

  One that ne'er dreamed a joy beyond his pleasure,

  And to that woman, when she has done most,

  Yet will I add an honor: a great patience.

WOLSEY

  Madam, you wander from the good we aim at.   138

KATHARINE

  My lord, I dare not make myself so guilty

  To give up willingly that noble title

---

112 mere distraction absolute frenzy **113 envy** malice **117 habits**
garments **123 above** more than **123–124 All . . . this** i.e., I challenge
you, in your clerical exertions, to devise a worse fate than I already
have **124 worse** i.e., than your wretchedness **125 speak** describe,
speak for **130 Still** always. **next** next to **131 superstitious** i.e., to the
point of idolatry **138 wander from** mistake

Your master wed me to. Nothing but death
Shall e'er divorce my dignities.

WOLSEY　　　　　　　　　　Pray, hear me.

KATHARINE
Would I had never trod this English earth
Or felt the flatteries that grow upon it!
Ye have angels' faces, but heaven knows your hearts.
What will become of me now, wretched lady?
I am the most unhappy woman living.
[*To her women.*] Alas, poor wenches, where are now
　your fortunes?
Shipwrecked upon a kingdom where no pity,
No friends, no hope, no kindred weep for me,
Almost no grave allowed me. Like the lily
That once was mistress of the field and flourished,
I'll hang my head and perish.

WOLSEY　　　　　　　　　If Your Grace
Could but be brought to know our ends are honest,　　154
You'd feel more comfort. Why should we, good lady,
Upon what cause, wrong you? Alas, our places,　　156
The way of our profession, is against it;
We are to cure such sorrows, not to sow 'em.
For goodness' sake, consider what you do,
How you may hurt yourself, ay, utterly
Grow from the King's acquaintance, by this carriage.　　161
The hearts of princes kiss obedience,
So much they love it; but to stubborn spirits
They swell and grow as terrible as storms.
I know you have a gentle, noble temper,　　165
A soul as even as a calm. Pray, think us　　166
Those we profess, peacemakers, friends, and servants.

CAMPEIUS
Madam, you'll find it so. You wrong your virtues
With these weak women's fears. A noble spirit,
As yours was put into you, ever casts　　170
Such doubts, as false coin, from it. The King loves you;
Beware you lose it not. For us, if you please

---

154 ends intentions.　**honest** honorable　**156 places** official positions
161 Grow from become estranged from.　**carriage** conduct　**165 temper**
disposition　**166 even** steadfast　**170 As . . . you** such as was given to you

To trust us in your business, we are ready
To use our utmost studies in your service.   174

KATHARINE
Do what ye will, my lords, and pray forgive me
If I have used myself unmannerly;   176
You know I am a woman, lacking wit
To make a seemly answer to such persons.
Pray, do my service to His Majesty.   179
He has my heart yet, and shall have my prayers
While I shall have my life. Come, reverend fathers,
Bestow your counsels on me. She now begs
That little thought when she set footing here   183
She should have bought her dignities so dear.

Exeunt.

❖

3.2   *Enter the Duke of Norfolk, Duke of Suffolk,
           Lord Surrey, and Lord Chamberlain.*

NORFOLK
If you will now unite in your complaints,
And force them with a constancy, the Cardinal   2
Cannot stand under them. If you omit   3
The offer of this time, I cannot promise   4
But that you shall sustain more new disgraces
With these you bear already.

SURREY   I am joyful
To meet the least occasion that may give me
Remembrance of my father-in-law, the Duke,   8
To be revenged on him.

SUFFOLK   Which of the peers
Have uncontemned gone by him, or at least   10
Strangely neglected? When did he regard   11

174 **studies** efforts   176 **used myself** conducted myself   179 **do my
service** pay my respects   183 **That** who

3.2. Location: London. Antechamber to the King's apartments.
2 **force** urge   3–4 **If . . . time** if you let this opportunity pass   8 **father-
in-law** i.e., Buckingham. (See 2.1.41–44 and note.)   10 **uncontemned**
unscorned   11 **Strangely neglected** i.e., not been strangely neglected

The stamp of nobleness in any person
Out of himself?
CHAMBERLAIN   My lords, you speak your pleasures.   13
What he deserves of you and me I know;
What we can do to him, though now the time
Gives way to us, I much fear. If you cannot   16
Bar his access to th' King, never attempt   17
Anything on him, for he hath a witchcraft   18
Over the King in 's tongue.
NORFOLK   O, fear him not;
His spell in that is out. The King hath found   20
Matter against him that forever mars
The honey of his language. No, he's settled,   22
Not to come off, in his displeasure.
SURREY   Sir,   23
I should be glad to hear such news as this
Once every hour.
NORFOLK   Believe it, this is true.
In the divorce his contrary proceedings   26
Are all unfolded, wherein he appears   27
As I would wish mine enemy.
SURREY   How came
His practices to light?
SUFFOLK   Most strangely.
SURREY   O, how, how?   29
SUFFOLK
The Cardinal's letters to the Pope miscarried,   30
And came to th' eye o' the King, wherein was read
How that the Cardinal did entreat His Holiness
To stay the judgment o' the divorce; for if   33
It did take place, "I do," quoth he; "perceive
My king is tangled in affection to
A creature of the Queen's, Lady Anne Bullen."   36
SURREY
Has the King this?
SUFFOLK   Believe it.

13 Out of excepting 16 Gives way to favors 17–18 attempt Anything
on attack, move against 20 out finished 22 settled fixed 23 come off
escape. his i.e., the King's 26 contrary contradictory, divisive
27 unfolded exposed 29 practices plots 30 miscarried went astray
33 stay stop, delay 36 creature dependent

SURREY   Will this work?

CHAMBERLAIN
  The King in this perceives him, how he coasts   38
  And hedges his own way. But in this point   39
  All his tricks founder, and he brings his physic   40
  After his patient's death. The King already
  Hath married the fair lady.

SURREY   Would he had!

SUFFOLK
  May you be happy in your wish, my lord,
  For I profess you have it.

SURREY   Now, all my joy
  Trace the conjunction!

SUFFOLK   My amen to 't!

NORFOLK   All men's!   45

SUFFOLK
  There's order given for her coronation.
  Marry, this is yet but young, and may be left   47
  To some ears unrecounted. But, my lords,
  She is a gallant creature, and complete   49
  In mind and feature. I persuade me, from her   50
  Will fall some blessing to this land, which shall
  In it be memorized.

SURREY   But will the King   52
  Digest this letter of the Cardinal's?   53
  The Lord forbid!

NORFOLK   Marry, amen!

SUFFOLK   No, no;
  There be more wasps that buzz about his nose
  Will make this sting the sooner. Cardinal Campeius
  Is stolen away to Rome, hath ta'en no leave,
  Has left the cause o' the King unhandled, and
  Is posted, as the agent of our cardinal,   59
  To second all his plot. I do assure you
  The King cried "Ha!" at this.

CHAMBERLAIN   Now, God incense him,
  And let him cry "Ha!" louder!

38–39 coasts And hedges goes a roundabout way, as by coast and hedge-row   40 physic medicine, cure   45 Trace follow   47 young recent, new   49 complete perfect, excellent   50 persuade me am confident   52 memorized caused to be remembered. (Refers prophetically to Queen Elizabeth.)   53 Digest put up with, "swallow"   59 Is posted has gone in haste

NORFOLK   But, my lord,
When returns Cranmer?
SUFFOLK
He is returned in his opinions, which   64
Have satisfied the King for his divorce,
Together with all famous colleges
Almost in Christendom. Shortly, I believe,
His second marriage shall be published, and   68
Her coronation. Katharine no more
Shall be called Queen, but Princess Dowager
And widow to Prince Arthur.
NORFOLK   This same Cranmer's
A worthy fellow, and hath ta'en much pain
In the King's business.
SUFFOLK   He has, and we shall see him
For it an archbishop.
NORFOLK   So I hear.
SUFFOLK   'Tis so.

Enter Wolsey and Cromwell.

The Cardinal!
NORFOLK   Observe, observe, he's moody.   75
              [*The nobles stand aside and observe.*]
WOLSEY
The packet, Cromwell, gave 't you the King?   76
CROMWELL
To his own hand, in 's bedchamber.
WOLSEY   Looked he
O' th' inside of the paper?
CROMWELL   Presently   78
He did unseal them, and the first he viewed
He did it with a serious mind; a heed   80
Was in his countenance. You he bade
Attend him here this morning.
WOLSEY   Is he ready
To come abroad?
CROMWELL   I think by this he is.   84
WOLSEY   Leave me awhile.   *Exit Cromwell.*

64 in his opinions having sent ahead his written opinions   **68 published**
proclaimed   **75 moody** angry   **76 packet** parcel of dispatches
78 Presently immediately   **80 heed** concern   **84 this** this time

[*To himself.*] It shall be to the Duchess of Alençon,
The French king's sister; he shall marry her.
Anne Bullen? No, I'll no Anne Bullens for him;
There's more in 't than fair visage. Bullen?
No, we'll no Bullens. Speedily I wish
To hear from Rome. The Marchioness of Pembroke?

NORFOLK
He's discontented.

SUFFOLK   Maybe he hears the King
Does whet his anger to him.

SURREY   Sharp enough,
Lord, for thy justice!

WOLSEY [*To himself*]
The late Queen's gentlewoman, a knight's daughter,   95
To be her mistress' mistress? The Queen's queen?
This candle burns not clear; 'tis I must snuff it,   97
Then out it goes. What though I know her virtuous
And well deserving? Yet I know her for
A spleeny Lutheran, and not wholesome to   100
Our cause, that she should lie i' the bosom of
Our hard-ruled king. Again, there is sprung up   102
An heretic, an arch one, Cranmer, one
Hath crawled into the favor of the King   104
And is his oracle.

NORFOLK   He is vexed at something.   105

*Enter King, reading of a schedule, [and Lovell.
Wolsey stands apart, not observing the King.]*

SURREY
I would 'twere something that would fret the string,   106
The master cord on 's heart.

SUFFOLK   The King, the King!   107

KING [*To himself*]
What piles of wealth hath he accumulated
To his own portion! And what expense by the hour
Seems to flow from him! How i' the name of thrift

---

95 late former   **97 clear** bright.   **snuff it** trim its wick   **100 spleeny**
staunch, contentious   **102 hard-ruled** hard to manage   **104 Hath** who
has   **105 s.d. schedule** scroll   **106 fret** gnaw through (with a pun on the
musical sense of pressing the string of a musical instrument against a
"fret" or bar, continued in the play on *cord/chord*)   **107 on 's** of his

Does he rake this together?—Now, my lords,
Saw you the Cardinal?

NORFOLK   My lord, we have
Stood here observing him. Some strange commotion
Is in his brain. He bites his lip, and starts,
Stops on a sudden, looks upon the ground,
Then lays his finger on his temple; straight   116
Springs out into fast gait, then stops again,
Strikes his breast hard, and anon he casts   118
His eye against the moon. In most strange postures
We have seen him set himself.

KING   It may well be
There is a mutiny in 's mind. This morning
Papers of state he sent me to peruse,
As I required; and wot you what I found   123
There—on my conscience, put unwittingly?
Forsooth, an inventory, thus importing   125
The several parcels of his plate, his treasure,   126
Rich stuffs and ornaments of household, which
I find at such proud rate that it outspeaks   128
Possession of a subject.

NORFOLK   It's heaven's will.   129
Some spirit put this paper in the packet
To bless your eye withal.

KING   If we did think   131
His contemplation were above the earth
And fixed on spiritual object, he should still
Dwell in his musings; but I am afraid
His thinkings are below the moon, not worth   135
His serious considering.

          King takes his seat; whispers [to] Lovell,
              who goes to the Cardinal [Wolsey].

WOLSEY   Heaven forgive me!
Ever God bless Your Highness!

KING   Good my lord,
You are full of heavenly stuff and bear the inventory
Of your best graces in your mind, the which

116 straight at once **118 anon** soon **123 wot** know **125 importing**
signifying **126 several parcels** various items. **plate** precious metal,
bullion **128–129 outspeaks . . . subject** describes possessions exceeding
what a subject should have **131 withal** with **135 below the moon** i.e.,
in the mortal sphere

You were now running o'er. You have scarce time
To steal from spiritual leisure a brief span
To keep your earthly audit. Sure in that
I deem you an ill husband, and am glad   143
To have you therein my companion.

WOLSEY   Sir,
For holy offices I have a time; a time
To think upon the part of business which
I bear i' the state; and nature does require
Her times of preservation, which perforce   148
I, her frail son, amongst my brethren mortal,
Must give my tendance to.

KING   You have said well.   150

WOLSEY
And ever may Your Highness yoke together,
As I will lend you cause, my doing well
With my well saying!

KING   'Tis well said again,
And 'tis a kind of good deed to say well;
And yet words are no deeds. My father loved you;
He said he did, and with his deed did crown   156
His word upon you. Since I had my office,
I have kept you next my heart, have not alone   158
Employed you where high profits might come home,
But pared my present havings, to bestow   160
My bounties upon you.

WOLSEY [Aside]   What should this mean?

SURREY [Aside]
The Lord increase this business!

KING   Have I not made you
The prime man of the state? I pray you, tell me   163
If what I now pronounce you have found true;   164
And if you may confess it, say withal
If you are bound to us or no. What say you?

WOLSEY
My sovereign, I confess your royal graces,   167

---

143 ill husband unthrifty manager   **148 perforce** necessarily
150 tendance attention   **156 crown** i.e., fulfill (by appointing Wolsey
chaplain in 1507 and Dean of Lincoln in 1509)   **158 next** nearest
160 pared . . . havings reduced my own wealth   **163 prime** principal
164 pronounce declare   **167 graces** favors

Show'red on me daily, have been more than could   168
My studied purposes requite, which went   169
Beyond all man's endeavors. My endeavors
Have ever come too short of my desires,
Yet filed with my abilities. Mine own ends   172
Have been mine so that evermore they pointed   173
To th' good of your most sacred person and
The profit of the state. For your great graces
Heaped upon me, poor undeserver, I
Can nothing render but allegiant thanks,   177
My prayers to heaven for you, my loyalty,
Which ever has and ever shall be growing,
Till death, that winter, kill it.

KING   Fairly answered.
A loyal and obedient subject is
Therein illustrated. The honor of it   182
Does pay the act of it, as, i' the contrary,   183
The foulness is the punishment. I presume   184
That, as my hand has opened bounty to you,   185
My heart dropped love, my power rained honor, more
On you than any, so your hand and heart,
Your brain, and every function of your power,
Should, notwithstanding that your bond of duty,   189
As 'twere in love's particular, be more   190
To me, your friend, than any.

WOLSEY   I do profess
That for Your Highness' good I ever labored
More than mine own; that am, have, and will be—   193
Though all the world should crack their duty to you   194
And throw it from their soul, though perils did
Abound as thick as thought could make 'em and
Appear in forms more horrid—yet my duty,
As doth a rock against the chiding flood,
Should the approach of this wild river break,   199
And stand unshaken yours.

168–169 more . . . requite more than I could devise means to repay
172 filed kept pace   **173 so that** only to the extent that   **177 allegiant**
loyal   **182 illustrated** made evident   **182–183 The honor . . . it** (Cf.
"Virtue is its own reward.")   **184 foulness** dishonor   **185 opened**
granted   **189 that . . . duty** i.e., your priestly vows   **190 in love's particulars** in the special devotion of friendship   **193 have** have been
194 crack violate   **199 break** check, hold back

KING   'Tis nobly spoken.
  Take notice, lords, he has a loyal breast,
  For you have seen him open 't. Read o'er this,
                              [*Giving him papers*]
  And after, this, and then to breakfast with
  What appetite you have.
                    Exit King, frowning upon the Cardinal
            [*Wolsey*]; *the nobles throng after him* [*the King*],
                  smiling and whispering, [*and so exeunt*].

WOLSEY   What should this mean?
  What sudden anger's this? How have I reaped it?   205
  He parted frowning from me, as if ruin
  Leaped from his eyes. So looks the chafèd lion   207
  Upon the daring huntsman that has galled him,   208
  Then makes him nothing. I must read this paper—   209
  I fear, the story of his anger. 'Tis so!
  This paper has undone me. 'Tis th' account
  Of all that world of wealth I have drawn together
  For mine own ends—indeed, to gain the popedom
  And fee my friends in Rome. O negligence,   214
  Fit for a fool to fall by! What cross devil   215
  Made me put this main secret in the packet   216
  I sent the King? Is there no way to cure this?
  No new device to beat this from his brains?
  I know 'twill stir him strongly; yet I know
  A way, if it take right, in spite of fortune   220
  Will bring me off again. What's this? "To th' Pope"?   221
  The letter, as I live, with all the business
  I writ to 's Holiness. Nay then, farewell!
  I have touched the highest point of all my greatness,
  And from that full meridian of my glory   225
  I haste now to my setting. I shall fall
  Like a bright exhalation in the evening,   227
  And no man see me more.

---

205 reaped i.e., deserved, incurred   **207 chafèd** angry   **208 galled**
wounded   **209 makes him nothing** destroys him (the hunter)   **214 fee**
pay, bribe   **215 cross** perverse   **216 main** weighty   **220 take right**
succeed   **221 bring me off** let me escape   **225 meridian** apex, sum-
mit   **227 exhalation** i.e., any astronomical phenomenon, such as a
meteor or a falling star

Enter to Wolsey the Dukes of Norfolk and
Suffolk, the Earl of Surrey, and the Lord
Chamberlain.

NORFOLK
Hear the King's pleasure, Cardinal, who commands you
To render up the great seal presently   230
Into our hands, and to confine yourself
To Asher House, my lord of Winchester's,
Till you hear further from His Highness.

WOLSEY   Stay,
Where's your commission, lords? Words cannot carry 234
Authority so weighty.

SUFFOLK   Who dare cross 'em,   235
Bearing the King's will from his mouth expressly?

WOLSEY
Till I find more than will or words to do it—
I mean your malice—know, officious lords,
I dare and must deny it. Now I feel
Of what coarse metal ye are molded—envy;   240
How eagerly ye follow my disgraces
As if it fed ye, and how sleek and wanton   242
Ye appear in everything may bring my ruin!
Follow your envious courses, men of malice!
You have Christian warrant for 'em, and no doubt   245
In time will find their fit rewards. That seal
You ask with such a violence, the King,
Mine and your master, with his own hand gave me;
Bade me enjoy it, with the place and honors,
During my life; and, to confirm his goodness,
Tied it by letters patents. Now, who'll take it?   251

SURREY
The King that gave it.

WOLSEY   It must be himself, then.

SURREY
Thou art a proud traitor, priest.

WOLSEY   Proud lord, thou liest!

---

230 presently immediately   **234 commission** authorizing warrant
235 cross oppose   **240 envy** malice   **242 sleek** fawning.   **wanton** merry,
frolicsome   **245 Christian warrant** i.e., the example of other uncharita-
ble Christians   **251 letters patents** formal and public bestowing of
rights or powers

Within these forty hours Surrey durst better
Have burnt that tongue than said so.

SURREY   Thy ambition,
Thou scarlet sin, robbed this bewailing land   256
Of noble Buckingham, my father-in-law.
The heads of all thy brother cardinals,
With thee and all thy best parts bound together,   259
Weighed not a hair of his. Plague of your policy!   260
You sent me deputy for Ireland,
Far from his succor, from the King, from all
That might have mercy on the fault thou gav'st him;   263
Whilst your great goodness, out of holy pity,
Absolved him with an ax.

WOLSEY   This, and all else
This talking lord can lay upon my credit,   266
I answer is most false. The Duke by law
Found his deserts. How innocent I was
From any private malice in his end   269
His noble jury and foul cause can witness.
If I loved many words, lord, I should tell you
You have as little honesty as honor,
That in the way of loyalty and truth   273
Toward the King, my ever royal master,
Dare mate a sounder man than Surrey can be,   275
And all that love his follies.

SURREY   By my soul,
Your long coat, priest, protects you; thou shouldst feel
My sword i' the lifeblood of thee else. My lords,
Can ye endure to hear this arrogance?
And from this fellow? If we live thus tamely,
To be thus jaded by a piece of scarlet,   281
Farewell nobility! Let His Grace go forward
And dare us with his cap, like larks.

WOLSEY   All goodness   283

---

256 Thou scarlet sin (Refers to his cardinal's cassock, described as
scarlet; see 3.1.103–104. See also Isaiah 1:18.)   **259 parts** qualities
260 Weighed equaled in weight.   **Plague of** a plague on.   **policy** scheming   **263 fault . . . him** offense you charged him (Buckingham) with
266 lay . . . credit charge against my good name   **269 From** of
273 That I that   **275 mate** rival, vie with   **281 jaded** intimidated, cowed
283 dare . . . larks dazzle us with his cardinal's hat as birds with a
mirror or a piece of scarlet cloth

Is poison to thy stomach.

SURREY   Yes, that goodness
Of gleaning all the land's wealth into one,
Into your own hands, Cardinal, by extortion;
The goodness of your intercepted packets
You writ to th' Pope against the King. Your goodness,
Since you provoke me, shall be most notorious.
My lord of Norfolk, as you are truly noble,
As you respect the common good, the state
Of our despised nobility, our issues,   292
Who, if he live, will scarce be gentlemen,
Produce the grand sum of his sins, the articles   294
Collected from his life. [*To Wolsey.*] I'll startle you
Worse than the sacring bell, when the brown wench   296
Lay kissing in your arms, Lord Cardinal.

WOLSEY
How much, methinks, I could despise this man,
But that I am bound in charity against it!

NORFOLK
Those articles, my lord, are in the King's hand;   300
But thus much, they are foul ones.

WOLSEY   So much fairer   301
And spotless shall mine innocence arise
When the King knows my truth.

SURREY   This cannot save you.   303
I thank my memory, I yet remember
Some of these articles, and out they shall.   305
Now, if you can blush and cry "Guilty," Cardinal,
You'll show a little honesty.

WOLSEY   Speak on, sir;
I dare your worst objections. If I blush,   308
It is to see a nobleman want manners.   309

SURREY
I had rather want those than my head. Have at you!
First, that without the King's assent or knowledge

---

292 issues sons   **294 articles** items of the indictment   **296 sacring bell**
bell rung at the most solemn portions of the Mass. (Surrey imagines a
scene in which Wolsey is startled in the midst of making love by hearing the Mass bell.)   **300 hand** possession   **301 thus much** (I can say)
this much   **303 truth** loyalty   **305 shall** i.e., shall come   **308 objections**
accusations   **309 want** lack

You wrought to be a legate, by which power   312
You maimed the jurisdiction of all bishops.

NORFOLK
Then, that in all you writ to Rome, or else
To foreign princes, *"Ego et Rex meus"*   315
Was still inscribed, in which you brought the King   316
To be your servant.

SUFFOLK   Then that, without the knowledge
Either of King or Council, when you went
Ambassador to the Emperor, you made bold
To carry into Flanders the great seal.

SURREY
Item, you sent a large commission   321
To Gregory de Cassado, to conclude,
Without the King's will or the state's allowance,   323
A league between His Highness and Ferrara.

SUFFOLK
That out of mere ambition you have caused   325
Your holy hat to be stamped on the King's coin.

SURREY
Then, that you have sent innumerable substance—   327
By what means got, I leave to your own conscience—
To furnish Rome, and to prepare the ways   329
You have for dignities, to the mere undoing   330
Of all the kingdom. Many more there are,
Which since they are of you, and odious,
I will not taint my mouth with.

CHAMBERLAIN   O my lord,
Press not a falling man too far! 'Tis virtue.
His faults lie open to the laws; let them,
Not you, correct him. My heart weeps to see him
So little of his great self.

SURREY   I forgive him.

---

312 wrought connived, worked.   **legate** representative of the Pope
315 Ego et Rex meus my king and I. (Literally, "I and my king"; Norfolk
accuses Wolsey of using the phrase in such a way as to make the King
his "servant" by naming himself first, but the Latin construction requires that "ego" precede any nouns parallel with it.)   **316 still** always
321 Item i.e., another item is.   **large** with full power to act   **323 allowance** assent   **325 mere** sheer   **327 innumerable substance** uncountable
wealth   **329 To furnish Rome** (Implies that Wolsey made gifts to Rome
as bribes to obtain his own advancement.)   **330 mere** utter

SUFFOLK

Lord Cardinal, the King's further pleasure is—
Because all those things you have done of late
By your power legative within this kingdom   340
Fall into the compass of a praemunire—   341
That therefore such a writ be sued against you,   342
To forfeit all your goods, lands, tenements,   343
Chattels, and whatsoever, and to be   344
Out of the King's protection. This is my charge.

NORFOLK

And so we'll leave you to your meditations
How to live better. For your stubborn answer
About the giving back the great seal to us,
The King shall know it and, no doubt, shall thank you.
So fare you well, my little good lord Cardinal.

                              Exeunt all but Wolsey.

WOLSEY

So farewell to the little good you bear me.
Farewell? A long farewell, to all my greatness!
This is the state of man: today he puts forth
The tender leaves of hopes; tomorrow blossoms,   354
And bears his blushing honors thick upon him;   355
The third day comes a frost, a killing frost,
And when he thinks, good easy man, full surely   357
His greatness is a-ripening, nips his root,
And then he falls as I do. I have ventured,
Like little wanton boys that swim on bladders,   360
This many summers in a sea of glory,
But far beyond my depth. My high-blown pride
At length broke under me and now has left me,
Weary and old with service, to the mercy
Of a rude stream that must forever hide me.   365
Vain pomp and glory of this world, I hate ye!
I feel my heart new opened. O, how wretched

---

340 legative as a papal legate   **341 Fall . . . praemunire** fall within the
penalties for violating a writ of praemunire, i.e., a writ by which one
could be charged with appealing to a foreign court (especially a papal
court) in an action involving an English subject and hence relevant to
the King's court   **342 sued** moved, issued   **343 tenements** properties
not owned outright but held for some set term   **344 Chattels** personal
possessions   **354 tender** young   **355 blushing** glowing   **357 easy** easy-
going   **360 wanton** sportful   **365 rude** rough

Is that poor man that hangs on princes' favors!
There is betwixt that smile we would aspire to,
That sweet aspect of princes, and their ruin,   370
More pangs and fears than wars or women have;
And when he falls, he falls like Lucifer,
Never to hope again.

> *Enter Cromwell, standing amazed.*

                              Why, how now, Cromwell?   373

CROMWELL
    I have no power to speak, sir.

WOLSEY   What, amazed   374
    At my misfortunes? Can thy spirit wonder
    A great man should decline? Nay, an you weep,   376
    I am fall'n indeed.

CROMWELL   How does Your Grace?

WOLSEY   Why, well;
    Never so truly happy, my good Cromwell.
    I know myself now, and I feel within me
    A peace above all earthly dignities,
    A still and quiet conscience. The King has cured me,
    I humbly thank His Grace, and from these shoulders,
    These ruined pillars, out of pity, taken
    A load would sink a navy—too much honor.
    O, 'tis a burden, Cromwell, 'tis a burden
    Too heavy for a man that hopes for heaven!

CROMWELL
    I am glad Your Grace has made that right use of it.

WOLSEY
    I hope I have. I am able now, methinks,
    Out of a fortitude of soul I feel,
    To endure more miseries and greater far
    Than my weakhearted enemies dare offer.
    What news abroad?

CROMWELL   The heaviest and the worst
    Is your displeasure with the King.

WOLSEY   God bless him!   393

CROMWELL
    The next is that Sir Thomas More is chosen
    Lord Chancellor in your place.

370 their ruin the ruin they bring about   **373 s.d.,   374 amazed**
stunned, astonished   **376 an** if   **393 displeasure** disgrace

WOLSEY   That's somewhat sudden.
But he's a learnèd man. May he continue
Long in His Highness' favor and do justice
For truth's sake and his conscience, that his bones,
When he has run his course and sleeps in blessings,
May have a tomb of orphans' tears wept on him!   400
What more?
CROMWELL   That Cranmer is returned with welcome,
Installed Lord Archbishop of Canterbury.
WOLSEY
That's news indeed.
CROMWELL   Last, that the Lady Anne,
Whom the King hath in secrecy long married,
This day was viewed in open as his queen,
Going to chapel, and the voice is now   406
Only about her coronation.
WOLSEY
There was the weight that pulled me down. O Cromwell,
The King has gone beyond me! All my glories   409
In that one woman I have lost forever.
No sun shall ever usher forth mine honors,
Or gild again the noble troops that waited   412
Upon my smiles. Go get thee from me, Cromwell!
I am a poor fall'n man, unworthy now
To be thy lord and master. Seek the King;
That sun, I pray, may never set! I have told him
What and how true thou art. He will advance thee;
Some little memory of me will stir him—
I know his noble nature—not to let
Thy hopeful service perish too. Good Cromwell,
Neglect him not; make use now, and provide   421
For thine own future safety.
CROMWELL   O my lord,
Must I then leave you? Must I needs forgo
So good, so noble, and so true a master?
Bear witness, all that have not hearts of iron,
With what a sorrow Cromwell leaves his lord.
The King shall have my service, but my prayers
Forever and forever shall be yours.

400 orphans' i.e., such as would be under the legal guardianship of the
Lord Chancellor   **406 voice** talk   **409 gone beyond** overreached
412 troops i.e., of retainers   **421 make use** take advantage

WOLSEY
  Cromwell, I did not think to shed a tear
  In all my miseries, but thou hast forced me,
  Out of thy honest truth, to play the woman.   431
  Let's dry our eyes. And thus far hear me, Cromwell,
  And when I am forgotten, as I shall be,
  And sleep in dull cold marble, where no mention
  Of me more must be heard of, say I taught thee;
  Say Wolsey, that once trod the ways of glory,
  And sounded all the depths and shoals of honor,   437
  Found thee a way, out of his wreck, to rise in,   438
  A sure and safe one, though thy master missed it.
  Mark but my fall, and that that ruined me.
  Cromwell, I charge thee, fling away ambition!
  By that sin fell the angels; how can man, then,
  The image of his Maker, hope to win by it?   443
  Love thyself last; cherish those hearts that hate thee.
  Corruption wins not more than honesty.
  Still in thy right hand carry gentle peace   446
  To silence envious tongues. Be just, and fear not.
  Let all the ends thou aim'st at be thy country's,
  Thy God's, and truth's; then if thou fall'st, O Cromwell,
  Thou fall'st a blessèd martyr!
  Serve the King, and—prithee, lead me in.
  There take an inventory of all I have,
  To the last penny; 'tis the King's. My robe,   453
  And my integrity to heaven, is all
  I dare now call mine own. O Cromwell, Cromwell!
  Had I but served my God with half the zeal
  I served my king, he would not in mine age
  Have left me naked to mine enemies.
CROMWELL
  Good sir, have patience.
WOLSEY   So I have. Farewell
  The hopes of court! My hopes in heaven do dwell.
                                  Exeunt.

❧

431 **play the woman** i.e., shed tears   437 **sounded** explored, fathomed
438 **wreck** shipwreck   443 **win** profit   446 **Still** always   453 **robe** i.e.,
clerical robe

4.1 *Enter two Gentlemen, meeting one another.*

FIRST GENTLEMAN
  You're well met once again.
SECOND GENTLEMAN   So are you.   1
FIRST GENTLEMAN
  You come to take your stand here and behold
  The Lady Anne pass from her coronation?
SECOND GENTLEMAN
  'Tis all my business. At our last encounter
  The Duke of Buckingham came from his trial.
FIRST GENTLEMAN
  'Tis very true. But that time offered sorrow;
  This, general joy.
SECOND GENTLEMAN   'Tis well. The citizens,
  I am sure, have shown at full their royal minds—   8
  As, let 'em have their rights, they are ever forward— 9
  In celebration of this day with shows,
  Pageants, and sights of honor.
FIRST GENTLEMAN   Never greater,
  Nor, I'll assure you, better taken, sir.   12
SECOND GENTLEMAN
  May I be bold to ask what that contains,
  That paper in your hand?
FIRST GENTLEMAN   Yes, 'tis the list
  Of those that claim their offices this day
  By custom of the coronation.
  The Duke of Suffolk is the first, and claims
  To be High Steward; next, the Duke of Norfolk,
  He to be Earl Marshal. You may read the rest.
                            [*He offers a paper.*]
SECOND GENTLEMAN
  I thank you, sir. Had I not known those customs,
  I should have been beholding to your paper.   21
  But, I beseech you, what's become of Katharine,
  The Princess Dowager? How goes her business?

4.1. Location: A street in Westminster.
1 You're well met i.e., I am happy to see you **8 royal minds** loyalty to
the crown **9 let . . . rights** to give them due credit. **forward** i.e., eager
to do **12 taken** received **21 beholding** beholden

FIRST GENTLEMAN
That I can tell you too. The Archbishop
Of Canterbury, accompanied with other
Learnèd and reverend fathers of his order,
Held a late court at Dunstable, six miles off   27
From Ampthill where the Princess lay, to which   28
She was often cited by them, but appeared not;   29
And, to be short, for not-appearance and   30
The King's late scruple, by the main assent   31
Of all these learnèd men she was divorced,
And the late marriage made of none effect;   33
Since which she was removed to Kimbolton,
Where she remains now sick.

SECOND GENTLEMAN   Alas, good lady!
                                    [*Trumpets.*]
The trumpets sound. Stand close, the Queen is
    coming.   *Hautboys.* 36

        The Order of the Coronation.
 1. *A lively flourish of Trumpets.*
 2. *Then, two* Judges.
 3. Lord Chancellor, *with purse and mace before him.*
 4. Choristers, *singing.* Music.
 5. Mayor of London, *bearing the mace. Then* Garter,
    *in his coat of arms, and on his head he wore a
    gilt copper crown.*
 6. Marquess Dorset, *bearing a scepter of gold, on his
    head a demi-coronal of gold. With him, the* Earl
    of Surrey, *bearing the rod of silver with the dove,
    crowned with an earl's coronet. Collars of S's.*
 7. Duke of Suffolk, *in his robe of estate, his coronet
    on his head, bearing a long white wand, as High
    Steward. With him, the* Duke of Norfolk, *with the
    rod of marshalship, a coronet on his head. Collars
    of* S's.

---

27 late recent (as also in ll. 31 and 33)   **28 lay** lodged   **29 cited** summoned   **30 short** brief   **31 main assent** general agreement   **33 of none
effect** void, invalid   **36 close** aside   **s.d. The Order of the Coronation:**
(3) **Lord Chancellor** i.e., Sir Thomas More. (4) **Music** musicians (as also
in l. 91). (5) **Garter** i.e., Garter King at Arms, a chief herald of the College of Arms. (6) **Collars of S's** golden chains of office made of flat,
broad S-shaped links, ornately decorated.

8. *A canopy borne by four of the* Cinque Ports; *under it, the* Queen *in her robe, in her hair, richly adorned with pearl, crowned. On each side her, the* Bishops of London *and* Winchester.

9. *The old* Duchess of Norfolk, *in a coronal of gold wrought with flowers, bearing the Queen's train.*

10. *Certain* Ladies *or* Countesses, *with plain circlets of gold without flowers.*

> *Exeunt, first passing over the stage in order and state, and then a great flourish of trumpets.*

SECOND GENTLEMAN
A royal train, believe me. These I know.   37
Who's that that bears the scepter?

FIRST GENTLEMAN   Marquess Dorset,
And that, the Earl of Surrey, with the rod.

SECOND GENTLEMAN
A bold brave gentleman. That should be
The Duke of Suffolk?

FIRST GENTLEMAN   'Tis the same: High Steward.

SECOND GENTLEMAN
And that, my lord of Norfolk?

FIRST GENTLEMAN   Yes.

SECOND GENTLEMAN [*Looking at the Queen*]
                         Heaven bless thee!
Thou hast the sweetest face I ever looked on.
Sir, as I have a soul, she is an angel;
Our King has all the Indies in his arms,
And more and richer, when he strains that lady.   46
I cannot blame his conscience.

FIRST GENTLEMAN   They that bear
The cloth of honor over her are four barons   48
Of the Cinque Ports.   49

---

(8) **Cinque Ports** barons of the Cinque Ports, a group of seaport towns (originally Dover, Hastings, Sandwich, Hythe, and Romney) situated on the southeast coast of England, in ancient times furnishing the chief parts of the English navy, in return for which they had many privileges and franchises.   **in her hair** with hair loosely hanging (customary for brides)   **37 train** procession   **46 strains** embraces   **48 cloth of honor** canopy   **49 Cinque Ports** (See l. 36 s.d. and note.)

SECOND GENTLEMAN
    Those men are happy, and so are all are near her.   50
    I take it she that carries up the train
    Is that old noble lady, Duchess of Norfolk.
FIRST GENTLEMAN
    It is, and all the rest are countesses.
SECOND GENTLEMAN
    Their coronets say so. These are stars indeed.
FIRST GENTLEMAN
    And sometimes falling ones.
SECOND GENTLEMAN   No more of that.   55
                            [*Exit procession.*]

        Enter a third Gentleman.

FIRST GENTLEMAN
    God save you, sir! Where have you been broiling?   56
THIRD GENTLEMAN
    Among the crowd i' th' Abbey, where a finger
    Could not be wedged in more. I am stifled
    With the mere rankness of their joy.
SECOND GENTLEMAN   You saw   59
    The ceremony?
THIRD GENTLEMAN   That I did.
FIRST GENTLEMAN   How was it?
THIRD GENTLEMAN
    Well worth the seeing.
SECOND GENTLEMAN   Good sir, speak it to us.   61
THIRD GENTLEMAN
    As well as I am able. The rich stream
    Of lords and ladies, having brought the Queen
    To a prepared place in the choir, fell off   64
    A distance from her, while Her Grace sat down
    To rest awhile, some half an hour or so,
    In a rich chair of state, opposing freely   67
    The beauty of her person to the people.
    Believe me, sir, she is the goodliest woman
    That ever lay by man; which when the people

50 **all** all who   55 **falling** (with a sexual pun)   56 **broiling** sweating
59 **mere rankness** sheer exuberance   61 **speak** describe   64 **fell off**
withdrew   67 **opposing** presenting in full view

Had the full view of, such a noise arose
As the shrouds make at sea in a stiff tempest,　　　72
As loud, and to as many tunes. Hats, cloaks—
Doublets, I think—flew up; and had their faces　　　74
Been loose, this day they had been lost. Such joy
I never saw before. Great-bellied women,
That had not half a week to go, like rams　　　77
In the old time of war, would shake the press　　　78
And make 'em reel before 'em. No man living
Could say "This is my wife" there, all were woven
So strangely in one piece.

SECOND GENTLEMAN　　　　　But what followed?

THIRD GENTLEMAN
At length Her Grace rose and with modest paces
Came to the altar, where she kneeled, and saintlike
Cast her fair eyes to heaven and prayed devoutly,
Then rose again and bowed her to the people;
When by the Archbishop of Canterbury
She had all the royal makings of a queen,
As holy oil, Edward Confessor's crown,　　　88
The rod, and bird of peace, and all such emblems
Laid nobly on her. Which performed, the choir,
With all the choicest music of the kingdom,　　　91
Together sung *Te Deum*. So she parted,　　　92
And with the same full state paced back again　　　93
To York Place, where the feast is held.

FIRST GENTLEMAN　　　　　Sir,
You must no more call it York Place; that's past,
For since the Cardinal fell that title's lost.
'Tis now the King's, and called Whitehall.

THIRD GENTLEMAN　　　　　I know it,
But 'tis so lately altered that the old name　　　98
Is fresh about me.

SECOND GENTLEMAN What two reverend bishops
Were those that went on each side of the Queen?

---

72 shrouds sail ropes　**74 Doublets** close-fitting jackets　**77 rams**
battering rams　**78 press** crowd　**88 As** such as, namely　**91 music** i.e.,
musicians　**92 Te Deum** (A hymn of thanksgiving, the opening words of
which are, *Te Deum laudamus*, "Thee, God, we praise.")　**parted** departed　**93 state** dignity　**98 lately** recently

THIRD GENTLEMAN
  Stokesley and Gardiner, the one of Winchester,   101
  Newly preferred from the King's secretary,   102
  The other, London.

SECOND GENTLEMAN   He of Winchester   103
  Is held no great good lover of the Archbishop's,
  The virtuous Cranmer.

THIRD GENTLEMAN   All the land knows that.
  However, yet there is no great breach; when it comes,
  Cranmer will find a friend will not shrink from him.   107

SECOND GENTLEMAN
  Who may that be, I pray you?

THIRD GENTLEMAN   Thomas Cromwell,
  A man in much esteem with the King, and truly
  A worthy friend. The King has made him Master
  O' the Jewel House,
  And one already of the Privy Council.

SECOND GENTLEMAN
  He will deserve more.

THIRD GENTLEMAN   Yes, without all doubt.
  Come, gentlemen, ye shall go my way, which
  Is to the court, and there ye shall be my guests.
  Something I can command. As I walk thither,   116
  I'll tell ye more.

BOTH   You may command us, sir.   *Exeunt.*

❖

4.2   *Enter Katharine, Dowager, sick, led between*
       Griffith, her gentleman usher, and Patience, her
       woman.

GRIFFITH
  How does Your Grace?

101–102 **Gardiner . . . secretary** (Gardiner, secretary to the King, was made Bishop of Winchester at the fall of Wolsey; he continued to act as secretary for several years.)   102 **preferred** promoted   103 **London** i.e., Bishop of London   107 **will not** who will not   116 **Something . . . command** i.e., I can provide refreshment

4.2. Location: Kimbolton Castle in Huntingtonshire. The Queen's apart-ments.

KATHARINE   O Griffith, sick to death!
My legs like loaden branches bow to th' earth,   2
Willing to leave their burden. Reach a chair. [*She sits.*]
So; now, methinks, I feel a little ease.
Didst thou not tell me, Griffith, as thou ledst me,
That the great child of honor, Cardinal Wolsey,
Was dead?
GRIFFITH   Yes, madam; but I think Your Grace,
Out of the pain you suffered, gave no ear to 't.
KATHARINE
Prithee, good Griffith, tell me how he died.
If well, he stepped before me happily   10
For my example.
GRIFFITH   Well, the voice goes, madam;   11
For after the stout Earl Northumberland   12
Arrested him at York, and brought him forward,
As a man sorely tainted, to his answer,   14
He fell sick suddenly and grew so ill
He could not sit his mule.
KATHARINE   Alas, poor man!
GRIFFITH
At last, with easy roads, he came to Leicester,   17
Lodged in the abbey, where the reverend abbot,
With all his convent, honorably received him;   19
To whom he gave these words, "O father Abbot,
An old man, broken with the storms of state,
Is come to lay his weary bones among ye;
Give him a little earth for charity!"
So went to bed, where eagerly his sickness
Pursued him still; and three nights after this,
About the hour of eight, which he himself
Foretold should be his last, full of repentance,
Continual meditations, tears, and sorrows,
He gave his honors to the world again,
His blessèd part to heaven, and slept in peace.
KATHARINE
So may he rest; his faults lie gently on him!

---

2 loaden laden, weighted down   **10 happily** fittingly   **11 the voice goes**
i.e., people say   **12 stout** brave   **14 sorely tainted** grievously discred-
ited.   **answer** i.e., trial   **17 roads** stages (of a journey)   **19 convent**
monastery

Yet thus far, Griffith, give me leave to speak him,   32
And yet with charity. He was a man
Of an unbounded stomach, ever ranking   34
Himself with princes; one that by suggestion   35
Tied all the kingdom. Simony was fair play;   36
His own opinion was his law. I' the presence   37
He would say untruths, and be ever double   38
Both in his words and meaning. He was never,
But where he meant to ruin, pitiful.   40
His promises were, as he then was, mighty;
But his performance, as he is now, nothing.
Of his own body he was ill, and gave   43
The clergy ill example.
GRIFFITH   Noble madam,
   Men's evil manners live in brass; their virtues
   We write in water. May it please Your Highness
   To hear me speak his good now?
KATHARINE   Yes, good Griffith;
   I were malicious else.
GRIFFITH   This cardinal,
   Though from an humble stock, undoubtedly
   Was fashioned to much honor. From his cradle
   He was a scholar, and a ripe and good one,
   Exceeding wise, fair-spoken, and persuading;
   Lofty and sour to them that loved him not,
   But, to those men that sought him, sweet as summer.
   And though he were unsatisfied in getting,   55
   Which was a sin, yet in bestowing, madam,
   He was most princely. Ever witness for him
   Those twins of learning that he raised in you,   58
   Ipswich and Oxford, one of which fell with him,   59
   Unwilling to outlive the good that did it;   60
   The other, though unfinished, yet so famous,
   So excellent in art, and still so rising,   62

---

32 speak describe   **34 stomach** ambition   **35 suggestion** crafty dealing   **36 Tied** fettered, controlled.   **Simony** the selling of ecclesiastical
offices   **37 presence** i.e., of the King   **38 double** duplicitous   **40 pitiful**
pitying, compassionate   **43 ill** i.e., sexually depraved   **55 getting** acquir-
ing wealth   **58 raised in you** built in your cities   **59 Ipswich and Oxford** (Wolsey founded a college, no longer extant, at Ipswich, where he
was born, and a college at Oxford that is now Christ Church.)   **60 good
that did** good man that founded   **62 art** learning

That Christendom shall ever speak his virtue.
His overthrow heaped happiness upon him;
For then, and not till then, he felt himself,   65
And found the blessedness of being little.   66
And, to add greater honors to his age
Than man could give him, he died fearing God.

KATHARINE
After my death I wish no other herald,
No other speaker of my living actions,   70
To keep mine honor from corruption
But such an honest chronicler as Griffith.
Whom I most hated living, thou hast made me,   73
With thy religious truth and modesty,   74
Now in his ashes honor. Peace be with him!
Patience, be near me still, and set me lower.
I have not long to trouble thee. Good Griffith,
Cause the musicians play me that sad note   78
I named my knell, whilst I sit meditating
On that celestial harmony I go to.
        Sad and solemn music. [*Katharine sleeps.*]

GRIFFITH
She is asleep. Good wench, let's sit down quiet,
For fear we wake her. Softly, gentle Patience.   82
                      [*They sit.*]

    *The vision. Enter, solemnly tripping one after
    another, six personages, clad in white robes,
    wearing on their heads garlands of bays, and
    golden vizards on their faces, branches of bays or
    palm in their hands. They first congee unto her,
    then dance; and, at certain changes, the first two
    hold a spare garland over her head, at which the
    other four make reverent curtsies. Then the two
    that held the garland deliver the same to the
    other next two, who observe the same order in
    their changes, and holding the garland over her
    head; which done, they deliver the same garland
    to the last two, who likewise observe the same*

65 felt knew **66 little** of humble station **70 living** while alive
73 Whom he whom **74 modesty** moderation **78 note** tune **82 s.d.**
The vision: bays bay leaves. **vizards** masks. **congee** make a congé, a
ceremonious bow. **changes** figures in the dance

order; at which, as it were by inspiration, she
makes in her sleep signs of rejoicing, and holdeth
up her hands to heaven; and so in their dancing
vanish, carrying the garland with them. The
music continues.

KATHARINE [*Waking*]
Spirits of peace, where are ye? Are ye all gone,
And leave me here in wretchedness behind ye?

GRIFFITH
Madam, we are here.

KATHARINE   It is not you I call for.
Saw ye none enter since I slept?

GRIFFITH   None, madam.

KATHARINE
No? Saw you not, even now, a blessèd troop
Invite me to a banquet, whose bright faces
Cast thousand beams upon me, like the sun?
They promised me eternal happiness,
And brought me garlands, Griffith, which I feel
I am not worthy yet to wear. I shall, assuredly.

GRIFFITH
I am most joyful, madam, such good dreams
Possess your fancy.

KATHARINE   Bid the music leave;   94
They are harsh and heavy to me.   *Music ceases.*

PATIENCE [*To Griffith*]   Do you note
How much Her Grace is altered on the sudden?
How long her face is drawn? How pale she looks,
And of an earthy cold? Mark her eyes!

GRIFFITH
She is going, wench. Pray, pray.

PATIENCE   Heaven comfort her!

     Enter a Messenger.

MESSENGER
An 't like Your Grace—

KATHARINE   You are a saucy fellow.   100
Deserve we no more reverence?

GRIFFITH [*To Messenger*]   You are too blame,   101

94 fancy imagination. **music leave** musicians cease **100 An 't like** if it
please **101 too blame** too blameworthy

Knowing she will not lose her wonted greatness,   102
To use so rude behavior. Go to, kneel.

MESSENGER [*Kneeling*]
I humbly do entreat Your Highness' pardon;
My haste made me unmannerly. There is staying   105
A gentleman, sent from the King, to see you.

KATHARINE
Admit him entrance, Griffith. But this fellow
Let me ne'er see again.   *Exit Messenger.*

   Enter Lord Capuchius [admitted by Griffith].

            If my sight fail not,
You should be Lord Ambassador from the Emperor,   109
My royal nephew, and your name Capuchius.

CAPUCHIUS
Madam, the same; your servant.

KATHARINE   O my lord,
The times and titles now are altered strangely
With me since first you knew me. But, I pray you,
What is your pleasure with me?

CAPUCHIUS   Noble lady,
First, mine own service to Your Grace; the next,
The King's request that I would visit you,
Who grieves much for your weakness, and by me
Sends you his princely commendations,
And heartily entreats you take good comfort.

KATHARINE
O my good lord, that comfort comes too late;
'Tis like a pardon after execution.
That gentle physic, given in time, had cured me,   122
But now I am past all comforts here but prayers.
How does His Highness?

CAPUCHIUS   Madam, in good health.

KATHARINE
So may he ever do, and ever flourish,
When I shall dwell with worms, and my poor name
Banished the kingdom!—Patience, is that letter
I caused you write yet sent away?

PATIENCE   No, madam.

---

102 lose forget.   **wonted** accustomed   **105 staying** waiting
109 Emperor i.e., Charles V   **122 physic** remedy.   **had** would have

KATHARINE
  Sir, I most humbly pray you to deliver
  This to my lord the King.
                  [*The letter is given to Capuchius.*]
CAPUCHIUS   Most willing, madam.
KATHARINE
  In which I have commended to his goodness
  The model of our chaste loves, his young daughter—   132
  The dews of heaven fall thick in blessings on her!—
  Beseeching him to give her virtuous breeding—   134
  She is young, and of a noble modest nature;
  I hope she will deserve well—and a little
  To love her for her mother's sake, that loved him,
  Heaven knows how dearly. My next poor petition
  Is that His Noble Grace would have some pity
  Upon my wretched women, that so long
  Have followed both my fortunes faithfully;   141
  Of which there is not one, I dare avow—
  And now I should not lie—but will deserve,   143
  For virtue and true beauty of the soul,
  For honesty and decent carriage,   145
  A right good husband. Let him be a noble;
  And sure those men are happy that shall have 'em.
  The last is for my men—they are the poorest,
  But poverty could never draw 'em from me—
  That they may have their wages duly paid 'em,
  And something over to remember me by.   151
  If heaven had pleased to have given me longer life
  And able means, we had not parted thus.   153
  These are the whole contents. And, good my lord,
  By that you love the dearest in this world,
  As you wish Christian peace to souls departed,
  Stand these poor people's friend, and urge the King
  To do me this last right.
CAPUCHIUS   By heaven, I will,
  Or let me lose the fashion of a man!   159

---

132 model image.　**young daughter** i.e., Mary, the only one of Katharine's
many children to live to maturity; she became Queen of England
(1553–1558) before her half-sister Elizabeth (1558–1603)　**134 breeding**
upbringing　**141 both my fortunes** i.e., good and ill　**143 now** i.e., on my
deathbed, when true speaking is of utmost spiritual importance
145 honesty . . . carriage chastity and proper behavior　**151 over** in
addition　**153 able** sufficient　**159 fashion** nature, characteristics

KATHARINE
  I thank you, honest lord. Remember me
  In all humility unto His Highness.
  Say his long trouble now is passing
  Out of this world. Tell him in death I blessed him,
  For so I will. Mine eyes grow dim. Farewell,
  My lord. Griffith, farewell. Nay, Patience,
  You must not leave me yet. I must to bed;
  Call in more women. When I am dead, good wench,
  Let me be used with honor. Strew me over
  With maiden flowers, that all the world may know   169
  I was a chaste wife to my grave. Embalm me,
  Then lay me forth; although unqueened, yet like   171
  A queen, and daughter to a king, inter me.
  I can no more.   *Exeunt, leading Katharine.* 173

❖

169 maiden flowers spring flowers, symbolic of chastity. (Compare *The Winter's Tale*, 4.4.113–129.)   **171 lay me forth** lay me out for burial   **173 can** can do

5.1 *Enter Gardiner, Bishop of Winchester, a Page with a torch before him, met by Sir Thomas Lovell.*

GARDINER
  It's one o'clock, boy, is 't not?

PAGE   It hath struck.

GARDINER
  These should be hours for necessities,
  Not for delights; times to repair our nature
  With comforting repose, and not for us
  To waste these times.—Good hour of night, Sir Thomas!
  Whither so late?

LOVELL   Came you from the King, my lord?

GARDINER
  I did, Sir Thomas, and left him at primero   7
  With the Duke of Suffolk.

LOVELL   I must to him too,
  Before he go to bed. I'll take my leave.

GARDINER
  Not yet, Sir Thomas Lovell. What's the matter?
  It seems you are in haste. An if there be   11
  No great offense belongs to 't, give your friend
  Some touch of your late business. Affairs that walk,   13
  As they say spirits do, at midnight, have
  In them a wilder nature than the business
  That seeks dispatch by day.

LOVELL   My lord, I love you,   16
  And durst commend a secret to your ear   17
  Much weightier than this work. The Queen's in labor,   18
  They say, in great extremity, and feared   19
  She'll with the labor end.

GARDINER   The fruit she goes with
  I pray for heartily, that it may find
  Good time, and live; but for the stock, Sir Thomas,   22
  I wish it grubbed up now.

LOVELL   Methinks I could   23

5.1. Location: London. A gallery in the palace.
7 primero gambling card game   **11 An if** if   **13 touch** hint.   **late** recent   **16 dispatch** accomplishment   **17 commend** entrust   **18 this work** i.e., what I am involved in   **19 feared** i.e., it is feared that   **22 Good time** good fortune, a good delivery.   **stock** trunk or main stem **23 grubbed up** rooted up

Cry the amen; and yet my conscience says   24
She's a good creature and, sweet lady, does
Deserve our better wishes.

GARDINER   But, sir, sir,
Hear me, Sir Thomas. You're a gentleman
Of mine own way. I know you wise, religious;   28
And, let me tell you, it will ne'er be well—
'Twill not, Sir Thomas Lovell, take 't of me—
Till Cranmer, Cromwell—her two hands—and she
Sleep in their graves.

LOVELL   Now, sir, you speak of two
The most remarked i' the kingdom. As for Cromwell,   33
Besides that of the Jewel House, is made Master   34
O' the Rolls, and the King's secretary; further, sir,   35
Stands in the gap and trade of more preferments,   36
With which the time will load him. Th' Archbishop   37
Is the King's hand and tongue, and who dare speak
One syllable against him?

GARDINER   Yes, yes, Sir Thomas,
There are that dare, and I myself have ventured
To speak my mind of him; and indeed this day,
Sir—I may tell it you, I think—I have
Incensed the lords o' the Council that he is—   43
For so I know he is, they know he is—
A most arch heretic, a pestilence
That does infect the land; with which they, moved,   46
Have broken with the King, who hath so far   47
Given ear to our complaint, of his great grace
And princely care foreseeing those fell mischiefs   49
Our reasons laid before him, hath commanded   50
Tomorrow morning to the Council board
He be convented. He's a rank weed, Sir Thomas,   52
And we must root him out. From your affairs
I hinder you too long. Good night, Sir Thomas.

24 **Cry the amen** give assent   28 **way** religious faith (opposed to Protestant reform)   33 **remarked** under the public eye   34–35 **Master . . .
Rolls** judge of the Court of Appeal   36 **gap and trade** open and beaten
path   37 **time** course of events   43 **Incensed** instigated, led to believe
46–47 **with . . . King** they, moved to anger at the idea, have disclosed it
to the King   49 **fell** terrible, cruel   50 **hath** (that) he has   52 **convented**
summoned

LOVELL
  Many good nights, my lord. I rest your servant.   55
                      Exeunt Gardiner and Page.

     Enter King and Suffolk.

KING
  Charles, I will play no more tonight.
  My mind's not on 't; you are too hard for me.   57
SUFFOLK
  Sir, I did never win of you before.
KING But little, Charles,
  Nor shall not, when my fancy's on my play.—   60
  Now, Lovell, from the Queen what is the news?
LOVELL
  I could not personally deliver to her
  What you commanded me, but by her woman
  I sent your message, who returned her thanks
  In the great'st humbleness and desired Your Highness
  Most heartily to pray for her.
KING   What sayst thou, ha?
  To pray for her? What, is she crying out?
LOVELL
  So said her woman, and that her sufferance made   68
  Almost each pang a death.
KING   Alas, good lady!
SUFFOLK
  God safely quit her of her burden, and   70
  With gentle travail, to the gladding of
  Your Highness with an heir!
KING   'Tis midnight, Charles.
  Prithee, to bed, and in thy prayers remember
  Th' estate of my poor queen. Leave me alone,   74
  For I must think of that which company
  Would not be friendly to.
SUFFOLK   I wish Your Highness
  A quiet night, and my good mistress will   77
  Remember in my prayers.
KING   Charles, good night.   78
                      Exit Suffolk.

---

55 rest remain   **57 hard** good a player   **60 fancy's** mind's   **68 sufferance** suffering   **70 God** may God.   **quit** release   **74 estate** condition   **77–78 and my . . . Remember** and I will remember my good mistress, i.e., the Queen

Enter Sir Anthony Denny.

Well, sir, what follows?
DENNY
  Sir, I have brought my lord the Archbishop,
  As you commanded me.
KING   Ha? Canterbury?
DENNY
  Ay, my good lord.
KING   'Tis true. Where is he, Denny?
DENNY
  He attends Your Highness' pleasure.
KING   Bring him to us.
                                    [*Exit Denny.*]
LOVELL [*Aside*]
  This is about that which the Bishop spake.   84
  I am happily come hither.   85

    Enter Cranmer and Denny.

KING
  Avoid the gallery. (*Lovell seems to stay.*) Ha? I have said.
    Begone.   86
  What?   *Exeunt Lovell and Denny.*
CRANMER [*Aside*] I am fearful. Wherefore frowns he thus?
  'Tis his aspect of terror. All's not well.   88
KING
  How now, my lord? You do desire to know
  Wherefore I sent for you.
CRANMER [*Kneeling*]   It is my duty   90
  T' attend Your Highness' pleasure.
KING   Pray you, arise,
  My good and gracious lord of Canterbury.
  Come, you and I must walk a turn together;
  I have news to tell you. Come, come, give me your hand.
                                    [*Cranmer rises.*]
  Ah, my good lord, I grieve at what I speak
  And am right sorry to repeat what follows.
  I have, and most unwillingly, of late
  Heard many grievous—I do say, my lord,

84 **the Bishop** i.e., Gardiner   85 **happily** luckily   86 **Avoid** vacate
88 **aspect** expression   90 **Wherefore** why

Grievous—complaints of you; which, being considered,
Have moved us and our Council that you shall
This morning come before us, where I know
You cannot with such freedom purge yourself   102
But that, till further trial in those charges
Which will require your answer, you must take
Your patience to you and be well contented
To make your house our Tow'r. You a brother of us,   106
It fits we thus proceed, or else no witness   107
Would come against you.

CRANMER [*Kneeling*]   I humbly thank Your Highness,
And am right glad to catch this good occasion
Most throughly to be winnowed, where my chaff   110
And corn shall fly asunder. For I know   111
There's none stands under more calumnious tongues   112
Than I myself, poor man.

KING   Stand up, good Canterbury!
Thy truth and thy integrity is rooted
In us, thy friend. Give me thy hand, stand up.
                              [*Cranmer rises.*]
Prithee, let's walk. Now, by my halidom,   116
What manner of man are you? My lord, I looked   117
You would have given me your petition that
I should have ta'en some pains to bring together
Yourself and your accusers, and to have heard you
Without endurance further.

CRANMER   Most dread liege,   121
The good I stand on is my truth and honesty.
If they shall fail, I, with mine enemies,
Will triumph o'er my person, which I weigh not,   124
Being of those virtues vacant. I fear nothing   125
What can be said against me.

KING   Know you not
How your state stands i' the world, with the whole
    world?

---

102 freedom ease and completeness. **purge** excuse, clear **106 brother
of us** fellow member of the Council **107 fits** is appropriate
110 throughly thoroughly **111 corn** grain **112 stands under** is the
object of. **calumnious** slandering **116 by my halidom** i.e., by something sacred **117 looked** expected **121 endurance** imprisonment
124–125 which . . . vacant i.e., which I do not value if it is void of those
virtues (*truth* and *honesty*) **125 nothing** not at all

Your enemies are many, and not small; their practices   128
Must bear the same proportion, and not ever   129
The justice and the truth o' the question carries   130
The due o' the verdict with it. At what ease   131
Might corrupt minds procure knaves as corrupt
To swear against you? Such things have been done.
You are potently opposed, and with a malice
Of as great size. Ween you of better luck,   135
I mean in perjured witness, than your master,   136
Whose minister you are, whiles here he lived
Upon this naughty earth? Go to, go to,   138
You take a precipice for no leap of danger
And woo your own destruction.

CRANMER   God and Your Majesty
Protect mine innocence, or I fall into
The trap is laid for me!

KING   Be of good cheer;   142
They shall no more prevail than we give way to.   143
Keep comfort to you, and this morning see
You do appear before them. If they shall chance,
In charging you with matters, to commit you,   146
The best persuasions to the contrary
Fail not to use, and with what vehemency
Th' occasion shall instruct you. If entreaties
Will render you no remedy, this ring
Deliver them, and your appeal to us
There make before them. [*He gives a ring.*] Look, the
    good man weeps!
He's honest, on mine honor. God's blest mother,
I swear he is truehearted, and a soul
None better in my kingdom. Get you gone,
And do as I have bid you. (*Exit Cranmer.*) He has
    strangled
His language in his tears.

    Enter Old Lady.

---

128 small insignificant.   **practices** schemes, plots   **129 bear . . . proportion** be correspondingly numerous and mighty   **129–131 not . . . it** i.e., the innocence of a person does not always ensure his acquittal   **131 At what ease** how easily   **135 Ween you of** do you expect   **136 master** i.e., Christ   **138 naughty** wicked   **142 is** that is   **143 give way to** allow   **146 commit** i.e., to prison

LOVELL (*Within*)   Come back! What mean you?

[*Enter Lovell, following her.*]

OLD LADY
I'll not come back. The tidings that I bring
Will make my boldness manners.—Now, good angels   159
Fly o'er thy royal head, and shade thy person
Under their blessèd wings!

KING   Now, by thy looks
I guess thy message. Is the Queen delivered?
Say ay, and of a boy.

OLD LADY   Ay, ay, my liege,
And of a lovely boy. The God of heaven
Both now and ever bless her! 'Tis a girl
Promises boys hereafter. Sir, your queen
Desires your visitation, and to be
Acquainted with this stranger. 'Tis as like you
As cherry is to cherry.

KING   Lovell!

LOVELL   Sir?

KING
Give her an hundred marks. I'll to the Queen.   170

                              Exit King.

OLD LADY
An hundred marks? By this light, I'll ha' more.
An ordinary groom is for such payment.   172
I will have more, or scold it out of him.
Said I for this the girl was like to him?
I'll have more, or else unsay 't; and now,
While 'tis hot, I'll put it to the issue.   176

                              Exit Lady [*with Lovell*].

❖

159 good angels may good angels   **170 an hundred marks** i.e., about 65
pounds   **172 for** suited for   **176 put it to** force

5.2   *Enter Cranmer, Archbishop of Canterbury,*
        [pursuivants, pages, etc., attending at the door].

CRANMER
   I hope I am not too late, and yet the gentleman
   That was sent to me from the Council prayed me
   To make great haste. All fast? What means this? Ho!   3
   Who waits there?

      Enter Keeper.

              Sure you know me?
KEEPER   Yes, my lord,
   But yet I cannot help you.
CRANMER   Why?
KEEPER
   Your Grace must wait till you be called for.

      Enter Doctor Butts.

CRANMER   So.
BUTTS [*Aside*]
   This is a piece of malice. I am glad
   I came this way so happily. The King
   Shall understand it presently.   *Exit Butts.*
CRANMER [*Aside*]   'Tis Butts,   10
   The King's physician. As he passed along,
   How earnestly he cast his eyes upon me!
   Pray heaven he sound not my disgrace! For certain   13
   This is of purpose laid by some that hate me—   14
   God turn their hearts! I never sought their malice—
   To quench mine honor. They would shame to make me   16
   Wait else at door, a fellow councillor,
   'Mong boys, grooms, and lackeys. But their pleasures

5.2. Location: London. Adjacent to the council chamber.
s.d. pursuivants messengers, subordinates (as also in l. 24).   **at the door**
i.e., at a stage door, as though guarding the entrance to the council
chamber   **3 fast** locked   **10 presently** at once   **13 sound** probe, search
out; or speak, proclaim   **14 laid** contrived as a trap   **16 quench mine**
honor destroy my reputation

Must be fulfilled, and I attend with patience.   19

    Enter the King and Butts at a window above.

BUTTS
  I'll show Your Grace the strangest sight—
KING   What's that, Butts?
BUTTS
  I think Your Highness saw this many a day.
KING
  Body o' me, where is it?
BUTTS   There, my lord:
  The high promotion of His Grace of Canterbury,
  Who holds his state at door, 'mongst pursuivants,   24
  Pages, and footboys.
KING   Ha? 'Tis he, indeed.
  Is this the honor they do one another?
  'Tis well there's one above 'em yet. I had thought   27
  They had parted so much honesty among 'em—   28
  At least good manners—as not thus to suffer
  A man of his place, and so near our favor,   30
  To dance attendance on their lordships' pleasures,   31
  And at the door too, like a post with packets.   32
  By holy Mary, Butts, there's knavery!
  Let 'em alone, and draw the curtain close.
  We shall hear more anon.
        [They conceal themselves behind the curtain.
        Cranmer remains waiting at the door, below.]

19 s.d. at a window above (The gallery over the stage, representing a
peephole through which the Council could be spied upon. The Folio text
makes no scene division between this and the following scene, so that
the Council would assemble under the view and in the hearing of the
King; and the main stage, imagined in scene 2 to be adjacent to the
council chamber, becomes in scene 3 the chamber itself.) **24 holds his
state** maintains his dignity   **27 one above** (Suggests Henry's role as a
godlike figure.)   **28 parted** shared   **30 place** official position   **31 dance
attendance** stand waiting around   **32 post** messenger.   **packets** letters

5.3　　*A council table brought in with chairs and*
stools, and placed under the state. Enter Lord
Chancellor; places himself at the upper end of
the table on the left hand, a seat being left void
above him, as for Canterbury's seat. Duke of
Suffolk, Duke of Norfolk, Surrey, Lord
Chamberlain, Gardiner, seat themselves in
order on each side. Cromwell at lower end, as
secretary. [Keeper at the door.]

CHANCELLOR
　Speak to the business, Master Secretary.
　Why are we met in council?
CROMWELL　　　　　　　　　　Please your honors,
　The chief cause concerns His Grace of Canterbury.
GARDINER
　Has he had knowledge of it?
CROMWELL　　　　　　　　Yes.
NORFOLK　　　　　　　　　　　Who waits there?
KEEPER
　Without, my noble lords?
GARDINER　　　　　　　　Yes.
KEEPER　　　　　　　　　　My lord Archbishop,　　5
　And has done half an hour, to know your pleasures.
CHANCELLOR
　Let him come in.
KEEPER　　　　　　　Your Grace may enter now.
　　　　　　　　Cranmer approaches the council table.
CHANCELLOR
　My good lord Archbishop, I'm very sorry
　To sit here at this present and behold　　　　9
　That chair stand empty. But we all are men,
　In our own natures frail, and capable　　　11
　Of our flesh—few are angels—out of which frailty　12
　And want of wisdom, you, that best should teach us,

5.3. Location: The council chamber. Scene is continuous with the previous.
s.d. **state** canopy　**5 Without** outside the door. (Although Cranmer seemingly has never exited, the stage has now become the room into which he
has been waiting to be admitted.)　**9 present** present time　**11–12 capable
. . . flesh** susceptible to the weaknesses of the flesh

Have misdemeaned yourself, and not a little,   14
Toward the King first, then his laws, in filling
The whole realm, by your teaching and your
    chaplains'—
For so we are informed—with new opinions,
Divers and dangerous, which are heresies
And, not reformed, may prove pernicious.   19

GARDINER
Which reformation must be sudden too,
My noble lords; for those that tame wild horses
Pace 'em not in their hands to make 'em gentle,   22
But stop their mouths with stubborn bits and spur 'em
Till they obey the manage. If we suffer,   24
Out of our easiness and childish pity   25
To one man's honor, this contagious sickness,
Farewell all physic! And what follows then?   27
Commotions, uproars, with a general taint
Of the whole state, as of late days our neighbors,
The upper Germany, can dearly witness,   30
Yet freshly pitied in our memories.

CRANMER
My good lords, hitherto, in all the progress
Both of my life and office, I have labored,
And with no little study, that my teaching
And the strong course of my authority
Might go one way, and safely; and the end
Was ever to do well. Nor is there living—
I speak it with a single heart, my lords—   38
A man that more detests, more stirs against,   39
Both in his private conscience and his place,   40
Defacers of a public peace than I do.
Pray heaven the King may never find a heart
With less allegiance in it! Men that make
Envy and crooked malice nourishment
Dare bite the best. I do beseech your lordships

---

14 misdemeaned yourself been guilty of misconduct   **19 pernicious**
deadly   **22 Pace . . . hands** i.e., don't lead them gently   **24 manage**
training, handling.   **suffer** allow   **25 easiness** laxness   **27 physic**
medicine, cure   **30 upper Germany** (Refers to the Peasants' Wars, 1524;
possibly to the massacre of the Anabaptists in 1535.)   **38 single** honest;
not given to double-dealing   **39 stirs** is active   **40 place** official capacity

That, in this case of justice, my accusers,
Be what they will, may stand forth face to face
And freely urge against me.

SUFFOLK   Nay, my lord,   48
That cannot be. You are a councillor,
And by that virtue no man dare accuse you.   50

GARDINER
My lord, because we have business of more moment,
We will be short with you. 'Tis His Highness' pleasure,
And our consent, for better trial of you,
From hence you be committed to the Tower,
Where, being but a private man again,
You shall know many dare accuse you boldly—
More than, I fear, you are provided for.   57

CRANMER
Ah, my good lord of Winchester, I thank you;
You are always my good friend. If your will pass,   59
I shall both find your lordship judge and juror,
You are so merciful. I see your end;
'Tis my undoing. Love and meekness, lord,
Become a churchman better than ambition.
Win straying souls with modesty again;   64
Cast none away. That I shall clear myself,
Lay all the weight ye can upon my patience,   66
I make as little doubt as you do conscience   67
In doing daily wrongs. I could say more,   68
But reverence to your calling makes me modest.

GARDINER
My lord, my lord, you are a sectary,   70
That's the plain truth. Your painted gloss discovers,   71
To men that understand you, words and weakness.   72

CROMWELL
My lord of Winchester, you're a little,
By your good favor, too sharp. Men so noble,   74

---

48 urge make accusation   **50 by that virtue** by virtue of that
57 provided prepared   **59 pass** prevail   **64 modesty** moderation
66 Lay . . . can i.e., no matter how hard you press   **67–68 I . . . In** I have
as little doubt (of my blamelessness) as you have scruples against
70 sectary follower of a heretical Protestant sect   **71 painted gloss**
discovers false exterior (in speech and acts) reveals   **72 words** i.e., mere
words   **74 By . . . favor** i.e., begging your pardon

However faulty, yet should find respect   75
For what they have been. 'Tis a cruelty
To load a falling man.

GARDINER   Good Master Secretary,   77
I cry your honor mercy; you may worst   78
Of all this table say so.

CROMWELL   Why, my lord?

GARDINER
Do not I know you for a favorer
Of this new sect? Ye are not sound.

CROMWELL   Not sound?   81

GARDINER
Not sound, I say.

CROMWELL   Would you were half so honest!
Men's prayers then would seek you, not their fears.

GARDINER
I shall remember this bold language.

CROMWELL   Do.
Remember your bold life too.

CHANCELLOR   This is too much.
Forbear, for shame, my lords.

GARDINER   I have done.

CROMWELL   And I.

CHANCELLOR [To Cranmer]
Then thus for you, my lord: it stands agreed,
I take it, by all voices, that forthwith
You be conveyed to the Tower a prisoner,
There to remain till the King's further pleasure
Be known unto us. Are you all agreed, lords?

ALL
We are.

CRANMER   Is there no other way of mercy,
But I must needs to the Tower, my lords?

GARDINER   What other   93
Would you expect? You are strangely troublesome.
Let some o' the guard be ready there.

        Enter the guard.

---

75 find be accorded   **77 load** burden   **78 I cry . . . mercy** I beg your
pardon.   **worst** with least justification   **81 sound** orthodox   **93 must
needs to** must necessarily go to

CRANMER   For me?
  Must I go like a traitor thither?
GARDINER   Receive him,
  And see him safe i' the Tower.
CRANMER   Stay, good my lords,
  I have a little yet to say. Look there, my lords.
                        [He shows the King's ring.]
  By virtue of that ring, I take my cause
  Out of the grips of cruel men and give it   100
  To a most noble judge, the King my master.
CHAMBERLAIN
  This is the King's ring.
SURREY   'Tis no counterfeit.
SUFFOLK
  'Tis the right ring, by heaven! I told ye all,
  When we first put this dangerous stone a-rolling,
  'Twould fall upon ourselves.
NORFOLK   Do you think, my lords,
  The King will suffer but the little finger
  Of this man to be vexed?
CHAMBERLAIN   'Tis now too certain.
  How much more is his life in value with him!   108
  Would I were fairly out on 't!
CROMWELL   My mind gave me,   109
  In seeking tales and informations
  Against this man, whose honesty the devil
  And his disciples only envy at,   112
  Ye blew the fire that burns ye. Now have at ye!   113

    Enter King, frowning on them; takes his seat.

GARDINER
  Dread sovereign, how much are we bound to heaven
  In daily thanks, that gave us such a prince,
  Not only good and wise, but most religious;
  One that in all obedience makes the Church
  The chief aim of his honor, and, to strengthen

100 grips clutches   **108 in value with** valued by.   **him** i.e., the King
109 on 't of it (this trouble).   **gave** told   **112 envy at** hate   **113 have at
ye** i.e., on guard, watch out. (Said as one attacks an opponent.)   **s.d.
Enter King** (The King has presumably come down behind the scene
from above. He enters on the main stage.)

That holy duty out of dear respect,   119
His royal self in judgment comes to hear
The cause betwixt her and this great offender.

KING
You were ever good at sudden commendations,   122
Bishop of Winchester. But know I come not
To hear such flattery now, and in my presence
They are too thin and base to hide offenses.
To me you cannot reach. You play the spaniel,
And think with wagging of your tongue to win me;
But whatsoe'er thou tak'st me for, I'm sure
Thou hast a cruel nature and a bloody.
[*To Cranmer.*] Good man, sit down. [*Cranmer sits.*] Now
    let me see the proudest
He, that dares most, but wag his finger at thee.   131
By all that's holy, he had better starve   132
Than but once think this place becomes thee not.

SURREY
May it please Your Grace—

KING   No, sir, it does not please me.
I had thought I had had men of some understanding
And wisdom of my Council, but I find none.
Was it discretion, lords, to let this man,
This good man—few of you deserve that title—
This honest man, wait like a lousy footboy
At chamber door? And one as great as you are?
Why, what a shame was this! Did my commission
Bid ye so far forget yourselves? I gave ye
Power as he was a councillor to try him,
Not as a groom. There's some of ye, I see,
More out of malice than integrity,
Would try him to the utmost, had ye means,
Which ye shall never have while I live.

CHANCELLOR   Thus far,
My most dread sovereign, may it like Your Grace   148
To let my tongue excuse all. What was purposed
Concerning his imprisonment was rather,
If there be faith in men, meant for his trial

---

119 dear respect heartfelt piety   **122 sudden commendations** unre-
hearsed compliments   **131 He** person   **132 starve** die   **148 like** please

And fair purgation to the world than malice,   152
  I'm sure, in me.

KING   Well, well, my lords, respect him.
  Take him, and use him well; he's worthy of it.
  I will say thus much for him: If a prince
  May be beholding to a subject, I   156
  Am, for his love and service, so to him.
  Make me no more ado, but all embrace him.
  Be friends, for shame, my lords! [*They all embrace*
    Cranmer.] My lord of Canterbury,
  I have a suit which you must not deny me:
  That is, a fair young maid that yet wants baptism;
  You must be godfather and answer for her.

CRANMER
  The greatest monarch now alive may glory
  In such an honor. How may I deserve it,
  That am a poor and humble subject to you?

KING
  Come, come, my lord, you'd spare your spoons. You
    shall have   166
  Two noble partners with you: the old Duchess of Norfolk
  And Lady Marquess Dorset. Will these please you?—
  Once more, my lord of Winchester, I charge you,
  Embrace and love this man.

GARDINER   With a true heart
  And brother-love I do it.   [*He embraces Cranmer.*]

CRANMER   And let heaven
  Witness how dear I hold this confirmation.

KING
  Good man, those joyful tears show thy true heart.
  The common voice, I see, is verified   174
  Of thee, which says thus, "Do my lord of Canterbury
  A shrewd turn, and he's your friend forever."   176
  Come, lords, we trifle time away; I long
  To have this young one made a Christian.
  As I have made ye one, lords, one remain;   179
  So I grow stronger, you more honor gain.   *Exeunt.*

❖

152 purgation clearing of himself   **156 beholding** beholden   **166 you'd
. . . spoons** (Said jestingly; spoons were a common christening gift.)
174 voice report, opinion   **176 shrewd** malicious   **179 one** united in
spirit

5.4   *Noise and tumult within. Enter Porter and his*
            Man.

PORTER   You'll leave your noise anon, ye rascals! Do you   1
  take the court for Paris Garden? Ye rude slaves, leave   2
  your gaping.   3
ONE (*Within*) Good Master Porter, I belong to the larder.   4
PORTER   Belong to the gallows, and be hanged, ye rogue!
  Is this a place to roar in?—Fetch me a dozen crab tree
  staves, and strong ones; these are but switches to 'em.—   7
  I'll scratch your heads. You must be seeing christen-
  ings? Do you look for ale and cakes here, you rude   9
  rascals?
MAN
  Pray, sir, be patient. 'Tis as much impossible—
  Unless we sweep 'em from the door with cannons—
  To scatter 'em as 'tis to make 'em sleep
  On May Day morning, which will never be.   14
  We may as well push against Paul's as stir 'em.   15
PORTER   How got they in, and be hanged?
MAN
  Alas, I know not. How gets the tide in?
  As much as one sound cudgel of four foot—   18
  You see the poor remainder—could distribute,
  I made no spare, sir.
PORTER   You did nothing, sir.   20
MAN
  I am not Samson, nor Sir Guy, nor Colbrand,   21
  To mow 'em down before me; but if I spared any
  That had a head to hit, either young or old,

5.4. Location: London. The palace yard.
1 leave stop. **anon** immediately   **2 Paris Garden** a bear garden on the
Bankside   **3 gaping** shouting   **4 I . . . larder** i.e., I am a servant of the
palace household, in the pantry   **7 to 'em** compared to them, i.e., to
cudgels made of crab tree   **9 ale and cakes** (Refreshments appropriate
to christenings and other festivals.)   **14 May Day morning** (Allusion to
the custom of rising before dawn on May Day for early morning festivities.)   **15 Paul's** Saint Paul's Cathedral   **18 cudgel** club   **20 made no
spare** exercised no frugality   **21 Samson** biblical character of great
strength.   **Sir Guy, Colbrand** (Colbrand was a legendary Danish giant
slain by Guy of Warwick in the popular English romance named after
its hero.)

He or she, cuckold or cuckold maker,
Let me ne'er hope to see a chine again;   25
And that I would not for a cow, God save her!   26

ONE (*Within*) Do you hear, Master Porter?

PORTER I shall be with you presently, good master
puppy.—Keep the door close, sirrah.

MAN What would you have me do?

PORTER What should you do, but knock 'em down by
the dozens? Is this Moorfields to muster in? Or have   32
we some strange Indian with the great tool come to   33
court, the women so besiege us? Bless me, what a fry   34
of fornication is at door! On my Christian conscience, 35
this one christening will beget a thousand; here will
be father, godfather, and all together.

MAN The spoons will be the bigger, sir. There is a fel- 38
low somewhat near the door—he should be a brazier   39
by his face, for, o' my conscience, twenty of the dog   40
days now reign in 's nose; all that stand about him are 41
under the line, they need no other penance. That fire- 42
drake did I hit three times on the head, and three   43
times was his nose discharged against me; he stands
there like a mortar-piece to blow us. There was a   45
haberdasher's wife of small wit near him that railed
upon me till her pinked porringer fell off her head for 47
kindling such a combustion in the state. I missed the   48
meteor once and hit that woman, who cried out   49

---

25 chine backbone; hence a joint of beef or other meat **26 for a cow**
i.e., for anything (*cow* perhaps being suggested by *chine*) **32 Moorfields**
an open space outside London walls, used among other things as a
training ground for the militia **33 tool** genitals. (This sentence alludes
to the Elizabethan excitement over exhibited Indians.) **34–35 fry of
fornication** swarm of would-be fornicators, or of bastards **38 spoons**
i.e., as christening presents. (See 5.3.166.) **39 brazier** worker in brass
40–41 dog days i.e., midsummer, when Sirius, the Dog Star, rises at
about the same time as the sun **42 under the line** on the equator
42–43 firedrake fiery dragon **45 mortar-piece** short cannon. **blow us**
(1) blow us up (2) blow his nose at us **47 pinked porringer** small close-
fitting cap ornamented with perforations **48 combustion** tumult. **in
the state** (1) in the commonwealth (2) in the brazier, whose inflamed
complexion, comically likened here to a miniature cosmos, seems made
up of meteors and discharging cannons **48–49 the meteor** i.e., the red-
faced brazier

"Clubs!" when I might see from far some forty trun- 50
cheoners draw to her succor, which were the hope o' 51
the Strand, where she was quartered. They fell on; I 52
made good my place. At length they came to the 53
broomstaff to me. I defied 'em still, when suddenly a 54
file of boys behind 'em, loose shot, delivered such a 55
shower of pebbles that I was fain to draw mine honor 56
in, and let 'em win the work. The devil was amongst 57
'em, I think, surely.

PORTER   These are the youths that thunder at a playhouse and fight for bitten apples, that no audience
but the tribulation of Tower Hill or the limbs of Lime- 61
house, their dear brothers, are able to endure. I have 62
some of 'em in *Limbo Patrum*, and there they are like 63
to dance these three days, besides the running ban- 64
quet of two beadles that is to come. 65

Enter Lord Chamberlain.

CHAMBERLAIN
Mercy o' me, what a multitude are here!
They grow still too; from all parts they are coming,
As if we kept a fair here! Where are these porters,
These lazy knaves? You've made a fine hand, fellows! 69
There's a trim rabble let in. Are all these 70
Your faithful friends o' the suburbs? We shall have 71
Great store of room, no doubt, left for the ladies, 72
When they pass back from the christening.

---

50 Clubs (The rallying cry for London apprentices to join in or stop a brawl.)   **50–51 truncheoners** men armed with cudgels   **52 Strand** a prosperous street of shops and residences.   **fell on** made their assault   **53 made . . . place** stood my ground   **54 broomstaff** i.e., close quarters   **55 loose shot** throwers or marksmen not attached to a particular company   **56 fain** obliged   **56–57 draw . . . in** i.e., withdraw from the fight   **57 work** fort   **61 tribulation** troublemakers, gang.   **limbs** lads; here, rowdies   **61–62 Limehouse** a dockyard area east of Tower Hill, a rough neighborhood   **63 Limbo Patrum** resting place for the pre-Christian patriarchs who had to remain there until the coming of Christ; hence, prison.   **like** likely   **64 dance** kick their heels   **64–65 running banquet** whipping following imprisonment (like a *banquet* or "dessert" after a meal)   **69 fine hand** fine job. (Said ironically.)   **70 trim** fine. (Said ironically.)   **71 suburbs** areas outside London walls and hence outside its legal jurisdiction   **72 store** plenty

PORTER   An 't please your honor,   73
  We are but men, and what so many may do,
  Not being torn a-pieces, we have done.
  An army cannot rule 'em.
CHAMBERLAIN   As I live,   76
  If the King blame me for 't, I'll lay ye all   77
  By th' heels, and suddenly, and on your heads   78
  Clap round fines for neglect. You're lazy knaves,   79
  And here ye lie baiting of bombards, when   80
  Ye should do service. [*A trumpet.*] Hark, the trumpets
    sound.
  They're come already from the christening.
  Go break among the press, and find a way out   83
  To let the troop pass fairly, or I'll find   84
  A Marshalsea shall hold ye play these two months.   85
PORTER
  Make way there for the Princess!
MAN   You great fellow,
  Stand close up, or I'll make your head ache.
PORTER
  You i' the camlet, get up o' the rail!   88
  I'll peck you o'er the pales else.   *Exeunt.*   89

5.5 *Enter trumpets, sounding; then two Aldermen,*
         Lord Mayor, Garter, Cranmer, Duke of Norfolk
         with his marshal's staff, Duke of Suffolk, two
         noblemen bearing great standing bowls for the
         christening gifts; then four noblemen bearing a
         canopy, under which the Duchess of Norfolk,
         godmother, bearing the child richly habited in

73 An 't if it   **76 rule** control   **77–78 lay . . . heels** put you in the stocks
or in chains   **79 round** heavy   **80 baiting of bombards** drinking from
leathern bottles   **83 press** crowd   **84 troop** royal retinue
85 Marshalsea prison in Southwark.   **hold ye play** keep you engaged
88 camlet a kind of fabric made with goat's hair. (Since no "crowd" is
onstage, the Porter may be speaking to his audience here as though it
were crowding to see the christening.)   **89 peck** pitch.   **pales** palings,
fence

5.5. Location: London. The royal court.
s.d. Garter Garter King at Arms, a chief herald of the College of Arms

a mantle, etc., train borne by a lady; then
follows the Marchioness Dorset, the other
godmother, and ladies. The troop pass once
about the stage, and Garter speaks.

GARTER Heaven, from thy endless goodness, send
   prosperous life, long, and ever happy, to the high and
   mighty Princess of England, Elizabeth!

   Flourish. Enter King and guard.

CRANMER [*Kneeling*]
   And to your royal Grace and the good Queen,
   My noble partners and myself thus pray
   All comfort, joy, in this most gracious lady
   Heaven ever laid up to make parents happy   7
   May hourly fall upon ye!
KING
   Thank you, good Lord Archbishop.
   What is her name?
CRANMER   Elizabeth.
KING   Stand up, lord.
         [*Cranmer rises. The King kisses the child.*]
   With this kiss take my blessing. God protect thee,
   Into whose hand I give thy life.
CRANMER   Amen.
KING
   My noble gossips, you've been too prodigal.   13
   I thank ye heartily; so shall this lady,
   When she has so much English.
CRANMER   Let me speak, sir,
   For heaven now bids me; and the words I utter
   Let none think flattery, for they'll find 'em truth.
   This royal infant—heaven still move about her!—   18
   Though in her cradle, yet now promises
   Upon this land a thousand thousand blessings,
   Which time shall bring to ripeness. She shall be—
   But few now living can behold that goodness—
   A pattern to all princes living with her,

7 laid up provided   **13 gossips** godparents   **18 still** ever

And all that shall succeed. Saba was never　　　　24
More covetous of wisdom and fair virtue
Than this pure soul shall be. All princely graces
That mold up such a mighty piece as this is,　　　27
With all the virtues that attend the good,
Shall still be doubled on her. Truth shall nurse her,
Holy and heavenly thoughts still counsel her.
She shall be loved and feared. Her own shall bless her;　31
Her foes shake like a field of beaten corn,　　　32
And hang their heads with sorrow. Good grows with her.
In her days every man shall eat in safety
Under his own vine what he plants, and sing
The merry songs of peace to all his neighbors.
God shall be truly known, and those about her
From her shall read the perfect ways of honor　　38
And by those claim their greatness, not by blood.　39
Nor shall this peace sleep with her; but as when　40
The bird of wonder dies, the maiden phoenix,　　41
Her ashes new-create another heir
As great in admiration as herself,　　　　43
So shall she leave her blessedness to one,　　　44
When heaven shall call her from this cloud of darkness,　45
Who from the sacred ashes of her honor
Shall starlike rise, as great in fame as she was,
And so stand fixed. Peace, plenty, love, truth, terror,　48
That were the servants to this chosen infant,
Shall then be his, and like a vine grow to him.
Wherever the bright sun of heaven shall shine,
His honor and the greatness of his name
Shall be, and make new nations. He shall flourish,
And like a mountain cedar reach his branches
To all the plains about him. Our children's children
Shall see this and bless heaven.

KING　　　　　　　　　　　　Thou speakest wonders.

---

24 Saba i.e., the Queen of Sheba, who visited Solomon to discover wisdom from him; see 1 Kings 10:1–10　**27 mighty piece** princely person　**31 own** i.e., own people　**32 beaten corn** wind-beaten grain　**38 read** learn　**39 greatness** nobility　**40 sleep** i.e., die　**41 phoenix** mythical bird believed to rise from its own ashes; a symbol of regeneration　**43 great in admiration** greatly wondered at　**44 she** i.e., Elizabeth.　**one** i.e., King James I　**45 cloud of darkness** i.e., mortal life　**48 terror** quality inspiring awe

CRANMER

> She shall be, to the happiness of England,
> An agèd princess; many days shall see her,
> And yet no day without a deed to crown it.   59
> Would I had known no more! But she must die,
> She must, the saints must have her; yet a virgin,
> A most unspotted lily shall she pass
> To th' ground, and all the world shall mourn her.

KING   O Lord Archbishop,

> Thou hast made me now a man! Never, before
> This happy child, did I get anything.   66
> This oracle of comfort has so pleased me
> That when I am in heaven I shall desire
> To see what this child does, and praise my Maker.
> I thank ye all. To you, my good Lord Mayor,
> And you, good brethren, I am much beholding;   71
> I have received much honor by your presence,
> And ye shall find me thankful. Lead the way, lords.
> Ye must all see the Queen, and she must thank ye;
> She will be sick else. This day, no man think   75
> H'as business at his house; for all shall stay.   76
> This little one shall make it holiday.   *Exeunt.*

❖

●

---

59 deed good deed   **66 get** beget; achieve   **71 beholding** beholden
75 sick unhappy   **76 H'as** (that) he has.   **stay** i.e., cease work

Epilogue   [*Enter the Epilogue.*]

EPILOGUE
   'Tis ten to one this play can never please
   All that are here. Some come to take their ease,
   And sleep an act or two; but those, we fear,
   We've frighted with our trumpets; so, 'tis clear,
   They'll say 'tis naught. Others to hear the city   5
   Abused extremely, and to cry "That's witty!"
   Which we have not done neither; that I fear   7
   All the expected good we're like to hear   8
   For this play at this time is only in
   The merciful construction of good women,   10
   For such a one we showed 'em. If they smile
   And say 'twill do, I know, within a while
   All the best men are ours; for 'tis ill hap   13
   If they hold when their ladies bid 'em clap. [*Exit.*]   14

Epilogue.
5 naught worthless **7 that** so that **8 expected good** anticipated approval, applause **10 construction** interpretation **13 ill hap** bad luck
14 hold hold back

Date and Text

The Famous History of the Life of King Henry the Eighth was first printed in the First Folio of 1623. The text is a good one, set from a careful transcript of Shakespeare's own manuscript. The stage directions are unusually elaborate. The first recorded performance was on June 29, 1613. A letter of July 2 in that year from Sir Henry Wotton to Sir Edmund Bacon tells of a performance of "a new play, called *All Is True*, representing some principal pieces of the reign of Henry VIII." During this performance, as King Henry was arriving as a masker at the house of Cardinal Wolsey (1.4), "certain chambers [cannons] being shot off at his entry, some of the paper, or other stuff, wherewith one of them was stopped, did light on the thatch, where being thought at first but an idle smoke, and their eyes more attentive to the show, it kindled inwardly, and ran round like a train, consuming within less than an hour the whole house to the very grounds." The identification of this *All Is True* with Shakespeare's play is certain. Other accounts include a letter from Thomas Lorkin to Sir Thomas Puckering, June 1613, asserting the fire to have started "while Burbage his company were acting at the Globe the play of Henry VIII," a letter of 8 July from John Chamberlain to Sir Ralph Winwood, and an account in John Stow's *Annals* as continued by Edmund Howe (1618).

Wotton calls it a new play, and stylistic considerations confirm this characterization. The play may also have helped provide entertainment for the betrothal and marriage of James I's daughter Elizabeth to the Elector Palatine earlier in 1613, though *Henry VIII* is not listed among the many plays acted on this occasion.

On the controversy over John Fletcher's purported share in the authorship of *Henry VIII*, see the play's Introduction.

Textual Notes

These textual notes are not a historical collation, either of the early folios or of more recent editions; they are simply a record of departures in this edition from the copy text. The reading adopted in this edition appears in boldface, followed by the rejected reading from the copy text, i.e., the First Folio. Only major alterations in punctuation are noted. Changes in lineation are not indicated, nor are some minor and obvious typographical errors.

Abbreviations used:
F the First Folio
s.d. stage direction
s.p. speech prefix

Copy text: the First Folio.

1.1. 42–45 All . . . function [assigned in F to Buckingham]   **47 as you guess** [assigned in F to Norfolk]   **63 'a** O   **69–70 that? . . . hell, the** that, . . . Hell? The   **115 s.p. [and elsewhere] Wolsey** Car   **120 venom** venom'd   **200 Hereford** Hertford   **219 Perk** Pecke   **chancellor** Councellour   **221 Nicholas** Michaell   **226 lord** Lords

1.2. 8 s.d. [F: A noyse within crying roome for the Queene, usher'd by the Duke of Norfolke. Enter the Queene, Norfolke and Suffolke: she kneels.] [etc.]   **9 s.p. [and elsewhere] Katharine** Queen   **67 business** basenesse   **156 feared** feare   **164 confession's** Commissions   **170 To gain** To   **180 him** this   **190 Bulmer** Blumer

1.3. s.d. Sands Sandys [elsewhere both **Sands** and **Sandys**]   **13 Or** A   **15 s.d.** [at. l. 16 in F]   **34 oui** wee   **59 wherewithal: in him** wherewithall in him;   **66 [and at 1.4. s.d. and elsewhere] Guildford** Guilford

1.4. 50 s.d. [at l. 49 in F]

2.1. 18 have him   **20 Perk** Pecke   **86 mark** make

2.2. 1 s.p. Chamberlain [not in F]

2.3. 61 of you of you, to you

2.4. 11 s.p. Katharine [not in F]   **125 s.p. Griffith** Gent. Ush   **131 s.d. Exeunt** Exit   **172 A** And

3.1. 3 s.p. Gentlewoman [not in F]   **23 s.d. Campeius** Campian   **61 your** our

3.2. 143 glad gald   **172 filed** fill'd   **293 Who** Whom   **344 Chattels** Castles

4.1. 20 s.p. Second Gentleman 1   **34 Kimbolton** Kymmalton   **55 s.p. First Gentleman** [not in F]   **101 Stokesley** Stokeley

4.2. 7 think thanke

5.1. 37 time Lime   **55 s.d. Exeunt** Exit [at l. 54 in F]   **78 s.d.** [at l. 79 in F]   **139 precipice** Precepit   **140 woo** woe   **157 s.p. Lovell** Gent

5.2. 4 s.d. Keeper [after "Sure you know me?" in F]   **8 piece** Peere

5.3. 86, 87 s.p. Chancellor Cham   **133 this** his   **173 heart** hearts
5.4. 4, 27 s.p. One [not in F]
5.5. 38 ways way

Shakespeare's Sources

Shakespeare's chief source for the first four acts of *Henry VIII*, as for many of his earlier history plays, was Raphael Holinshed's *Chronicles* (1587 edition). Holinshed presented him with conflicting views of Cardinal Wolsey, however, and traces of the conflict remain in Shakespeare's play. Much of Holinshed is actually a compilation of the writings of earlier historiographers. In this case, some of Holinshed's material is from the bitterly anti-Wolseyan *Anglica Historia* (1534) of Polydore Vergil. Accordingly, Holinshed gives decidedly unfavorable interpretations of Wolsey's animosity toward the Duke of Buckingham and his unscrupulous meddling in the question of the King's marriage. Vergil was particularly distressed by the way in which Katharine had been shabbily treated; he (and Holinshed) report her speeches in her own behalf with manifest approval. Shakespeare preserves this alignment of sympathies in which Katharine is the wrongly accused wife and Wolsey the scheming Machiavel.

Other portions of Holinshed, on the other hand, derive from George Cavendish's *The Life and Death of Thomas Wolsey*, written some time around 1557 and extensively used by the chroniclers, though not separately printed until 1641. Cavendish was a gentleman usher in the household of Cardinal Wolsey from 1526 to 1530. Although he moralizes about the lesson to be learned from Wolsey's ambitious rise and sudden fall, Cavendish speaks admiringly of the Cardinal as an extraordinarily great man. He captures in minutely observed detail the magnificence of Wolsey's prosperous estate. He gives a moving portrait of Wolsey after his fall, on his sickbed and near the end, saying to a companion: "If I had served God as diligently as I have done the King, he would not have given me over in my gray hairs." This passage, borrowed verbatim by Holinshed from Cavendish, produces in turn the famous lines from Shakespeare: "Had I but served my God with half the zeal / I served my king, he would not in mine age / Have left me naked to mine enemies" (3.2.456–458).

For his fifth act, Shakespeare turned to John Foxe's *Acts*

and Monuments of Martyrs (1583 edition). Here he encountered a particularly rabid Protestant point of view, which
has left its impression not only on the fifth act but on portrayals of Wolsey (whom Foxe naturally deplored) in earlier
scenes. Foxe's hero, Thomas Cranmer, emerges as the victor of Shakespeare's play. Although the triumphantly Protestant ending contrasts oddly with Shakespeare's earlier
manifest sympathy for Queen Katharine, the duality of attitudes is somehow plausible and perhaps even typically
Elizabethan: Katharine suffered lamentably, and Henry
and Wolsey treated her shabbily, but these great events
did after all lead to the English Reformation and the
rule of Queen Elizabeth. The ambiguity so often noted in
Henry VIII, then, is an essential part of Shakespeare's
sources, not merely because he used conflicting accounts
but because many Elizabethan Englishmen necessarily felt
mixed emotions toward this chapter of their past.

   Shakespeare may also have read in Edward Hall's *The
Union of the Two Noble and Illustre Families of Lancaster
and York* (1542), and in John Speed's *History of Great Britain* (1611). In addition, he probably knew a dramatic version of the reign of Henry VIII that had appeared about
eight years before, *When You See Me You Know Me* by Samuel Rowley (1603–1605).

The Third Volume of Chronicles (1587 edition)
Compiled by Raphael Holinshed

HENRY THE SEVENTH

[In his account of the reign of Henry VII, Holinshed tells a
story very much like that in which a secret account of Cardinal Wolsey's great wealth is inadvertently delivered into
the hands of King Henry VIII; see *Henry VIII*, 3.2.121 ff.
The blunderer in this present story is Thomas Ruthall,
made Bishop of Durham in 1508 by Henry VII and commissioned by him to write "a book of the whole estate of the
kingdom."]

Afterwards, the King commanded Cardinal Wolsey to go to
this bishop and to bring the book away with him to deliver

to His Majesty. But see the mishap! That a man in all other things so provident should now be so negligent, and at that time most forget himself when, as it after fell out, he had most need to have remembered himself. For this bishop, having written two books, the one to answer the King's command and the other entreating of[1] his own private affairs, did bind them both after one sort in vellum, just of one length, breadth, and thickness, and in all points in such like proportion answering one another as the one could not by any especial note be discerned from the other, both which he also laid up together in one place of his study.

Now when the Cardinal came to demand the book due to the King, the Bishop unadvisedly commanded his servant to bring him the book bound in white vellum lying in his study in such a place. The servant, doing accordingly, brought forth one of those books so bound, being the book entreating of the state of the Bishop, and delivered the same unto his master, who, receiving it, without further consideration or looking on gave it to the Cardinal to bear unto the King. The Cardinal, having the book, went from the Bishop, and after, in his study by himself, understanding the contents thereof, he greatly rejoiced, having now occasion (which he long sought for) offered unto him to bring the Bishop into the King's disgrace.

Wherefore he went forthwith to the King, delivered the book into his hands, and briefly informed the King of the contents thereof; putting further into the King's head that if at any time he were destitute of a mass of money, he should not need to seek further therefor than to the coffers of the Bishop, who by the tenor of his own book had accounted his proper riches and substance to the value of a hundred thousand pounds. Of all which when the Bishop had intelligence . . . he was stricken with such grief of the same that he shortly through extreme sorrow ended his life at London.

HENRY THE EIGHTH

[Beginning his account of the reign of Henry VIII in 1509, Holinshed comes at length to 1519–1520 and the handing over of Tournai to the French King.]

1 entreating of dealing with

During this time remained in the French court divers young gentlemen of England, and they with the French King rode daily disguised through Paris, throwing eggs, stones, and other foolish trifles at the people; which light demeanor of a king was much discommended and jested at. And when these young gentlemen came again into England, they were all French in eating, drinking, and apparel, yea, and in French vices and brags, so that all the estates[2] of England were by them laughed at. The ladies and gentlewomen were dispraised, so that nothing by them was praised but if it were after the French turn, which after turned them to displeasure, as you shall hear. . . .

Then the King's Council caused the Lord Chamberlain to call before them divers of the privy chamber, which had been in the French court, and banished them the court for divers considerations, laying nothing particularly to their charges, and they that had offices were commanded to go to their offices. Which discharge out of court grieved sore the hearts of these young men, which were called the King's minions. . . .

The King specially rebuked Sir William Bulmer, knight, because he, being his servant sworn, refused the King's service and became servant to the Duke of Buckingham. . . .

The French King,[3] desirous to continue the friendship lately begun betwixt him and the King of England, made means unto the Cardinal that they might in some convenient place come to an interview together, that he might have further knowledge of King Henry and likewise King Henry of him. But the fame[4] went that the Cardinal desired greatly, of himself, that the two Kings might meet, who, measuring by his will what was convenient, thought it should make much with his glory if in France also at some high assembly of noblemen he should be seen in his vain pomp and show of dignity. He therefore breaketh with the King of that matter, declaring how honorable, necessary, and convenient it should be for him to gratify his friend[5] therein; and thus with his persuasions the King began to conceive an earnest desire to see the French King, and

---

2 estates noblemen **3 French King** i.e., Francis I **4 fame** rumor **5 his friend** i.e., Francis I

thereupon appointed to go over to Calais and so in the marches[6] of Guînes to meet with him. . . .

Herewith were letters written to all such lords, ladies, gentlemen, and gentlewomen which should give their attendance on the King and Queen, which incontinently[7] put themselves in a readiness after the most sumptuous sort. Also it was appointed that the King of England and the French King, in a camp between Ardres and Guînes, with eighteen aides, should in June next ensuing abide all comers, being gentlemen, at the tilt, at tourney, and at barriers. . . .[8]

Moreover, now that it was concluded that the Kings of England and France should meet, as ye have heard, then both the Kings committed the order and manner of their meeting, and how many days the same should continue, and what preeminence each should give to other, unto the Cardinal of York, which, to set all things in a certainty, made an instrument containing an order and direction concerning the premises by him devised and appointed.

[Holinshed prints the instrument of direction made by Cardinal Wolsey.]

The peers of the realm, receiving letters to prepare themselves to attend the King in this journey and no apparent necessary cause expressed why nor wherefore, seemed to grudge that such a costly journey should be taken in hand, to their importunate charges and expenses, without consent of the whole board of the Council. But namely[9] the Duke of Buckingham, being a man of a lofty courage but not most liberal,[10] sore repined that he should be at so great charges for his furniture forth[11] at this time, saying that he knew not for what cause so much money should be spent about the sight of a vain talk to be had and communication to be ministered of things of no importance. Wherefore he

---

6 marches boundaries, frontiers   **7 incontinently** immediately
8 barriers military exercises named for the railings down the center of the tilting or tournament arena, on opposite sides of which the combatants rode toward one another. (The date is 1520.)   **9 namely** especially
10 of a . . . liberal of great spirit but not generous   **11 charges . . . forth** expenses to furnish himself for the event

sticked[12] not to say that it was an intolerable matter to obey such a vile and importunate person.

The Duke indeed could not abide the Cardinal, and specially he had of late conceived an inward malice against him for Sir William Bulmer's cause, whose trouble was only procured by the Cardinal, who first caused him to be cast in prison. Now such grievous words as the Duke thus uttered against him came to the Cardinal's ear, whereupon he cast beforehand all ways possible to have him in a trip, that he might cause him to leap headless.[13] But because he doubted[14] his friends, kinsmen, and allies, and chiefly the Earl of Surrey, Lord Admiral, which had married the Duke's daughter, he thought good first to send him somewhither out of the way lest he might cast a trump[15] in his way. There was great enmity betwixt the Cardinal and the Earl for that, on a time, when the Cardinal took upon him to check the Earl, he had like to have[16] thrust his dagger into the Cardinal.

At length there was occasion offered him to compass his purpose, by occasion of the Earl of Kildare his coming out of Ireland. For the Cardinal . . . accused him to the King of that he had not borne himself uprightly in his office in Ireland, where he was the King's lieutenant. Such accusations were framed against him, when no bribes would come, that he was committed to prison, and then by the Cardinal's good preferment the Earl of Surrey was sent into Ireland as the King's deputy in lieu of the said Earl of Kildare, there to remain rather as an exile than as lieutenant to the King, even at the Cardinal's pleasure, as he himself well perceived. . . .

Now it chanced that the Duke, coming to London with his train of men to attend the King into France, went before into Kent unto a manor place which he had there. And whilst he stayed in that country till the King set forward, grievous complaints were exhibited to him by his farmers and tenants against Charles Knevet, his surveyor,[17] for such bribing as he had used there amongst them. Whereupon the Duke

12 **sticked** hesitated   13 **to have him . . . headless** to trip him (the Duke) up in such a way as to cause him to be beheaded   14 **doubted** feared   15 **trump** i.e., obstruction. (The metaphor is from card playing.)   16 **check . . . he had like to have** rebuke . . . he nearly   17 **surveyor** overseer

took such displeasure against him that he deprived him of his office, not knowing how that in so doing he procured his own destruction, as after appeared.

[The Emperor Charles V visits England in May 1520 to see his aunt, the Queen, "of whom ye may be sure he was most joyfully received and welcomed."]

The chief cause that moved the Emperor to come thus on land at this time was to persuade[18] that by word of mouth which he had before done most earnestly by letters; which was, that the King should not meet with the French King at any interview. For he doubted lest, if the King of England and the French King should grow into some great friendship and faithful bond of amity, it might turn him to displeasure.[19]

But now that he perceived how the King was forward on his journey, he did what he could to procure that no trust should be committed to the fair words of the Frenchmen; and that, if it were possible, the great friendship that was now in breeding betwixt the two Kings might be dissolved. And forsomuch as he knew the Lord Cardinal to be won with rewards, as a fish with a bait, he bestowed on him great gifts and promised him much more so that he would be his friend and help to bring his purpose to pass. The Cardinal . . . promised to the Emperor that he would so use the matter as his purpose should be sped.[20]

[King Henry sails from Dover in late May and early June 1520 for his meeting with King Francis I at the Field of the Cloth of Gold.]

The day of the meeting was appointed to be on the Thursday, the seventh of June, upon which day the two Kings met in the vale of Andren, accompanied with such a number of the nobility of both realms, so richly appointed in apparel and costly jewels, as chains, collars of S's, and other the like ornaments to set forth their degrees and estates, that a

18 persuade urge   **19 turn him to displeasure** i.e., cause him, the Emperor, trouble and sorrow   **20 as his . . . sped** so that his, the Emperor's, purpose should prosper

wonder it was to behold and view them in their order and
rooms,[21] which every man kept according to his appointment.

The two Kings meeting in the field, either saluted other in
most loving wise, first on horseback, and after alighting on
foot eftsoons[22] embraced with courteous words, to the great
rejoicing of the beholders; and after they had thus saluted
each other, they went both together into a rich tent of cloth
of gold there set up for the purpose, in the which they
passed the time in pleasant talk, banqueting, and loving devices till it drew toward the evening, and then departed for
that night, the one to Guînes, the other to Ardres.

[Holinshed gives a long description of the tilting, in which
all did "right valiantly," but "the two Kings surmounted all
the rest in prowess and valiantness."]

On Monday, the eighteenth of June, was such an hideous
storm of wind and weather that many conjectured it did
prognosticate trouble and hatred shortly after to follow between princes.

[In 1521, some months after King Henry's return to England, trouble breaks out between Wolsey and Buckingham.]

The Cardinal, boiling in hatred against the Duke of Buckingham and thirsting for his blood, devised to make Charles
Knevet, that had been the Duke's surveyor and put from
him[23] (as ye have heard), an instrument to bring the Duke to
destruction. This Knevet, being had in examination before
the Cardinal, disclosed all the Duke's life. And first he uttered that the Duke was accustomed, by way of talk, to say
how he meant so to use the matter that he would attain to
the crown if King Henry chanced to die without issue; and
that he had talk and conference of that matter on a time
with George Neville, Lord of Abergavenny, unto whom he
had given his daughter in marriage; and also that he threatened to punish the Cardinal for his manifold misdoings, being without cause his mortal enemy.

21 rooms places   **22 eftsoons** immediately   **23 put from him** dismissed

The Cardinal, having gotten that which he sought for, encouraged, comforted, and procured[24] Knevet, with many comfortable words and great promises, that he should with a bold spirit and countenance object and lay these things to the Duke's charge, with more if he knew it when time required. Then Knevet, partly provoked with desire to be revenged and partly moved with hope of reward, openly confessed that the Duke had once fully determined to devise means how to make the King away, being brought into a full hope that he should be king by a vain prophecy which one Nicholas Hopkins, a monk of an house of the Chartreux order beside Bristol, called Henton, sometime his confessor, had opened[25] unto him.

The Cardinal, having thus taken the examination of Knevet, went unto the King and declared unto him that his person was in danger by such traitorous purpose as the Duke of Buckingham had conceived in his heart, and showed how that[26] now there is manifest tokens of his wicked pretense;[27] wherefore he exhorted the King to provide for his own surety with speed. The King, hearing the accusation enforced to the uttermost by the Cardinal, made this answer: "If the Duke have deserved to be punished, let him have according to his deserts." The Duke hereupon was sent for up to London and, at his coming thither, was straightways attached[28] and brought to the Tower by Sir Henry Marney, Captain of the Guard, the sixteenth of April. There was also attached the foresaid Chartreux monk, Master John de la Car alias de la Court, the Duke's confessor, and Sir Gilbert Perke, priest, the Duke's chancellor.[29]

After the apprehension of the Duke, inquisitions were taken in divers shires of England of him, so that by the knights and gentlemen he was indicted of high treason for certain words spoken (as before ye have heard) by the same Duke at Blechingley to the Lord of Abergavenny; and therewith was the same lord attached for concealment, and so likewise was the Lord Montacute, and both led to the Tower.

[Holinshed gives the counts in the indictment of Buckingham for high treason, including the following:]

24 **procured** induced   25 **opened** revealed, expounded   26 **showed how that** explained how   27 **pretense** intent   28 **attached** arrested
29 **chancellor** secretary

. . . the same Duke . . . said unto one Charles Knevet, esquire, after that the King had reproved the Duke for retaining William Bulmer, knight, into his service, that if he had
perceived that he should have been committed to the Tower
(as he doubted[30] he should have been), he would have so
wrought that the principal doers therein should not have
had cause of great rejoicing, for he would have played the
part which his father intended to have put in practice
against King Richard the Third at Salisbury, who made earnest suit to have come unto the presence of the same King
Richard; which suit if he might have obtained, he, having a
knife secretly about him, would have thrust it into the body
of King Richard as he had made semblance to kneel down
before him. And in speaking these words, he maliciously
laid his hand upon his dagger and said that, if he were so
evil used, he would do his best to accomplish his pretensed[31] purpose, swearing to confirm his word by the
blood of our Lord.

Besides all this, the same Duke . . . at London in a place
called the Rose, within the parish of St. Lawrence Poultney,
in Canwick Street Ward, demanded of the said Charles
Knevet, esquire, what was the talk amongst the Londoners
concerning the King's journey beyond the seas? And the
said Charles told him that many stood in doubt[32] of that
journey, lest the Frenchmen meant some deceit towards the
King. Whereto the Duke answered that it was to be feared
lest it would come to pass, according to the words of a certain holy monk. "For there is," saith he, "a Chartreux
monk that divers times hath sent to me, willing me to send
unto him my chancellor; and I did send unto him John de la
Court, my chaplain, unto whom he would not declare anything till de la Court had sworn unto him to keep all things
secret and to tell no creature living what he should hear of
him, except it were to me.

"And then the said monk told de la Court that neither the
King nor his heirs should prosper and that I should endeavor myself to purchase the good wills of the commonalty of England, for I, the same Duke, and my blood should
prosper and have the rule of the realm of England." Then
said Charles Knevet, "The monk may be deceived through

30 doubted feared   **31 pretensed** intended   **32 doubt** fear

the devil's illusion," and that it was evil to meddle with such matters. "Well," said the Duke, "it cannot hurt me," and so (saith the indictment) the Duke seemed to rejoice in the monk's words. And further, at the same time, the Duke told the said Charles that, if the King had miscarried now in his last sickness, he would have chopped off the heads of the Cardinal, of Sir Thomas Lovell, knight, and of others; and also said that he had rather die for it than to be used as he had been.

[Popular opinion blames the Cardinal for Buckingham's fall.]

I trust I may without offense say that, as the rumor then went, the Cardinal chiefly procured the death of this nobleman, no less favored and beloved of the people of this realm in that season than the Cardinal himself was hated and envied. Which thing caused the Duke's fall the more to be pitied and lamented, sith[33] he was the man of all other that chiefly went about to cross the Cardinal in his lordly demeanor and heady proceedings. But to the purpose. Shortly after that the Duke had been indicted, as before ye have heard, he was arraigned in Westminster Hall, before the Duke of Norfolk. . . . When the lords had taken their place, the Duke was brought to the bar, and upon his arraignment pleaded not guilty and put himself upon[34] his peers. Then was his indictment read, which the Duke denied to be true and, as he was an eloquent man, alleged reasons to falsify[35] the indictment, pleading the matter for his own justification very pithily and earnestly. The King's attorney, against the Duke's reasons, alleged the examinations, confessions, and proofs of witnesses.

The Duke desired that the witnesses might be brought forth. And then came before him Charles Knevet, Perke, de la Court, and Hopkins the monk of the priory of the Charterhouse beside Bath, which like a false hypocrite had induced the Duke to the treason with his false, forged prophecies. Divers presumptions[36] and accusations were

---

33 sith since **34 put himself upon** submitted his case to **35 falsify** confute, prove false **36 presumptions** inferences, allegations

laid unto him by Charles Knevet, which he would fain have covered.[37] The depositions were read and the deponents delivered as prisoners to the officers of the Tower.

[Buckingham is commanded to withdraw. The peers confer and find him guilty by vote of all the lords present.]

The Duke was brought to the bar sore chafing, and sweat marvelously; and after he had made his reverence, he paused awhile. The Duke of Norfolk, as judge, said: "Sir Edward, you have heard how you be indicted of high treason. You pleaded thereto not guilty, putting yourself to the peers of the realm, which have found you guilty." Then the Duke of Norfolk wept and said, "You shall be led to the King's prison and there laid on a hurdle[38] and so drawn to the place of execution, and there be hanged, cut down alive, your members cut off and cast into the fire, your bowels burnt before you, your head smitten off, and your body quartered and divided at the King's will, and God have mercy on your soul. Amen."

The Duke of Buckingham said: "My lord of Norfolk, you have said as a traitor should be said unto, but I was never any; but, my lords, I nothing malign for that you have done to me, but the eternal God forgive you my death, and I do. I shall never sue to the King for life, howbeit he is a gracious prince, and more grace may come from him than I desire. I desire you, my lords and all my fellows, to pray for me." Then was the edge of the ax turned towards him and he led into a barge. Sir Thomas Lovell desired him to sit on the cushions and carpet ordained for him. He said, "Nay, for when I went to Westminster I was Duke of Buckingham; now I am but Edward Bohun, the most caitiff[39] of the world." Thus they landed at the Temple, where received him Sir Nicholas Vaux and Sir William Sands, baronets, and led him through the city, who desired ever the people to pray for him, of whom some wept and lamented.

[Buckingham is led to the scaffold on Tower Hill, May 17, 1521.]

---

37 fain have covered gladly have concealed   **38 hurdle** frame or sledge for dragging prisoners to execution   **39 caitiff** wretched, miserable

He said he had offended the King's Grace through negligence and lack of grace, and desired all noblemen to beware by him and all men to pray for him and that he trusted to die the King's true man. Thus meekly with an ax he took his death.

[Holinshed takes this occasion to provide "A convenient collection concerning the High Constables of England, which office ceased and took end at the Duke of Buckingham above-mentioned." The present duke and his father are thus the last of the line.]

Henry Stafford . . . was High Constable of England and Duke of Buckingham. This man, raising war against Richard the Third usurping the crown, was in the first year of the reign of the said Richard . . . betrayed by his man Humphrey Banister (to whom being in distress he fled for succor) and . . . was beheaded without arraignment or judgment. . . .

Edward Stafford, son to Henry, Duke of Buckingham, being also Duke of Buckingham after the death of his father, was Constable of England, Earl of Hereford, Stafford, and Northampton, being in the first year of Henry the Seventh, in the year of our redemption 1485, restored to his father's dignities and possessions. He is termed . . . to be the flower and mirror of all courtesy. This man (as before is touched) was by Henry the Seventh restored to his father's inheritance, in recompense of the loss of his father's life.

[Some years later, in 1525, Cardinal Wolsey uses the King's determination to make war in France as his excuse for devising new and unpopular taxes.]

Wherefore by the Cardinal there was devised strange[40] commissions and sent in the end of March into every shire . . . that the sixth part of every man's substance should be paid in money or plate to the King without delay for the furniture[41] of his war. Hereof followed such cursing, weeping, and exclamation against both King and Cardinal that pity it was to hear. . . .

40 strange unprecedented **41 furniture** equipping

The Duke of Suffolk, sitting in commission about this subsidy in Suffolk, persuaded by courteous means the rich clothiers to assent thereto; but when they came home and went about to discharge and put from them their spinners, carders, fullers, weavers, and other artificers, which they kept in work aforetime, the people began to assemble in companies. . . . The rage of the people increased. . . . And herewith there assembled together after the manner of rebels four thousand men. . . .

The King then came to Westminster to the Cardinal's palace, and assembled there a great Council, in the which he openly protested that his mind was never to ask anything of his commons which might sound to the breach of his laws, wherefore he willed to know by whose means the commissions were so strictly given forth, to demand the sixth part of every man's goods.

The Cardinal excused himself and said that . . . by the consent of the whole Council it was done, and took God to witness that he never desired the hindrance of the commons, but like a true councillor devised how to enrich the King. The King indeed was much offended that his commons were thus entreated and thought it touched his honor that his Council should attempt such a doubtful matter in his name and to be denied both of the spirituality and temporality. Therefore he would no more of that trouble, but caused letters to be sent into all shires that the matter should no further be talked of; and he pardoned all them that had denied the demand openly or secretly. The Cardinal, to deliver himself of the evil will of the commons purchased by procuring and advancing of this demand, affirmed and caused it to be bruited[42] abroad that through his intercession the King had pardoned and released all things.

[Some two years later, in 1527, rumors circulate about King Henry's marriage.]

There rose a secret bruit in London that the King's confessor, Dr. Longland, and divers other great clerks had told the King that the marriage between him and the Lady Kath-

42 **bruited** rumored

arine, late wife to his brother Prince Arthur, was not lawful; whereupon the King should sue a divorce and marry the Duchess of Alençon, sister to the French King, at the town of Calais this summer; and that the Viscount Rochford had brought with him the picture of the said lady. The King was offended with those tales and sent for Sir Thomas Seymour, Mayor of the city of London, secretly charging him to see that the people ceased from such talk. . . .

The truth is that, whether this doubt was first moved by the Cardinal or by the said Longland, being the King's confessor, the King was not only brought in doubt whether it was a lawful marriage or no but also determined to have the case examined, cleared, and adjudged by learning, law, and sufficient authority. The Cardinal verily was put in most blame for this scruple now cast into the King's conscience for the hate he bare to the Emperor because he would not grant to him the archbishopric of Toledo, for the which he was a suitor. And therefore he did not only procure the King of England to join in friendship with the French King but also sought a divorce betwixt the King and the Queen that the King might have had in marriage the Duchess of Alençon, sister unto the French King; and, as some have thought, he travailed[43] in that matter with the French King at Amiens; but the Duchess would not give ear thereunto.

But howsoever it came about that the King was thus troubled in conscience concerning his marriage, this followed, that, like a wise and sage prince, to have the doubt clearly removed, he called together the best learned of the realm, which were of several opinions. Wherefore he thought to know the truth by indifferent judges, lest peradventure the Spaniards and other also in favor of the Queen would say that his own subjects were not indifferent[44] judges in this behalf. And therefore he wrote his cause to Rome and also sent to all the universities in Italy and France and to the great clerks of all Christendom to know their opinions, and desired the court of Rome to send into his realm a legate, which should be indifferent and of a great and profound judgment, to hear the cause debated. At whose request the whole consistory of the College of Rome sent thither

43 travailed labored **44 indifferent** impartial

Laurence Campeius, a priest cardinal, a man of great wit and experience . . . and with him was joined in commission the Cardinal of York and legate of England. . . .

The place where the cardinals should sit to hear the cause of matrimony betwixt the King and the Queen was ordained to be at the Blackfriars in London, where in the great hall was preparation made of seats, tables, and other furniture according to such a solemn session and royal appearance. The court was platted in tables and benches in manner of a consistory,[45] one seat raised higher for the judges to sit in. Then, as it were in the midst of the said judges, aloft above them three degrees high was a cloth of estate[46] hanged, with a chair royal under the same, wherein sat the King, and besides him, some distance from him, sat the Queen, and under the judges' feet sat the scribes and other officers. The chief scribe was Doctor Steevens,[47] and the caller of the court was one Cook of Winchester.

Then before the King and the judges within the court sat the Archbishop of Canterbury, Warham, and all the other bishops. . . . The judges commanded silence whilst their commission was read both to the court and to the people assembled. That done, the scribes commanded the crier to call the King by the name of "King Henry of England, come into the court," etc. With that the King answered and said, "Here." Then called he the Queen by the name of "Katharine, Queen of England, come into the court," etc.; who made no answer, but rose out of her chair.

And because she could not come to the King directly, for the distance severed between them, she went about by the court and came to the King, kneeling down at his feet, to whom she said in effect as followeth: "Sir," quoth she, "I desire you to do me justice and right and take some pity upon me, for I am a poor woman and a stranger,[48] born out of your dominion, having here no indifferent counsel and less assurance of friendship. Alas, sir, what have I offended you or what occasion of displeasure have I showed you in-

---

45 platted . . . consistory arranged, laid out in tables and benches according to a plan of an ecclesiastical tribunal or court of judgment **46 cloth of estate** canopy spread over a throne **47 Doctor Steevens** i.e., Stephen Gardiner, just recently appointed to a position of royal adviser in place of Doctor Pace **48 stranger** foreigner

tending thus to put me from you after this sort? I take God to my judge, I have been to you a true and humble wife, ever conformable to your will and pleasure, that never contraried or gainsaid anything thereof, and being always contented with all things wherein you had any delight, whether little or much, without grudge or displeasure. I loved for your sake all them whom you loved, whether they were my friends or enemies.

"I have been your wife these twenty years and more, and you have had by me divers children. If there be any just cause that you can allege against me, either of dishonesty[49] or matter lawful to put me from you, I am content to depart to my shame and rebuke; and if there be none, then I pray you to let me have justice at your hand. The King your father was in his time of excellent wit, and the King of Spain, my father Ferdinando, was reckoned one of the wisest princes that reigned in Spain many years before. It is not to be doubted but that they had gathered as wise counselors unto them of every realm as to their wisdoms they thought meet, who deemed the marriage between you and me good and lawful, etc. Wherefore I humbly desire you to spare me until I may know what counsel my friends in Spain will advertise[50] me to take, and if you will not, then your pleasure be fulfilled." With that she arose up, making a low curtsy to the King, and departed from thence.

The King, being advertised that she was ready to go out of the house, commanded the crier to call her again, who called her by these words: "Katharine, Queen of England, come into the court." With that, quoth Master Griffith,[51] "Madam, you be called again." "On, on," quoth she, "it maketh no matter, I will not tarry; go on your ways." And thus she departed without any further answer at that time or any other, and never would appear after in any court. The King, perceiving she was departed, said these words in effect: "Forasmuch," quoth he, "as the Queen is gone, I will in her absence declare to you all that she hath been to me as true, as obedient, and as conformable a wife as I would wish or desire. She hath all the virtuous qualities that ought to be in a woman of her dignity or in any other of a

---

49 dishonesty unchastity   **50 advertise** advise   **51 Master Griffith** the Queen's gentleman usher; see *Henry VIII*, dramatis personae

baser estate. She is also surely a noblewoman born; her conditions[52] will well declare the same."

With that, quoth Wolsey the Cardinal: "Sir, I most humbly require[53] Your Highness to declare before all this audience whether I have been the chief and first mover of this matter unto Your Majesty or no, for I am greatly suspected herein." "My Lord Cardinal," quoth the King, "I can well excuse you in this matter. Marry," quoth he, "you have been rather against me in the tempting hereof than a setter forward or mover of the same. The special cause that moved me unto this matter was a certain scrupulosity that pricked my conscience upon certain words spoken at a time when it was by the Bishop of Bayonne, the French ambassador, who had been hither sent upon the debating of a marriage to be concluded between our daughter, the Lady Mary, and the Duke of Orleans, second son to the King of France.

"Upon the resolution and determination whereof, he desired respite to advertise[54] the King his master thereof, whether our daughter Mary should be legitimate in respect of this my marriage with this woman, being sometime[55] my brother's wife. Which words, once conceived within the secret bottom of my conscience, engendered such a scrupulous doubt that my conscience was incontinently accumbered,[56] vexed, and disquieted; whereby I thought myself to be greatly in danger of God's indignation—which appeared to be (as meseemed) the rather for that He sent us no issue male, and all such issues male as my said wife had by me died incontinent[57] after they came into the world, so that I doubted[58] the great displeasure of God in that behalf.

"Thus my conscience being tossed in the waves of a scrupulous mind, and partly in despair to have any other issue than I had already by this lady now my wife, it behooved me further to consider the state of this realm and the danger it stood in for lack of a prince to succeed me. I thought it good, in release of the weighty burden of my weak conscience and also the quiet estate of this worthy realm, to attempt[59] the law therein, whether I may lawfully take an-

---

52 **conditions** personal qualities 53 **require** ask 54 **advertise** advise
55 **sometime** formerly 56 **incontinently accumbered** immediately
encumbered 57 **incontinent** immediately 58 **doubted** feared
59 **attempt** essay to engage with

other wife more lawfully, by whom God may send me more issue, in case this my first copulation was not good; without any carnal concupiscence and not for any displeasure or misliking of the Queen's person and age, with whom I would be as well contented to continue, if our marriage may stand with the laws of God, as with any woman alive.

"In this point consisteth all this doubt that we go about now to try, by the learning, wisdom, and judgment of you our prelates and pastors of all this our realm and dominions now here assembled for that purpose, to whose conscience and learning I have committed the charge and judgment according to the which I will, God willing, be right well content to submit myself and, for my part, obey the same. Wherein, after that I perceived my conscience so doubtful, I moved it in confession to you, my lord of Lincoln, then ghostly father.[60] And forsomuch as then you yourself were in some doubt, you moved me to ask the counsel of all these my lords; whereupon I moved you, my lord of Canterbury, first to have your license, inasmuch as you were metropolitan,[61] to put this matter in question. And so I did of all you, my lords; to which you granted, under your seals, here to be showed." "That is truth," quoth the Archbishop of Canterbury. After that the King rose up, and the court was adjourned until another day.

Here is to be noted that the Queen, in presence of the whole court, most grievously accused the Cardinal of untruth, deceit, wickedness, and malice, which had sown dissension betwixt her and the King her husband; and therefore openly protested that she did utterly abhor, refuse, and forsake such a judge as was not only a most malicious enemy to her but also a manifest adversary to all right and justice; and therewith did she appeal unto the Pope, committing her whole cause to be judged of him. But notwithstanding this appeal, the legates sat weekly . . . and still they assayed if they could by any means procure the Queen to call back her appeal, which she utterly refused to do. The King would gladly have had an end in the matter, but when the legates drave time[62] and determined upon no certain point, he conceived a suspicion that this was done

60 ghostly father confessor   **61 metropolitan** archbishop   **62 drave time** i.e., delayed matters

of purpose, that their doings might draw to none effect or conclusion. . . .

And thus this court passed from sessions to sessions and day to day, till at certain of their sessions the King sent the two cardinals to the Queen (who was then in Bridewell)[63] to persuade[64] with her by their wisdoms and to advise her to surrender the whole matter into the King's hands by her own consent and will, which should be much better to her honor than to stand to the trial of law and thereby to be condemned, which should seem much to her dishonor.

The Cardinals being in the Queen's chamber of presence,[65] the gentleman usher advertised the Queen that the Cardinals were come to speak with her. With that she rose up and, with a skein of white thread about her neck, came into her chamber of presence, where the Cardinals were attending. At whose coming, quoth she, "What is your pleasure with me?" "If it please Your Grace," quoth Cardinal Wolsey, "to go into your privy chamber, we will show you the cause of our coming." "My lord," quoth she, "if ye have anything to say, speak it openly before all these folk, for I fear nothing that ye can say against me but that I would all the world should hear and see it, and therefore speak your mind." Then began the Cardinal to speak to her in Latin. "Nay, good my lord," quoth she, "speak to me in English."

"Forsooth," quoth the Cardinal, "good madam, if it please you, we come both to know your mind how you are disposed to do in this matter between the King and you and also to declare secretly our opinions and counsel unto you; which we do only for very zeal and obedience we bear unto Your Grace." "My lord," quoth she, "I thank you for your good will, but to make you answer in your request I cannot so suddenly, for I was set among my maids at work, thinking full little of any such matter, wherein there needeth a longer deliberation and a better head than mine to make answer; for I need counsel in this case, which toucheth me so near, and for[66] any counsel or friendship that I can find in England, they are not for my profit. What think you, my lords, will any Englishman counsel me or be friend to me

---

63 Bridewell (At this time a house owned by the King.) **64 persuade** use persuasion **65 chamber of presence** presence chamber, reception room in a palace **66 for** as for

against the King's pleasure that is his subject?[67] Nay, forsooth. And as for my council in whom I will put my trust, they be not here; they be in Spain in my own country.

"And, my lords, I am a poor woman, lacking wit, to answer to any such noble persons of wisdom as you be in so weighty a matter. Therefore I pray you be good to me, poor woman, destitute of friends here in a foreign region, and your counsel also I will be glad to hear." And therewith she took the Cardinal by the hand and led him into her privy chamber with the other cardinal, where they tarried a season talking with the Queen.

[Some time later, the King comes to the court to hear judgment given.]

That done, the King's counsel at the bar called for judgment. With that, quoth Cardinal Campeius: "I . . . will adjourn this court for this time, according to the order of the court of Rome." And with that the court was dissolved and no more done. This protracting of the conclusion of the matter King Henry took very displeasantly. Then Cardinal Campeius took his leave of the King and returned towards Rome.

Whilst these things were thus in hand, the Cardinal of York was advised that the King had set his affection upon a young gentlewoman named Anne, the daughter of Sir Thomas Bullen, Viscount Rochford, which did wait upon the Queen. This was a great grief unto the Cardinal, as he that perceived aforehand that the King would marry the said gentlewoman if the divorce took place. Wherefore he began with all diligence to disappoint[68] that match, which, by reason of the misliking that he had to the woman, he judged ought to be avoided more than present death. While the matter stood in this state, and that the cause of the Queen was to be heard and judged at Rome by reason of the appeal which by her was put in, the Cardinal required[69] the Pope by letters and secret messengers that in any wise he should defer the judgment of the divorce till he might frame the King's mind to his purpose.

67 that is his subject who is subject to the King   **68 disappoint** frustrate   **69 required** requested

Howbeit he went about nothing so secretly but that the
same came to the King's knowledge, who took so high displeasure with such his cloaked dissimulation that he determined to abase his degree, sith[70] as an unthankful person he
forgot himself and his duty towards him that had so highly
advanced him to all honor and dignity. When the nobles of
the realm perceived the Cardinal to be in displeasure, they
began to accuse him of such offenses as they knew might be
proved against him, and thereof they made a book containing certain articles, to which divers of the King's Council
set their hands. The King, understanding more plainly by
those articles the great pride, presumption, and covetousness of the Cardinal, was sore moved against him; but yet
kept his purpose secret for a while. . . .

In the meantime the King, being informed that all those
things that the Cardinal had done by his power legantine
within this realm were in the case of the praemunire and
provision,[71] caused his attorney, Christopher Hales, to sue
out a writ of praemunire against him, in the which he licensed him to make his attorney.[72] And further, the seventeenth of November, the King sent the two Dukes of Norfolk
and Suffolk to the Cardinal's place at Westminster, who
went as they were commanded; and finding the Cardinal
there, they declared that the King's pleasure was that he
should surrender up the Great Seal into their hands and to
depart simply unto Asher, which was an house situate nigh
unto Hampton Court belonging to the bishopric of Winchester. The Cardinal demanded of them their commission
that gave them such authority; who answered again that
they were sufficient commissioners and had authority to do
no less by the King's mouth. Notwithstanding, he would in
no wise agree in that behalf without further knowledge of
their authority, saying that the Great Seal was delivered
him by the King's person to enjoy the ministration thereof,

---

70 abase his degree, sith reduce his (Wolsey's) authority and lower his station,
since   **71 by his power . . . provision** i.e., by his power as papal legate
within the realm of England came under the provisions of the assertion
of papal jurisdiction in England, thus denying the ecclesiastical supremacy of the King. (A *writ of praemunire* charges the sheriff to
summon a person, here Wolsey, accused of violating English law in this
way.)   **72 in the which . . . attorney** i.e., in which the King licensed
Hales to act as his (the King's) attorney

with the room[73] of the chancellor for the term of his life, whereof for his surety he had the King's letters patents.

This matter was greatly debated between them with many great words, insomuch that the Dukes were fain to depart again without their purpose, and rode to Windsor to the King and made report accordingly; but the next day they returned again, bringing with them the King's letters. Then the Cardinal delivered unto them the Great Seal and was content to depart simply, taking with him nothing but only certain provision for his house. . . . Then the Cardinal called all his officers before him and took account of them for all such stuff whereof they had charge. And in his gallery were set divers tables whereupon lay a great number of goodly rich stuff. . . .

There was laid, on every table, books reporting the contents of the same, and so was there inventories of all things, in order against the King's coming. . . . Then had he two chambers adjoining to the gallery, the one most commonly called the gilt chamber and the other the council chamber, wherein were set up two broad and long tables upon trestles, whereupon was set such a number of plate[74] of all sorts as was almost incredible. . . .

After this, in the King's Bench,[75] his matter for the praemunire being called upon, two attorneys, which he had authorized by his warrant signed with his own hand, confessed the action and so had judgment to forfeit all his lands, tenements, goods, and chattels, and to be out of the King's protection. . . .

During this Parliament was brought down to the Commons the book of articles which the Lords had put to the King against the Cardinal, the chief whereof were these:

1. First, that he without the King's assent had procured to be a legate, by reason whereof he took away the right of all bishops and spiritual persons.

2. Item, in all writings which he wrote to Rome or any other foreign prince he wrote *Ego et rex meus*, I and my King, as who would say that the King were his servant.

---

73 room position   74 plate objects of precious metal   75 the King's Bench a supreme court of common law

3. Item, that he hath slandered the Church of England in the court of Rome. . . .

4. Item, he without the King's assent carried the King's Great Seal with him into Flanders when he was sent ambassador to the Emperor.

5. Item, he without the King's assent sent a commission to Sir Gregory de Cassado, knight, to conclude a league between the King and the Duke of Ferrar without the King's knowledge.

6. Item, that he, having the French pox,[76] presumed to come and breathe on the King.

7. Item, that he caused the Cardinal's hat to be put on the King's coin.

8. Item, that he would not suffer the King's clerk of the market to sit at Saint Albans.

9. Item, that he had sent innumerable substance to Rome for the obtaining of his dignities, to the great impoverishment of the realm.

[Holinshed reports that, in the Lenten season of 1530, Wolsey is licensed to go to his diocese of York and not return south without express permission. Among those who leave his service is Thomas Cromwell, now serving the King in the suppressing of the monasteries. Wolsey is subsequently arrested for treason at Cawood by the Earl of Northumberland. On the way south he becomes very ill with dysentery.]

The next day he rode to Nottingham and there lodged that night more sick; and the next day he rode to Leicester Abbey, and by the way waxed so sick that he was almost fallen from his mule; so that it was night before he came to the Abbey of Leicester, where, at his coming in at the gates, the abbot with all his convent met him with divers torches light,[77] whom they honorably received and welcomed.

To whom the Cardinal said: "Father abbot, I am come hither to lay my bones among you." . . . And as soon as he was in his chamber he went to bed. This was on the Saturday at night, and then increased he sicker and sicker until Monday, that all men thought he would have died. So on Tuesday, Saint Andrew's Even, Master Kingston came to

76 French pox syphilis   **77 light** lighted

him and bade him good morrow. . . . "Sir," quoth he, "I tarry but the pleasure of God to render up my poor soul into his hands." . . .

"Well, well, Master Kingston," quoth the Cardinal, "I see the matter how it is framed. But if I had served God as diligently as I have done the King, he would not have given me over in my gray hairs. . . ."

Then they did put him in remembrance of Christ His passion . . . and incontinent[78] the clock struck eight, and then he gave up the ghost and departed this present life; which caused some to call to remembrance how he said the day before that at eight of the clock they should lose their master.

Here is the end and fall of pride and arrogancy of men exalted by fortune to dignity; for in his time he was the haughtiest man in all his proceedings alive, having more respect to the honor of his person than he had to his spiritual profession, wherein should be showed all meekness, humility, and charity. . . .

This Cardinal, as Edmund Campian in his *History of Ireland* describeth him, was a man undoubtedly born to honor. "I think," saith he, "some prince's bastard, no butcher's son; exceeding wise, fair-spoken, high-minded; full of revenge; vicious of his body; lofty to his enemies, were they never so big; to those that accepted and sought his friendship, wonderful courteous; a ripe schoolman; thrall to affections;[79] brought abed with flattery; insatiable to get,[80] and more princely in bestowing, as appeareth by his two colleges at Ipswich and Oxenford, the one overthrown with his fall, the other unfinished, and yet as it lieth for an house of students, considering all the appurtenances, incomparable thorough Christendom . . . a great preferrer[81] of his servants . . . stout in every quarrel; never happy till this his overthrow, wherein he showed such moderation and ended so perfectly that the hour of his death did him more honor than all the pomp of his life past." . . .

This Thomas Wolsey was a poor man's son of Ipswich, in

---

78 incontinent immediately   **79 ripe schoolman . . . affections** mature scholar in divinity; enslaved to passions   **80 brought abed with flattery . . . get** i.e., debilitated by his proneness to flattery . . . acquire   **81 preferrer** one who gives advancement

the county of Suffolk, and there born; and, being but a child,[82] very apt to be learned. . . .

[Holinshed describes Wolsey's career at length, including the ceremonial honors he insisted upon for himself, such as two great crosses of silver that were borne before him wherever he went. Particularly impressive is the order of procession attending his daily going in to Westminster Hall during term:]

Before him was borne first the Broad Seal of England and his cardinal's hat by a lord or some gentleman of worship, right solemnly, and as soon as he was once entered into his chamber of presence his two great crosses were there attending to be borne before him. Then cried the gentlemen ushers, going before him bareheaded, and said: "On before, my lords and masters, on before! Make way for my lord's Grace!" Thus went he down through the hall with a sergeant-of-arms before him, bearing a great mace of silver, and two gentlemen carrying two great pillars of silver. . . .

Thus in great honor, triumph, and glory he reigned a long season, ruling all things within the realm appertaining unto the King. His house was resorted to with[83] noblemen and gentlemen, feasting and banqueting ambassadors divers times, and all other right nobly. And when it pleased the King for his recreation to repair to the Cardinal's house, as he did divers times in the year, there wanted no preparations or furniture.[84] Banquets were set forth with masques and mummeries in so gorgeous a sort and costly manner that it was an heaven to behold. There wanted no dames or damosels meet or apt to dance with the maskers or to garnish the place for the time; then was there all kind of music and harmony, with fine voices both of men and children.

On a time the King came suddenly thither in a masque with a dozen maskers all in garments like shepherds made of fine cloth of gold and crimson satin paned[85] and caps of the same, with visors of good physiognomy, their hairs[86] and beards either of fine goldwire silk or black silk; having

---

82 being but a child even when he was still a child   **83 with** by
84 furniture things provided for lavish entertainment   **85 paned** bordered or lined with fur   **86 hairs** wigs

sixteen torchbearers, besides their drums[87] and other persons with visors all clothed in satin of the same color. And before his entering into the hall, he came by water to the water gate without any noise, where were laid divers chambers and guns charged with shot, and at his landing they were shot off, which made such a rumble in the air that it was like thunder. It made all the noblemen, gentlemen, ladies, and gentlewomen to muse what it should mean, coming so suddenly, they sitting quiet at a solemn banquet, after this sort.[88]

First ye shall understand that the tables were set in the chamber of presence just[89] covered, and the Lord Cardinal sitting under the cloth of estate, there having all his service alone; and then was there set a lady with a nobleman, or a gentleman and a gentlewoman, throughout all the tables in the chamber on the one side, which were made and joined as it were but one table, all which order and device was done by the Lord Sands, then Lord Chamberlain to the King, and by Sir Henry Guildford, Comptroller of the King's Majesty's house. Then immediately after, the Great Chamberlain and the said Comptroller sent to look what it should mean (as though they knew nothing of the matter), who, looking out of the windows into the Thames, returned again and showed[90] him that it seemed they were noblemen and strangers that arrived at his bridge,[91] coming as ambassadors from some foreign prince.

With that quoth the Cardinal: "I desire you, because you can speak French, to take the pains to go into the hall, there to receive them according to their estates and to conduct them into this chamber, where they shall see us and all these noble personages being merry at our banquet; desiring them to sit down with us and to take part of our fare." Then went he incontinent down into the hall, whereas[92] they received them with twenty new torches and conveyed them up into the chamber with such a noise of drums and flutes as seldom had been heard the like. At their entering into the chamber, two and two together, they went directly before the Cardinal where he sat, and saluted him reverently.

87 drums drummers   **88 after this sort** in this manner   **89 just** appropriately   **90 showed** informed   **91 bridge** gangway or movable landing stage for boats   **92 whereas** where

To whom the Lord Chamberlain for them said: "Sir, forasmuch as they be strangers and cannot speak English, they have desired me to declare unto you that they, having understanding of this your triumphant banquet where was assembled such a number of excellent dames, they could do no less, under support of Your Grace, but to repair hither to view as well their incomparable beauty as for to accompany them at mumchance[93] and then to dance with them; and, sir, they require[94] of Your Grace license to accomplish the said cause of their coming." To whom the Cardinal said he was very well content they should so do. Then went the maskers and first saluted all the dames, and returned to the most worthy and there opened their great cup of gold filled with crowns and other pieces of gold; to whom they set certain pieces of gold to cast at.

Thus, perusing all the ladies and gentlewomen, to some they lost and of some they won; and marking after this manner all the ladies, they returned to the Cardinal with great reverence, pouring down all their gold so left in their cup, which was above two hundred crowns. "At all!" quoth the Cardinal, and so cast the dice and wan them, whereat was made a great noise and joy. Then quoth the Cardinal to the Lord Chamberlain: "I pray you," quoth he, "that you would show[95] them that meseemeth there should be a nobleman amongst them who is more meet to occupy this seat and place than I am, to whom I would most gladly surrender the same according to my duty, if I knew him."

Then spake the Lord Chamberlain to them in French, and they rounding[96] him in the ear, the Lord Chamberlain said to my Lord Cardinal: "Sir," quoth he, "they confess that among them there is such a noble personage whom, if Your Grace can appoint him out from the rest, he is content to disclose himself and to accept your place." With that the Cardinal, taking good advisement[97] among them, at the last quoth he, "Meseemeth the gentleman with the black beard should be even he." And with that he arose out of his chair and offered the same to the gentleman in the black beard, with his cap in his hand. The person to whom he offered the chair was Sir Edward Neville, a comely knight, that much

---

93 mumchance a dicing game **94 require** request **95 show** inform
96 rounding whispering to **97 good advisement** careful scrutiny

more resembled the King's person in that masque than any other.

The King, perceiving the Cardinal so deceived, could not forbear laughing, but pulled down his visor and Master Neville's also and dashed out such a pleasant countenance and cheer that all the noble estates there assembled, perceiving the King to be there among them, rejoiced very much. The Cardinal eftsoons[98] desired His Highness to take the place of estate. To whom the King answered that he would go first and shift his apparel, and so departed into my Lord Cardinal's chamber and there new appareled him; in which time the dishes of the banquet were clean taken up and the tables spread again with new, clean, perfumed cloths, every man and woman sitting still until the King with all his maskers came among them again all new appareled.

Then the King took his seat under the cloth of estate, commanding every person to sit still as they did before. In came a new banquet before the King and to all the rest throughout all the tables, wherein were served two hundred divers dishes of costly devices and subtleties. Thus passed they forth the night with banqueting, dancing, and other triumphs, to the great comfort of the King and pleasant regard of the nobility there assembled. . . .

This Cardinal, as you may perceive in this story,[99] was of a great stomach,[100] for he counted himself equal with princes and by crafty suggestion gat into his hands innumerable treasure. He forced little on simony,[101] and was not pitiful, and stood affectionate[102] in his own opinion. In open presence he would lie and say untruth and was double both in speech and meaning; he would promise much and perform little. He was vicious of his body and gave the clergy evil example.

[In 1532 King Henry creates Anne Boleyn Marchioness of Pembroke. He marries her secretly on November 14. Order is given that Katharine is to be called Princess Dowager rather than Queen.]

---

98 eftsoons very soon afterward   **99 story** history   **100 stomach** haughtiness   **101 forced little on simony** had few scruples about the selling of church offices   **102 affectionate** obstinate

After that the King perceived his new wife to be with child, he caused all officers necessary to be appointed to her, and so on Easter Even she went to her closet openly as Queen; and then the King appointed the day of her coronation to be kept on Whitsunday[103] next following. And writings were sent to all sheriffs to certify the names of men of forty pounds to receive the order of knighthood or else to make fine. The assessment of the fine was appointed to Thomas Cromwell, Master of the King's Jewel House and councillor to the King, a man newly received into high favor. He so used the matter that a great sum of money was raised to the King's use by those fines. The matter of the Queen's appeal, whereunto she still sticked and by no means could be removed from it, was communed of[104] both in the Parliament House and also in the Convocation House, where it was so handled that many were of opinion that not only her appeal but also all other appeals made to Rome were void and of none effect; for that in ancient councils it had been determined that a cause rising in one province should be determined in the same.

This matter was opened with all the circumstances[105] to the Lady Katharine Dowager (for so was she then called), the which persisted still in her former opinion and would revoke by no means her appeal to the court of Rome. Whereupon the Archbishop of Canterbury, accompanied with the Bishops of London, Winchester, Bath, Lincoln, and divers other learned men in great number, rode to Dunstable, which is six miles from Ampthill, where the Princess Dowager lay. And there by one Doctor Lee she was cited to appear before the said Archbishop in cause of matrimony in the said town of Dunstable; and at the day of appearance, she appeared not but made default, and so she was called peremptory[106] every day fifteen days together; and at the last, for lack of appearance, by the assent of all the learned men there present she was divorced from the King and the marriage declared to be void and of none effect.

[Anne's coronation in May 1533 is an occasion of ceremonial splendor.]

103 Whitsunday the seventh Sunday after Easter   **104 communed of** discussed   **105 opened with all the circumstances** laid out in full detail **106 peremptory** by decree

First went gentlemen, then esquires, then knights, then the aldermen of the city in their cloaks of scarlet; after them the judges in their mantles of scarlet and coifs.[107] Then followed the Knights of the Bath, being no lords, every man having a white lace on his left sleeve; then followed barons and viscounts in their parliament robes of scarlet. After them came earls, marquesses, and dukes, in their robes of estate of crimson velvet furred with ermine, powdered according to their degrees. After them came the Lord Chancellor in a robe of scarlet open before, bordered with lettice.[108] After him came the King's chapel and the monks solemnly singing with procession; then came abbots and bishops mitered, then sergeants- and officers-of-arms; then after them went the Mayor of London with his mace, and Garter[109] in his coat of arms. Then went the Marquess Dorset in a robe of estate, which bare[110] the scepter of gold, and the Earl of Arundel, which bare the rod of ivory with the dove, both together.

Then went alone the Earl of Oxford, High Chamberlain of England, which bare the crown; after him went the Duke of Suffolk in his robe of estate also, for that day being High Steward of England, having a long white rod in his hand; and the Lord William Howard, with the rod of the marshalship; and every Knight of the Garter had on his collar of the order. Then proceeded forth the Queen in a surcoat and robe of purple velvet furred with ermine, in her hair, coif, and circlet[111] as she had the Saturday; and over her was borne the canopy by four of the Five Ports,[112] all crimson with points[113] of blue and red hanging on their sleeves; and the Bishops of London and Winchester bare up the laps[114] of the Queen's robe. The Queen's train, which was very long, was borne by the old Duchess of Norfolk; after her followed ladies, being lords' wives, which had surcoats of scarlet. . . .

When she was thus brought to the high place made in the midst of the church, between the choir and the high altar,

---

107 **coifs** close-fitting caps   108 **lettice** whitish gray fur   109 **Garter** Garter King at Arms, a chief herald   110 **which bare** who bore   111 **in her hair, coif, and circlet** with her hair unbound, in a close-fitting cap and metal headband   112 **the Five Ports** the barons of the Five Cinque Ports on the English southern coast; see *Henry VIII*, 4.1.36 s.d. 113 **points** laces for fastening clothing   114 **laps** folds or flaps

she was set in a rich chair. And after that she had rested
awhile she descended down to the high altar and there prostrate[115] herself while the Archbishop of Canterbury said
certain collects.[116] Then she rose, and the Bishop anointed
her on the head and on the breast; and then she was led up
again where, after divers orisons said, the Archbishop set
the crown of Saint Edward on her head and then delivered
her the scepter of gold in her right hand and the rod of ivory
with the dove in the left hand; and then all the choir sung *Te
Deum*,[117] etc. Which done, the Bishop took off the crown of
Saint Edward, being heavy, and set on the crown made for
her. Then went she to Saint Edward's shrine and there offered, after which offering done she withdrew her into a little place made for the nonce on the one side of the choir.

Now in the mean season, every duchess had put on their
bonnets a coronal of gold wrought with flowers, and every
marquess put on a demicoronal of gold, every countess a
plain circlet of gold without flowers, and every King of
Arms put on a crown of copper and gilt, all which were
worn till night. When the Queen had a little reposed her, the
company returned in the same order that they set forth, and
the Queen went crowned, and so did the ladies aforesaid. . . .
Now when she was out of the sanctuary and appeared
within the palace, the trumpets played marvelous freshly.
Then she was brought to Westminster Hall and so to her
withdrawing chamber.

[Anne gives birth to a child some four months later, 1533.]

The seventh of September, being Sunday, between three
and four of the clock in the afternoon, the Queen was delivered of a fair young lady. On which day the Duke of Norfolk
came home to the christening, which was appointed on the
Wednesday next following and was accordingly accomplished on the same day with all such solemn ceremonies as
were thought convenient. The godfather at the font was the
Lord Archbishop of Canterbury, the godmothers the old
Duchess of Norfolk and the old Marchioness Dorset,

---

115 prostrate prostrated   **116 collects** short prayers   **117 Te Deum** We
praise you O God. (A hymn of thanksgiving.)

widow; and at the confirmation[118] the Lady Marchioness of Exeter was godmother. The child was named Elizabeth.

[The christening is an elaborate ceremonial occasion.]

When the ceremonies and christening were ended, Garter Chief King of Arms cried aloud, "God of his infinite goodness send prosperous life and long to the high and mighty Princess of England, Elizabeth!" and then the trumpets blew. Then the Archbishop of Canterbury gave to the Princess a standing cup of gold, the Duchess of Norfolk gave to her a standing cup of gold fretted with pearl, the Marchioness of Dorset gave three gilt bowls, pounced,[119] with a cover, and the Marchioness of Exeter gave three standing bowls, graven, all gilt, with a cover. Then was brought in wafers, comfits, and hippocras[120] in such plenty that every man had as much as he would desire. Then they set forwards, the trumpets going before in the same order, towards the King's palace.

[Katharine, as Princess Dowager, lives in isolation until early 1536.]

The Princess Dowager, lying at Kimbolton, fell into her last sickness, whereof the King, being advertised, appointed the Emperor's ambassador that was ledger[121] here with him, named Eustachius Capucius, to go to visit her and to do his commendations to her and will her to be of good comfort. The ambassador with all diligence did his duty therein, comforting her the best he might; but she, within six days after, perceiving herself to wax very weak and feeble and to feel death approaching at hand, caused one of her gentlewomen to write a letter to the King commending to him her daughter and his, beseeching him to stand good father unto her, and further desired him to have some consideration of her gentlewomen that had served her

---

118 the confirmation a rite administered to baptized persons to confirm or strengthen the practice of the Christian faith; in more recent days, normally done after the child has been able to learn and study the articles of faith   **119 pounced** embossed   **120 hippocras** a spicy wine drink   **121 ledger** resident

and to see them bestowed in marriage. Further, that it would please him to appoint that her servants might have their due wages and a year's wages besides. This in effect was all that she requested; and so, immediately hereupon, she departed this life the eighth of January at Kimbolton aforesaid and was buried at Peterborough. The nine-and-twentieth of January, Queen Anne was delivered of a child before her time, which was born dead.

The second edition of Raphael Holinshed's *Chronicles* was published in 1587. This selection is based on that edition, Volume 3, folios 796 and 850–939. Some proper names have been regularized: Ardres (Ard), Guînes (Guisnes), etc.

Acts and Monuments of Martyrs (1583 edition)
By John Foxe

[Foxe describes the machinations of certain Catholic members of the King's Privy Council, especially Stephen Gardiner, the Bishop of Winchester, to bring down the Protestant reforming Archbishop of Canterbury, Thomas Cranmer.]

It came into a common proverb: Do unto my lord of Canterbury displeasure or a shrewd turn, and then you may be sure to have him your friend whiles he liveth. . . .

Notwithstanding, not long after that, certain of the Council, whose names need not to be repeated, by the enticement and provocation of his ancient enemy the Bishop of Winchester and other of the same sect, attempted[1] the King against him, declaring plainly that the realm was so infected with heresies and heretics that it was dangerous to His Highness farther to permit it unreformed,[2] lest peradventure by long suffering[3] such contention should arise and ensue in the realm among his subjects that thereby might spring horrible commotions and uproars, like as in some

---

1 attempted tried to influence   **2 permit it unreformed** permit it (Protestant heresy) to continue uncorrected   **3 by long suffering** by being long tolerated

parts of Germany it did not long ago; the enormity whereof they could not impute to any so much as to the Archbishop of Canterbury, who, by his own preaching and his chaplains', had defiled the whole realm full of divers pernicious heresies. The King would needs know[4] his accusers. They answered that forasmuch as he was a councillor no man durst take upon him to accuse him, but if it would please His Highness to commit him to the Tower for a time there would be accusations and proofs enough against him. . . .

The King, perceiving their importunate suit against the Archbishop (but yet meaning not to have him wronged and utterly given over unto their hands), granted unto them that they should the next day commit him to the Tower for his trial. When night came, the King sent Sir Anthony Denny, about midnight, to Lambeth to the Archbishop, willing him forthwith to resort unto him at the court. The message done, the Archbishop speedily addressed himself[5] to the court, and coming into the gallery where the King walked and tarried for him, His Highness said: "Ah, my lord of Canterbury, I can tell you news. For divers weighty considerations, it is determined by me and the Council that you, tomorrow at nine of the clock, shall be committed to the Tower, for that you and your chaplains (as information is given us) have taught and preached and thereby sown within the realm such a number of execrable heresies that it is feared, the whole realm being infected with them, no small contention and commotions will rise thereby amongst my subjects, as of late days the like was in divers parts of Germany; and therefore the Council have requested me, for the trial of the matter, to suffer them to commit you to the Tower, or else no man dare come forth as witness in these matters, you being a councillor."

When the King had said his mind, the Archbishop kneeled down and said: "I am content, if it please Your Grace, with all my heart to go thither at Your Highness's commandment, and I most humbly thank Your Majesty that I may come to my trial, for there be that[6] have many ways slandered me, and now this way I hope to try[7] myself not worthy of such report."

---

4 would needs know wished to know the names of   **5 addressed himself** betook himself   **6 there be that** there are those who   **7 try** prove

The King, perceiving the man's uprightness joined with such simplicity, said: "Oh, lord, what manner o' man be you? What simplicity is in you? I had thought that you would rather have sued to us[8] to have taken the pains to have heard you and your accusers together for your trial without any such indurance.[9] Do not you know what state you be in with the whole world and how many great enemies you have? Do you not consider what an easy thing it is to procure[10] three or four false knaves to witness against you? Think you to have better luck that way than your master Christ had? I see by it you will run headlong to your undoing if I would suffer you. Your enemies shall not so prevail against you, for I have otherwise devised with myself to keep you out of their hands. Yet notwithstanding, tomorrow when the Council shall sit and send for you, resort unto them, and if in charging you with this matter they do commit you to the Tower, require[11] of them, because you are one of them—a councillor—that you may have your accusers brought before them without any further indurance, and use for yourself as good persuasions that way as you may devise, and if no entreaty or reasonable request will serve, then deliver unto them this my ring" (which when the King delivered unto the Archbishop) "and say unto them, 'If there be no remedy, my lords, but that I must needs go to the Tower, then I revoke[12] my cause from you and appeal to the King's own person by this his token unto you all.' For," said the King then unto the Archbishop, "so soon as they shall see this my ring, they know it so well that they shall understand that I have resumed the whole cause into mine own hands and determination, and that I have discharged them thereof."

The Archbishop, perceiving the King's benignity so much to him wards,[13] had much ado to forbear tears. "Well," said the King, "go your ways, my lord, and do as I have bidden you." My lord, humbling himself with thanks, took his leave of the King's Highness for that night.

On the morrow, about nine of the clock before noon, the Council sent a gentleman usher for the Archbishop, who,

---

8 us i.e., me. (The royal plural.)   **9 indurance** imprisonment   **10 to procure** i.e., for your enemies to procure   **11 require** request   **12 revoke** call back, withdraw   **13 to him wards** toward him

when he came to the Council chamber door, could not be let in, but of purpose (as it seemed) was compelled there to wait among the pages, lackeys, and servingmen all alone. Dr. Butts, the King's physician, resorting that way and espying how my lord of Canterbury was handled, went to the King's Highness and said: "My lord of Canterbury, if it please Your Grace, is well promoted; for now he is become a lackey or a servingman, for yonder he standeth this half hour at the Council chamber door amongst them." "It is not so," quoth the King, "I trow, nor the Council hath not so little discretion as to use the metropolitan[14] of the realm in that sort, specially being one of their own number. But let them alone," said the King, "and we shall hear more soon."

Anon the Archbishop was called into the Council chamber, to whom was alleged as before is rehearsed. The Archbishop answered in like sort as the King had advised him; and in the end, when he perceived that no manner of persuasion or entreaty could serve, he delivered them the King's ring, revoking his cause into the King's hands. The whole Council being thereat somewhat amazed, the Earl of Bedford with a loud voice, confirming his words with a solemn oath, said: "When you first began the matter, my lords, I told you what would come of it. Do you think that the King will suffer this man's finger to ache? Much more, I warrant you, will he defend his life against brabbling varlets.[15] You do but cumber[16] yourselves to hear tales and fables against him." And so, incontinently[17] upon the receipt of the King's token, they all rose and carried to the King his ring, surrendering that matter, as the order and use[18] was, into his own hands.

When they were all come to the King's presence, His Highness, with a severe countenance, said unto them: "Ah, my lords, I thought I had had wiser men of my Council than now I find you. What discretion was this in you thus to make the primate[19] of the realm, and one of you in office, to wait at the Council chamber door amongst servingmen? You might have considered that he was a councillor as well as you, and you had no such commission of me so to handle

---

14 metropolitan archbishop   **15 brabbling varlets** quibbling, quarrelsome rascals   **16 cumber** trouble, undo, confound   **17 incontinently** immediately   **18 use** custom, practice   **19 primate** archbishop

him. I was content that you should try him as a councillor and not as a mean[20] subject. But now I well perceive that things be done against him maliciously, and if some of you might have had your minds,[21] you would have tried him to the uttermost. But I do you all to wit,[22] and protest that if a prince may be beholding unto his subject" (and so, solemnly laying his hand upon his breast, said), "by the faith I owe to God, I take this man here, my lord of Canterbury, to be of all other a most faithful subject unto us and one to whom we are much beholding, giving him great commendations otherwise." And with that, one or two of the chiefest of the Council, making their excuse, declared that, in requesting his indurance, it was rather meant for his trial and his purgation against the common fame[23] and slander of the world than for any malice conceived against him. "Well, well, my lords," quoth the King, "take him and well use him, as he is worthy to be, and make no more ado." And with that every man caught him by the hand and made fair weather of altogethers,[24] which might easily be done with that man.

Text based on *The Second Volume of the Ecclesiastical History, Containing the Acts and Monuments of Martyrs . . . newly recognized and enlarged by the author, John Foxe, 1583. . . . Printed by John Day*, pp. 1863, 1866–1867. The first edition of this work appeared in 1563.

20 mean of ordinary rank   **21 minds** intents   **22 do you all to wit** wish you all to know   **23 fame** rumor, reputation   **24 of altogethers** altogether

Further Reading

Anderson, Judith H. "Shakespeare's *Henry VIII:* The Changing Relation of Truth to Fiction." *Biographical Truth: The Representation of Historical Persons in Tudor–Stuart Writing.* New Haven, Conn.: Yale Univ. Press, 1984. Anderson examines *Henry VIII*'s treatment of its historical source material, as it exposes and explores the provocative ironies of the play's apparent subtitle, *All Is True.* Anderson claims "divorce" is not merely a central historical event in the play but a crucial metaphor for the disjunctions that exist throughout the play between private and public lives as well as between objective and subjective understandings of the truth.

Baillie, William M. "*Henry VIII:* A Jacobean History." *Shakespeare Studies* 12 (1979): 247–266. Baillie argues that in dramatizing the reign of Henry VIII Shakespeare holds a mirror up to political concerns of the time. The play's presentation of Henry's reign is designed to comment on the central political issues of James's court in 1613: concerns about state divorce, the role of a court favorite, and the limits of royal power.

Berry, Edward I. "*Henry VIII* and the Dynamics of Spectacle." *Shakespeare Studies* 12 (1979): 229–246. Berry examines the way Shakespeare blends the play's archaic tragic pattern of political falls with stylized and spectacular elements derived from the masque. The play thus reveals both a serious concern with the world of historical flux and a powerful impulse toward political idealization.

Bertram, Paul. "Henry VIII: The Conscience of the King." In *In Defense of Reading: A Reader's Approach to Literary Criticism,* ed. Reuben A. Brower and Richard Poirier. New York: E. P. Dutton, 1962. Bertram discovers the play's design in its presentation of Henry's progression from a king who merely reigns to one who effectively rules. The entire fifth act celebrates the new Henrician order and affirms a festive union of King and people that overshadows and transcends the private tragedies of Katharine and Wolsey.

Bliss, Lee. "The Wheel of Fortune and the Maiden Phoenix

of Shakespeare's *King Henry the Eighth.*" *ELH* 42 (1975): 1–25. Bliss emphasizes the disturbing political and moral realities revealed in the world of the play: Henry understands that power rather than truth or integrity succeeds and that justice is at best provisional and expedient. Cranmer's prophecy in Act 5, however, offers an alternative to the disillusioned political world of Henry's rule; it provides an ideal, hortatory portrait of what England and its ruler should be.

Cespedes, Frank V. " 'We are one in fortunes': The Sense of History in *Henry VIII.*" *English Literary Renaissance* 10 (1980): 413–438. In Cespedes's view, *Henry VIII* is above all a history play, though one suffused with irony. The play exploits the tension between the fortunate progress toward Elizabeth's reign and the unfortunate fate of the individuals whose personal tragedies lead up to that event. Throughout, Shakespeare emphasizes the disparity between what his characters and what his Jacobean audience know about the outcome of sixteenth-century English history.

Cox, John D. "*Henry the Eighth* and the Masque." *ELH* 45 (1978): 390–409. Cox examines how Shakespeare in *Henry VIII* adapted the principles of the Jacobean court masque to the popular stage. While the masque typically celebrates Jacobean kingship, the play is able to exploit and modify this adulation, exploring the ambiguities of divine right as it combines masque elements with older, popular theatrical traditions.

Felperin, Howard. "Tragical-Comical-Historical-Pastoral: *Cymbeline* and *Henry VIII.*" *Shakespearean Romance.* Princeton, N.J.: Princeton Univ. Press, 1972. *Henry VIII*, Felperin argues, enacts a pattern of secular fall and spiritual regeneration that differentiates the play from the earlier histories and relates it to the idealizing concerns of the late romances. Felperin feels that the insistent redemptive design never succeeds in firmly grounding the romance vision in history; rather it abandons history— not perfecting but distorting the world of fact in its myth of the Tudor golden age.

Foakes, R. A. "Epilogue: A Note on *King Henry VIII.*" *Shakespeare, The Dark Comedies to the Last Plays: From Satire to Celebration.* Charlottesville, Va.: The Univ. Press of Virginia, 1971. Foakes finds that in *Henry VIII* the instruments of rule are flawed and incapable of insuring justice, but that human history is redeemed by the operation of a benign providence. Henry's emergence as a capable ruler is part of a providential action in which suffering and injustice are transcended as the truth of heaven's grace is finally revealed.

Harris, Bernard. " 'What's Past is Prologue': *Cymbeline* and *Henry VIII.*" In *Later Shakespeare*, ed. John Russell Brown and Bernard Harris. New York: St. Martin's Press, 1967. Harris focuses on the play's final prophecy, a vision of England's past history and future security, in which Shakespeare addresses the political situation facing James I, especially the religious and economic confrontation with England's Catholic foes.

Johnson, Samuel. *Johnson on Shakespeare*, ed. Arthur Sherbo. *The Yale Edition of the Works of Samuel Johnson*, vol. 8. New Haven, Conn.: Yale Univ. Press, 1968. Johnson considers *Henry VIII* among the least successful of Shakespeare's histories; nonetheless, he admires "the splendour of its pageantry," which largely accounted for its popularity on the eighteenth-century stage, and the pathos of Katharine's fall, tenderly depicted in "some scenes which may be justly numbered among the greatest efforts of tragedy."

Kermode, Frank. "What Is Shakespeare's *Henry VIII* About?" *Durham University Journal* 40, n.s. 9 (1948): 48–55. Rpt. in *Shakespeare, the Histories: A Collection of Critical Essays*, ed. Eugene M. Waith. Englewood Cliffs, N.J.: Prentice-Hall, 1965; and in *Shakespeare's Histories: An Anthology of Modern Criticism*, ed. William A. Armstrong. Baltimore, Md.: Penguin, 1972. With Henry, as God's deputy, standing at the center of the play, Kermode sees *Henry VIII* as an anthology of literary tragedies organized around a providential theme. The falls of "Good Queen, Ambitious Prelate, Virtuous Prelate, or merely Great Man" not only exhibit individual variations on the familiar moralistic pattern of the inevitable decline from greatness but also participate together in a larger providential design that moves toward the establishment of a reformed church and Elizabeth's great reign.

Knight, G. Wilson. "*Henry VIII* and the Poetry of Conversion." *The Crown of Life: Essays in Interpretation of Shakespeare's Final Plays*. London: Oxford Univ. Press, 1947. *Henry VIII*, Knight argues, powerfully binds Shakespeare's entire dramatic achievement into a whole. In a wide-ranging essay, Knight explores the play's synthesis of the tragic, historical, and theological strands of Shakespeare's earlier plays, a synthesis that is realized in the humility and charity achieved by the fallen characters and in the play's emphasis on ceremony and ritual. In Cranmer's prophecy, the play moves beyond mere political affirmation to its transcendent vision of power and peace.

Leech, Clifford. "The Structure of the Last Plays." *Shakespeare Survey* 11 (1958): 19–30. The structures of Shakespeare's last plays, for Leech, resist any decisive closure (and deny the claims of transcendence that have been made for the romances), enacting instead cyclical patterns of flux and repetition. This is most strongly realized in *Henry VIII*, where the repeated falls from high position and the foreshadowing of future events by the action of the play declare the cyclical process of history and the inherent instability of any new order.

Leggatt, Alexander. "*Henry VIII* and the Ideal England." *Shakespeare Survey* 38 (1985): 131–143. In extending its idealizing prophecy from Elizabeth to James, Cranmer's speech, Leggatt argues, encourages an audience to set the "ideal vision against our sense of the world as it really is." For Leggatt, this double perspective enacts the historical vision of the play itself. *Henry VIII* acknowledges the tensions and contradictions of history as well as the powerful impulse to purify these, revealing the "close relationship between what we dream of and what we are."

Richmond, H. M. "Shakespeare's *Henry VIII*: Romance Redeemed by History." *Shakespeare Studies* 4 (1968): 334–349. Richmond regards *Henry VIII* as a play in which the values of the romances are tested and vindicated by history. In locating the redemptive pattern of these values in an overtly historical world, Shakespeare articulates the substantiality of the romance vision, asserting its ability to operate not merely in the exotic worlds of the other late plays but in a world of ordinary causality and circumstantial fact.

Saccio, Peter. "Henry VIII: The Supreme Head." *Shakespeare's English Kings: History, Chronicle, and Drama*. New York: Oxford Univ. Press, 1977. Saccio distinguishes between *Henry VIII* and Henry VIII—between Shakespeare's romance and historical reality. He reviews the events of Henry's reign and examines how Shakespeare reorders and reshapes the historical material into drama.

Memorable Lines

King John

Sweet, sweet, sweet poison for the age's tooth.
(BASTARD   1.1.213)

For courage mounteth with occasion.   (AUSTRIA   2.1.82)

Mad world, mad kings, mad composition!
(BASTARD   2.1.562)

That smooth-faced gentleman, tickling Commodity,
Commodity, the bias of the world.   (BASTARD   2.1.574–575)

Since kings break faith upon commodity,
Gain, be my lord, for I will worship thee.
(BASTARD   2.1.598–599)

I will instruct my sorrows to be proud,
For grief is proud and makes his owner stoop.
(CONSTANCE   3.1.68–69)

What earthy name to interrogatories
Can taste the free breath of a sacred king?
(KING JOHN   3.1.147–148)

Bell, book, and candle shall not drive me back.
(BASTARD   3.3.12)

KING JOHN   Dost thou understand me?
  Thou art his keeper.
HUBERT   And I'll keep him so
  That he shall not offend Your Majesty.
KING JOHN   Death.
HUBERT
  My lord?
KING JOHN   A grave.

HUBERT   He shall not live.
KING JOHN   Enough.   (3.3.63–66)

Grief fills the room up of my absent child,
Lies in his bed, walks up and down with me,
Puts on his pretty looks, repeats his words,
Remembers me of all his gracious parts,
Stuffs out his vacant garments with his form.
                              (CONSTANCE   3.4.93–97)

Life is as tedious as a twice-told tale
Vexing the dull ear of a drowsy man.   (LEWIS   3.4.108–109)

How green you are and fresh in this old world!
                              (PANDULPH   3.4.145)

                    Will you put out mine eyes?
These eyes that never did nor never shall
So much as frown on you?   (ARTHUR   4.1.56–58)

To gild refinèd gold, to paint the lily . . .
Is wasteful and ridiculous excess.   (SALISBURY   4.2.11–16)

In this the antique and well-noted face
Of plain old form is much disfigurèd.
                              (SALISBURY   4.2.21–22)

O me! My uncle's spirit is in these stones.
Heaven take my soul, and England keep my bones!
                              (ARTHUR   4.3.9–10)

Now my soul hath elbowroom.   (KING JOHN   5.7.28)

                    I do not ask you much—
I beg cold comfort . . .   (KING JOHN   5.7.41–42)

This England never did, nor never shall,
Lie at the proud foot of a conqueror.   (BASTARD   5.7.112–113)

Memorable Lines

Henry VIII

No man's pie is freed
From his ambitious finger.   (BUCKINGHAM   1.1.52–53)

The force of his own merit makes his way—
                              (NORFOLK   1.1.64)

We may outrun
By violent swiftness that which we run at,
And lose by overrunning.   (NORFOLK   1.1.141–143)

Go with me like good angels to my end,
And, as the long divorce of steel falls on me,
Make of your prayers one sweet sacrifice,
And lift my soul to heaven.   (BUCKINGHAM   2.1.75–78)

Heaven has an end in all.   (BUCKINGHAM   2.1.124)

CHAMBERLAIN
  It seems the marriage with his brother's wife
  Has crept too near his conscience.
SUFFOLK   No, his conscience
  Has crept too near another lady.   (2.2.16–18)

. . . 'tis better to be lowly born,
And range with humble livers in content,
Than to be perked up in a glistering grief
And wear a golden sorrow.   (ANNE   2.3.19–22)

. . . I would not be a queen
For all the world.   (ANNE   2.3.45–46)

Heaven is above all yet; there sits a judge
That no king can corrupt.   (KATHARINE   3.1.100–101)

I have touched the highest point of all my greatness,
And from that full meridian of my glory
I haste now to my setting. I shall fall
Like a bright exhalation in the evening,
And no man see me more.   (WOLSEY   3.2.224–228)

Press not a falling man too far!   (CHAMBERLAIN   3.2.334)

Farewell? A long farewell, to all my greatness!
                                    (WOLSEY   3.2.352)

              I have ventured,
Like little wanton boys that swim on bladders,
This many summers in a sea of glory,
But far beyond my depth.   (WOLSEY   3.2.359–362)

Vain pomp and glory of this world, I hate ye!
I feel my heart new opened. O, how wretched
Is that poor man that hangs on princes' favors!
                                    (WOLSEY   3.2.366–368)

Mark but my fall, and that that ruined me.
Cromwell, I charge thee, fling away ambition!
By that sin fell the angels . . .   (WOLSEY   3.2.440–442)

Had I but served my God with half the zeal
I served my king, he would not in mine age
Have left me naked to mine enemies. (WOLSEY   3.2.456–458)

              He was a man
Of an unbounded stomach.   (KATHARINE   4.2.33–34)

He was a scholar, and a ripe and good one,
Exceeding wise, fair-spoken, and persuading.
                                    (GRIFFITH   4.2.51–52)

              She shall be—
But few now living can behold that goodness—
A pattern to all princes living with her,
And all that shall succeed.   (CRANMER   5.5.21–24)

              Truth shall nurse her,
Holy and heavenly thoughts still counsel her.
She shall be loved and feared. Her own shall bless her.
                                    (CRANMER   5.5.29–31)

              Some come to take their ease,
And sleep an act or two.   (EPILOGUE   2–3)

Contributors

DAVID BEVINGTON, Phyllis Fay Horton Professor of Humanities at the University of Chicago, is editor of *The Complete Works of Shakespeare* (Scott, Foresman, 1980) and of *Medieval Drama* (Houghton Mifflin, 1975). His latest critical study is *Action Is Eloquence: Shakespeare's Language of Gesture* (Harvard University Press, 1984).

DAVID SCOTT KASTAN, Professor of English and Comparative Literature at Columbia University, is the author of *Shakespeare and the Shapes of Time* (University Press of New England, 1982).

JAMES HAMMERSMITH, Associate Professor of English at Auburn University, has published essays on various facets of Renaissance drama, including literary criticism, textual criticism, and printing history.

ROBERT KEAN TURNER, Professor of English at the University of Wisconsin–Milwaukee, is a general editor of the New Variorum Shakespeare (Modern Language Association of America) and a contributing editor to *The Dramatic Works in the Beaumont and Fletcher Canon* (Cambridge University Press, 1966–).

JAMES SHAPIRO, who coedited the bibliographies with David Scott Kastan, is Assistant Professor of English at Columbia University.

❖

JOSEPH PAPP, one of the most important forces in theater today, is the founder and producer of the New York Shakespeare Festival, America's largest and most prolific theatrical institution. Since 1954 Mr. Papp has produced or directed all but one of Shakespeare's plays—in Central Park, in schools, off and on Broadway, and at the Festival's permanent home, The Public Theater. He has also produced such award-winning plays and musical works as *Hair, A Chorus Line, Plenty*, and *The Mystery of Edwin Drood*, among many others.